Take the Next Step
in Your IT Career

D1459909

Save
10%
on Exam Vouchers*

(up to a $35 value)

CompTIA.

Get details at
sybex.com/go/comptiavoucher

*Some restrictions apply. See web page for details.

CompTIA®
Security+®
Practice Tests
Exam SY0-501

S. Russell Christy

Chuck Easttom

Senior Acquisitions Editor: Kenyon Brown
Development Editor: Kathi Duggan
Technical Editors: Josh More and Warren Wyrostek
Senior Production Editor: Christine O'Connor
Copy Editor: Elizabeth Welch
Editorial Manager: Mary Beth Wakefield
Production Manager: Kathleen Wisor
Executive Editor: Jim Minatel
Book Designers: Judy Fung and Bill Gibson
Proofreader: Louise Watson, Word One New York
Indexer: Jack Lewis
Project Coordinator, Cover: Brent Savage
Cover Designer: Wiley
Cover Image: Getty Images Inc./Jeremy Woodhouse

Copyright © 2018 by John Wiley & Sons, Inc., Indianapolis, Indiana

Published simultaneously in Canada

ISBN: 978-1-119-41692-0
ISBN: 978-1-119-41698-2 (ebk.)
ISBN: 978-1-119-41696-8 (ebk.)

Manufactured in the United States of America

For general information on our other products and services or to obtain technical support, please contact our Customer Care Department within the U.S. at (877) 762-2974, outside the U.S. at (317) 572-3993 or fax (317) 572-4002.

Wiley publishes in a variety of print and electronic formats and by print-on-demand. Some material included with standard print versions of this book may not be included in e-books or in print-on-demand. If this book refers to media such as a CD or DVD that is not included in the version you purchased, you may download this material at http://booksupport.wiley.com. For more information about Wiley products, visit www.wiley.com.

Library of Congress Control Number: 2018937837

For my beautiful and wonderful wife, thank you for all your support.
—Russ Christy

Acknowledgments

I would like to thank Ken Brown and Kathi Duggan for all their support during my journey on this project; and all those at Wiley who worked on this title. The dedication of the team at Wiley cannot be overstated.

Thanks are also due to my family, who supported me through my endless work hours—my wonderful wife Leigh Ann, my children Zackary and Katelyn, and my mom. I love you all!
—Russ Christy

About the Authors

S. Russell Christy is a technical trainer in Memphis, Tennessee, who delivers traditional and online classroom learning for adults, covering a wide variety of products. He specializes in computer maintenance and network and security; Microsoft Office applications; and web and print design. For over 20 years, he has deployed new desktops and operating systems, servers, and network hardware and software, while simultaneously troubleshooting various hardware and software issues. Russ holds a bachelor's degree in business administration from the University of Memphis. He has additionally gained industry certifications in CompTIA A+, CompTIA Network+, CompTIA Security+, CompTIA CySA+, CompTIA Server+, MTA Windows Server Administration Fundamentals, Network Fundamentals, Security Fundamentals, and Windows OS Fundamentals, Microsoft Office Specialist 2013 Master, and Adobe Education Trainer.

Chuck Easttom is a researcher, consultant, and trainer in computer science and computer security. He has expertise in software engineering, operating systems, databases, web development, and computer networking. He travels the world teaching and consulting on digital forensics, cyber security, cryptology, and related topics. He has authored 22 books and counting, as well as dozens of research papers. Chuck is additionally an inventor with 10 patented computer science inventions. He also frequently works as an expert witness in computer-related cases. His website is http://chuckeasttom.com/.

About the Authors

Contents at a Glance

Contents

CompTIA.

Becoming a CompTIA Certified IT Professional is Easy

It's also the best way to reach greater professional opportunities and rewards.

Why Get CompTIA Certified?

Growing Demand

Labor estimates predict some technology fields will experience growth of over 20% by the year 2020.* CompTIA certification qualifies the skills required to join this workforce.

Higher Salaries

IT professionals with certifications on their resumes command better jobs, earn higher salaries, and have more doors open to new multi-industry opportunities.

Verified Strengths

91% of hiring managers indicate CompTIA certifications are valuable in validating IT expertise, making certification the best way to demonstrate your competency and knowledge to employers.**

Universal Skills

CompTIA certifications are vendor neutral—which means that certified professionals can proficiently work with an extensive variety of hardware and software found in most organizations.

 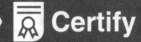 

Learn more about what the exam covers by reviewing the following:

- Exam objectives for key study points

- Sample questions for a general overview of what to expect on the exam and examples of question format

- Visit online forums, like LinkedIn, to see what other IT professionals say about CompTIA exams.

Purchase a voucher at a Pearson VUE testing center or at CompTIAstore.com.

- Register for your exam at a Pearson VUE testing center:

  Visit pearsonvue.com/CompTIA to find the closest testing center to you.

- Schedule the exam online. You will be required to enter your voucher number or provide payment information at registration.

- Take your certification exam.

Congratulations on your CompTIA certification!

- Make sure to add your certification to your resume.

- Check out the CompTIA Certification Roadmap to plan your next career move.

Learn more: **Certification.CompTIA.org/securityplus**

* Source: CompTIA 9th Annual Information Security Trends study: 500 U.S. IT and Business Executives Responsible for Security
** Source: CompTIA Employer Perceptions of IT Training and Certification

Introduction

Congratulations on your purchase of *CompTIA Security+ Practice Tests*. This book will serve as a preparation tool for the CompTIA Security+ certification exam (SY0-501) as well as your career in the IT security field.

The objective of this book is to prepare you for the CompTIA Security+ exam by explaining the terminology and technology that will be tested on the exam. The main focus of this book is to help you pass the exam. We don't always cover every aspect of the related field, so some of the aspects of the technology will be covered only to the extent necessary to help you understand what you will need to know to pass the exam. We hope this book will become a valuable resource for you after you achieve the certification.

It Pays to Get Certified

In a digital world, digital literacy is an essential survival skill. Certification proves that you have the knowledge and skill to solve business problems in virtually any business environment.

Certification makes you more competitive and employable. Research has shown that people who study technology get hired. In the competition for entry-level jobs, applicants with high school diplomas or college degrees who included IT coursework in their academic load consistently fared better in job interviews and were hired in significantly higher numbers. If considered a compulsory part of a technology education, testing for certification can be an invaluable competitive distinction for IT professionals.

How Certification Helps Your Career

Security is one of the highest-demand job categories.   The U.S. Bureau of Labor Statistics (BLS) predicts that information security analysts will be the fastest growing overall job category, with 37 percent overall growth between 2012 and 2022.

Get your foot in the door.   According to CompTIA's Employer Perceptions of IT Training and Certification study, 91 percent of hiring managers today believe that IT certifications are valuable in validating expertise.

Network security administrators earn a good income.   According to Glassdoor, network security administrators earn a national average of almost $70,000 per year.

CompTIA Security+ is the first step in starting your career as a network security administrator or systems security administrator.   Professionals who are CompTIA Security+ certified are 85 percent more likely to believe that they have the knowledge and skills needed to fulfill their jobs successfully.

CompTIA Security+ certification is popular.   More than 250,000 individuals worldwide are CompTIA Security+ certified.

CompTIA Security+ is regularly used in organizations.   Companies such as Hitachi Systems, Fuji Xerox, HP, Dell, and a variety of major U.S. government contractors use CompTIA Security+.

CompTIA Security+ is approved by the U.S. Department of Defense (DoD).   CompTIA Security+ is approved by the DoD as one of the required certification options in the DoD 8570.01-M directive for Information Assurance Technical Level II and Management Level I job roles.

Steps to Getting Certified and Staying Certified

Review exam objectives.   Review the certification objectives to make sure that you know what is covered in the exam:

> http://certification.comptia.org/examobjectives.aspx

Practice for the exam.   After you have studied for the certification, review and answer as many sample questions as you can to prepare for the exam.

Purchase an exam voucher.   Purchase exam vouchers on the CompTIA Marketplace:

> www.comptiastore.com

Take the test!   Go to the Pearson VUE website and schedule a time to take your exam:

> www.pearsonvue.com/comptia/locate/

Stay certified with continuing education.   New CompTIA Security+ certifications are valid for three years from the date of certification. There are a number of ways that the certification can be renewed. For more information, check the CompTIA site.

How to Obtain More Information

- Visit CompTIA (http://certification.comptia.org/home.aspx) to learn more about getting CompTIA certified.
- Contact CompTIA: Call 866-835-8020 and choose Option 2, or email questions@comptia.org.
- Connect with CompTIA on LinkedIn, Facebook, Twitter, Flicker, and YouTube.

Taking the Exam

Once you are fully prepared to take the exam, you can visit the CompTIA website to purchase your exam voucher:

www.comptiastore.com/Articles.asp?ID=265&category=vouchers

CompTIA partners with Pearson VUE's testing centers, so your next step will be to locate a testing center near you. In the United States, you can do this based on your address or your ZIP code, while non-U.S. test takers may find it easier to enter their city and country. You can search for a test center near you at the Pearson VUE website, where you will need to navigate to "Find a test center":

www.pearsonvue.com/comptia/

Now that you know where you'd like to take the exam, simply set up a Pearson VUE testing account and schedule an exam:

https://certification.comptia.org/testing/schedule-exam

On the day of the test, take two forms of identification, and make sure to show up with plenty of time before the exam starts. Remember that you will not be able to take your notes, electronic devices (including smartphones and watches), or other materials in with you.

How This Book Is Organized

This book consists of six chapters based on each of the domains in the CompTIA Security+ Exam SY0-501. The book also has one chapter that is meant to simulate the exam based on a variety of the questions from all six domains. The chapters are organized as follows:

Chapter 1: Threats, Attacks, and Vulnerabilities (Domain 1)   Explain various types of attacks, such as wireless, application, and social engineering. Explain various types of malware.

Chapter 2: Technologies and Tools (Domain 2)   Apply various types of mitigation and deterrent techniques to various attacks. Use appropriate tools and techniques to discover security threats and vulnerabilities.

Chapter 3: Architecture and Design (Domain 3)   Explain network design elements and components and implement common protocols and services. Implement security configuration parameters on network devices and other types of technologies.

Chapter 4: Identity and Access Management (Domain 4)   Compare and contrast the function and purpose of authentication services. Install and configure security controls when performing account management.

Chapter 5: Risk Management (Domain 5)   Implement appropriate risk mitigation strategies and basic forensic procedures. Explain the importance of risk-related concepts and summarize risk management best practices.

Chapter 6: Cryptography and PKI (Domain 6)   Understand general cryptography concepts and use the appropriate methods. Use appropriate PKI, certificate management, and associated components.

Chapter 7: Practice Test   The practice test simulates the actual exam. Although the questions are different, they test your knowledge of the objectives and your understanding of basic concepts.

How to Use This Book and the Interactive Online Learning Environment and Test Bank

This book includes 1,000 practice test questions, which will help you get ready to pass the Security+ exam. The interactive online learning environment that accompanies the CompTIA Security+ Practice Tests provides a robust test bank to help you prepare for the certification exam and increase your chances of passing it the first time. By using this test bank, you can identify weak areas up front and then develop a solid studying strategy using each of the robust testing features.

The test bank also includes a practice exam. Take the practice exam just as if you were taking the actual exam (without any reference material). If you get more than 90 percent of the answers correct, you're ready to take the certification exam.

> You can access the Sybex Interactive Online Test Bank at www.wiley.com/go/Sybextestprep.

Security+ Exam Objective Map

The following objective map will help you to find the book chapter that covers each objective for the exam.

> Exam domains and objectives are subject to change at any time without prior notice and at CompTIA's sole discretion. Please visit their website at www.comptia.org for the most current information.

1.0 Threats, Attacks, and Vulnerabilities

2.0 Technologies and Tools

3.0 Architecture and Design

Identity and Access Management

5.0 Risk Management

6.0 Cryptography and PKI

Exam domains and objectives are subject to change at any time without prior notice and at CompTIA's sole discretion. Please visit their website at www.comptia.org for the most current information.

Chapter

1

Threats, Attacks, and Vulnerabilities

THE COMPTIA SECURITY+ EXAM SYO-501 TOPICS COVERED IN THIS CHAPTER INCLUDE THE FOLLOWING:

✓ **1.1 Given a scenario, analyze indicators of compromise and determine the type of malware.**

- Viruses
- Crypto-malware
- Ransomware
- Worm
- Trojan
- Rootkit
- Keylogger
- Adware
- Spyware
- Bots
- RAT
- Logic bomb
- Backdoor

✓ **1.2 Compare and contrast types of attacks.**

- Social engineering
  - Phishing
  - Spear phishing
  - Whaling
  - Vishing
  - Tailgating
  - Impersonation

- Dumpster diving
- Shoulder surfing
- Hoax
- Watering hole attack
- Principles (reasons for effectiveness)
  - Authority
  - Intimidation
  - Consensus
  - Scarcity
  - Familiarity
  - Trust
  - Urgency
- Application/service attacks
  - DoS
  - DDoS
  - Man-in-the-middle
  - Buffer overflow
  - Injection
  - Cross-site scripting
  - Cross-site request forgery
  - Privilege escalation
  - ARP poisoning
  - Amplification
  - DNS poisoning
  - Domain hijacking
  - Man-in-the-browser
  - Zero day
  - Replay
  - Pass the hash
  - Hijacking and related attacks
    - Clickjacking
    - Session hijacking

- URL hijacking
- Typo squatting
- Driver manipulation
  - Shimming
  - Refactoring
- MAC spoofing
- IP spoofing
- Wireless attacks
  - Replay
  - IV
  - Evil twin
  - Rogue AP
  - Jamming
  - WPS
  - Bluejacking
  - Bluesnarfing
  - RFID
  - NFC
  - Disassociation
- Cryptographic attacks
  - Birthday
  - Known plain text/cipher text
  - Rainbow tables
  - Dictionary
  - Brute force
    - Online vs. offline
  - Collision
  - Downgrade
  - Replay
  - Weak implementations

✓ **1.3 Explain threat actor types and attributes.**

- Types of actors
  - Script kiddies
  - Hacktivist
  - Organized crime
  - Nation states/APT
  - Insiders
  - Competitors
- Attributes of actors
  - Internal/external
  - Level of sophistication
  - Resources/funding
  - Intent/motivation
- Use of open-source intelligence

✓ **1.4 Explain penetration testing concepts.**

- Active reconnaissance
- Passive reconnaissance
- Pivot
- Initial exploitation
- Persistence
- Escalation of privilege
- Black box
- White box
- Gray box
- Pen testing vs. vulnerability scanning

✓ **1.5 Explain vulnerability scanning concepts.**

- Passively test security controls
- Identify vulnerability
- Identify lack of security controls
- Identify common misconfigurations

- Intrusive vs. non-intrusive
- Credentialed vs. non-credentialed
- False positive

✓ **1.6 Explain the impact associated with types of vulnerabilities.**

- Race conditions
- Vulnerabilities due to:
    - End-of-life systems
    - Embedded systems
    - Lack of vendor support
- Improper input handling
- Improper error handling
- Misconfiguration/weak configuration
- Default configuration
- Resource exhaustion
- Untrained users
- Improperly configured accounts
- Vulnerable business processes
- Weak cipher suites and implementations
- Memory/buffer vulnerability
    - Memory leak
    - Integer overflow
    - Buffer overflow
    - Pointer dereference
    - DLL injection
- System sprawl/undocumented assets
- Architecture/design weaknesses
- New threats/zero day
- Improper certificate and key management

1. John is analyzing strange behavior on computers in his network. He believes there is malware on the machines. The symptoms include strange behavior that persists, even if he boots the machine to a Linux Live CD. What is the most likely cause?

    A. Ransomware

    B. Boot sector virus

    C. Rootkit

    D. Key logger

2. Ahmed is a sales manager with a major insurance company. He has received an email that is encouraging him to click on a link and fill out a survey. He is suspicious of the email, but it does mention a major insurance association, and that makes him think it might be legitimate. Which of the following best describes this attack?

    A. Phishing

    B. Social engineering

    C. Spear phishing

    D. Trojan horse

3. You are a security administrator for a medium-sized bank. You have discovered a piece of software on your bank's database server that is not supposed to be there. It appears that the software will begin deleting database files if a specific employee is terminated. What best describes this?

    A. Worm

    B. Logic bomb

    C. Trojan horse

    D. Rootkit

4. You are responsible for incident response at Acme bank. The Acme bank website has been attacked. The attacker used the login screen, but rather than enter login credentials, he or she entered some odd text: ' or '1' = '1. What is the best description for this attack?

    A. Cross-site scripting

    B. Cross-site request forgery

    C. SQL injection

    D. ARP poisoning

5. Juanita is a network administrator for a small accounting firm. The users on her network are complaining of slow connectivity. When she examines the firewall logs, she observes a large number of half-open connections. What best describes this attack?

    A. DDoS

    B. SYN flood

    C. Buffer overflow

    D. ARP poisoning

6. Frank is deeply concerned about attacks to his company's e-commerce server. He is particularly worried about cross-site scripting and SQL injection. Which of the following would best defend against these two specific attacks?

   A. Encrypted web traffic

   B. Filtering user input

   C. A firewall

   D. An IDS

7. You are responsible for network security at Acme Company. Users have been reporting that personal data is being stolen when using the wireless network. They all insist they only connect to the corporate wireless access point (WAP). However, logs for the WAP show that these users have not connected to it. Which of the following could best explain this situation?

   A. Session hijacking

   B. Clickjacking

   C. Rogue access point

   D. Bluejacking

8. What type of attack depends on the attacker entering JavaScript into a text area that is intended for users to enter text that will be viewed by other users?

   A. SQL injection

   B. Clickjacking

   C. Cross-site scripting

   D. Bluejacking

9. A sales manager at your company is complaining about slow performance on his computer. When you thoroughly investigate the issue, you find spyware on his computer. He insists that the only thing he has downloaded recently was a freeware stock trading application. What would best explain this situation?

   A. Logic bomb

   B. Trojan horse

   C. Rootkit

   D. Macro virus

10. Your company outsourced development of an accounting application to a local programming firm. After three months of using the product, one of your accountants accidently discovers a way to log in and bypass all security and authentication. What best describes this?

   A. Logic bomb

   B. Trojan horse

   C. Backdoor

   D. Rootkit

11. Teresa is the security manager for a mid-sized insurance company. She receives a call from law enforcement, telling her that some computers on her network participated in a massive denial-of-service (DoS) attack. Teresa is certain that none of the employees at her company would be involved in a cybercrime. What would best explain this scenario?

   A. It is a result of social engineering.

   B. The machines all have backdoors.

   C. The machines are bots.

   D. The machines are infected with crypto-viruses.

12. Mike is a network administrator with a small financial services company. He has received a popup window that states his files are now encrypted and he must pay .5 bitcoins to get them decrypted. He tries to check the files in question, but their extensions have changed, and he cannot open them. What best describes this situation?

   A. Mike's machine has a rootkit.

   B. Mike's machine has ransomware.

   C. Mike's machine has a logic bomb.

   D. Mike's machine has been the target of whaling.

13. Terrance is examining logs for the company e-commerce web server. He discovers a number of redirects that cannot be explained. After carefully examining the website, he finds some attacker performed a watering hole attack by placing JavaScript in the website and is redirecting users to a phishing website. Which of the following techniques would be best at preventing this in the future?

   A. An SPI firewall

   B. An active IDS/IPS

   C. Checking buffer boundaries

   D. Checking user input

14. What type of attack is based on sending more data to a target variable than the data can actually hold?

   A. Bluesnarfing

   B. Buffer overflow

   C. Bluejacking

   D. DDoS

15. You have been asked to test your company network for security issues. The specific test you are conducting involves primarily using automated and semiautomated tools to look for known vulnerabilities with the various systems on your network. Which of the following best describes this type of test?

   A. Vulnerability scan

   B. Penetration test

   C. Security audit

   D. Security test

16. Jared discovers that attackers have breached his WiFi network. They have gained access via the wireless access point (WAP) administrative panel, and have logged on with the credentials the WAP shipped with. What best describes this issue?

    A. Default configuration

    B. Race conditions

    C. Failure to patch

    D. Weak encryption

17. Joanne is concerned about social engineering. She is particularly concerned that this technique could be used by an attacker to obtain information about the network, including possibly even passwords. What countermeasure would be most effective in combating social engineering?

    A. SPI firewall

    B. An IPS

    C. User training

    D. Strong policies

18. You are responsible for incident response at a mid-sized bank. You have discovered that someone was able to successfully breach your network and steal data from your database server. All servers are configured to forward logs to a central logging server. However, when you examine that central log, there are no entries after 2:13 a.m. two days ago. You check the servers, and they are sending logs to the right server, but they are not getting there. Which of the following would be most likely to explain this?

    A. Your log server has a backdoor.

    B. Your log server has been hit with a buffer overflow attack.

    C. Your switches have been hit with ARP poisoning.

    D. Your IDS is malfunctioning and blocking log transmissions.

19. Coleen is the web security administrator for an online auction website. A small number of users are complaining that when they visit the website and log in, they are told the service is down and to try again later. Coleen checks and she can visit the site without any problem, even from computers outside the network. She also checks the web server log and there is no record of those users ever connecting. Which of the following might best explain this?

    A. Typosquatting

    B. SQL injection

    C. Cross-site scripting

    D. Cross-site request forgery

20. Mahmoud is responsible for managing security at a large university. He has just performed a threat analysis for the network, and based on past incidents and studies of similar networks, he has determined that the most prevalent threat to his network is low-skilled attackers who wish to breach the system, simply to prove they can or for

some low-level crime, such as changing a grade. Which term best describes this type of attacker?

A. Hacktivist

B. Amateur

C. Insider

D. Script kiddie

21. Which of the following best describes a collection of computers that have been compromised and are being controlled from one central point?

A. Zombienet

B. Botnet

C. Nullnet

D. Attacknet

22. John is conducting a penetration test of a client's network. He is currently gathering information from sources such as `archive.org`, `netcraft.com`, social media, and information websites. What best describes this stage?

A. Active reconnaissance

B. Passive reconnaissance

C. Initial exploitation

D. Pivot

23. One of the salespeople in your company reports that his computer is behaving sluggishly. You check but don't see any obvious malware. However, in his temp folder you find JPEGs that look like screenshots of his desktop. Which of the following is the most likely cause?

A. He is stealing data from the company.

B. There is a backdoor on his computer.

C. There is spyware on his computer.

D. He needs to update his Windows.

24. What type of attack is based on entering fake entries into a target networks domain name server?

A. DNS poisoning

B. ARP poisoning

C. Bluesnarfing

D. Bluejacking

25. Frank has been asked to conduct a penetration test of a small bookkeeping firm. For the test, he has only been given the company name, the domain name for their website, and the IP address of their gateway router. What best describes this type of test?

A. White-box test

B. External test

C. Black-box test

D. Threat test

26. You work for a security company that performs penetration testing for clients. You are conducting a test of an e-commerce company. You discover that after compromising the web server, you can use the web server to launch a second attack into the company's internal network. What best describes this?

    A. Internal attack

    B. White-box testing

    C. Black-box testing

    D. A pivot

27. While investigating a malware outbreak on your company network, you discover something very odd. There is a file that has the same name as a Windows system DLL, and even has the same API interface, but handles input very differently, in a manner to help compromise the system, and it appears that applications have been attaching to this file, rather than the real system DLL. What best describes this?

    A. Shimming

    B. Trojan horse

    C. Backdoor

    D. Refactoring

28. Your company has hired a penetration testing firm to test the network. For the test, you have given the company details on operating systems you use, applications you run, and network devices. What best describes this type of test?

    A. White-box test

    B. External test

    C. Black-box test

    D. Threat test

29. Frank is a network administrator for a small college. He discovers that several machines on his network are infected with malware. That malware is sending a flood of packets to a target external to the network. What best describes this attack?

    A. SYN flood

    B. DDoS

    C. Botnet

    D. Backdoor

30. John is a salesman for an automobile company. He recently downloaded a program from an unknown website, and now his client files have their file extensions changed, and he cannot open them. He has received a popup window that states his files are now encrypted and he must pay .5 bitcoins to get them decrypted. What has happened?

    A. His machine has a rootkit.

    B. His machine has a logic bomb.

    C. His machine has a boot sector virus.

    D. His machine has ransomware.

31. When phishing attacks are so focused that they target a specific individual, they are called what?

   A. Spear phishing

   B. Targeted phishing

   C. Phishing

   D. Whaling

32. You are concerned about a wide range of attacks that could affect your company's web server. You have recently read about an attack wherein the attacker sends more data to the target than the target is expecting. If done properly, this could cause the target to crash. What would best prevent this type of attack?

   A. An SPI firewall

   B. An active IDS/IPS

   C. Checking buffer boundaries

   D. Checking user input

33. You work for a large retail company that processes credit card purchases. You have been asked to test your company network for security issues. The specific test you are conducting involves primarily checking policies, documentation, and past incident reports. Which of the following best describes this type of test?

   A. Vulnerability scan

   B. Penetration test

   C. Security audit

   D. Security test

34. Maria is a salesperson with your company. After a recent sales trip, she discovers that many of her logins have been compromised. You carefully scan her laptop and cannot find any sign of any malware. You do notice that she had recently connected to a public WiFi at a coffee shop, and it is only since that connection that she noticed her logins had been compromised. What would most likely explain what has occurred?

   A. She connected to a rogue AP.

   B. She downloaded a Trojan horse.

   C. She downloaded spyware.

   D. She is the victim of a buffer overflow attack.

35. You are the manager for network operations at your company. One of the accountants sees you in the hall and thanks you for your team keeping his antivirus software up to date. When you ask him what he means, he mentions that one of your staff, named Mike, called him and remotely connected to update the antivirus. You don't have an employee named Mike. What has occurred?

   A. IP spoofing

   B. MAC spoofing

   C. Man-in-the-middle attack

   D. Social engineering

36. You are a security administrator for a bank. You are very interested in detecting any breaches or even attempted breaches of your network, including those from internal personnel. But you don't want false positives to disrupt work. Which of the following devices would be the best choice in this scenario?

A. IPS

B. WAF

C. SIEM

D. IDS

37. One of your users cannot recall the password for their laptop. You want to recover that password for them. You intend to use a tool/technique that is popular with hackers, and it consists of searching tables of precomputed hashes to recover the password. What best describes this?

A. Rainbow table

B. Backdoor

C. Social engineering

D. Dictionary attack

38. You have noticed that when in a crowded area, you sometimes get a stream of unwanted text messages. The messages end when you leave the area. What describes this attack?

A. Bluejacking

B. Bluesnarfing

C. Evil twin

D. Rogue access point

39. Someone has been rummaging through your company's trash bins seeking to find documents, diagrams, or other sensitive information that has been thrown out. What is this called?

A. Dumpster diving

B. Trash diving

C. Social engineering

D. Trash engineering

40. You have noticed that when in a crowded area, data from your cell phone is stolen. Later investigation shows a Bluetooth connection to your phone, one that you cannot explain. What describes this attack?

A. Bluejacking

B. Bluesnarfing

C. Evil twin

D. RAT

41. Louis is investigating a malware incident on one of the computers on his network. He has discovered unknown software that seems to be opening a port, allowing someone to remotely connect to the computer. This software seems to have been installed at the same time as a small shareware application. Which of the following best describes this malware?

    A. RAT

    B. Backdoor

    C. Logic bomb

    D. Rootkit

42. This is a common security issue that is extremely hard to control in large environments. It occurs when a user has more computer rights, permissions, and privileges than what is required for the tasks the user needs to perform. What best describes this scenario?

    A. Excessive rights

    B. Excessive access

    C. Excessive permissions

    D. Excessive privileges

43. Jared is responsible for network security at his company. He has discovered behavior on one computer that certainly appears to be a virus. He has even identified a file he thinks might be the virus. However, using three separate antivirus programs, he finds that none can detect the file. Which of the following is most likely to be occurring?

    A. The computer has a RAT.

    B. The computer has a zero-day exploit.

    C. The computer has a logic bomb.

    D. The computer has a rootkit.

44. There are some computers on your network that use Windows XP. They have to stay on Windows XP due to a specific application they are running. That application won't run on newer operating systems. What security concerns does this situation give you?

    A. No special concerns; this is normal.

    B. The machines cannot be patched; XP is no longer supported.

    C. The machines cannot coordinate with an SIEM since XP won't support that.

    D. The machines are more vulnerable to DoS attacks.

45. Farès has discovered that attackers have breached his wireless network. They seem to have used a brute-force attack on the WiFi-protected setup PIN to exploit the WAP and recover the WPA2 password. What is this attack called?

    A. Evil twin

    B. Rogue WAP

    C. IV attack

    D. WPS Attack

46. Your wireless network has been breached. It appears the attacker modified a portion of data used with the stream cipher and utilized this to expose wirelessly encrypted data. What is this attack called?

    A. Evil twin

    B. Rogue WAP

    C. IV attack

    D. WPS Attack

47. John is concerned about disgruntled employees stealing company documents and exfiltrating them from the network. He is looking for a solution that will detect likely exfiltration and block it. What type of system is John looking for?

    A. IPS

    B. SIEM

    C. Honeypot

    D. Firewall

48. Some users on your network use Acme Bank for their personal banking. Those users have all recently been the victim of an attack, wherein they visited a fake Acme Bank website and their logins were compromised. They all visited the bank website from your network, and all of them insist they typed in the correct URL. What is the most likely explanation for this situation?

    A. Trojan horse

    B. IP spoofing

    C. Clickjacking

    D. DNS poisoning

49. Users are complaining that they cannot connect to the wireless network. You discover that the WAPs are being subjected to a wireless attack designed to block their WiFi signals. Which of the following is the best label for this attack?

    A. IV attack

    B. Jamming

    C. WPS attack

    D. Botnet

50. What type of attack involves users clicking on something different on a website than what they intended to click on?

    A. Clickjacking

    B. Bluesnarfing

    C. Bluejacking

    D. Evil twin

51. What type of attack exploits the trust that a website has for an authenticated user to attack that website by spoofing requests from the trusted user?

    A. Cross-site scripting

    B. Cross-site request forgery

    C. Bluejacking

    D. Evil twin

52. John is a network administrator for Acme Company. He has discovered that someone has registered a domain name that is spelled just one letter different than his company's domain. The website with the misspelled URL is a phishing site. What best describes this attack?

    A. Session hijacking

    B. Cross-site request forgery

    C. Typosquatting

    D. Clickjacking

53. Frank has discovered that someone was able to get information from his smartphone using a Bluetooth connection. The attacker was able to get his contact list and some emails he had received. What is this type of attack called?

    A. Bluesnarfing

    B. Session hijacking

    C. Backdoor attack

    D. CSRF

54. Juanita is a network administrator for Acme Company. Some users complain that they keep getting dropped from the network. When Juanita checks the logs for the wireless access point (WAP), she finds that a deauthentication packet has been sent to the WAP from the users' IP addresses. What seems to be happening here?

    A. Problem with users' WiFi configuration

    B. Disassociation attack

    C. Session hijacking

    D. Backdoor attack

55. John has discovered that an attacker is trying to get network passwords by using software that attempts a number of passwords from a list of common passwords. What type of attack is this?

    A. Dictionary

    B. Rainbow table

    C. Brute force

    D. Session hijacking

56. You are a network security administrator for a bank. You discover that an attacker has exploited a flaw in OpenSSL and forced some connections to move to a weak cipher suite version of TLS, which the attacker could breach. What type of attack was this?

   A. Disassociation attack

   B. Downgrade attack

   C. Session hijacking

   D. Brute force

57. When an attacker tries to find an input value that will produce the same hash as a password, what type of attack is this?

   A. Rainbow table

   B. Brute force

   C. Session hijacking

   D. Collision attack

58. Farès is the network security administrator for a company that creates advanced routers and switches. He has discovered that his company's networks have been subjected to a series of advanced attacks over a period of time. What best describes this attack?

   A. DDoS

   B. Brute force

   C. APT

   D. Disassociation attack

59. You are responsible for incident response at Acme Company. One of your jobs is to attempt to attribute attacks to a specific type of attacker. Which of the following would not be one of the attributes you consider in attributing the attack?

   A. Level of sophistication

   B. Resources/funding

   C. Intent/motivation

   D. Amount of data stolen

60. John is running an IDS on his network. Users sometimes report that the IDS flags legitimate traffic as an attack. What describes this?

   A. False positive

   B. False negative

   C. False trigger

   D. False flag

61. You are performing a penetration test of your company's network. As part of the test, you will be given a login with minimal access and will attempt to gain administrative access with this account. What is this called?

   A. Privilege escalation

   B. Session hijacking

   C. Root grabbing

   D. Climbing

62. Mary has discovered that a web application used by her company does not always handle multithreading properly, particularly when multiple threads access the same variable. This could allow an attacker who discovered this vulnerability to exploit it and crash the server. What type of error has Mary discovered?

   A. Buffer overflow

   B. Logic bomb

   C. Race conditions

   D. Improper error handling

63. An attacker is trying to get access to your network. He is sending users on your network a link to a freeware stock-monitoring program. However, that stock-monitoring program has attached to it software that will give the attacker access to any machine that it is installed on. What type of attack is this?

   A. Rootkit

   B. Trojan horse

   C. Spyware

   D. Boot sector virus

64. Acme Company uses its own internal certificate server for all internal encryption. However, their certificate authority only publishes a CRL once per week. Does this pose a danger, and if so what?

   A. Yes, this means a revoked certificate could be used for up to seven days.

   B. No, this is standard for all certificate authorities.

   C. Yes, this means it would be easy to fake a certificate.

   D. No, since this is being used only internally.

65. When a program has variables, especially arrays, and does not check the boundary values before inputting data, what attack is the program vulnerable to?

   A. XSS

   B. CRSF

   C. Buffer overflow

   D. Logic bomb

66. Which of the following best describes malware that will execute some malicious activity when a particular condition is met (i.e., if condition is met, then execute)?

   A. Boot sector virus

   B. Logic bomb

   C. Buffer overflow

   D. Sparse infector virus

67. Gerald is a network administrator for Acme Company. Users are reporting odd behavior on their computers. He believes this may be due to malware, but the behavior is different on different computers. What might best explain this?

   A. It is not malware, but hardware failure.

   B. It is a boot sector virus.

   C. It is a macro virus.

   D. It is a polymorphic virus.

68. Teresa is a security officer at ACME Inc. She has discovered an attack where the attacker sent multiple broadcast messages to the network routers, spoofing an IP address of one of the network servers. This caused the network to send a flood of packets to that server and it is no longer responding. What is this attack called?

   A. Smurf attack

   B. DDoS attack

   C. TCP hijacking attack

   D. TCP SYN flood attack

69. Which type of virus is able to alter its own code to avoid being detected by antivirus software?

   A. Boot sector

   B. Hoax

   C. Polymorphic

   D. Stealth

70. Gerald is a network administrator for a small financial services company. Users are reporting odd behavior that appears to be caused by a virus on their machines. After isolating the machines that he believes are infected, Gerald analyzes them. He finds that all the infected machines received an email purporting to be from accounting, with an Excel spreadsheet, and the users opened the spreadsheet. What is the most likely issue on these machines?

   A. A macro virus

   B. A boot sector virus

   C. A Trojan horse

   D. A RAT

71. Fred is on the incident response team for a major insurance company. His specialty is malware analysis. He is studying a file that is suspected of being a virus that infected the company network last month. The file seems to intermittently have bursts of malicious activity, interspersed with periods of being dormant. What best describes this malware?

    A. A macro virus

    B. A logic bomb

    C. A sparse infector virus

    D. A polymorphic virus

72. What is the term used to describe a virus that can infect both program files and boot sectors?

    A. Polymorphic

    B. Multipartite

    C. Stealth

    D. Multiple encrypting

73. Your company has hired an outside security firm to perform various tests of your network. During the vulnerability scan you will provide that company with logins for various systems (i.e., database server, application server, web server, etc.) to aid in their scan. What best describes this?

    A. A white-box test

    B. A gray-box test

    C. A privileged scan

    D. An authenticated user scan

74. Which of the following is commonly used in a distributed denial of service (DDoS) attack?

    A. Phishing

    B. Adware

    C. Botnet

    D. Trojan

75. You are investigating a recent breach at Acme Company. You discover that the attacker used an old account of someone no longer at the company. The account was still active. Which of the following best describes what caused this vulnerability to exist?

    A. Improperly configured accounts

    B. Untrained users

    C. Using default configuration

    D. Failure to patch systems

76. Juan is responsible for incident response at a large financial institution. He discovers that the company WiFi has been breached. The attacker used the same login credentials that ship with the wireless access point (WAP). The attacker was able to use those credentials

to access the WAP administrative console and make changes. Which of the following best describes what caused this vulnerability to exist?

A. Improperly configured accounts

B. Untrained users

C. Using default configuration

D. Failure to patch systems

77. Elizabeth is investigating a network breach at her company. She discovers a program that was able to execute code within the address space of another process by using the target process to load a specific library. What best describes this attack?

A. Logic bomb

B. Session hijacking

C. Buffer overflow

D. DLL injection

78. Zackary is a malware investigator with a cybersecurity firm. He is investigating malware that is able to compromise a target program by finding null references in the target program and dereferencing them, causing an exception to be generated. What best describes this type of attack?

A. DLL injection

B. Buffer overflow

C. Memory leak

D. Pointer dereference

79. Frank has just taken over as CIO of a mid-sized insurance company. One of the first things he does is order a thorough inventory of all network equipment. He discovers two routers that are not documented. He is concerned that if they are not documented, they might not be securely configured, tested, and safe. What best describes this situation?

A. Poor user training

B. System sprawl

C. Failure to patch systems

D. Default configuration

80. What is the primary difference between an intrusive and a nonintrusive vulnerability scan?

A. An intrusive scan is a penetration test.

B. A nonintrusive scan is just a document check.

C. An intrusive scan could potentially disrupt operations.

D. A nonintrusive scan won't find most vulnerabilities.

81. Daryl is investigating a recent breach of his company's web server. The attacker used sophisticated techniques and then defaced the website, leaving messages that were denouncing the company's public policies. He and his team are trying to determine the type of actor who most likely committed the breach. Based on the information provided, who was the most likely threat actor?

    A. A script

    B. A nation-state

    C. Organized crime

    D. Hacktivists

82. When investigating breaches and attempting to attribute them to specific threat actors, which of the following is not one of the indicators of an APT?

    A. Long-term access to the target

    B. Sophisticated attacks

    C. The attack comes from a foreign IP address.

    D. The attack is sustained over time.

83. What type of attack uses a second wireless access point (WAP) that broadcasts the same SSID as a legitimate access point, in an attempt to get users to connect to the attacker's WAP?

    A. Evil twin

    B. IP spoofing

    C. Trojan horse

    D. MAC spoofing

84. You are investigating a breach of a large technical company. You discover that there have been several different attacks over a period of a year. The attacks were sustained, each lasting several weeks of continuous attack. The attacks were somewhat sophisticated and originated from a variety of IP addresses, but all the IP addresses are within your country. Which threat actor would you most suspect of being involved in this attack?

    A. Nation-state

    B. Hacktivist

    C. Script kiddie

    D. A lone highly skilled hacker

85. Which of the following best describes a zero-day vulnerability?

    A. A vulnerability that has been known to the vendor for zero days

    B. A vulnerability that has not yet been breached

    C. A vulnerability that can be quickly exploited (i.e., in zero days)

    D. A vulnerability that will give the attacker brief access (i.e., zero days)

86. You have discovered that there are entries in your network's domain name server that point legitimate domains to unknown and potentially harmful IP addresses. What best describes this type of attack?

A. A backdoor

B. An APT

C. DNS poisoning

D. A Trojan horse

87. What best describes an attack that attaches some malware to a legitimate program so that when the user installs the legitimate program, they inadvertently install the malware?

A. Backdoor

B. Trojan horse

C. RAT

D. Polymorphic virus

88. Which of the following best describes software that will provide the attacker with remote access to the victim's machine, but that is wrapped with a legitimate program in an attempt to trick the victim into installing it?

A. RAT

B. Backdoor

C. Trojan horse

D. Macro virus

89. Which of the following is an attack that seeks to attack a website, based on the website's trust of an authenticated user?

A. XSS

B. CSRF

C. Buffer overflow

D. RAT

90. John is analyzing what he believes is a malware outbreak on his network. Many users report their machines are behaving strangely. The anomalous behavior seems to occur sporadically and John cannot find a pattern. What is the most likely cause?

A. APT

B. Boot sector virus

C. Sparse infector virus

D. Key logger

91. Farès is the CISO of a bank. He has received an email that is encouraging him to click on a link and fill out a survey. Being security conscious, he normally does not click on links. However, this email calls him by name and claims to be a follow-up to a recent conference he attended. Which of the following best describes this attack?

    A. Clickjacking

    B. Social engineering

    C. Spear phishing

    D. Whaling

92. You are responsible for technical support at your company. Users are all complaining of very slow Internet connectivity. When you examine the firewall, you find a large number of incoming connections that are not completed, all packets coming from a single IP address. What best describes this attack?

    A. DDoS

    B. SYN flood

    C. Buffer overflow

    D. ARP poisoning

93. An attacker is trying to get malformed queries sent to the backend database to circumvent the web page's security. What type of attack depends on the attacker entering text into text boxes on a web page that is not normal text, but rather odd-looking commands that are designed to be inserted into database queries?

    A. SQL injection

    B. Clickjacking

    C. Cross-site scripting

    D. Bluejacking

94. Tyrell is responsible for selecting cryptographic products for his company. The company wants to encrypt the drives of all laptops. The product they have selected uses 128-bit AES encryption for full disk encryption, and users select a password to decrypt the drive. What, if any, would be the major weakness in this system?

    A. None; this is a good system.

    B. The 128-bit AES key is too short.

    C. The passwords users select are the weak link.

    D. The AES algorithm is the problem; they should use DES.

95. Valerie is responsible for security testing applications in her company. She has discovered that a web application, under certain conditions, can generate a memory leak. What, type of attack would this leave the application vulnerable to?

    A. DoS

    B. Backdoor

    C. SQL injection

    D. Buffer overflow

96. When a multithreaded application does not properly handle various threads accessing a common value, what flaw is this?

   A. Memory leak

   B. Buffer overflow

   C. Integer overflow

   D. Race condition

97. Acme Company is using smart cards that use near-field communication (NFC) rather than needing to be swiped. This is meant to make physical access to secure areas more secure. What vulnerability might this also create?

   A. Tailgating

   B. Eavesdropping

   C. IP spoofing

   D. Race conditions

98. John is responsible for physical security at a large manufacturing plant. Employees all use a smart card in order to open the front door and enter the facility. Which of the following is a common way attackers would circumvent this system?

   A. Phishing

   B. Tailgating

   C. Spoofing the smart card

   D. RFID spoofing

99. Which of the following is the term for an attack wherein malware inserts itself as a library, such as a DLL, between an application and the real system library the application is attempting to communicate with?

   A. Application spoofing

   B. Jamming

   C. Evil twin

   D. Shimming

100. You are responsible for incident response at Acme Corporation. You have discovered that someone has been able to circumvent the Windows authentication process for a specific network application. It appears that the attacker took the stored hash of the password and sent it directly to the backend authentication service, bypassing the application. What type of attack is this?

   A. Hash spoofing

   B. Evil twin

   C. Shimming

   D. Pass the hash

101. A user in your company reports that she received a call from someone claiming to be from the company technical support team. The caller stated that there was a virus spreading through the company and he needed immediate access to the employee's computer to stop it from being infected. What social-engineering principles did the caller use to try to trick the employee?

    A. Urgency and intimidation

    B. Urgency and authority

    C. Authority and trust

    D. Intimidation and authority

102. Ahmed has discovered that someone has manipulated tables in one of the company's switches. The manipulation has changed the tables so that data destined for one specific MAC address will now be routed elsewhere. What type of attack is this?

    A. ARP poisoning

    B. DNS poisoning

    C. Man-in-the-middle

    D. Backdoor

103. You are investigating incidents at Acme Corporation and have discovered malware on several machines. It appears that this malware infects system files in the `Windows/System32/` directory and also affects the boot sector. What type of malware is this?

    A. Multipartite

    B. Boot sector

    C. Macro virus

    D. Polymorphic virus

104. What type of attack uses Bluetooth to access the data from a cell phone when in range?

    A. Phonejacking

    B. Bluejacking

    C. Bluesnarfing

    D. Evil twin

105. An attacker is using a table of precomputed hashes in order to try to get a Windows password. What type of technique is being used?

    A. Dictionary

    B. Brute force

    C. Pass the hash

    D. Rainbow table

106. Carlos works in incident response for a mid-sized bank. Users inform him that internal network connections are fine, but connecting to the outside world is very slow. Carlos reviews logs on the external firewall and discovers tens of thousands of ICMP packets coming from a wide range of different IP addresses. What type of attack is occurring?

   A. Smurf

   B. DoS

   C. DDoS

   D. SYN flood

107. What type of attack is it when the attacker attempts to get the victim's communication to abandon a high-quality/secure mode in favor of a lower-quality/less secure mode?

   A. Downgrade

   B. Brute force

   C. Rainbow table

   D. Bluesnarfing

108. What type of penetration test is being done when the tester is given extensive knowledge of the target network?

   A. White-box

   B. Full disclosure

   C. Black-box

   D. Red team

109. Your company is instituting a new security awareness program. You are responsible for educating end users on a variety of threats, including social engineering. Which of the following best defines social engineering?

   A. Illegal copying of software

   B. Gathering information from discarded manuals and printouts

   C. Using people skills to obtain proprietary information

   D. Phishing emails

110. Which of the following attacks can be caused by a user being unaware of their physical surroundings?

   A. ARP poisoning

   B. Phishing

   C. Shoulder surfing

   D. Smurf attack

111. Francine is a network administrator for Acme Corporation. She has noticed that one of the servers is now unreachable. After carefully reviewing various logs, she discovers that a large number of broadcast packets were sent to the network router, spoofing the server's IP address. What type of attack is this?

    A. SYN flood

    B. ICMP flood

    C. Buffer overflow

    D. Smurf attack

112. An attacker enters code into a text box on a website. That text box is used for product reviews. The attacker wants his code to execute the next time a visitor visits that page. What is this attack called?

    A. SQL injection

    B. Logic bomb

    C. Cross-site scripting

    D. Session hijacking

113. A user is redirected to a different website when the user requests the DNS record www.xyz.com. Which of the following is this an example of?

    A. DNS poisoning

    B. DoS

    C. DNS caching

    D. Smurf attack

114. Tom is the network administrator for a small accounting firm. As soon as he comes in to work, users report to him that they cannot connect to the network. After investigating, Tom discovers that none of the workstations can connect to the network and all have an IP address in the form of 169.254.x.x. What has occurred?

    A. Smurf attack

    B. Man-in-the-middle attack

    C. DDoS

    D. DHCP starvation

115. Which of the following would most likely use a group of bots to stop a web server from accepting new requests?

    A. DoS

    B. DDoS

    C. Buffer overflow

    D. Trojan horse

116. Which of the following would a former employee most likely plant on a server before leaving to cause disruption to the network?

A. Worm

B. Logic bomb

C. Trojan

D. Virus

117. A SYN flood is a DoS attack in which an attacker deliberately violates the three-way handshake and opens a large number of half-open TCP connections. The signature of a SYN flood attack is:

A. The source and destination address having the same value

B. The source and destination port numbers having the same value

C. A large number of SYN packets appearing on a network without the corresponding ACK packets

D. A large number of SYN packets appearing on a network with the corresponding reply RST

118. What does white-box testing mean?

A. The tester has full knowledge of the environment.

B. The tester has no knowledge of the environment.

C. The tester has permission to access the system.

D. The tester has no permission to access the system.

119. Ahmed has been hired to perform a penetration test of Acme Corporation. He begins by looking at IP address ranges owned by the company and details of domain name registration. He also visits social media and newsgroups to see if they contain any sensitive information or have any technical details online. Within the context of penetration-examining methodology, what phase is Ahmed conducting?

A. Passive information gathering

B. Active information gathering

C. Initial exploitation

D. Vulnerability scanning

120. Mary works for a large insurance company, on their cybersecurity team. She is investigating a recent incident and discovers that a server was breached using an authorized user's account. After investigating the incident further, Mary believes that the authorized user logged on, and then someone else took over their session. What best describes this attack?

A. Man-in-the-middle

B. Session hijacking

C. Backdoor

D. Smurf attack

121. Which of the following type of testing utilizes an automated process of proactively identifying vulnerabilities of the computing systems present on a network?

   A. Security audit

   B. Vulnerability scanning

   C. White-box test

   D. Black-box test

122. What type of attack is an NFC most susceptible to?

   A. Eavesdropping

   B. Man-in-the-middle

   C. Buffer overflow

   D. Smurf attack

123. John has been asked to do a penetration test of a company. He has been given general information but no details about the network. What kind of test is this?

   A. Gray-box

   B. White-box

   C. Partial

   D. Masked

124. Under which type of attack does an attacker's system appear to be the server to the real client and appear to be the client to the real server?

   A. Denial of service

   B. Replay

   C. Eavesdropping

   D. Man-in-the-middle

125. You are a security administrator for Acme Corporation. You have discovered malware on some of your company's machines. This malware seems to intercept calls from the web browser to libraries, and then manipulates the browser calls. What type of attack is this?

   A. Man-in-the-browser

   B. Man-in-the-middle

   C. Buffer overflow

   D. Session hijacking

126. Your company has hired a penetration testing firm to test the company network security. The penetration tester has just been able to achieve guest-level privileges on one low-security system. What best describes this phase of the test?

   A. Vulnerability scanning

   B. Initial exploit

   C. Black-box testing

   D. White-box testing

127. What is the primary risk from using outdated software?

    A. It may not have all the features you need.

    B. It may not have the most modern security features.

    C. It may no longer be supported by the vendor.

    D. It may be easier to break into than newer software.

128. You are responsible for software testing at Acme Corporation. You want to check all software for bugs that might be used by an attacker to gain entrance into the software or your network. You have discovered a web application that would allow a user to attempt to put a 64-bit value into a 4-byte integer variable. What is this type of flaw?

    A. Memory overflow

    B. Buffer overflow

    C. Variable overflow

    D. Integer overflow

129. Which type of virus is most difficult to analyze by reverse engineering?

    A. Polymorphic

    B. Macro

    C. Armored

    D. Boot sector

130. What type of attack attempts to deauthorize users from a resource, such as a wireless access point (WAP)?

    A. Disassociation

    B. Session hijacking

    C. Man-in-the-middle

    D. Smurf attack

131. John is a network administrator for a large retail chain. He has discovered that his DNS server is being attacked. The attack involves false DNS requests from spoofed IP addresses. The requests are far larger than normal. What type of attack is this?

    A. Amplification

    B. DNS poisoning

    C. DNS spoofing

    D. Smurf attack

132. Heidi is a security officer for an investment firm. Many of the employees in her firm travel frequently and access the company intranet from remote locations. Heidi is concerned about users logging in from public WiFi, as well as other people seeing information such as login credentials or customer data. Which of the following is Heidi's most significant concern?

    A. Social engineering

    B. Shoulder surfing

    C. Man-in-the-middle attack

    D. CSRF

133. Cross-site scripting is an attack on the _____ that is based on the _____ trusting the _____.

   A. user, user, website
   B. user, website, user
   C. website, website, user
   D. user, website, website

134. You are a security officer for a large investment firm. Some of your stock traders handle very valuable accounts with large amounts of money. You are concerned about someone targeting these specific traders to get their login credentials and access account information. Which of the following best describes the attack you are concerned about?

   A. Spear phishing
   B. Man-in-the-middle
   C. Target phishing
   D. Vishing

135. You lead an incident response team for a large retail chain store. You have discovered what you believe is spyware on the point-of-sale systems. But the malware in question is encrypted, preventing you from analyzing it. What best describes this?

   A. An armored virus
   B. Ransomware
   C. Polymorphic virus
   D. Trojan horse

136. Jared has discovered malware on the workstations of several users. This particular malware provides administrative privileges for the workstation to an external hacker. What best describes this malware?

   A. Trojan horse
   B. Logic bomb
   C. Multipartite virus
   D. Rootkit

137. Users in your company report someone has been calling their extension and claiming to be doing a survey for a large vendor. Based on the questions asked in the survey, you suspect that this is a scam to elicit information from your company's employees. What best describes this?

   A. Spear phishing
   B. Vishing
   C. War dialing
   D. Robocalling

138. Cross-site request forgery is an attack on the _____ that is based on the _____ trusting the _____.

   A. website, website, user

   B. user, user website

   C. website, user, website

   D. user, website, user

139. What type of virus can infect both a file in the operating system and the boot sector?

   A. Multipartite

   B. Rootkit

   C. Ransomware

   D. Worm

140. John is analyzing a recent malware infection on his company network. He discovers malware that can spread rapidly and does not require any interaction from the user. What best describes this malware?

   A. Worm

   B. Virus

   C. Logic bomb

   D. Trojan horse

141. Your company has issued some new security directives. One of these new directives is that all documents must be shredded before being thrown out. What type of attack is this trying to prevent?

   A. Phishing

   B. Dumpster diving

   C. Shoulder surfing

   D. Man-in-the-middle

142. What type of attack embeds malicious code into a document or spreadsheet?

   A. Logic bomb

   B. Rootkit

   C. Trojan horse

   D. Macro virus

143. You are a network security analyst for an online retail website. Users report that they have visited your site and had their credit cards stolen. You cannot find any evidence of any breach of your website. You begin to suspect that these users were lured to a fake site. You have found a website that is spelled exactly like your company site, with one letter different. What is this attack called?

   A. URL hijacking

   B. DNS poisoning

    C. Cross-site scripting

    D. Man-in-the-middle

144. You have discovered that someone has been trying to log on to your web server. The person has tried a wide range of likely passwords. What type of attack is this?

    A. Rainbow table

    B. Birthday attack

    C. Dictionary attack

    D. Spoofing

145. You have just started a new job as a security administrator for Acme Corporation. You discover they have weak authentication protocols. You are concerned that an attacker might simply capture and re-send a user's login credentials. What type of attack is this?

    A. Replay attack

    B. IP spoofing

    C. Login spoofing

    D. Session hijacking

146. What is the primary difference between active and passive reconnaissance?

    A. Active will be done manually, passive with tools.

    B. Active is done with black-box tests and passive with white-box tests.

    C. Active is usually done by attackers and passive by testers.

    D. Active will actually connect to the network and could be detected; passive won't.

147. What is the primary difference between a vulnerability scan and a penetration test?

    A. Vulnerability scans are done by employees and penetration tests by outside teams.

    B. Vulnerability scans only use tools; penetration tests are manual.

    C. Vulnerability scans just identify issues; penetration tests attempt to exploit them.

    D. Vulnerability scans are usually white-box tests; penetration tests are black-box tests.

148. When an attacker breaches one system and uses that as a base to attack a related system, what is this called?

    A. Man-in-the-middle

    B. Pivot

    C. Shimming

    D. Vishing

149. Terrance is conducting a penetration test for a client. The client is a major e-commerce company and is primarily concerned about security for their web server. He has just finished running Nmap and OWASP Zap on the target web server. What is this activity called?

   A. Passive scanning

   B. Black-box testing

   C. Active scanning

   D. White-box testing

150. You have just taken over as the CISO for a large bank. You are concerned about making sure all systems are secure. One major concern you have is security misconfiguration. Which of the following is not a common security misconfiguration?

   A. Unpatched operating system

   B. Default accounts with passwords

   C. Unneeded services running

   D. No firewall running

Chapter

2

Technologies and Tools

THE COMPTIA SECURITY+ EXAM SY0-501 TOPICS COVERED IN THIS CHAPTER INCLUDE THE FOLLOWING:

✓ **2.1 Install and configure network components, both hardware- and software-based, to support organizational security.**

- Firewall
    - ACL
    - Application-based vs. network-based
    - Stateful vs. stateless
    - Implicit deny
- VPN concentrator
    - Remote access vs. site-to-site
    - IPSec
        - Tunnel mode
        - Transport mode
        - AH
        - ESP
    - Split tunnel vs. full tunnel
    - TLS
    - Always-on VPN
- NIPS/NIDS
    - Signature-based
    - Heuristic/behavioral
    - Anomaly
    - Inline vs. passive
    - In-band vs. out-of-band
    - Rules

- Analytics
  - False positive
  - False negative
- Router
  - ACLs
  - Antispoofing
- Switch
  - Port security
  - Layer 2 vs. Layer 3
  - Loop prevention
  - Flood guard
- Proxy
  - Forward and reverse proxy
  - Transparent
  - Application/multipurpose
- Load balancer
  - Scheduling
    - Affinity
    - Round-robin
  - Active-passive
  - Active-active
  - Virtual IPs
- Access point
  - SSID
  - MAC filtering
  - Signal strength
  - Band selection/width
  - Antenna types and placement
  - Fat vs. thin
  - Controller-based vs. standalone
- SIEM
  - Aggregation

- Correlation
- Automated alerting and triggers
- Time synchronization
- Event deduplication
- Logs/WORM
- DLP
  - USB blocking
  - Cloud-based
  - Email
- NAC
  - Dissolvable vs. permanent
  - Host health checks
  - Agent vs. agentless
- Mail gateway
  - Spam filter
  - DLP
  - Encryption
- Bridge
- SSL/TLS accelerators
- SSL decryptors
- Media gateway
- Hardware security module

✓ **2.2 Given a scenario, use appropriate software tools to assess the security posture of an organization.**

- Protocol analyzer
- Network scanners
  - Rogue system detection
    - Network mapping
- Wireless scanners/cracker
- Password cracker
- Vulnerability scanner
- Configuration compliance scanner

- Exploitation frameworks
- Data sanitization tools
- Steganography tools
- Honeypot
- Backup utilities
- Banner grabbing
- Passive vs. active
- Command line tools
  - ping
  - netstat
  - tracert
  - nslookup/dig
  - arp
  - ipconfig/ip/ifconfig
  - tcpdump
  - nmap
  - netcat

✓ **2.3 Given a scenario, troubleshoot common security issues.**

- Unencrypted credentials/clear text
- Logs and events anomalies
- Permission issues
- Access violations
- Certificate issues
- Data exfiltration
- Misconfigured devices
  - Firewall
  - Content filter
  - Access points
- Weak security configurations
- Personnel issues
  - Policy violation

- Insider threat
- Social engineering
- Social media
- Personal email
- Unauthorized software
- Baseline deviation
- License compliance violation (availability/integrity)
- Asset management
- Authentication issues

✓ **2.4 Given a scenario, analyze and interpret output from security technologies.**

- HIDS/HIPS
- Antivirus
- File integrity check
- Host-based firewall
- Application whitelisting
- Removable media control
- Advanced malware tools
- Patch management tools
- UTM
- DLP
- Data execution prevention
- Web application firewall

✓ **2.5 Given a scenario, deploy mobile devices securely.**

- Connection methods
  - Cellular
  - WiFi
  - SATCOM
  - Bluetooth
  - NFC
  - ANT

- Infrared
- USB
- Mobile device management concepts
  - Application management
  - Content management
  - Remote wipe
  - Geofencing
  - Geolocation
  - Screen locks
  - Push notification services
  - Passwords and pins
  - Biometrics
  - Context-aware authentication
  - Containerization
  - Storage segmentation
  - Full device encryption
- Enforcement and monitoring for:
  - Third-party app stores
  - Rooting/jailbreaking
  - Sideloading
  - Custom firmware
  - Carrier unlocking
  - Firmware OTA updates
  - Camera use
  - SMS/MMS
  - External media
  - USB OTG
  - Recording microphone
  - GPS tagging
  - WiFi direct/ad hoc
  - Tethering
  - Payment methods

- Deployment models
    - BYOD
    - COPE
    - CYOD
    - Corporate-owned
    - VDI

✓ **2.6 Given a scenario, implement secure protocols.**

- Protocols
    - DNSSEC
    - SSH
    - S/MIME
    - SRTP
    - LDAPS
    - FTPS
    - SFTP
    - SNMPv3
    - SSL/TLS
    - HTTPS
    - Secure POP/IMAP
- Use cases
    - Voice and video
    - Time synchronization
    - Email and web
    - File transfer
    - Directory services
    - Remote access
    - Domain name resolution
    - Routing and switching
    - Network address allocation
    - Subscription services

1. John is looking for a new firewall for a small company. He is concerned about DoS attacks, particularly the SYN flood. Which type of firewall would give the best protection against the SYN flood?

   A. Packet filter

   B. Application gateway

   C. Bastion

   D. SPI

2. You are responsible for network security at an insurance company. A lot of employees bring their own devices. You have security concerns about this. You have decided to implement a process whereby when users connect to your network, their devices are scanned. If a device does not meet your minimum security requirements, it is not allowed to connect. What best describes this?

   A. NAC

   B. SPI

   C. IDS

   D. BYOD

3. Ahmed is responsible for VPN connections at his company. His company uses IPSec exclusively. He has decided to implement IPSec in a mode that encrypts the data of only the packet, not the headers. What is this called?

   A. Tunneling

   B. IKE

   C. ESP

   D. Transport

4. Maria is responsible for monitoring IDS activity on her company's network. Twice in the past month there has been activity reported on the IDS that investigation has shown was legitimate traffic. What best describes this?

   A. False negative

   B. Passive

   C. Active

   D. False positive

5. Juanita is a network administrator for a large university. The university has numerous systems, each with logs she must monitor and analyze. What would be the best approach for her to view and analyze logs from a central server?

   A. NAC

   B. Port forwarding

   C. IDS

   D. SIEM

6. Enrique is responsible for web application security at his company. He is concerned about attacks such as SQL injection. Which of the following devices would provide the best protection for web attacks on his web application server?

A. ACL

B. SPI

C. WAF

D. IDS

7. ACME Company has several remote offices. The CIO wants to set up permanent secure connections between the remote offices and the central office. What would be the best solution for this?

A. L2TP VPN

B. IPSEC VPN

C. Site-to-site VPN

D. Remote-access VPN

8. Mary is responsible for network security at a medium-sized insurance company. She is concerned that the offices are too open to public traffic and someone could simply connect a laptop to an open RJ45 jack and access the network. Which of the following would best address this concern?

A. ACL

B. IDS

C. VLAN

D. Port security

9. You are the network administrator for an e-commerce company. You are responsible for the web server cluster. You are concerned about not only failover, but also load-balancing and using all the servers in your cluster to accomplish load-balancing. What should you implement?

A. Active-active

B. Active-passive

C. Affinity

D. Round-robin

10. Donald is working as a network administrator. He is responsible for the database cluster. Connections are load-balanced in the cluster by each new connection being simply sent to the next server in the cluster. What type of load-balancing is this?

A. Round-robin

B. Affinity

C. Weighted

D. Rotating

11. Gerald is setting up new wireless access points throughout his company's building. The wireless access points have just the radio transceiver, with no additional functionality. What best describes these wireless access points?

    A. Fat

    B. Repeater

    C. Thick

    D. Thin

12. Mohaned is an IT manager for a hotel. His hotel wants to put wireless access points on each floor. The specifications state that the wireless access points should have minimal functionality, with all the configuration, authentication, and other functionality centrally controlled. What type of wireless access points should Mohaned consider purchasing?

    A. Fat

    B. Controller-based

    C. Stand-alone

    D. 801.11i

13. What IPSec protocol provides authentication and encryption?

    A. AH

    B. ESP

    C. IKE

    D. ISAKMP

14. Terrance is implementing IPSec. He wants to ensure that the packets are encrypted, and that the packet and all headers are authenticated. What should he implement?

    A. AH

    B. ESP

    C. AH and ESP

    D. IKE

15. You are responsible for security at your company. One of management's biggest concerns is that employees might exfiltrate sensitive data. Which of the following would you implement first?

    A. IPS

    B. Routine audits of user machines

    C. VLAN

    D. USB blocking

16. You are responsible for email server security in your company. You want to implement encryption of all emails, using third-party authenticated certificates. What protocol should you implement?

    A. IMAP

    B. S/MIME

    C. PGP

    D. SMTP-S

17. Joanne is responsible for all remote connectivity to her company's network. She knows that administrators frequently log in to servers remotely to execute command-line commands and Linux shell commands. She wants to make sure this can only be done if the transmission is encrypted. What protocol should she use?

    A. HTTPS

    B. RDP

    C. Telnet

    D. SSH

18. You are responsible for network management at your company. You have been using SNMP for many years. You are currently using SNMP v2. A colleague has recently suggested you upgrade to SNMP v3. What is the primary benefit of SNMP v3?

    A. It is much faster.

    B. It integrates with SIEM.

    C. It uses CHAP authentication.

    D. It is encrypted.

19. Employees in your company are allowed to use tablets. They can select a tablet from four different models approved by the company but purchased by the employee. What best describes this?

    A. BYOD

    B. CYOD

    C. COPE

    D. BYOE

20. Mahmoud is considering moving all company desktops to a VDI deployment. Which of the following would be a security advantage of VDI?

    A. Employees can work from any computer in the company.

    B. VDI is more resistant to malware.

    C. Patch management is centrally controlled.

    D. It eliminates man-in-the-middle attacks.

21. You have been assigned to select a backup communication method for your company to use in case of significant disasters that disrupt normal communication. Which option would provide the most reliability?

    A. Cellular

    B. WiFi

    C. SATCOM

    D. VoIP

22. John is concerned about the security of data on smartphones and tablets that his company issues to employees. Which of the following would be most effective in preventing data loss, should a device be stolen?

   A. Remote wipe

   B. Geolocation

   C. Strong PIN

   D. Limited data storage

23. What does geofencing accomplish?

   A. Provides the location for a mobile device.

   B. Limits the range a mobile device can be used in.

   C. Determines WiFi coverage areas.

   D. Segments the WiFi.

24. What best describes mobile device content management?

   A. Limiting how much content can be stored.

   B. Limiting the type of content that can be stored.

   C. Blocking certain websites.

   D. Digitally signing authorized content.

25. Frank believes there could be a problem accessing the DHCP server from a specific client. He wants to check by getting a new dynamic IP. What command will do this?

   A. `ipconfig /request`

   B. `NETSTAT -renew`

   C. `ipconfig /renew`

   D. `NETSTAT /request`

26. Teresa is responsible for network administration at a health club chain. She is trying for find a communication technology that uses low power and can spend long periods in low-power sleep modes. Which of the following technologies would be the best fit?

   A. WiFi

   B. Cellular

   C. Bluetooth

   D. ANT

27. What technology was first introduced in Windows Vista and still exists in Windows that helps prevent malware by requiring user authorization to run executables?

   A. DEP

   B. DLP

   C. UTM

   D. ANT

28. John is responsible for security of his company's new e-commerce server. He wants to ensure that online transactions are secure. What technology should he use?

   A. L2TP

   B. IPSec

   C. SSL

   D. TLS

29. Frank is a network administrator for a small college. The college has implemented a simple NIDS. However, the NIDS seems to only catch well-known attacks. What technology is this NIDS likely missing?

   A. Heuristic scanning

   B. Signature scanning

   C. Passive scanning

   D. Active scanning

30. You are concerned about an attacker enumerating all of your network. What protocol might help at least mitigate this issue?

   A. HTTPS

   B. TLS

   C. IPSec

   D. LDAPS

31. You have been asked to implement a secure protocol for transferring files that uses digital certificates. Which protocol would be the best choice?

   A. FTP

   B. SFTP

   C. FTPS

   D. SCP

32. Ahmed is responsible for VoIP at his company. He has been directed to ensure that all VoIP calls have the option to be encrypted. What protocol is best suited for security VoIP calls?

   A. SIP

   B. TLS

   C. SRTP

   D. SSH

33. What is the purpose of screen locks on mobile devices?

   A. To encrypt the device

   B. To limit access to the device

   C. To load a specific user's apps

   D. To connect to WiFi

34. Maria is a security engineer with a large bank. Her CIO has asked her to investigate the use of context-aware authentication for online banking. Which of the following best describes context-aware authentication?

   A. In addition to username and password, authentication is based on the entire context (location, time of day, action being attempted, etc.).

   B. Without a username or password, authentication is based on the entire context (location, time of day, action being attempted, etc.).

   C. Authentication that requires a username and password, but in the context of a token or digital certificate

   D. Authentication that requires a username and password, but not in the context of a token or digital certificate

35. What does application management accomplish for mobile devices?

   A. Only allows applications from the iTunes store to be installed

   B. Ensures the company has a list of all applications on the devices

   C. Ensures only approved applications are installed on the devices

   D. Updates patches on all applications on mobile devices

36. Dominick is responsible for security at a medium-sized insurance company. He is very concerned about detecting intrusions. The IDS he has purchased states that he must have an IDS on each network segment. What type of IDS is this?

   A. Active

   B. IPS

   C. Passive

   D. Inline

37. Remote employees at your company frequently need to connect to both the secure company network via VPN and open public websites, simultaneously. What technology would best support this?

   A. Split tunnel

   B. IPSec

   C. Full tunnel

   D. TLS

38. Denish is looking for a solution that will allow his network to retrieve information from a wide range of web resources, while all traffic passes through a proxy. What would be the best solution?

   A. Forward proxy

   B. Reverse proxy

   C. SPI

   D. Open proxy

39. Someone has been rummaging through your company's trash bins seeking to find documents, diagrams, or other sensitive information that has been thrown out. What is this called?

   A. Dumpster diving

   B. Trash diving

   C. Social engineering

   D. Trash engineering

40. Derrick is responsible for a web server cluster at his company. The cluster uses various load-balancing protocols. Derrick wants to ensure that clients connecting from Europe are directed to a specific server in the cluster. What would be the best solution to his problem?

   A. Affinity

   B. Binding

   C. Load balancing

   D. Round-robin

41. Teresa is responsible for WiFi security in her company. Her main concern is that there are many other offices in the building her company occupies and that someone could easily attempt to breach their WiFi from one of these locations. What technique would be best in alleviating her concern?

   A. Using thin WAPs

   B. Geofencing

   C. Securing the Admin screen

   D. WAP placement

42. Juan is responsible for the SIEM in his company. The SIEM aggregates logs from 12 servers. In the event that a breach is discovered, which of the following would be Juan's most important concern?

   A. Event duplication

   B. Time synchronization

   C. Impact assessment

   D. Correlation

43. When you are considering an NIDS or NIPS, what are your two most important concerns?

   A. Cost and false positives

   B. False positives and false negatives

   C. Power consumption and cost

   D. Management interface and cost

44. Shelly is very concerned about unauthorized users connecting to the company routers. She would like to prevent spoofing. What is the most essential antispoofing technique for routers?

   A. ACL

   B. Logon

   C. NIPS

   D. NIDS

45. Farès has implemented a flood guard. What type of attack is this most likely to defend against?

   A. SYN attack

   B. DNS poisoning

   C. MAC spoofing

   D. ARP spoofing

46. Terrance is trying to get all of his users to connect to a certificate server on his network. However, some of the users are using machines that are incompatible with the certificate server, and changing those machines is not an option. Which of the following would be the best solution for Terrance?

   A. Use an application proxy for the certificate server.

   B. Use NAT with the certificate server.

   C. Change the server.

   D. Implement a protocol analyzer.

47. John is implementing virtual IP load-balancing. He thinks this might alleviate network slowdowns, and perhaps even mitigate some of the impact of a denial-of-service attack. What is the drawback of virtual IP load-balancing?

   A. It is resource-intensive.

   B. Most servers don't support it.

   C. It is connection-based, not load-based.

   D. It works only on Unix/Linux servers.

48. There has been a breach of the ACME network. John manages the SIEM at ACME. Part of the attack disrupted NTP; what SIEM issue would this most likely impact?

   A. Time synchronization

   B. Correlation

   C. Event duplication

   D. Events not being logged

49. What command would produce the image shown here?

    A. `ping -n 6 -l 100 192.168.1.1`

    B. `ping 192.168.1.1 -n 6 -s 100`

    C. `ping #6 s 100 192.168.1.1`

    D. `ping -s 6 -w 100 192.168.1.1`

50. You are a security officer for a large law firm. You are concerned about data loss prevention. You have limited the use of USBs and other portable media, you use an IDS to look for large volumes of outbound data, and a guard searches all personnel and bags before they leave the building. What is a key step in DLP that you have missed?

    A. Portable drives

    B. Email

    C. Bluetooth

    D. Optical media

51. Which of the following email security measures would have the most impact on phishing emails?

    A. Email encryption

    B. Hardening the email server

    C. Digitally signing email

    D. Spam filter

52. Joanne has implemented TLS for communication with many of her networks servers. She wants to ensure that the traffic cannot be sniffed. However, users now complain that this is slowing down connectivity. Which of the following is the best solution?

    A. Increase RAM on servers.

    B. Change routers to give more bandwidth to traffic to these servers.

    C. Implement TLS accelerators.

    D. Place all servers in clusters with extensive load-balancing.

53. Olivia has discovered steganography tools on an employee's computer. What is the greatest concern regarding employees having steganography tools?

    A. Password cracking

    B. Data exfiltration

    C. Hiding network traffic

    D. Malware

54. What command would generate the output shown here?

```
Proto  Local Address          Foreign Address         State        PID
TCP    127.0.0.1:15485        DESKTOP-CV8KNU2:57688   ESTABLISHED  2212
TCP    127.0.0.1:57688        DESKTOP-CV8KNU2:15485   ESTABLISHED  7204
TCP    127.0.0.1:57691        DESKTOP-CV8KNU2:57692   ESTABLISHED  960
TCP    127.0.0.1:57692        DESKTOP-CV8KNU2:57691   ESTABLISHED  960
```

    A. `netstat -a`

    B. `netstat -o`

    C. `arp -a`

    D. `arp -g`

55. John has discovered that an attacker is trying to get network passwords by using software that attempts a number of passwords from a list of common passwords. What type of attack is this?

    A. Dictionary

    B. Rainbow table

    C. Brute force

    D. Session hijacking

56. Isabella has found netcat installed on an employee's computer. That employee is not authorized to have netcat. What security concern might this utility present?

    A. It is a password cracker.

    B. It is a packet sniffer.

    C. It is a network communication utility.

    D. It is a DoS tool.

57. Omar is a network administrator for ACME Company. He is responsible for the certificate authorities within the corporate network. The CAs publish their CRLs once per week. What, if any, security issue might this present?

    A. Revoked certificates still being used

    B. Invalid certificates being issued

    C. No security issue

    D. Certificates with weak keys

58. Hans is a network administrator for a large bank. He is concerned about employees violating software licenses. What would be the first step in addressing this issue?

    A. Performing software audits

    B. Scanning the network for installed applications

    C. Establishing clear policies

    D. Blocking the ability of users to install software

59. You are responsible for authentication methods at your company. You have implemented fingerprint scanners to enter server rooms. Frequently people are being denied access to the server room, even though they are authorized. What problem is this?

A. FAR

B. FRR

C. CER

D. EER

60. John is responsible for network security at a very small company. Due to both budget constraints and space constraints, John can select only one security device. What should he select?

A. Firewall

B. Antivirus

C. IDS

D. UTM

61. You are responsible for security at Acme Company. Recently, 20 new employee network accounts were created, with the default privileges for the network. You have discovered that eight of these have privileges that are not needed for their job tasks. Which security principle best describes how to avoid this problem in the future?

A. Least privileges

B. Separation of duties

C. Implicit deny

D. Weakest link

62. Mary is concerned that SIEM logs at her company are not being stored long enough, or securely enough. She is aware that it is possible a breach might not be discovered until long after it occurs. This would require the company to analyze older logs. It is important that Mary find an SIEM log backup solution that can a) handle all the aggregate logs of the SIEM, b) be maintained for a long period of time, and c) be secure. What solution would be best for her?

A. Back up to large-capacity external drives.

B. Back up to large-capacity backup tapes.

C. Back up to WORM storage.

D. Back up to tapes that will be stored off-site.

63. Elizabeth is responsible for SIEM systems in her company. She monitors the company's SIEM screens every day, checking every hour. What, if any, would be a better approach for her to keep up with issues that appear in the logs?

A. Automatic alerts

B. Having logs forwarded to her email

C. Nothing, this is fine.

D. Review SIEM logs primarily when an incident occurs.

64. You are responsible for network security at a university. Faculty members are issued laptops. However, many of the faculty members leave the laptops in their offices most of the time (sometimes even for weeks). You are concerned about theft of laptops. In this scenario, what would be the most cost-effective method of securing the laptops?

A. FDE

B. GPS tagging

C. Geofencing

D. Tethering

65. You work at a defense contracting company. You are responsible for mobile device security. Some researchers in your company use company-issued tablets for work. These tablets may contain sensitive, even classified data. What is the most important security measure for you to implement?

A. FDE

B. GPS tagging

C. Geofencing

D. Content management

66. When using any HIDS/HIPS or NIDS/NIPS, the output is specific to the vendor. However, what is the basic set of information that virtually all HIDSs/HIPSs or NIDSs/NIPSs provide?

A. IP addresses (sender and receiver), ports (sender and receiver), and protocol

B. IP addresses (sender and receiver), ports (sender and receiver), and attack type

C. IP addresses (sender and receiver), ports (sender and receiver), usernames, and machine names

D. Usernames, machine names, and attack type

67. You are responsible for firewalls in your company. You are reviewing the output of the gateway firewall. What basic information would any firewall have in its logs?

A. For all traffic: the source and destination IP and port, protocol, and whether it was allowed or denied

B. For only blocked traffic: the source and destination IP and port as well as the reason for the traffic being denied/blocked

C. For all traffic: the source and destination IP and port, whether it was allowed or denied, and the reason it was denied/blocked

D. For only blocked traffic: the source and destination IP, protocol, and the reason it was denied/blocked

68. Teresa is responsible for incident response at ACME Company. There was a recent breach of the network. The breach was widespread and affected many computers. As part of the incident response process, Teresa will collect the logs from the SIEM, which aggregates logs from 20 servers. Which of the following should she do first?

A. Event de-duplication

B. Log forwarding

    C. Identify the nature of the attack

    D. Identify the source IP of the attack

69. Hector is responsible for NIDS/NIPS in his company. He is configuring a new NIPS solution. What part of the NIPS collects data?

    A. Sensor

    B. Data source

    C. Manager

    D. Analyzer

70. Gerald is a network administrator for a small financial services company. He is responsible for controlling access to resources on his network. What mechanism is responsible for blocking access to a resource based on the requesting IP address?

    A. ACL

    B. NIPS

    C. HIPS

    D. Port blocking

71. Elizabeth is responsible for secure communications at her company. She wants to give administrators the option to log in remotely and to execute command-line functions, but she wants this to only be possible via a secure, encrypted connection. What action should she take on the firewall?

    A. Block port 23 and allow ports 20 and 21.

    B. Block port 22 and allow ports 20 and 21.

    C. Block port 22 and allow port 23.

    D. Block port 23 and allow port 22.

72. Mark is looking for a proxy server for his network. The purpose of the proxy server is to ensure that the web servers are hidden from outside clients. All of the different web servers should appear to the outside world as if they were the proxy server. What type of proxy server would be best for Mark to consider?

    A. Forward

    B. Reverse

    C. Transparent

    D. Firewall

73. Your company has hired an outside security firm to perform various tests of your network. During the vulnerability scan you will provide that company with logins for various systems (i.e., database server, application server, web server, etc.) to aid in their scan. What best describes this?

    A. A white-box test

    B. A gray-box test

    C. A credentialed scan

    D. A logged-in scan

74. Lars is responsible for incident response at ACME Company. He is particularly concerned about the network segment that hosts the corporate web servers. He wants a solution that will detect potential attacks and notify the administrator so the administrator can take whatever action he or she deems appropriate. Which of the following would be the best solution for Lars?

   A. HIDS

   B. HIPS

   C. NIDS

   D. NIPS

75. Mia is responsible for security devices at her company. She is concerned about detecting intrusions. She wants a solution that would work across entire network segments. However, she wants to ensure that false positives do not interrupt work flow. What would be the best solution for Mia to consider?

   A. HIDS

   B. HIPS

   C. NIDS

   D. NIPS

76. Abigail is a security manager for a small company. Many employees want to use handheld devices, such as smartphones and tablets. The employees want to use these devices both for work and outside of work. Abigail is concerned about security issues. Which of the following would be the most secure solution?

   A. COPE

   B. CYOD

   C. Geotagging

   D. BYOD

77. You are responsible for always-on VPN connectivity for your company. You have been told that you must use the most secure mode for IPSec that you can. Which of the following would be the best for you to select?

   A. Tunneling

   B. AH

   C. IKE

   D. Transport

78. Debra is the network administrator for her company. Her company's web servers are all in a cluster. Her concern is this: if one of the servers in the cluster fails, will the backup server be capable of running for a significant amount of time? She wants to make sure that the backup won't soon fail. What would be her best choice in clustering?

   A. Active-active

   B. Round-robin

   C. Affinity

   D. Active-passive

79. Omar is responsible for wireless security in his company. He wants completely different WiFi access (i.e., a different SSID, different security levels, and different authentication methods) in different parts of the company. What would be the best choice for Omar to select in WAPs?

A. Fat

B. Thin

C. Repeater

D. Full

80. Lilly is a network administrator for a medium-sized financial services company. She wants to implement company-wide encryption and digital signing of emails. But she is concerned about cost, since there is a very limited budget for this. What would be her best choice?

A. SMTPS

B. S/MIME

C. IMAPS

D. PGP

81. Edward is a security manager for a bank. He has recently been reading a great deal about malware that accesses system memory. He wants to find a solution that would stop programs from utilizing system memory. Which of the following would be the best solution?

A. DEP

B. FDE

C. UTM

D. IDS

82. Sarah is the CIO for a small company. She recently had the entire company's voice calls moved to VoIP. Her new VoIP system is using SIP with RTP. What might be the concern with this?

A. SIP is not secure.

B. RTP is not secure.

C. RTP is too slow.

D. SIP is too slow.

83. What command would generate the output shown here?

A. `nslookup`

B. `ipconfig`

C. `netstat -a`

D. `dig`

84. Emiliano is a network administrator for a large web-hosting company. His company also issues digital certificates to web-hosting clients. He wants to ensure that a digital certificate will not be used once it has been revoked. He also wants to ensure that there will be no delay between when the certificate is revoked and when browsers are made aware that it is revoked. What solution would be best for this?

    A. OCSP

    B. X.509

    C. CRL

    D. PKI

85. Elizabeth is responsible for security at a defense contracting company. She is concerned about users within her network exfiltrating data by attaching sensitive documents to emails. What solution would best address this concern?

    A. Email encryption

    B. USB blocking

    C. NIPS

    D. Content filtering

86. Victor is concerned about data security on BYOD and COPE. He is concerned specifically about data exposure should the device become lost or stolen. Which of the following would be most effective in countering this concern?

    A. Geofencing

    B. Screen lock

    C. GPS tagging

    D. Device encryption

87. Gabriel is using nmap to scan one of his servers whose IP address is 192.168.1.1. He wants to perform a ping scan, but the network blocks ICMP, so he will try a TCP ping scan and do so very slowly. Which of the following would accomplish that?

    A. `nmap -0 -PT -T1 192.168.1.1`

    B. `nmap -0 - T3 192.168.1.1`

    C. `nmap -T -T1 192.168.1.1`

    D. `nmap -PT -T5 192.168.1.1`

88. Mary is a network administrator for ACME Company. She sometimes needs to run a packet sniffer so that she can view the network traffic. She wants to find a well-known packet sniffer that works on Linux. Which of the following would be her best choice?

    A. Ophcrack

    B. Nmap

    C. Wireshark

    D. Tcpdump

89. What command produced the output shown here?

```
1    5 ms     3 ms     2 ms   aca80001.ipt.aol.com [172.168.0.1]
2    6 ms    15 ms     7 ms   185.108.243.33
3    4 ms     5 ms     7 ms   192.168.194.1
4    5 ms     4 ms    12 ms   static-185-29-95-0.mobily.com.sa [185.29.95.97]
5    6 ms     8 ms     7 ms   ae2.0.igw.sbc.sr2.mobily.com.sa [86.51.2.62]
6    *         *        *     Request timed out.
7    9 ms     7 ms    19 ms   dam-adm-igw-br-02 [86.51.2.136]
8    8 ms     7 ms     8 ms   adma-mgn-msr-02 [86.51.65.141]
9  175 ms   185 ms   176 ms   pos-0-0-2-0.mgn.ashb.msr1.mobily.com.sa [86.51.65.67]
10 193 ms   174 ms   197 ms   exchange-cust1.dc2.equinix.net [206.126.236.16]
```

A. tracert -h 10 www.chuckeasttom.com

B. tracert www.chuckeasttom.com

C. netstat www.chuckeasttom.com

D. nmap www.chuckeasttom.com

90. Daryll has been using a packet sniffer to observe traffic on his company's network. He has noticed that traffic between the web server and the database server is sent in clear text. He wants a solution that will not only encrypt that traffic, but also leverage the existing digital certificate infrastructure his company has. Which of the following would be the best solution for Daryll?

A. TLS

B. SSL

C. IPSec

D. WPA2

91. Jarod is concerned about DLP in his organization. Employees all have cloud-based solutions for data storage. What DLP-related security hazard, if any, might this create?

A. No security hazard

B. Malware from the cloud

C. Data exfiltration through the cloud

D. Security policies don't apply to the cloud.

92. Derrick is a network administrator for a large company. The company network is segmented into zones of high security, medium security, low security, and the DMZ. He is concerned about external intruders and wishes to install a honeypot. Which is the most important zone to put the honeypot in?

A. High security

B. Medium security

C. Low security

D. DMZ

93. Sheila is responsible for data backups for all the company servers. She is concerned about frequency of backup and about security of the backup data. Which feature, found in some backup utility software, would be most important to her?

    A. Using data encryption

    B. Digitally signing the data

    C. Using automated backup scheduling

    D. Hashing the backup data

94. Frank is a web server administrator for a large e-commerce company. He is concerned about someone using netcat to connect to the company web server and retrieving detailed information about the server. What best describes his concern?

    A. Passive reconnaissance

    B. Active reconnaissance

    C. Banner grabbing

    D. Vulnerability scanning

95. Mike is responsible for testing security at his company. He is using a tool that identifies vulnerabilities and provides mechanisms to test them by attempting to exploit them. What best describes this type of tool?

    A. Vulnerability scanner

    B. Exploit framework

    C. Metasploit

    D. Nessus

96. William is a security officer for a large bank. When executives' laptops are decommissioned, he wants to ensure that the data on those laptops is completely wiped so that it cannot be recovered, even using forensic tools. How many times should William wipe a hard drive?

    A. 1

    B. 3

    C. 5

    D. 7

97. You are responsible for firewalls in your organization. You are concerned about ensuring that all firewalls are properly configured. The gateway firewall is configured as follows: to only allow inbound traffic on a very few specific, required ports; all traffic (allowed or blocked) is logged and logs forwarded to the SIEM. What, if anything, is missing from this configuration?

    A. Nothing, it is a good configuration.

    B. Encrypting all traffic

    C. Outbound connection rules

    D. Digital certificate authentication for inbound traffic

98. Charles is responsible for security for web servers in his company. Some web servers are used for an internal intranet, and some for external websites. He has chosen to encrypt all web traffic, and he is using self-signed X.509 certificates. What, if anything, is wrong with this approach?

    A. He cannot encrypt all HTTP traffic.

    B. He should use PGP certificates.

    C. He should not use self-signed certificates.

    D. Nothing; this is an appropriate configuration.

99. You are responsible for the security of web servers at your company. You are configuring the WAF and want to allow only encrypted traffic to and from the web server, including traffic from administrators using a command-line interface. What should you do?

    A. Open port 80 and 23, and block port 443.

    B. Open port 443 and 23, and block port 80.

    C. Open port 443 and 22, and block port 80 and 23.

    D. Open port 443, and block all other ports.

100. Francis is a security administrator at a large law firm. She is concerned that confidential documents, with proprietary information, might be leaked. The leaks could be intentional or accidental. She is looking for a solution that would embed some identifying information into documents in such a way that it would not be seen by the reader but could be extracted with the right software. What technology would best meet Francis's needs?

    A. Symmetric encryption

    B. Steganography

    C. Hashing

    D. Asymmetric encryption

101. You are responsible for the gateway firewall for your company. You need to configure a firewall to allow only email that is encrypted to be sent or received. What action should you take?

    A. Allow ports 25, 110, and 143. Block ports 465, 993, and 995.

    B. Block ports 25, 110, and 143. Allow ports 465, 993, and 995.

    C. Allow ports 25, 110, and 443. Block ports 465, 993, and 143.

    D. Block ports 465, 994, and 464. Allow ports 25, 110, and 80.

102. Mark is responsible for security for a small bank. He has a firewall at the gateway as well as one at each network segment. Each firewall logs all accepted and rejected traffic. Mark checks each of these logs regularly. What is the first step Mark should take to improve his firewall configuration?

    A. Integrate with SIEM.

    B. Add a honeypot.

    C. Integrate with AD.

    D. Add a honeynet.

103. You are setting up VPNs in your company. You are concerned that anyone running a packet sniffer could obtain metadata about the traffic. You have chosen IPSec. What mode should you use to accomplish your goals of preventing metadata being seen?

A. AH

B. ESP

C. Tunneling

D. Transport

104. John is responsible for configuring security devices in his network. He has implemented a robust NIDS in his network. However, on two occasions the NIDS has missed a breach. What configuration issue should John address?

A. False negative

B. Port blocking

C. SPI

D. False positive

105. You are responsible for communications security at your company. Your company has a large number of remote workers, including traveling salespeople. You wish to make sure that when they connect to the network, it is in a secure manner. What should you implement?

A. L2TP VPN

B. IPSec VPN

C. Site-to-site VPN

D. Remote-access VPN

106. Your company is issuing portable devices to employees for them to use for both work and personal use. This is done so the company can control the security of the devices. What, if anything, is an issue this process will cause?

A. Personal information being exposed

B. Company data being exfiltrated

C. Devices being insecurely configured

D. No issues

107. Marsha is responsible for mobile device security. Her company uses COPE for mobile devices. All phones and tablets have a screen lock and GPS tagging. What is the next, most important step for Marsha to take to secure the phones?

A. Implement geofencing.

B. Implement application management.

C. Implement geolocation.

D. Implement remote wipe.

108. Valerie is responsible for mobile device security at her company. The company is using BYOD. She is concerned about employees' personal device usage compromising company data on the phones. What technology would best address this concern?

A. Containerization

B. Screen lock

   C. Full disk encryption

   D. Biometrics

109. Jack is a chief information security officer (CISO) for a small marketing company. The company's sales staff travel extensively and all use mobile devices. He has recently become concerned about sideloading. Which of the following best describes sideloading?

   A. Installing applications to Android devices via USB

   B. Loading software on any device via WiFi

   C. Bypassing the screen lock

   D. Loading malware on a device without the user being aware

110. You are responsible for DLP at a large company. Some employees have COPE and others BYOD. What DLP issue might these devices present?

   A. COPE can be USB OTG.

   B. BYOD can be USB OTG.

   C. COPE and BYOD can be USB OTG.

   D. Only jailbroken COPE or BYOD can be USB OTG.

111. John is responsible for network security at a large company. He is concerned about a variety of attacks but DNS poisoning in particular. Which of the following protocols would provide the most help in mitigating this issue?

   A. IPSec

   B. DNSSEC

   C. L2TP

   D. TLS

112. You are responsible for network security at your company. You have discovered that NTP is not functioning properly. What security protocol will most likely be affected by this?

   A. Radius

   B. DNSSEC

   C. IPSec

   D. Kerberos

113. Frank is concerned about DHCP starvation attacks. He is even more worried since he learned that anyone can download software called a "gobbler" and execute a DHCP starvation attack. What technology would most help him mitigate this risk?

   A. Encrypt all DHCP communication with TLS.

   B. FDE on the DHCP server

   C. Network Address Allocation

   D. IPSec for all DHCP communications

114. You are trying to allocate appropriate numbers of IP addresses for various subnets in your network. What would be the proper CIDR notation for an IP v4 subnet with 59 nodes?

A. /27

B. /29

C. /24

D. /26

115. Lydia is trying to reduce costs at her company and at the same time centralize network administration and maintain direct control of the network. Which of the following solutions would provide the most network administration centralization and control while reducing costs?

A. Outsourcing network administration

B. IaaS

C. PaaS

D. Moving all OSs to open source

116. You are investigating a remote access protocol for your company to use. The protocol needs to fully encrypt the message, use reliable transport protocols, and support a range of network protocols. Which of the following would be the best choice?

A. RADIUS

B. Diameter

C. TACACS +

D. IPSec

117. Carrol is responsible for network connectivity in her company. The sales department is transitioning to VoIP. What are two protocols she must allow through the firewall?

A. RADIUS and SNMP

B. TCP and UDP

C. SIP and RTP

D. RADIUS and SIP

118. John is setting up all the database servers on their own subnet. He has placed them on 10.10.3.3/29. How many nodes can be allocated in this subnet?

A. 32

B. 16

C. 8

D. 6

119. Carlos is a security manager for a small company that does medical billing and records management. He is using application blacklisting to prevent malicious applications from being installed. What, if anything, is the weakness with this approach?

A. None, this is the right approach.

B. It might block legitimate applications.

    C. It might fail to block malicious applications.

    D. It will limit productivity.

120. Joanne is a security administrator for a large company. She discovered that approximately 100 machines on her network were recently attacked by a major virus. She is concerned because there was a patch available that would have stopped the virus from having any impact. What is the best solution for her to implement on her network?

    A. Installing patch management software

    B. Using automatic updates

    C. Putting unpatched machines on a Bridge

    D. Scanning all machines for patches every day

121. A review of your company's network traffic shows that most of the malware infections are caused by users visiting illicit websites. You want to implement a solution that will block these websites, scan all web traffic for signs of malware, and block the malware before it enters the company network. Which of the following technologies would be the best solution?

    A. IDS

    B. Firewall

    C. UTM

    D. SIEM

122. You work for a large bank. The bank is trying to limit the risk associated with the use of unapproved USB devices to copy documents. Which of the following would be the best solution to this problem?

    A. IDS

    B. DLP

    C. Content filtering

    D. NIPS

123. Match the letter of the functionality with the device in the following table.

    A. Detect intrusions on a single machine

    B. Use aggregate logs

    C. Filter network packets based on a set of rules

    D. Detect intrusions on a network segment

Firewall	
HIDS	
SIEM	
NIDS	

124. Francine is concerned about employees in her company jailbreaking their COPE devices. What would be the most critical security concern for jailbroken devices?

   A. They would no longer get security patches.

   B. It would disable FDE.

   C. Unauthorized applications could be installed.

   D. Data could be exfiltrated on these devices.

125. You are responsible for mobile device security in your company. Employees have COPE devices. Many employees only enter the office infrequently, and you are concerned that their devices are not receiving firmware updates on time. What is the best solution for this problem?

   A. Scheduled office visits for updates

   B. OTA updates

   C. Moving from COPE to BYOD

   D. A policy that requires users to update their firmware regularly

126. Frank is looking for a remote authentication and access protocol. It must be one that uses UDP due to firewall rules. Which of the following would be the best choice?

   A. RADIUS

   B. Diameter

   C. TACACS +

   D. IPSec

127. You have discovered that one of the employees at your company tethers her smartphone to her work PC to bypass the corporate web security and access prohibited websites while connected to the LAN. What would be the best way to prevent this?

   A. Disable wireless access.

   B. Implement a WAF.

   C. Implement a policy against tethering.

   D. Implement an HIPS.

128. You work for a large bank. One of your responsibilities is to ensure that web banking logins are as secure as possible. You are concerned that a customer's account login could be compromised and someone else would use that login to access the customer's account. What is the best way to mitigate this threat?

   A. Use SMS authentication for any logins from an unknown location or computer.

   B. Encrypt all traffic via TLS.

   C. Require strong passwords.

   D. Do not allow customers to log on from any place other than their home computer.

129. You have discovered that some employees in your company have installed custom firmware on their portable devices. What security flaw would this most likely lead to?

    A. Unauthorized software can run on the device.

    B. The device may not connect to the network.

    C. The device will overheat.

    D. This is not really a security issue.

130. You are configuring BYOD access for your company. You want the absolute most robust security for the BYOD on your network. What would be the best solution?

    A. Agentless NAC

    B. Agent NAC

    C. Digital certificate authentication

    D. Two-factor authentication

131. You work for a large law firm and are responsible for network security. It is common for guests to come to the law firm (clients, expert witnesses, etc.) who need to connect to the firm's WiFi. You wish to ensure that you provide the maximum security when these guests connect with their own devices, but you also wish to provide assurance to the guest that you will have minimal impact on their device. What is the best solution?

    A. Permanent NAC agent

    B. Agentless NAC

    C. Dissolvable NAC agent

    D. Implement COPE

132. Tom is concerned about how his company can best respond to breaches. He is interested in finding a way to identify files that have been changed during the breach. What would be the best solution for him to implement?

    A. NAC

    B. NIDS

    C. File integrity checker

    D. Vulnerability scanner

133. Mary works for a large insurance company and is responsible for cybersecurity. She is concerned about insiders and wants to detect malicious activity on the part of insiders. But she wants her detection process to be invisible to the attacker. What technology best fits these needs?

    A. Hybrid NIDS

    B. Out-of-band NIDS

    C. NIPS

    D. NNIDS

134. Denish is responsible for security at a large financial services company. The company frequently uses SSL/TLS for connecting to external resources. He has concerns that an insider might exfiltrate data using an SSL/TLS tunnel. What would be the best solution to this issue?

   A. NIPS

   B. SSL decryptor

   C. NIDS

   D. SSL accelerator

135. You want to allow a media gateway to be accessible through your firewall. What ports should you open? (Choose two.)

   A. 2427

   B. 1707

   C. 2227

   D. 1727

136. Match the letter with the protocol in the following table.

   A. Wireless security

   B. Voice over IP

   C. VPN

   D. Secure command-line interface

IPSec	
WPA2	
SSH	
SIP	

137. Dennis is implementing wireless security throughout his network. He is using WPA2. However, there are some older machines that cannot connect to WPA2—they only support WEP. At least for now, he must keep these machines. What is the best solution for this problem?

   A. Put those machines on a different VLAN.

   B. Deny wireless capability for those machines.

   C. Put those machines on a separate wireless network with separate WAP.

   D. Encrypt their traffic with TLS.

138. You are a security administrator for Acme Company. Employees in your company routinely upload and download files. You are looking for a method that allows users to remotely upload or download files in a secure manner. The solution must also support more advanced file operations such as creating directories, deleting files, and so forth. What is the best solution for this?

   A. SFTP

   B. SSH

C. SCP

D. IPSec

139. Your company allows BYOD on the network. You are concerned about the risk of malicious apps being introduced to your network. Which of the following policies would be most helpful in mitigating that risk?

   A. Prohibiting apps from third-party stores

   B. Application blacklisting

   C. Antimalware scanning

   D. Requiring FDE on BYOD

140. John is the CISO for a small company. The company has password policies, but John is not sure the policies are adequate. He is concerned that someone might be able to "crack" company passwords. What is the best way for John to determine whether his passwords are vulnerable?

   A. Run a good vulnerability scan.

   B. Perform a password policy audit.

   C. Use one or more password crackers himself.

   D. Ensure that passwords are stored as a hash.

141. You are scanning your network using a packet sniffer. You are seeing traffic on ports 25 and 110. What security flaw would you most likely notice on these ports?

   A. Website vulnerabilities

   B. Unencrypted credentials

   C. Misconfigured FTP

   D. Digital certificate errors

142. Abigail is a network administrator with ACME Company. She believes that a network breach has occurred in the data center as a result of a misconfigured router access list, allowing outside access to an SSH server. Which of the following should she search for in the logs to confirm if such a breach occurred?

   A. Traffic on port 23

   B. Traffic on port 22

   C. Unencrypted credentials

   D. Malformed network packets

143. Gianna is evaluating the security of her company. The company has a number of mobile apps that were developed in house for use on COPE devices. She wants to ensure that these apps are updated as soon as an update is available. What should she ensure is being used?

   A. Firmware OTA

   B. Push notifications

   C. Scheduled updates

   D. A policy against custom firmware

144. Liam is concerned about the security of both COPE and BYOD devices. His company uses a lot of Android-based devices, and he is concerned about users getting administrative access and altering security features. What should he prohibit in his company?

A. Third-party app stores

B. Jailbreaking

C. Custom firmware

D. Rooting

145. Heidi works for a large company that issues various mobile devices (tablets and phones) to employees. She is concerned about unauthorized access to mobile devices. Which of the following would be the best way to mitigate that concern?

A. Biometrics

B. Screen lock

C. Context-aware authentication

D. Storage segmentation

146. You are looking for a point-to-point connection method that would allow two devices to synchronize data. The solution you pick should not be affected by EMI (electromagnetic interference) and should be usable over distances exceeding 10 meters, provided there is a line-of-sight connection. What would be the best solution?

A. Bluetooth

B. WiFi

C. Infrared

D. RF

147. You wish to use nmap to scan one of your servers, whose IP address is 192.168.1.16. The target is one of your own Windows servers. You want a scan that is the most thorough, and you are not concerned about it being detected. Which of the following would best accomplish that?

A. `nmap -sW -sL -T1 192.168.1.16/24`

B. `nmap -sW -sT -T1 192.168.1.16`

C. `nmap -sW -sT -T5 192.168.1.16/24`

D. `nmap -sW -sT -sO -T5 192.168.1.16`

148. What command would produce the output shown here?

A. `nestat -a`

B. `arp -a`

C. `arp -s`

D. `netstat -s`

149. Ethan has noticed some users on his network accessing inappropriate videos. His network uses a proxy server that has content filtering with blacklisting. What is the most likely cause of this issue?

A. Sites not on the blacklist

B. Misconfigured content filtering

C. Misconfigured proxy server

D. Someone circumventing the proxy server

150. You are looking for tools to assist in penetration testing your network. Which of the following best describes Metasploit?

A. Hacking tool

B. Vulnerability scanner

C. Exploit framework

D. Network scanner

151. Logan is responsible for enforcing security policies in his company. There are a number of policies regarding the proper configuration of public-facing servers. Which of the following would be the best way for Logan to check to see if such policies are being enforced?

A. Periodically audit selected servers.

B. Implement a configuration compliance scanning solution.

C. Conduct routine penetration tests of those servers.

D. Implement a vulnerability scanning solution.

Chapter

3

Architecture and Design

THE COMPTIA SECURITY+ EXAM SY0-501 TOPICS COVERED IN THIS CHAPTER INCLUDE THE FOLLOWING:

✓ **3.1 Explain use cases and purpose for frameworks, best practices and secure configuration guides.**

- Industry-standard frameworks and reference architectures
    - Regulatory
    - Non-regulatory
    - National vs. international
    - Industry-specific frameworks
- Benchmarks/secure configuration guides
    - Platform/vendor-specific guides
        - Web server
        - Operating system
        - Application server
        - Network infrastructure devices
    - General purpose guides
- Defense-in-depth/layered security
    - Vendor diversity
    - Control diversity
        - Administrative
        - Technical
    - User training

✓ **3.2 Given a scenario, implement secure network architecture concepts.**

- Zones/topologies
    - DMZ

- Extranet
- Intranet
- Wireless
- Guest
- Honeynets
- NAT
- Ad hoc
- Segregation/segmentation/isolation
  - Physical
  - Logical (VLAN)
  - Virtualization
  - Air gaps
- Tunneling/VPN
  - Site-to-site
  - Remote access
- Security device/technology placement
  - Sensors
  - Collectors
  - Correlation engines
  - Filters
  - Proxies
  - Firewalls
  - VPN concentrators
  - SSL accelerators
  - Load balancers
  - DDoS mitigator
  - Aggregation switches
  - Taps and port mirror
- SDN

✓ **3.3 Given a scenario, implement secure systems design.**

- Hardware/firmware security
    - FDE/SED
    - TPM
    - HSM
    - UEFI/BIOS
    - Secure boot and attestation
    - Supply chain
    - Hardware root of trust
    - EMI/EMP
- Operating systems
    - Types
        - Network
        - Server
        - Workstation
        - Appliance
        - Kiosk
        - Mobile OS
    - Patch management
    - Disabling unnecessary ports and services
    - Least functionality
    - Secure configurations
    - Trusted operating system
    - Application whitelisting/blacklisting
    - Disable default accounts/passwords
- Peripherals
    - Wireless keyboards
    - Wireless mice
    - Displays
    - WiFi-enabled MicroSD cards
    - Printers/MFDs
    - External storage devices
    - Digital cameras

✓ **3.4 Explain the importance of secure staging deployment concepts.**

- Sandboxing
- Environment
  - Development
  - Test
  - Staging
  - Production
- Secure baseline
- Integrity measurement

✓ **3.5 Explain the security implications of embedded systems.**

- SCADA/ICS
- Smart devices/IoT
  - Wearable technology
  - Home automation
- HVAC
- SoC
- RTOS
- Printers/MFDs
- Camera systems
- Special purpose
  - Medical devices
  - Vehicles
  - Aircraft/UAV

✓ **3.6 Summarize secure application development and deployment concepts.**

- Development life-cycle models
  - Waterfall vs. Agile
- Secure DevOps
  - Security automation
  - Continuous integration

- Cloud deployment models
  - SaaS
  - PaaS
  - IaaS
  - Private
  - Public
  - Hybrid
  - Community
- On-premise vs. hosted vs. cloud
- VDI/VDE
- Cloud access security broker
- Security as a Service

✓ **3.8 Explain how resiliency and automation strategies reduce risk.**

- Automation/scripting
  - Automated courses of action
  - Continuous monitoring
  - Configuration validation
- Templates
- Master image
- Non-persistence
  - Snapshots
  - Revert to known state
  - Rollback to known configuration
  - Live boot media
- Elasticity
- Scalability
- Distributive allocation
- Redundancy
- Fault tolerance
- High availability
- RAID

✓ **3.9 Explain the importance of physical security controls.**

- Lighting
- Signs
- Fencing/gate/cage
- Security guards
- Alarms
- Safe
- Secure cabinets/enclosures
- Protected distribution/Protected cabling
- Airgap
- Mantrap
- Faraday cage
- Lock types
- Biometrics
- Barricades/bollards
- Tokens/cards
- Environmental controls
  - HVAC
  - Hot and cold aisles
  - Fire suppression
- Cable locks
- Screen filters
- Cameras
- Motion detection
- Logs
- Infrared detection
- Key management

1. Caroline has been asked to find a standard to guide her company's choices in implementing information security management systems. She is looking for a standard that is international. Which of the following would be the best choice for her?

   A. ISO 27002

   B. ISO 27017

   C. NIST 800-12

   D. NIST 800-14

2. You are responsible for network security at an e-commerce company. You want to ensure that you are using best practices for the e-commerce website your company hosts. What standard would be the best for you to review?

   A. OWASP

   B. NERC

   C. NIST

   D. ISA/IEC

3. Cheryl is responsible for cybersecurity at a mid-sized insurance company. She has decided to utilize a different vendor for network antimalware than she uses for host antimalware. Is this a recommended action, and why or why not?

   A. This is not recommended; you should use a single vendor for a particular security control.

   B. This is recommended; this is described as vendor diversity.

   C. This is not recommended; this is described as vendor forking.

   D. It is neutral. This does not improve or detract from security.

4. Maria is a security administrator for a large bank. She is concerned about malware, particularly spyware that could compromise customer data. Which of the following would be the best approach for her to mitigate the threat of spyware?

   A. Computer usage policies, network antimalware, and host antimalware

   B. Host antimalware and network antimalware

   C. Host and network antimalware, computer usage policies, and website whitelisting

   D. Host and network antimalware, computer usage policies, and employee training

5. Gabriel is setting up a new e-commerce server. He is concerned about security issues. Which of the following would be the best location to place an e-commerce server?

   A. DMZ

   B. Intranet

   C. Guest network

   D. Extranet

6. Enrique is concerned about backup data being infected by malware. The company backs up key servers to digital storage on a backup server. Which of the following would be most effective in preventing the backup data being infected by malware?

   A. Place the backup server on a separate VLAN.

   B. Air-gap the backup server.

   C. Place the backup server on a different network segment.

   D. Use a honeynet.

7. Janelle is the security administrator for a small company. She is trying to improve security throughout the network. Which of the following steps should she take first?

   A. Implement antimalware on all computers.

   B. Implement acceptable use policies.

   C. Turn off unneeded services on all computers.

   D. Turn on host-based firewalls on all computers.

8. Mary is the CISO for a mid-sized company. She is attempting to mitigate the danger of computer viruses. Which administrative control can she implement to help achieve this goal?

   A. Implement host-based antimalware.

   B. Implement policies regarding email attachments and file downloads.

   C. Implement network-based antimalware.

   D. Block portable storage devices from being connected to computers.

9. You are the network administrator for a large company. Your company frequently has nonemployees in the company such as clients and vendors. You have been directed to provide these nonemployees with access to the Internet. Which of the following is the best way to implement this?

   A. Establish a guest network.

   B. Allow nonemployees to connect only to the DMZ.

   C. Allow nonemployees to connect only to the intranet.

   D. Establish limited accounts on your network for nonemployees to use.

10. Juan is a network administrator for an insurance company. His company has a number of traveling salespeople. He is concerned about confidential data on their laptops. What is the best way for him to address this?

    A. FDE

    B. TPM

    C. SDN

    D. DMZ

11. Terrance is responsible for secure communications on his company's network. The company has a number of traveling salespeople who need to connect to network resources. What technology would be most helpful in addressing this need?

    A. VPN concentrator

    B. SSL accelerator

    C. DMZ

    D. Guest network

12. Mohaned is concerned about malware infecting machines on his network. One of his concerns is that malware would be able to access sensitive system functionality that requires administrative access. What technique would best address this issue?

    A. Implementing host-based antimalware

    B. Using a nonadministrative account for normal activities

    C. Implementing FDE

    D. Making certain the operating systems are patched

13. John works for an insurance company. His company uses a number of operating systems, including Windows and Linux. In this mixed environment, what determines the network operating system?

    A. The OS of the DNS server

    B. The OS of the domain controller

    C. The OS of the majority of servers

    D. The OS of the majority of client computers

14. Juanita is implementing virtualized systems in her network. She is using Type I hypervisors. What operating system should be on the machines for her to install the hypervisor?

    A. None

    B. Windows

    C. Any operating system

    D. Windows or Linux

15. You are responsible for security at your company. You want to improve cloud security by following the guidelines of an established international standard. What standard would be most helpful?

    A. NIST 800-14

    B. NIST 800-53

    C. ISO 27017

    D. ISO 27002

16. You are responsible for setting up a kiosk computer that will be in your company's lobby. It will be accessible for visitors to locate employee offices, obtain the guest WiFi password, and retrieve general public company information. What is the most important thing to consider when configuring this system?

    A. Using a strong administrator password

    B. Limiting functionality to only what is needed

    C. Using good antivirus protection

    D. Implementing a host-based firewall

17. You are concerned about peripheral devices being exploited by an attacker. Which of the following is the first step you should take to mitigate this threat?

    A. Disable WiFi for any peripheral that does not absolutely need it.

    B. Enable BIOS protection for peripheral devices.

    C. Use strong encryption on all peripheral devices.

    D. Configure antivirus on all peripherals.

18. Which design concept limits access to systems from outside users while protecting users and systems inside the LAN?

    A. DMZ

    B. VLAN

    C. Router

    D. Guest network

19. Which of the following is the equivalent of a VLAN from a physical security perspective?

    A. Perimeter security

    B. Partitioning

    C. Security zones

    D. Firewall

20. In an attempt to observe hacker techniques, a security administrator configures a nonproduction network to be used as a target so that he can covertly monitor network attacks. What is this type of network called?

    A. Active detection

    B. False subnet

    C. IDS

    D. Honeynet

21. You have instructed all administrators to disable all nonessential ports on servers at their sites. Why are nonessential protocols a security issue that you should be concerned about?

    A. Nonessential ports provide additional areas of attack.

    B. Nonessential ports can't be secured.

    C. Nonessential ports are less secure.

    D. Nonessential ports require more administrative effort to secure.

22. Which type of firewall examines the content and context of each packet it encounters?

   A. Packet filtering firewall

   B. Stateful packet filtering firewall

   C. Application layer firewall

   D. Gateway firewall

23. Which of the following would prevent a user from installing a program on a company-owned mobile device?

   A. Whitelisting

   B. Blacklisting

   C. ACL

   D. HIDS

24. You're designing a new network infrastructure so that your company can allow unauthenticated users connecting from the Internet to access certain areas. Your goal is to protect the internal network while providing access to those areas. You decide to put the web server on a separate subnet open to public contact. What is this subnet called?

   A. Guest network

   B. DMZ

   C. Intranet

   D. VLAN

25. Upper management has decreed that a firewall must be put in place immediately, before your site suffers an attack similar to one that struck a sister company. Responding to this order, your boss instructs you to implement a packet filter by the end of the week. A packet filter performs which function?

   A. Prevents unauthorized packets from entering the network

   B. Allows all packets to leave the network

   C. Allows all packets to enter the network

   D. Eliminates collisions in the network

26. You're outlining your plans for implementing a wireless network to upper management. Which protocol was designed to provide security for a wireless network and is considered equivalent to the security of a wired network?

   A. WAP

   B. WPA

   C. WPA2

   D. WEP

27. An IV attack is usually associated with which of the following wireless protocols?

   A. WEP

   B. WAP

    C.   WPA

    D.   WPA2

28. Suzan is responsible for application development in her company. She wants to have all web applications tested prior to being deployed live. She wants to use a test system that is identical to the live server. What is this called?

    A.   Production server

    B.   Development server

    C.   Test server

    D.   Predeployment server

29. John is responsible for security in his company. He is implementing a kernel integrity subsystem for key servers. What is the primary benefit of this action?

    A.   To detect malware

    B.   To detect whether files have been altered

    C.   To detect rogue programs being installed

    D.   To detect changes to user accounts

30. You are responsible for BIOS security in your company. Which of the following is the most fundamental BIOS integrity technique?

    A.   Verifying the BIOS version

    B.   Using a TPM

    C.   Managing BIOS passwords

    D.   Backing up the BIOS

31. You have been asked to implement security for SCADA systems in your company. Which of the following standards will be most helpful to you?

    A.   NIST 800-82

    B.   PCI-DSS

    C.   NIST 800-30

    D.   ISO 27002

32. Joanne works for a large insurance company. Some employees have wearable technology, such as smart watches. What is the most significant security concern from such devices?

    A.   These devices can distract employees.

    B.   These devices can be used to carry data in and out of the company.

    C.   These devices may not have encrypted drives.

    D.   These devices may not have strong passwords.

33. John is installing an HVAC system in his datacenter. What will this HVAC have the most impact on?

   A. Confidentiality

   B. Availability

   C. Fire suppression

   D. Monitoring access to the datacenter

34. Maria is a security engineer with a manufacturing company. During a recent investigation, she discovered that an engineer's compromised workstation was being used to connect to SCADA systems while the engineer was not logged in. The engineer is responsible for administering the SCADA systems and cannot be blocked from connecting to them. What should Maria do to mitigate this threat?

   A. Install host-based antivirus software on the engineer's system.

   B. Implement account usage auditing on the SCADA system.

   C. Implement an NIPS on the SCADA system.

   D. Use FDE on the engineer's system.

35. Lucy works as a network administrator for a large company. She needs to administer several servers. Her objective is to make it easy to administer and secure these servers, as well as making the installation of new servers more streamlined. Which of the following best addresses these issues?

   A. Setting up a cluster

   B. Virtualizing the servers

   C. Putting the servers on a VLAN

   D. Putting the servers on a separate subnet

36. Gerard is responsible for secure communications with his company's e-commerce server. All communications with the server use TLS. What is the most secure option for Gerard to store the private key on the e-commerce server?

   A. HSM

   B. FDE

   C. SED

   D. SDN

37. You are the security officer for a large company. You have discovered malware on one of the workstations. You are concerned that the malware might have multiple functions and might have caused more security issues with the computer than you can currently detect. What is the best way to test this malware?

   A. Leave the malware on that workstation until it is tested.

   B. Place the malware in a sandbox environment for testing.

   C. It is not important to test it; just remove it from the machine.

   D. Place the malware on a honeypot for testing.

38. Web developers in your company currently have direct access to the production server and can deploy code directly to it. This can lead to unsecure code, or simply code flaws being deployed to the live system. What would be the best change you could make to mitigate this risk?

   A. Implement sandboxing.

   B. Implement virtualized servers.

   C. Implement a staging server.

   D. Implement deployment policies.

39. Denish is concerned about the security of embedded devices in his company. He is most concerned about the operating system security for such devices. Which of the following would be the best option for mitigating this threat?

   A. RTOS

   B. SCADA

   C. FDE

   D. TPM

40. Which of the following 802.11 standards is supported in WPA2, but not in WEP or WPA?

   A. 802.11a

   B. 802.11b

   C. 802.11i

   D. 802.11n

41. Teresa is responsible for WiFi security in her company. Which wireless security protocol uses TKIP?

   A. WPA

   B. CCMP

   C. WEP

   D. WPA2

42. Juan is responsible for wireless security in his company. He has decided to disable the SSID broadcast on the single AP the company uses. What will the effect be on client machines?

   A. They will no longer be able to use wireless networking.

   B. They will no longer see the SSID as a preferred network when they are connected.

   C. They will no longer see the SSID as an available network.

   D. They will be required to make the SSID part of their HomeGroup.

43. Which cloud service model provides the consumer with the infrastructure to create applications and host them?

   A. SaaS

   B. PaaS

   C. IaaS

   D. CaaS

44. Which cloud service model gives the consumer the ability to use applications provided by the cloud provider over the Internet?

   A. SaaS

   B. PaaS

   C. IaaS

   D. CaaS

45. Which feature of cloud computing involves dynamically provisioning (or deprovisioning) resources as needed?

   A. Multitenancy

   B. Elasticity

   C. CMDB

   D. Sandboxing

46. Which type of hypervisor implementation is known as "bare metal"?

   A. Type I

   B. Type II

   C. Type III

   D. Type IV

47. Mohaned is a security analyst and has just removed malware from a virtual server. What feature of virtualization would he use to return the virtual server to a last known good state?

   A. Sandboxing

   B. Hypervisor

   C. Snapshot

   D. Elasticity

48. Lisa is concerned about fault tolerance for her database server. She wants to ensure that if any single drive fails, it can be recovered. What RAID level would support this goal while using distributed parity bits?

   A. RAID 0

   B. RAID 1

   C. RAID 3

   D. RAID 5

49. Jarod is concerned about EMI affecting a key escrow server. Which method would be most effective in mitigating this risk?

   A. VLAN

   B. SDN

   C. Trusted platform module

   D. Faraday cage

50. John is responsible for physical security at his company. He is particularly concerned about an attacker driving a vehicle into the building. Which of the following would provide the best protection against this threat?

A. A gate

B. Bollards

C. A security guard on duty

D. Security cameras

51. Mark is responsible for cybersecurity at a small college. There are many computer labs that are open for students to use. These labs are monitored only by a student worker, who may or may not be very attentive. Mark is concerned about the theft of computers. Which of the following would be the best way for him to mitigate this threat?

A. Cable locks

B. FDE on the lab computers

C. Strong passwords on the lab computers

D. Having a lab sign-in sheet

52. Joanne is responsible for security at a power plant. The facility is very sensitive and security is extremely important. She wants to incorporate two-factor authentication with physical security. What would be the best way to accomplish this?

A. Smart cards

B. A mantrap with a smart card at one door and a pin keypad at the other door

C. A mantrap with video surveillance

D. A fence with a smart card gate access

53. Which of the following terms refers to the process of establishing a standard for security?

A. Baselining

B. Security evaluation

C. Hardening

D. Normalization

54. You are trying to increase security at your company. You're currently creating an outline of all the aspects of security that will need to be examined and acted on. Which of the following terms describes the process of improving security in a trusted OS?

A. FDE

B. Hardening

C. SED

D. Baselining

55. Which level of RAID is a "stripe of mirrors"?

A. RAID 1+0

B. RAID 6

C. RAID 0

D. RAID 1

56. Isabella is responsible for database management and security. She is attempting to remove redundancy in the database. What is this process called?

   A. Integrity checking

   B. Deprovisioning

   C. Baselining

   D. Normalization

57. A list of applications approved for use on your network would be known as which of the following?

   A. Blacklist

   B. Red list

   C. Whitelist

   D. Orange list

58. Hans is a security administrator for a large company. Users on his network visit a wide range of websites. He is concerned they might get malware from one of these many websites. Which of the following would be his best approach to mitigate this threat?

   A. Implement host-based antivirus.

   B. Blacklist known infected sites.

   C. Set browsers to allow only signed components.

   D. Set browsers to block all active content (ActiveX, JavaScript, etc.).

59. Elizabeth has implemented agile development for her company. What is the primary difference between agile development and the waterfall method?

   A. Agile has fewer phases.

   B. Waterfall has fewer phases.

   C. Agile is more secure.

   D. Agile repeats phases.

60. John is using the waterfall method for application development. At which phase should he implement security measures?

   A. Requirements

   B. Design

   C. Implementation

   D. All

61. You are responsible for database security at your company. You are concerned that programmers might pass badly written SQL commands to the database, or that an attacker might exploit badly written SQL in applications. What is the best way to mitigate this threat?

   A. Programmer training

   B. Programming policies

    C. Agile programming

    D. Stored procedures

62. Mary is concerned about application security for her company's application development. Which of the following is the most important step for addressing application security?

    A. Proper error handling

    B. Regular data backups

    C. Encrypted data transmission

    D. Strong authentication

63. Farès is responsible for managing the many virtual machines on his company's networks. Over the past two years, the company has increased the number of virtual machines significantly. Farès is no longer able to effectively manage the large number of machines. What is the term for this situation?

    A. VM overload

    B. VM sprawl

    C. VM spread

    D. VM zombies

64. Mary is responsible for virtualization management in her company. She is concerned about VM escape. Which of the following methods would be the most effective in mitigating this risk?

    A. Only share resources between the VM and host if absolutely necessary.

    B. Keep the VM patched.

    C. Use a firewall on the VM.

    D. Use host-based antimalware on the VM.

65. You work at a large company. You are concerned about ensuring that all workstations have a common configuration, no rogue software is installed, and all patches are kept up to date. Which of the following would be the most effective for accomplishing this?

    A. Use VDE.

    B. Implement strong policies.

    C. Use an image for all workstations.

    D. Implement strong patch management.

66. Juan is responsible for the physical security of the company server room. He has been asked to recommend a type of fire suppression system for the server room. Which of the following would be the best choice?

    A. Wet pipe

    B. Deluge

    C. Pre-action

    D. Halon

67. You are responsible for server room security for your company. You are concerned about physical theft of the computers. Which of the following would be best able to detect theft or attempted theft?

    A. Motion sensor–activated cameras

    B. Smart card access to the server rooms

    C. Strong deadbolt locks for the server rooms

    D. Logging everyone who enters the server room

68. Teresa has deployed session tokens on her network. These would be most effective against which of the following attacks?

    A. DDoS

    B. Replay

    C. SYN flood

    D. Malware

69. Hector is using infrared cameras to verify that servers in his datacenter are being properly racked. Which of the following datacenter elements is he concerned about?

    A. EMI blocking

    B. Humidity control

    C. Hot and cold aisles

    D. HVAC

70. Gerald is concerned about unauthorized people entering the company's building. Which of the following would be most effective in preventing this?

    A. Alarm systems

    B. Fencing

    C. Cameras

    D. Security guards

71. Which of the following is the most important benefit from implementing SDN?

    A. It will stop malware.

    B. It provides scalability.

    C. It will detect intrusions.

    D. It will prevent session hijacking.

72. Mark is an administrator for a health care company. He has to support an older, legacy application. He is concerned that this legacy application might have vulnerabilities that would affect the rest of the network. What is the most efficient way to mitigate this?

    A. Use an application container.

    B. Implement SDN.

    C. Run the application on a separate VLAN.

    D. Insist on an updated version of the application.

73. Lars is auditing the physical security of a company. The company uses chain-link fences on its perimeter. The fence is over pavement, not soft ground. How close to the ground should the bottom of the fence be?

   A. Touching the ground

   B. Within 4 inches

   C. There is no standard for this.

   D. Within 2 inches

74. Mia has to deploy and support a legacy application. The configuration for this application and the OS it runs on are very specific and cannot be changed. What is the best approach for her to deploy this?

   A. Use an immutable server.

   B. Use a VM.

   C. Set permissions on the application so it cannot be changed.

   D. Place the application on a separate VLAN.

75. To mitigate the impact of a software vendor going out of business, a company that uses vendor software should require which one of the following?

   A. A detailed credit investigation prior to acquisition

   B. A third-party source-code escrow

   C. Substantial penalties for breach of contract

   D. Standby contracts with other vendors

76. Abigail is responsible for datacenters in a large, multinational company. She has to support multiple datacenters in diverse geographic regions. What would be the most effective way for her to manage these centers consistently across the enterprise?

   A. Hire datacenter managers for each center.

   B. Implement enterprise-wide SDN.

   C. Implement Infrastructure as Code (IaC).

   D. Automate provisioning and deprovisioning.

77. Olivia is responsible for web application security for her company's e-commerce server. She is particularly concerned about XSS and SQL injection. Which technique would be most effective in mitigating these attacks?

   A. Proper error handling

   B. The use of stored procedures

   C. Proper input validation

   D. Code signing

78. Sophia wants to test her company's web application to see if it is handling input validation and data validation properly. Which testing method would be most effective for this?

    A. Static code analysis

    B. Fuzzing

    C. Baselining

    D. Version control

79. Omar is using the waterfall method for software development in his company. Which of the following is the proper sequence for the waterfall method?

    A. Requirements, design, implementation, testing, deployment, maintenance

    B. Planning, designing, coding, testing, deployment

    C. Requirements, planning, designing, coding, testing, deployment

    D. Design, coding, testing, deployment, maintenance

80. Lilly is responsible for security on web applications for her company. She is checking to see that all applications have robust input validation. What is the best way to implement validation?

    A. Server-side validation

    B. Client-side validation

    C. Validate in transit

    D. Client-side and server-side validation

81. Edward is responsible for web application security at a large insurance company. One of the applications that he is particularly concerned about is used by insurance adjusters in the field. He wants to have strong authentication methods to mitigate misuse of the application. What would be his best choice?

    A. Authenticate the client with a digital certificate.

    B. Implement a very strong password policy.

    C. Secure application communication with TLS.

    D. Implement a web application firewall (WAF).

82. Sarah is the CIO for a small company. The company uses several custom applications that have complicated interactions with the host operating system. She is concerned about ensuring that systems on her network are all properly patched. What is the best approach in her environment?

    A. Implement automatic patching.

    B. Implement a policy that has individual users patch their systems.

    C. Delegate patch management to managers of departments so they can find the best patch management for their departments.

    D. Immediately deploy patches to a test environment, then as soon as testing is complete have a staged rollout to the network.

83. John is examining the logs for his company's web applications. He discovers what he believes is a breach. After further investigation, it appears as if the attacker executed code from one of the libraries the application uses, code that is no longer even used by the application. What best describes this attack?

A. Buffer overflow

B. Code reuse attack

C. DoS attack

D. Session hijacking

84. Emiliano is a network administrator and is concerned about the security of peripheral devices. Which of the following would be a basic step he could take to improve security for those devices?

A. Implement FDE.

B. Turn off remote access (SSH, telnet, etc.) if not needed.

C. Utilize fuzzy testing for all peripherals.

D. Implement digital certificates for all peripherals.

85. Ixxia is a software development team manager. She is concerned about memory leaks in code. What type of testing is most likely to find memory leaks?

A. Fuzzing

B. Stress testing

C. Static code analysis

D. Normalization

86. Victor is a network administrator for a medium-sized company. He wants to be able to access servers remotely so that he can perform small administrative tasks from remote locations. Which of the following would be the best protocol for him to use?

A. SSH

B. Telnet

C. RSH

D. SNMP

87. Mark is responsible for a server that runs sensitive software for a major research facility. He is very concerned that only authorized software execute on this server. He is also concerned about malware masquerading as legitimate, authorized software. What technique would best address this concern?

A. Secure boot

B. Software attestation

C. Sandboxing

D. TPM

88. Hannah is a programmer with a large software company. She is interested in ensuring that the module she just created will work well with a module created by another program. What type of testing is this?

   A. Unit testing

   B. Regression testing

   C. Stress testing

   D. Integration testing

89. Erik is responsible for the security of a SCADA system. Availability is a critical issue. Which of the following is most important to implement?

   A. SIEM

   B. IPS

   C. Automated patch control

   D. Honeypot

90. You are concerned about the security of new devices your company has implemented. Some of these devices use SoC technology. What would be the best security measure you could take for these?

   A. Using a TPM

   B. Ensuring each has its own cryptographic key

   C. Using SED

   D. Using BIOS protection

91. Vincent works for a company that manufactures portable medical devices, such as insulin pumps. He is concerned about ensuring these devices are secure. Which of the following is the most important step for him to take?

   A. Ensure all communications with the device are encrypted.

   B. Ensure the devices have FDE.

   C. Ensure the devices have individual antimalware.

   D. Ensure the devices have been fuzz tested.

92. Emile is concerned about securing the computer systems in vehicles. Which of the following vehicle types has significant cybersecurity vulnerabilities?

   A. UAV

   B. Automobiles

   C. Airplanes

   D. All of the above

93. Ariel is responsible for software development in her company. She is concerned that the software development team integrate well with the network system. She wants to ensure that software development processes are aligned with the security needs of the entire network. Which of the following would be most important for her to implement?

   A. Integration testing

   B. Secure DevOps

C. Clear policies

D. Employee training

94. Greg is a programmer with a small company. He is responsible for the web application. He has become aware that one of the modules his web application uses may have a security flaw allowing an attacker to circumvent authentication. There is an update available for this module that fixes the flaw. What is the best approach for him to take to mitigate this threat?

A. Submit an RFC.

B. Immediately apply the update.

C. Place the update on a test server, then if it works apply it to the production server.

D. Document the issue.

95. You are using a sophisticated system that models various attacks on your networks. You intend for this system to help your team realize weak areas and improve response to incidents. What is the most important step to take before relying on data from this system?

A. Get approval from a CAB.

B. Thoroughly review the systems documentation.

C. Verify the models being used.

D. Perform integration testing on the system.

96. Your company has an accounting application that was developed in-house. It has been in place for 36 months, and functioning very well, with very few issues. You have just made a minor change to the tax calculation based on a change in tax law. What should be your next step?

A. Deploy the change.

B. Get CAB approval for the change.

C. Perform stress testing.

D. Perform regression testing.

97. Tom works as a software development manager for a large company. He is trying to explain to management the difference between compiled code and runtime code. What is the biggest advantage of compiled code?

A. Better performance

B. Platform independence

C. More secure

D. Faster development time

98. Your company is interested in keeping data in the cloud. Management feels that public clouds are not secure but is concerned about the cost of a private cloud. What is the solution you would recommend?

A. Tell them there are no risks with public clouds.

B. Tell them they will have to find a way to budget for a private cloud.

C. Suggest that they consider a community cloud.

D. Recommend against a cloud solution at this time.

99. Your development team primarily uses Windows, but they need to develop a specific solution that will run on Linux. What is the best solution to getting your programmers access to Linux systems for development and testing?

    A. Set their machines to dual-boot Windows and Linux.

    B. PaaS

    C. Set up a few Linux machines for them to work with as needed.

    D. IaaS

100. Daniel works for a mid-sized financial institution. The company has recently moved some of its data to a cloud solution. Daniel is concerned that the cloud provider may not support the same security policies as the company's internal network. What is the best way to mitigate this concern?

    A. Implement a cloud access security broker.

    B. Perform integration testing.

    C. Establish cloud security policies.

    D. Implement Security as a Service.

101. Hanz is responsible for the e-commerce servers at his company. He is concerned about how they will respond to a DoS attack. Which software testing methodology would be most helpful in determining this?

    A. Regression testing

    B. Stress testing

    C. Integration testing

    D. Fuzz testing

102. You are the CIO for a small company. The company wants to use cloud storage for some of its data, but cost is a major concern. Which of the following cloud deployment models would be best?

    A. Community cloud

    B. Private cloud

    C. Public cloud

    D. Hybrid cloud

103. Alisha is monitoring security for a mid-sized financial institution. Under her predecessor there were multiple high-profile breaches. Management is very concerned about detecting any security issues or breach of policy as soon as possible. Which of the following would be the best solution for this?

    A. Monthly audits

    B. NIPS

    C. NIDS

    D. Continuous monitoring

104. Helga works for a bank and is responsible for secure communications with the online banking application. The application uses TLS to secure all customer communications. She has noticed that since migrating to larger encryption keys, the server's performance has declined. What would be the best way to address this issue?

A. Implement a VPN concentrator.

B. Implement an SSL accelerator.

C. Return to smaller encryption keys.

D. Upgrade all servers.

105. What is the primary advantage of allowing only signed code to be installed on computers?

A. It guarantees that malware will not be installed.

B. It improves patch management.

C. It verifies who created the software.

D. It executes faster on computers with a TPM.

106. Which of the following is the best description for VM sprawl?

A. When VMs on your network outnumber physical machines

B. When there are more VMs than IT can effectively manage

C. When a VM on a computer begins to consume too many resources

D. When VMs are spread across a wide area network

107. Which of the following is the best description of a stored procedure?

A. Code that is in a DLL, rather than the executable

B. Server-side code that is called from a client

C. SQL statements compiled on the database server as a single procedure that can be called

D. Procedures that are kept on a separate server from the calling application, such as in middleware

108. Farès is responsible for security at his company. He has had bollards installed around the front of the building. What is Farès trying to accomplish?

A. Gated access for people entering the building

B. Video monitoring around the building

C. Protecting against EMI

D. Preventing a vehicle from being driven into the building

109. Jane is concerned about servers in her datacenter. She is particularly worried about EMI. What damage might EMI most likely cause to servers?

A. Damage to chips (CPU or RAM)

B. Temperature control issues

C. Malware infections

D. The staff could be locked out of the servers.

110. You are concerned about VM escape attacks. Which of the following would provide the most protection against this?

    A. Completely isolate the VM from the host.

    B. Install a host-based antivirus on both the VM and the host.

    C. Implement FDE on both the VM and the host.

    D. Use a TPM on the host.

111. Teresa is the network administrator for a small company. The company is interested in a robust and modern network defense strategy but lacks the staff to support it. What would be the best solution for Teresa to use?

    A. Implement SDN.

    B. Use automated security.

    C. Use Security as a Service.

    D. Implement only as much security controls as they can support.

112. Dennis is trying to set up a system to analyze the integrity of applications on his network. He wants to make sure that the applications have not been tampered with or Trojaned. What would be most useful in accomplishing this goal?

    A. Implement NIPS.

    B. Use cryptographic hashes.

    C. Sandbox the applications in question.

    D. Implement NIDS.

113. George is a network administrator at a power plant. He notices that several turbines had unusual ramp-ups in cycles last week. After investigating, he finds that an executable was uploaded to the system control console and caused this. Which of the following would be most effective in preventing this from affecting the SCADA system in the future?

    A. Implement SDN.

    B. Improve patch management.

    C. Place the SCADA system on a separate VLAN.

    D. Implement encrypted data transmissions.

114. Tom is responsible for VPN connections in his company. His company uses IPSec for VPNs. What is the primary purpose of AH in IPSec?

    A. Encrypt the entire packet.

    B. Encrypt just the header.

    C. Authenticate the entire packet.

    D. Authenticate just the header.

115. Mia is a network administrator for a bank. She is responsible for secure communications with her company's customer website. Which of the following would be the best for her to implement?

    A. SSL

    B. PPTP

C. IPSec

D. TLS

116. Abigail is responsible for setting up an NIPS on her network. The NIPS is located in one particular network segment. She is looking for a passive method to get a copy of all traffic to the NIPS network segment so that it can analyze the traffic. Which of the following would be her best choice?

A. Using a network tap

B. Using port mirroring

C. Setting the NIPS on a VLAN that is connected to all other segments

D. Setting up an NIPS on each segment

117. Janice is explaining how IPSec works to a new network administrator. She is trying to explain the role of IKE. Which of the following most closely matches the role of IKE in IPSec?

A. It encrypts the packet.

B. It establishes the SAs.

C. It authenticates the packet.

D. It establishes the tunnel.

118. Jeff is the security administrator for an e-commerce site. He is concerned about DoS attacks. Which of the following would be the most effective in addressing this?

A. DDoS mitigator

B. WAF with SPI

C. NIPS

D. Increased available bandwidth

119. Doug is a network administrator for a small company. The company has recently implemented an e-commerce server. This has placed a strain on network bandwidth. What would be the most cost-effective means for him to address this issue?

A. Isolate the new server on a separate network segment.

B. Upgrade the network to CAT 7.

C. Move to fiber optic.

D. Implement aggregation switches.

120. Liam is responsible for monitoring security events in his company. He wants to see how diverse events may connect. He is interested in identifying different indicators of compromise that may point to the same breach. Which of the following would be most helpful for him to implement?

A. NIDS

B. SIEM

C. Correlation engine

D. Aggregation switch

121. Emily manages the IDS/IPS for her network. She has an NIPS installed and properly configured. It is not detecting obvious attacks on one specific network segment. She has verified that the NIPS is properly configured and working properly. What would be the most efficient way for her to address this?

    A. Implement port mirroring for that segment.

    B. Install an NIPS on that segment.

    C. Upgrade to a more effective NIPS.

    D. Isolate that segment on its own VLAN.

122. You have been instructed to find a VPN solution for your company. Your company uses TACACS+ for remote access. Which of the following would be the best VPN solution for your company?

    A. PPTP

    B. RADIUS

    C. L2TP

    D. CHAP

123. Jacob is the CIO for a mid-sized company. His company has very good security policies and procedures. The company has outsourced its web application development to a well-known web programming company. Which of the following should be the most important security issue for Jacob to address?

    A. The web application vendor's hiring practices

    B. The financial stability of the web application vendor

    C. Security practices of the web application vendor

    D. Having an escrow for the source code

124. Gerard is responsible for physical security at his company. He is considering using cameras that would detect a burglar entering the building at night. Which of the following would be most useful in accomplishing this goal?

    A. Motion-sensing camera

    B. Infrared-sensing camera

    C. Sound-activated camera

    D. HD camera

125. Tim is implementing a Faraday cage around his server room. What is the primary purpose of a Faraday cage?

    A. Regulate temperature

    B. Regulate current

    C. Block intrusions

    D. Block EMI

126. You are working for a large company. You are trying to find a solution that will provide controlled physical access to the building and record every employee who enters the building. Which of the following would be the best for you to implement?

   A. A security guard with a sign-in sheet

   B. Smart card access

   C. A camera by the entrance

   D. A sign-in sheet by the front door

127. David is responsible for cryptographic keys in his company. What is the best way to deauthorize a public key?

   A. Send out a network alert.

   B. Delete the digital certificate.

   C. Publish that certificate in the CRL.

   D. Notify the RA.

128. Thomas is trying to select the right fire extinguisher for his company's server room. Which of the following would be his best choice?

   A. Type A

   B. Type B

   C. Type C

   D. Type D

129. Carole is concerned about security for her server room. She wants the most secure lock she can find for the server room door. Which of the following would be the best choice for her?

   A. Combination lock

   B. Key-in-knob

   C. Deadbolt

   D. Padlock

130. What is the ideal humidity range for a server room?

   A. 70% to 80%

   B. 40% to 60%

   C. Below 30%

   D. Above 70%

131. Molly is implementing biometrics in her company. Which of the following should be her biggest concern?

   A. FAR

   B. FRR

   C. CER

   D. EER

132. Daniel is responsible for physical security in his company. All external doors have electronic smart card access. In an emergency such as a power failure, how should the doors fail?

A. Fail secure

B. Fail closed

C. Fail open

D. Fail locked

133. Donald is responsible for networking for a defense contractor. He is concerned that emanations from UTP cable could reveal classified information. Which of the following would be his most effective way to address this?

A. Migrate to CAT 7 cable.

B. Implement protected cabling.

C. Place all cable in a Faraday cage.

D. Don't send any classified information over the cable.

134. Fred is responsible for physical security in his company. He wants to find a good way to protect the USB thumb drives that have BitLocker keys stored on them. Which of the following would be the best solution for this situation?

A. Store the drives in a secure cabinet.

B. Encrypt the thumb drives.

C. Don't store BitLocker keys on these drives.

D. Lock the thumb drives in desk drawers.

135. Juanita is responsible for servers in her company. She is looking for a fault-tolerant solution that can handle two drives failing. Which of the following should she select?

A. RAID 1+0

B. RAID 3

C. RAID 5

D. RAID 6

136. You are a network administrator for a mid-sized company. You need all workstations to have the same configuration. What would be the best way for you to accomplish this?

A. Push out a configuration file.

B. Implement a policy requiring all workstations to be configured the same way.

C. Ensure all computers have the same version of the operating system and the same applications installed.

D. Use a master image that is properly configured and image all workstations from that.

137. Mike is a network administrator for an e-commerce company. There have been several updates to the operating system, the web server software, and the web application, all within the last 24 hours. It appears that one of these updates has caused a significant security problem. What would be the best approach for Mike to take to correct this problem?

   A. Remove the updates one at a time to see which corrects the problem.

   B. Roll the server back to the last known good state.

   C. Investigate and find out which update caused the problem, and remove only that update.

   D. Investigate and find out which update caused the problem, and find a patch for that issue.

138. Which device would most likely process the following rules?

```
PERMIT IP ANY EQ 443
DENY IP ANY ANY
```

   A. NIPS

   B. HIPS

   C. Content filter

   D. Firewall

139. Ixxia is responsible for security at a mid-sized company. She wants to prevent users on her network from visiting job-hunting sites while at work. Which of the following would be the best device to accomplish this goal?

   A. Proxy server

   B. NAT

   C. Firewall

   D. NIPS

140. You are responsible for an e-commerce site. The site is hosted in a cluster. Which of the following techniques would be best in assuring availability?

   A. A VPN concentrator

   B. Aggregate switching

   C. An SSL accelerator

   D. Load balancing

141. When you are concerned about application security, what is the most important issue in memory management?

   A. Never allocate a variable any larger than is needed.

   B. Always check bounds on arrays.

   C. Always declare a variable where you need it (i.e., at function or file level if possible).

   D. Make sure you release any memory you allocate.

142. Darrel is looking for a cloud solution for his company. One of the requirements is that the IT staff can make the transition with as little change to the existing infrastructure as possible. Which of the following would be his best choice?

   A. Off-premises cloud

   B. On-premises cloud

   C. Hybrid solution

   D. Use only a community cloud

143. Ryan is concerned about the security of his company's web application. Since the application processes confidential data, he is most concerned about data exposure. Which of the following would be the most important for him to implement?

   A. WAF

   B. TLS

   C. NIPS

   D. NIDS

144. Arjun has just taken over web application security for a small company. He notices that some values are temporarily stored in hidden fields on one of the web pages. What is this called and how would it be best characterized?

   A. This is obfuscation, a weak security measure.

   B. This is data hiding, a weak security measure.

   C. This is obfuscation, a possible security flaw.

   D. This is data hiding, a possible security flaw.

145. What is the primary reason a company would consider implementing Agile programming?

   A. To speed up development time

   B. To improve development documentation

   C. To focus more on design

   D. To focus more on testing

146. When you're implementing security cameras in your company, which of the following is the most important concern?

   A. High-definition video

   B. Large storage capacity

   C. How large an area the camera can cover

   D. Security of the camera and video storage

147. What is the primary security issue presented by monitors?

   A. Unauthorized users may see confidential data.

   B. Data can be detected from electromagnetic emanations.

   C. Poor authentication

   D. Screen burn

148. Clark is responsible for mobile device security in his company. Which of the following is the most important security measure for him to implement?

  A. Encrypted drives

  B. Patch management

  C. Remote wiping

  D. Geotagging

149. Which of the following security measures is most effective against phishing attacks?

  A. User training

  B. NIPS

  C. Spam filters

  D. Content filter

150. You are the CISO for a mid-sized health care company. Which of the following is the most important for you to implement?

  A. Industry best practices

  B. Contractual requirements

  C. Strong security policies

  D. Regulatory requirements

Chapter

4

Identity and Access Management

THE COMPTIA SECURITY+ EXAM SY0-501 TOPICS COVERED IN THIS CHAPTER INCLUDE THE FOLLOWING:

✓ **4.1 Compare and contrast identity and access management concepts.**

- Identification, authentication, authorization and accounting (AAA)
- Multifactor authentication
  - Something you are
  - Something you have
  - Something you know
  - Somewhere you are
  - Something you do
- Federation
- Single sign-on
- Transitive trust

✓ **4.2 Given a scenario, install and configure identity and access services.**

- LDAP
- Kerberos
- TACACS+
- CHAP
- PAP
- MSCHAP
- RADIUS
- SAML
- OpenID Connect

- OAUTH
- Shibboleth
- Secure token
- NTLM

✓ **4.3 Given a scenario,implement identity and access management controls.**

- Access control models
  - MAC
  - DAC
  - ABAC
  - Role-based access control
  - Rule-based access control
- Physical access control
  - Proximity cards
  - Smart cards
- Biometric factors
  - Fingerprint scanner
  - Retinal scanner
  - Iris scanner
  - Voice recognition
  - Facial recognition
  - False acceptance rate
  - False rejection rate
  - Crossover error rate
- Tokens
  - Hardware
  - Software
  - HOTP/TOTP
- Certificate-based authentication
  - PIV/CAC/smart card
  - IEEE 802.1x

- File system security

- Database security

✓ **4.4 Given a scenario, differentiate common account management practices.**

- Account types
  - User account
  - Shared and generic accounts/credentials
  - Guest accounts
  - Service accounts
  - Privileged accounts
- General Concepts
  - Least privilege
  - Onboarding/offboarding
  - Permission auditing and review
  - Usage auditing and review
  - Time-of-day restrictions
  - Recertification
  - Standard naming convention
  - Account maintenance
  - Group-based access control
  - Location-based policies
- Account policy enforcement
  - Credential management
  - Group policy
  - Password complexity
  - Expiration
  - Recovery
  - Disablement
  - Lockout
  - Password history
  - Password reuse
  - Password length

1. Jack is using smart cards for authentication. He is trying to classify the type of authentication for a report to his CIO. What type of authentication is Jack using?

   A. Type I

   B. Type II

   C. Type III

   D. Strong

2. Carole is responsible for various network protocols at her company. The network time protocol has been intermittently failing. Which of the following would be most affected?

   A. Kerberos

   B. RADIUS

   C. CHAP

   D. LDAP

3. You are selecting an authentication method for your company's servers. You are looking for a method that periodically reauthenticates clients to prevent session hijacking. Which of the following would be your best choice?

   A. PAP

   B. SPAP

   C. CHAP

   D. OAUTH

4. Emiliano is working for a small company. His company is concerned about authentication and wants to implement biometrics using facial recognition and fingerprint scanning. How would this authentication be classified?

   A. Type I

   B. Type II

   C. Type III

   D. Strong

5. Lisa is setting up accounts for her company. She wants to set up accounts for the Oracle database server. Which of the following would be the best type of account to assign to the database service?

   A. User

   B. Guest

   C. Admin

   D. Service

6. You have been asked to select an authentication method that will support single sign-on, integrate with SAML, and work well over the Internet. Which of the following would be your best choice?

   A. Shibboleth

   B. OAUTH

   C. SPAP

   D. CHAP

7. Which authentication method was used as a native default for older versions of Microsoft Windows?

   A. PAP

   B. CHAP

   C. OAUTH

   D. NTLM

8. Carl has been asked to set up access control for a server. The requirements state that users at a lower privilege level should not be able to see or access files or data at a higher privilege level. What access control model would best fit these requirements?

   A. MAC

   B. DAC

   C. RBAC

   D. SAML

9. Clarice is concerned about an attacker getting information regarding network resources in her company. Which protocol should she implement that would be most helpful in mitigating this risk?

   A. LDAP

   B. TLS

   C. SNMP

   D. LDAPS

10. Ahmed is looking for an authentication protocol for his network. He is very concerned about highly skilled attackers. As part of mitigating that concern, he wants an authentication protocol that never actually transmits a user's password, in any form. Which authentication protocol would be a good fit for Ahmed's needs?

   A. CHAP

   B. Kerberos

   C. RBAC

   D. Type II

11. You work for a social media website. You wish to integrate your users' accounts with other web resources. To do so, you need to allow authentication to be used across different domains, without exposing your users' passwords to these other services. Which of the following would be most helpful in accomplishing this goal?

   A. Kerberos

   B. SAML

   C. OAUTH

   D. OpenID

12. Mary is trying to set up remote access to her network for salespeople in her company. Which protocol would be most helpful in accomplishing this goal?

   A. RADIUS

   B. Kerberos

   C. CHAP

   D. OpenID

13. Victor is trying to identify the protocol used by Windows for authentication to a server that is not part of the network domain. Which of the following would be most useful for Victor?

   A. Kerberos

   B. NTLM

   C. OpenID

   D. CHAP

14. You have been asked to find an authentication service that is handled by a third party. The service should allow users to access multiple websites, as long as they support the third-party authentication service. What would be your best choice?

   A. OpenID

   B. Kerberos

   C. NTLM

   D. Shibboleth

15. Abigail is implementing biometrics for her company. She is trying to get the false rejection rate and false acceptance rate to the same level. What is the term used for this?

   A. Crossover error rate

   B. Leveling

   C. Balanced error rate

   D. Remediation

16. Mia is responsible for website security for a bank. When a user forgets their password, she wants a method to give them a temporary password. Which of the following would be the best solution for this situation?

   A. Facial recognition

   B. Digital certificate authentication

   C. RBAC

   D. TOTP

17. George wants a secure authentication protocol that can integrate with RADIUS and can use digital certificates. Which of the following would be his best choice?

   A. CHAP

   B. 802.11i

  C. 802.1x

  D. OAUTH

18. Jacob is responsible for database server security in his company. He is very concerned about preventing unauthorized access to the databases. Which of the following would be the most appropriate for him to implement?

  A. ABAC

  B. TOTP

  C. HIDS

  D. DAMP

19. Mason is responsible for security at a company that has traveling salespeople. The company has been using ABAC for access control to the network. Which of the following is an issue that is specific to ABAC and might cause it to incorrectly reject logins?

  A. Geographic location

  B. Wrong password

  C. Remote access is not allowed by ABAC.

  D. Firewalls usually block ABAC.

20. You work for a U.S. defense contractor. You are setting up access cards that have chips embedded in them to provide access control for users in your company. Which of the following types of cards would be best for you to use?

  A. CAC

  B. PIV

  C. NFC

  D. Smart card

21. Darrell is concerned that users on his network have too many passwords to remember and might write down their passwords, thus creating a significant security risk. Which of the following would be most helpful in mitigating this issue?

  A. OAUTH

  B. SSO

  C. OpenID

  D. Kerberos

22. Fares is a security administrator for a large company. Occasionally, a user needs to access a specific resource that they don't have permission to access. Which access control methodology would be most helpful in this situation?

  A. Mandatory Access Control

  B. Discretionary Access Control

  C. Role-based Access Control

  D. Rule-based Access Control

23. You are comparing biometric solutions for your company, and the product you pick must have an appropriate False Acceptance Rate (FAR). Which of the following best describes FAR?

    A. How often an unauthorized user is granted access by mistake

    B. How readily users accept the new technology, based on ease of use

    C. How often an authorized user is not granted access

    D. How frequently the system is offline

24. Amelia is looking for a network authentication method that can use digital certificates and does not require end users to remember passwords. Which of the following would best fit her requirements?

    A. OAUTH

    B. Tokens

    C. OpenID

    D. RBAC

25. You are responsible for setting up new accounts for your company network. What is the most important thing to keep in mind when setting up new accounts?

    A. Password length

    B. Password complexity

    C. Account age

    D. Least privileges

26. Stefan just became the new security officer for a university. He is concerned that student workers who work late on campus could try and log in with faculty credentials. Which of the following would be most effective in preventing this?

    A. Time of day restrictions

    B. Usage auditing

    C. Password length

    D. Credential management

27. Jennifer is concerned that some people in her company have more privileges than they should. This has occurred due to people moving from one position to another, and having cumulative rights that exceed the requirements of their current jobs. Which of the following would be most effective in mitigating this issue?

    A. Permission auditing

    B. Job rotation

    C. Preventing job rotation

    D. Separation of duties

28. Chloe has noticed that users on her company's network frequently have simple passwords made up of common words. Thus, they have weak passwords. How could Chloe best mitigate this issue?

    A. Increase minimum password length.

    B. Have users change passwords more frequently.

    C. Require password complexity.

    D. Implement Single Sign-On (SSO).

29. Bart is looking for a remote access protocol for his company. It is important that the solution he selects support multiple protocols and use a reliable network communication protocol. Which of the following would be his best choice?

    A. RADIUS

    B. TACACS+

    C. NTLM

    D. CHAP

30. You are looking for an authentication method that has one-time passwords and works well with the Initiative for Open Authentication. However, the user should have unlimited time to use the password. Which of the following would be your best choice?

    A. CHAP

    B. TOTP

    C. HOTP

    D. ABAC

31. Gerard is trying to find a flexible remote access protocol that can use either TCP or UDP. Which of the following should he select?

    A. RADIUS

    B. DIAMETER

    C. TACACS+

    D. TACACS

32. Emiliano is considering voice recognition as part of his access control strategy. What is one weakness with voice recognition?

    A. People's voices change.

    B. Systems require training.

    C. High false negative rate

    D. High false positive rate

33. You are explaining facial recognition to a colleague. What is the most significant drawback to implementing facial recognition?

   A. These systems can be expensive.

   B. These systems can be fooled with facial hair, glasses, etc.

   C. These systems have a high false positive rate.

   D. The systems require a long time to observe a face.

34. Mohanned is responsible for account management at his company. He is very concerned about hacking tools that rely on rainbow tables. Which of the following would be most effective in mitigating this threat?

   A. Password complexity

   B. Password age

   C. Password expiration

   D. Password length

35. Mary is a security administrator for a mid-sized company. She is trying to securely off-board employees. What should she do with the network account for an employee who is being off-boarded?

   A. Disable the account.

   B. Delete the account.

   C. Change the account password.

   D. Leave the account as is.

36. Your supervisor tells you to implement security based on your users' physical characteristics. Under which type of security would hand scanning and retina scanning fall?

   A. CHAP

   B. Multifactor

   C. Biometrics

   D. Token

37. What port does TACACS use?

   A. TCP 143

   B. TCP and UDP 49

   C. TCP 443

   D. UDP 53

38. A company-wide policy is being created to define various security levels. Which of the following systems of access control would use documented security levels like Confidential or Secret for information?

   A. RBAC

   B. MAC

   C. DAC

   D. BBC

39. There is a common security issue that is extremely hard to control in large environments. It occurs when a user has more computer rights, permissions, and privileges than what is required for the tasks the user needs to fulfill. This is the opposite of what principle?

    A. Separation of duties

    B. Least privileges

    C. Transitive trust

    D. Account management

40. Users in your network are able to assign permissions to their own shared resources. Which of the following access control models is used in your network?

    A. DAC

    B. RBAC

    C. MAC

    D. ABAC

41. John is performing a port scan of a network as part of a security audit. He notices that the domain controller is using secure LDAP. Which of the following ports would lead him to that conclusion?

    A. 53

    B. 389

    C. 443

    D. 636

42. Which of the following access control methods grants permissions based on the user's position in the organization?

    A. MAC

    B. RBAC

    C. DAC

    D. ABAC

43. Which of the following can be used as a means for dual-factor authentication?

    A. Password and PIN number

    B. RADIUS and L2TP

    C. LDAP and WPA

    D. Iris scan and password

44. Kerberos uses which of the following to issue tickets?

    A. Authentication service

    B. Certificate authority

    C. Ticket-granting service

    D. Key distribution center

45. A company requires that a user's credentials include providing something they know and something they are in order to gain access to the network. Which of the following types of authentication is being described?

    A. Token

    B. Two-factor

    C. Kerberos

    D. Biometrics

46. Samantha is looking for an authentication method that incorporates the X.509 standard and will allow authentication to be digitally signed. Which of the following authentication methods would best meet these requirements?

    A. Certificate-based authentication

    B. OAUTH

    C. Kerberos

    D. Smart cards

47. Your company relies heavily on cloud and SaaS service providers such as salesforce.com, Office365, and Google. Which of the following would you have security concerns about?

    A. LDAP

    B. TACACS+

    C. SAML

    D. Transitive trust

48. Greg is responsible for database security for his company. He is concerned about authentication and permissions. Which of the following should be his first step?

    A. Implement minimum password length.

    B. Implement password lockout.

    C. Conduct a permissions audit.

    D. Ensure least privileges.

49. Which of the following is a step in account maintenance?

    A. Implement two-factor authentication.

    B. Check for time of day restrictions.

    C. Review onboarding processes.

    D. Check to see that all accounts are for active employees.

50. Tyrell works as a security officer for a mid-sized bank. All the employees only work in the office; there are no employees who work remotely or travel for company business. Tyrell is concerned about someone using an employee's login credentials to access the bank's network. Which of the following would be most effective in mitigating this threat?

    A. Kerberos authentication

    B. TOTP

    C. Location-based policies

    D. Group-based access control

51. Henry is an employee at Acme Company. The company requires him to change his password every three months. He has trouble remembering new passwords, so he keeps switching between just two passwords. Which policy would be most effective in preventing this?

    A. Password complexity

    B. Password history

    C. Password length

    D. Password age

52. Sheila is concerned that some users on her network may be accessing files that they should not—specifically, files that are not required for their job tasks. Which of the following would be most effective in determining if this is happening?

    A. Usage auditing and review

    B. Permissions auditing and review

    C. Account maintenance

    D. Policy review

53. In which of the following scenarios would using a shared account pose the least security risk?

    A. For a group of tech support personnel

    B. For guest Wi-Fi access

    C. For students logging in at a university

    D. For accounts with few privileges

54. Which of the following is not a part of password complexity?

    A. Using both uppercase and lowercase letters

    B. Minimum password length

    C. Using numbers

    D. Using symbols (such as $, #, etc.)

55. Jane is setting up login accounts for federated identities. She wants to avoid requiring the users to remember login credentials and allow them to use their logins from the originating network. Which of the following technologies would be most suitable for implementing this?

    A. Credential management

    B. OAUTH

    C. Kerberos

    D. Shibboleth

56. Sam is responsible for password management at a large company. Sometimes users cannot recall their passwords. What would be the best solution for him to address this?

    A. Changing password history length

    B. Implementing password recovery

    C. Eliminating password complexity

    D. Lengthening password age

57. You are a security administrator for an insurance company. You have discovered that there are a few active accounts for employees who left the company over a year ago. Which of the following would best address this issue?

    A. Password complexity

    B. Offboarding procedures

    C. Onboarding procedures

    D. Password expiration

58. Maria is responsible for security at a small company. She is concerned about unauthorized devices being connected to the network. She is looking for a device authentication process. Which of the following would be the best choice for her?

    A. CHAP

    B. Kerberos

    C. 802.11i

    D. 802.1x

59. Laura is a security admin for a mid-sized mortgage company. She wants to ensure that the network is using the most secure login and authentication scheme possible. Which of the following would be her best choice?

    A. Iris scanning

    B. Fingerprint scanning

    C. Multifactor authentication

    D. Smart cards

60. Charles is a CISO for an insurance company. He recently read about an attack wherein an attacker was able to enumerate all the network resources, and was able to make some resources unavailable. All this was done by exploiting a single protocol. Which protocol should Charles secure to mitigate this attack?

    A. SNMP

    B. LDAP

    C. HTTP

    D. DHCP

61. Robert is using PAP for authentication in his network. What is the most significant weakness in PAP?

    A. Unsigned authentication

    B. Single factor

    C. Credentials sent in cleartext

    D. PAP does not support TACACS+.

62. You are responsible for account access control and authorization at a large university. There are approximately 30,000 students and 1,200 faculty/staff for whom you must manage accounts. Which of the following would be the best access control/account management approach?

    A. Group-based

    B. Location-based

    C. MAC

    D. DAC

63. Which of the following is most important in managing account permissions?

    A. Account recertification

    B. Usage auditing

    C. Standard naming conventions

    D. Account recovery

64. Which of the following would be the best choice for naming the account of John Smith, who is a domain administrator?

    A. dm_jsmith

    B. jsmithAdmin

    C. AdministratorSmith

    D. jsmith

65. Megan is very concerned about file system security on her network servers. Which of the following is the most basic form of file system security?

    A. Encryption

    B. Access control

    C. Auditing

    D. RAID

66. Karen is responsible for account security in her company. She has discovered a receptionist whose account has a six-character password that has not been changed in two years, and her password history is not being maintained. What is the most significant problem with this account?

    A. Nothing, this is adequate for a low-security position.

    B. The password length is the most significant problem.

    C. The lack of password history is the most significant problem.

    D. The age of the password is the most significant problem.

67. When you're offboarding an employee, which of the following is the first thing you should do?

    A. Audit their computer.

    B. Conduct an out-processing questionnaire.

    C. Disable accounts.

    D. Delete accounts.

68. Which of the following is a difference between TACACS and TACACS+?

    A. TACACS uses TCP, TACACS+ uses UDP

    B. TACACS uses UDP, TACACS+ uses TCP

    C. TACACS uses TCP or UDP, TACACS+ uses UDP

    D. TACACS uses UDP, TACACS+ uses UDP or TCP

69. Greg is considering using CHAP or MS-CHAPv2 for authenticating remote users. Which of the following is a major difference between the two protocols?

    A. CHAP uses a hash for the challenge, MS-CHAPv2 uses AES.

    B. CHAP provides mutual authentication, MS-CHAPv2 does not.

    C. CHAP uses AES for the challenge, MS-CHAPv2 uses a hash.

    D. MS-CHAPv2 provides mutual authentication, CHAP does not.

70. Terrance is looking for a physical access solution that uses asymmetric cryptography (public key cryptography) to authorize the user. What type of solution is this?

    A. Asynchronous password token

    B. Challenge response token

    C. TOTP token

    D. Static password token

71. Which access control model is based on the Trusted Computer System Evaluation Criteria (TCSEC)?

    A. ABAC

    B. MAC

    C. RBAC

    D. DAC

72. Mary is responsible for the security of database servers at a mortgage company. The servers are Windows Server 2016. She is concerned about file system security. Which of the following Microsoft features would be most helpful to her in implementing file system security?

    A. Password policies

    B. EFS

    C. Account lockout

    D. UAC

73. Santiago manages database security for a university. He is concerned about ensuring that appropriate security measures are implemented. Which of the following would be most important to database security?

   A. Password policies

   B. Antivirus

   C. EFS

   D. Access control policies

74. Ingrid is reviewing her company's recertification policy. Which of the following is the best reason to recertify?

   A. To audit usage

   B. To enhance onboarding

   C. To audit permissions

   D. To manage credentials

75. Emma is concerned about credential management. Users on her network often have over a half-dozen passwords to remember. She is looking for a solution to this problem. Which of the following would be the best way to address this issue?

   A. Implement a manager.

   B. Use shorter passwords.

   C. Implement OAUTH.

   D. Implement Kerberos.

76. Magnus is concerned about someone using a password cracker on computers in his company. He is concerned that crackers will attempt common passwords in order to log in to a system. Which of the following would be best for mitigating this threat?

   A. Password age restrictions

   B. Password minimum length requirements

   C. Account lockout policies

   D. Account usage auditing

77. Lucas is looking for an XML-based open standard for exchanging authentication information. Which of the following would best meet his needs?

   A. SAML

   B. OAUTH

   C. RADIUS

   D. NTLM

78. Which of the following processes transpires when a user provides a correct username and password?

   A. Identification

   B. Authentication

   C. Authorization

   D. Accounting

79. Min-seo is looking for a type of access control that enforces authorization rules by the operating system. Users cannot override authentication or access control policies. Which of the following best fits this description?

   A. DAC

   B. MAC

   C. RBAC

   D. ABAC

80. Hinata is considering biometric access control solutions for her company. She is concerned about the crossover error rate (CER). Which of the following most accurately describes the CER?

   A. The rate of false acceptance

   B. The rate of false rejection

   C. The point at which false rejections outpace false acceptances

   D. The point at which false rejections and false acceptances are equal

81. Joshua is looking for an authentication protocol that would be effective at stopping session hijacking. Which of the following would be his best choice?

   A. CHAP

   B. PAP

   C. SPAP

   D. RADIUS

82. David is trying to select an authentication method for his company. He needs one that will support REST as well as multiple web-based and mobile clients. Which of the following would be his best choice?

   A. Shibboleth

   B. RADIUS

   C. OpenID Connect

   D. OAuth

83. Phillip is examining options for controlling physical access to the server room at his company. He wants a hands-free solution. Which of the following would be his best choice?

   A. Smart cards

   B. Proximity cards

    C. Tokens

    D. Fingerprint scanner

84. Which of the following is the most significant disadvantage of federated identities?

    A. They cannot be used with Kerberos.

    B. They don't implement least privileges.

    C. Poor password management

    D. Transitive trust

85. Max is implementing type II authentication for his company. Which of the following would be an example of type II authentication?

    A. Strong passwords

    B. Retinal scan

    C. Smart cards

    D. Timed one-time passwords

86. Nicole is implementing a server authentication method that depends on a TPM in the server. Which of the following best describes this approach?

    A. Hardware-based access control

    B. Software-based access control

    C. Digital certificate–based access control

    D. Chip-based access control

Chapter

5

Risk Management

THE COMPTIA SECURITY+ EXAM SY0-501 TOPICS COVERED IN THIS CHAPTER INCLUDE THE FOLLOWING:

✓ **5.1 Explain the importance of policies, plans and procedures related to organizational security.**

- Standard operating procedure
- Agreement types
  - BPA
  - SLA
  - ISA
  - MOU/MOA
- Personnel management
  - Mandatory vacations
  - Jot rotation
  - Separation of duties
  - Clean desk
  - Background checks
  - Exit interviews
  - Role-based awareness training
    - Data owner
    - System administrator
    - System owner
    - User
    - Privileged user
    - Executive user
  - NDA
  - Onboarding
  - Continuing education
  - Acceptable use policy/rules of behavior
  - Adverse actions

- General security policies
  - Social media networks/applications
  - Personal email

✓ **5.2 Summarize business impact analysis concepts.**

- RTO/RPO
- MTBF
- MTTR
- Mission-essential functions
- Identification of critical systems
- Single point of failure
- Impact
  - Life
  - Property
  - Safety
  - Finance
  - Reputation
- Privacy impact assessment
- Privacy threshold assessment

✓ **5.3 Explain risk management processes and concepts.**

- Threat assessment
  - Environmental
  - Manmade
  - Internal vs external
- Risk assessment
- SLE
- ALE
- ARO
- Asset value
- Risk register
- Likelihood of occurrence
- Supply chain assessment
- Impact
- Quantitative

- Qualitative
- Testing
    - Penetration testing authorization
    - Vulnerability testing authorization
- Risk response techniques
    - Accept
    - Transfer
    - Avoid
    - Mitigate
- Change Management

✓ **5.4 Given a scenario, follow incident response procedures.**

- Incident response plan
    - Documented incident types/category definitions
    - Roles and responsibilities
    - Reporting requirements/escalation
    - Cyber-incident response teams
    - Exercise
- Incident response process
    - Preparation
    - Identification
    - Containment
    - Eradication
    - Recovery
    - Lessons learned

✓ **5.5 Summarize basic concepts of forensics.**

- Order of volatility
- Chain of custody
- Legal hold
- Data acquisition
    - Capture system image
    - Network traffic and logs
    - Capture video
    - Record time offset

- Take hashes
- Screenshots
- Witness interviews
- Preservation
- Recovery
- Strategic intelligence/counterintelligence gathering
  - Active logging
- Track man-hours

✓ **5.6 Explain disaster recovery and continuity of operation concepts.**

- Recovery sites
  - Hot site
  - Warm site
  - Cold site
- Order of restoration
- Backup concepts
  - Differential
  - Incremental
  - Snapshots
  - Full
- Geographic considerations
  - Off-site backups
  - Distance
  - Location selection
  - Legal implications
  - Data sovereignty
- Continuity of operation planning
  - Exercises/tabletop
  - After-action reports
  - Failover
  - Alternate processing sites
  - Alternate business practices

✓ **5.7 Compare and contrast various types of controls.**

- Deterrent
- Preventive
- Detective
- Corrective
- Compensating
- Technical
- Administrative
- Physical

✓ **5.8 Given a scenario, carry out data security and privacy practices.**

- Data destruction and media sanitization
  - Burning
  - Shredding
  - Pulping
  - Pulverizing
  - Degaussing
  - Purging
  - Wiping
- Data sensitivity labeling and handling
  - Confidential
  - Private
  - Public
  - Proprietary
  - PII
  - PHI
- Data roles
  - Owner
  - Steward/custodian
  - Privacy officer
- Data retention
- Legal and compliance

1. You are a manager of a bank and you suspect one of your tellers has stolen money from their station. After talking with your supervisor, you place the employee on leave with pay, suspend their computer account, and obtain their proximity card and keys to the building. Which of the following policies did you follow?

    A. Mandatory vacations

    B. Exit interviews

    C. Adverse actions

    D. Onboarding

2. Which of the following principles stipulates that multiple changes to a computer system should not be made at the same time?

    A. Due diligence

    B. Acceptable use

    C. Change management

    D. Due care

3. Why are penetration test often not advised?

    A. It can be disruptive for the business activities.

    B. It is able to measure and authenticate the efficiency of a company's defensive mechanisms.

    C. It's able to find both known and unknown hardware or software weaknesses.

    D. It permits the exploration of real risks and gives a precise depiction of a company's IT infrastructure security posture at any given time.

4. You are a security engineer and discovered an employee using the company's computer systems to operate their small business. The employee installed their personal software on the company's computer and is using the computer hardware, such as the USB port. What policy would you recommend the company implement to prevent any risk of the company's data and network being compromised?

    A. Acceptable use policy

    B. Clean desk policy

    C. Mandatory vacation policy

    D. Job rotation policy

5. What should be done to back up tapes that are stored off-site?

    A. Generate a file hash for each backup file.

    B. Scan the backup data for viruses.

    C. Perform a chain of custody on the backup tape.

    D. Encrypt the backup data.

6. Which recovery site is the easiest to test?

    A. Warm site

    B. Cold site

    C. Hot site

    D. Medium site

7. Katelyn is a network technician for a manufacturing company. She is testing a network forensic capturing software and plugs her laptop into an Ethernet switch port and begins capturing network traffic. Later she begins to analyze the data and notices some broadcast and multicast packets, as well as her own laptop's network traffic. Which of the following statements best describes why Katelyn was unable to capture all network traffic on the switch?

    A. Each port on the switch is an isolated broadcast domain.

    B. Each port on the switch is an isolated collision domain.

    C. Promiscuous mode must be enabled on the NIC.

    D. Promiscuous mode must be disabled on the NIC.

8. Which of the following is not a step of the incident response process?

    A. Snapshot

    B. Preparation

    C. Recovery

    D. Containment

9. Which of the following is another term for technical controls?

    A. Access controls

    B. Logical controls

    C. Detective controls

    D. Preventive controls

10. You are a security manager for your company and need to reduce the risk of employees working in collusion to embezzle funds. Which of the following policies would you implement?

    A. Mandatory vacations

    B. Clean desk

    C. NDA

    D. Continuing education

11. You are a security administrator, and your manager has asked you about protecting the privacy of personally identifiable information (PII) that is collected. Which of the following would be the best option to fulfill the request?

    A. PIA

    B. BIA

    C. RTO

    D. SPF

12. Which of the following plans best identifies critical systems and components to ensure the assets are protected?

    A. DRP

    B. BCP

    C. IT contingency plan

    D. Succession plan

13. After your company implemented a clean desk policy, you have been asked to secure physical documents every night. Which of the following would be the best solution?

    A. Department door lock

    B. Locking cabinets and drawers

    C. Proximity card

    D. Onboarding

14. Your manager has instructed the team to test certain systems based on the business continuity plan to ensure they are operating properly. The manager wants to ensure there are no overlaps in the plan before implementing the test. Which continuity of operation planning concept is your manager referring to?

    A. After-action report

    B. Failover

    C. Eradication

    D. Tabletop exercise

15. Which of the following is an example of PHI?

    A. Passport number

    B. Criminal record

    C. Fingerprints

    D. Name of school attended

16. Which of the following techniques attempts to predict the likelihood a threat will occur and assigns monetary values should a loss occur?

    A. Change management

    B. Vulnerability assessment

    C. Qualitative risk assessment

    D. Quantitative risk assessment

17. Your competitors are offering a new service that is predicted to sell strong. After much careful research, your company has decided not to launch a competing service due to the uncertainty of the market and the enormous investment required. Which of the following best describes the company's decision?

    A. Risk transfer

    B. Risk avoidance

   C.   Risk acceptance

   D.   Risk mitigation

18. Which of the following agreements is less formal than a traditional contract but still has a certain level of importance to all parties involved?

   A.   SLA

   B.   BPA

   C.   ISA

   D.   MOU

19. Your company is considering moving its mail server to a hosting company. This will help reduce hardware and server administrator costs at the local site. Which of the following documents would formally state the reliability and recourse if the reliability is not met?

   A.   MOU

   B.   SLA

   C.   ISA

   D.   BPA

20. You have an asset that is valued at $16,000, the exposure factor of a risk affecting that asset is 35%, and the annualized rate of occurrence if 75%. What is the SLE?

   A. $5,600

   B. $5,000

   C. $4,200

   D. $3,000

21. During a meeting, you present management with a list of access controls used on your network. Which of the following controls is an example of a corrective control?

   A.   IDS

   B.   Audit logs

   C.   Antivirus software

   D.   Router

22. You are the new security administrator and have discovered your company lacks deterrent controls. Which of the following would you install that satisfies your needs? (Choose two.)

   A.   Lighting

   B.   Motion sensor

   C.   No trespassing signs

   D.   Antivirus scanner

23. Your company's security policy includes system testing and security awareness training guidelines. Which of the following control types is this?

   A. Detective technical control

   B. Preventive technical control

   C. Detective administrative control

   D. Preventive administrative control

24. Which step of the incident response process occurs after containment?

   A. Preparation

   B. Recovery

   C. Identification

   D. Eradication

25. You are a security administrator for your company and you identify a security risk. You decide to continue with the current security plan. However, you develop a contingency plan in case the security risk occurs. Which of the following type of risk response technique are you demonstrating?

   A. Accept

   B. Transfer

   C. Avoid

   D. Mitigate

26. Which of the following best visually shows the state of a computer at the time it was collected by law enforcement?

   A. Screenshots

   B. Identification

   C. Tabletop exercise

   D. Generate hash values

27. You are asked to protect the company's data should a complete disaster occur. Which action would be the best option for this request?

   A. Back up all data to tape, and store those tapes at an alternate location within the city.

   B. Back up all data to tape, and store those tapes at an alternate location in another city.

   C. Back up all data to disk, and store the disk in a safe in the company's basement.

   D. Back up all data to disk, and store the disk in a safe at the network administrator's home.

28. Which of the following would *not* be a purpose of a privacy threshold analysis?

   A. Identify programs and systems that are privacy-sensitive.

   B. Demonstrate the inclusion of privacy considerations during the review of a program or system.

   C. Identify systems that are considered a single point of failure.

   D. Demonstrate compliance with privacy laws and regulations.

29. You have purchased new laptops for your salespeople. You plan to dispose of the hard drives of the former laptops as part of a company computer sale. Which of the following methods would you use to properly dispose of the hard drives?

   A. Destruction

   B. Shredding

   C. Purging

   D. Formatting

30. You are the head of the IT department of a school and are looking for a way to promote safe and responsible use of the Internet for students. With the help of the teachers, you develop a document for students to sign that describes methods of accessing the Internet on the school's network. Which of the following best describes this document?

   A. Service level agreement

   B. Acceptable use policy

   C. Incident response plan

   D. Chain of custody

31. You are the security administrator and have discovered a malware incident. Which of the following responses should you do first?

   A. Recovery

   B. Eradication

   C. Containment

   D. Identification

32. You are an IT administrator for a company and you are adding new employees to an organization's identity and access management system. Which of the following best describes the process you are performing?

   A. Onboarding

   B. Offboarding

   C. Adverse action

   D. Job rotation

33. Your company is partnering with another company and requires systems to be shared. Which of the following agreements would outline how the shared systems should be interfaced?

   A. BPA

   B. MOU

   C. SLA

   D. ISA

34. Mark is an office manager at a local bank branch. He wants to ensure customer information isn't compromised when the deskside employees are away from their desks for the day. What security concept would Mark use to mitigate this concern?

   A. Clean desk

   B. Background checks

   C. Continuing education

   D. Job rotation

35. You are a security administrator and advise the web development team to include a CAPTCHA on the web page where users register for an account. Which of the following controls is this referring to?

   A. Deterrent

   B. Detective

   C. Compensating

   D. Degaussing

36. Which of the following is *not* a common security policy type?

   A. Acceptable use policy

   B. Social media policy

   C. Password policy

   D. Parking policy

37. As the IT security officer, you are configuring data label options for your company's research and development file server. Regular users can label documents as contractor, public, or internal. Which label should be assigned to company trade secrets?

   A. High

   B. Top secret

   C. Proprietary

   D. Low

38. Users are currently accessing their personal email through company computers, so you and your IT team have created a security policy for email use. What is the next step after creating and approving the email use policy?

   A. Encrypt all user email messages.

   B. Provide security user awareness training.

   C. Provide every employee with their own device to access their personal email.

   D. Forward all personal emails to their company email account.

39. Which of the following is not a physical security control?

   A. Motion detector

   B. Fence

   C. Antivirus software

   D. CCTV

40. Which of the following might you find in a DRP?

    A. Single point of failure

    B. Prioritized list of critical computer systems

    C. Exposure factor

    D. Asset value

41. Your security manager wants to decide which risks to mitigate based on cost. What is this an example of?

    A. Quantitative risk assessment

    B. Qualitative risk assessment

    C. Business impact analysis

    D. Threat assessment

42. Your company has outsourced its proprietary processes to Acme Corporation. Due to technical issues, Acme Corporation wants to include a third-party vendor to help resolve the technical issues. Which of the following must Acme Corporation consider before sending data to the third party?

    A. This data should be encrypted before it is sent to the third-party vendor.

    B. This may constitute unauthorized data sharing.

    C. This may violate the privileged user role-based awareness training.

    D. This may violate a nondisclosure agreement.

43. Zack is a security administrator who has been given permission to run a vulnerability scan on the company's wireless network infrastructure. The results show TCP ports 21 and 23 open on most hosts. What port numbers do these refer to? (Choose two.)

    A. FTP

    B. SMTP

    C. Telnet

    D. DNS

44. Which of the following backup concepts is the quickest backup but slowest restore?

    A. Incremental

    B. Differential

    C. Full

    D. Snapshots

45. Which of the following operations should you undertake to avoid mishandling of tapes, removal drives, CDs, and DVDs?

    A. Degaussing

    B. Acceptable use

    C. Data labeling

    D. Wiping

46. Which of the following can be classified as a single point of failure?

    A. Failover

    B. A cluster

    C. Load balancing

    D. A configuration

47. Which of the following are considered detective controls?

    A. Closed-circuit television (CCTV)

    B. Guard

    C. Firewall

    D. IPS

48. Your CIO wants to move the company's large sets of sensitive data to an SaaS cloud provider to limit the storage and infrastructure costs. Both the cloud provider and the company are required to have a clear understanding of the security controls that will be applied to protect the sensitive data. What type of agreement would the SaaS cloud provider and your company initiate?

    A. MOU

    B. BPA

    C. SLA

    D. ISA

49. Which of the following is typically included in a BPA?

    A. Clear statements detailing the expectation between a customer and a service provider

    B. The agreement that a specific function or service will be delivered at the agreed-upon level of performance

    C. Sharing of profits and losses and the addition or removal of a partner

    D. Security requirements associated with interconnecting IT systems

50. Your team powered off the SQL database server for over 7 hours to perform a test. Which of the following is the most likely reason for this?

    A. Business impact analysis

    B. Succession plan

    C. Continuity of operations plan

    D. Service level agreement

51. Which of the following role-based positions should receive training on how to manage a particular system?

    A. Users

    B. Privileged users

    C. Executive users

    D. System owners

52. You maintain a network of 150 computers and must determine which hosts are secure and which are not. Which of the following tools would best meet your need?

    A. Vulnerability scanner

    B. Protocol analyzer

    C. Port scanner

    D. Password cracker

53. You have been instructed to introduce an affected system back into the company's environment and be sure that it will not lead to another incident. You test, monitor, and validate that the system is not being compromised by any other means. Which of the incident response processes have you completed?

    A. Lessons learned

    B. Preparation

    C. Recovery

    D. Containment

54. You discover that an investigator made a few mistakes during a recent forensic investigation. You want to ensure the investigator follows the appropriate process for the collection, analysis, and preservation of evidence. Which of the following terms should you use for this process?

    A. Incident handling

    B. Legal hold

    C. Order of volatility

    D. Chain of custody

55. You receive a call from the help desk manager stating that there has been an increase in calls from users reporting their computers are infected with malware. Which of the following incident response steps should be completed first?

    A. Containment

    B. Eradication

    C. Lessons learned

    D. Identification

56. Which of the following are examples of custodian security roles? (Choose two.)

    A. Human resources employee

    B. Sales executive

    C. CEO

    D. Server backup operator

57. You are the network administrator of your company, and the manager of a retail site located across town has complained about the loss of power to their building several times this year. The branch manager is asking for a compensating control to overcome the power outage. What compensating control would you recommend?

   A. Firewall

   B. Security guard

   C. IDS

   D. Backup generator

58. James is a security administrator and is attempting to block unauthorized access to the desktop computers within the company's network. He has configured the computers' operating systems to lock after 5 minutes of no activity. What type of security control has James implemented?

   A. Preventive

   B. Corrective

   C. Deterrent

   D. Detective

59. Which of the following terms best describes sensitive medical information?

   A. AES

   B. PHI

   C. PII

   D. TLS

60. An accounting employee changes roles with another accounting employee every 4 months. What is this an example of?

   A. Separation of duties

   B. Mandatory vacation

   C. Job rotation

   D. Onboarding

61. Which of the following are considered inappropriate places to store backup tapes? (Choose two.)

   A. Near a workstation

   B. Near a speaker

   C. Near a CRT monitor

   D. Near an LCD screen

62. You are a member of your company's security response team and have discovered an incident within your network. You are instructed to remove and restore the affected system. You restore the system with the original disk image and then install patches and disable any unnecessary services to harden the system against any future attacks. Which incident response process have you completed?

   A. Eradication

   B. Preparation

C. Containment

D. Recovery

63. You are a security administrator and have decided to implement a unified threat management (UTM) appliance within your network. This appliance will provide antimalware, spam filtering, and content inspection along with other protections. Which of the following statements best describes the potential problem with this plan?

   A. The protections can only be performed one at a time.

   B. This is a complex plan because you will manage several complex platforms.

   C. This could create the potential for a single point of failure.

   D. You work with a single vendor and its support department.

64. You are attending a risk analysis meeting and are asked to define internal threats. Which of the following is not considered an internal threat?

   A. Employees accessing external websites through the company's hosts

   B. Embezzlement

   C. Threat actors compromising a network through a firewall

   D. Users connecting a personal USB thumb drive to a workstation

65. You are the network director and are creating the following year's budget. You submit forensic dollar amounts for the cyber incident response team. Which of the following would you not submit? (Choose two.)

   A. ALE amounts

   B. SLE amounts

   C. Training expenses

   D. Man-hour expenses

66. Computer evidence of a crime is preserved by making an exact copy of the hard disk. Which of the following does this demonstrate?

   A. Chain of custody

   B. Order of volatility

   C. Capture system image

   D. Taking screenshots

67. Which option is an example of a workstation not hardened?

   A. Risk

   B. Threat

   C. Exposure

   D. Mitigate

68. Which of the following elements should not be included in the preparation phase of the incident response process?

   A. Policy

   B. Lesson learned documentation

   C. Response plan/strategy

   D. Communication

69. Which of the following does not minimize security breaches committed by internal employees?

   A. Job rotation

   B. Separation of duties

   C. Nondisclosure agreements signed by employees

   D. Mandatory vacations

70. You find one of your employees posting negative comments about the company on Facebook and Twitter. You also discover the employee is sending negative comments from their personal email on the company's computer. You are asked to implement a policy to help the company avoid any negative reputation in the marketplace. Which of the following would be the best option to fulfill the request?

   A. Account policy enforcement

   B. Change management

   C. Security policy

   D. Risk assessment

71. Which of the following statements best describes a differential backup?

   A. Only the changed portions of files are backed up.

   B. All files are copied to storage media.

   C. Files that have changed since the last full backup are backed up.

   D. Only files that have changed since the last full or incremental backup are backed up.

72. During which step of the incident response process does root cause analysis occur?

   A. Preparation

   B. Lessons learned

   C. Containment

   D. Recovery

73. Which of the following types of testing can help identify risks? (Choose two.)

   A. Quantitative

   B. Penetration testing

   C. Vulnerability testing

   D. Qualitative

74. What can a company do to prevent sensitive data from being retrieved by dumpster diving?

   A. Degaussing

   B. Capture system image

   C. Shredding

   D. Wiping

75. You are a network administrator and have been asked to send a large file that contains PII to an accounting firm. Which of the following protocols would it be best to use?

   A. Telnet

   B. FTP

   C. SFTP

   D. SMTP

76. Zackary is a network backup engineer and performs a full backup each Sunday evening and an incremental backup Monday through Friday evenings. One of the company's network servers crashes on Thursday afternoon. How many backups will Zack need to do to restore the server?

   A. Two

   B. Three

   C. Four

   D. Five

77. Your company website is hosted by an Internet service provider. Which of the following risk response techniques is in use?

   A. Risk avoidance

   B. Risk register

   C. Risk acceptance

   D. Risk mitigation

78. A call center leases a new space across town, complete with a functioning computer network that mirrors the current live site. A high-speed network link continuously synchronizes data between the two sites. Which of the following describes the site at the new leased location?

   A. Cold site

   B. Warm site

   C. Hot site

   D. Differential site

79. A security administrator is reviewing the company's continuity plan, and it specifies an RTO of 4 hours and an RPO of 1 day. Which of the following is the plan describing?

    A. Systems should be restored within 1 day and should remain operational for at least 4 hours.

    B. Systems should be restored within 4 hours and no later than 1 day after the incident.

    C. Systems should be restored within 1 day and lose, at most, 4 hours' worth of data.

    D. Systems should be restored within 4 hours with a loss of 1 day's worth of data at most.

80. Which of the following statements is true regarding a data retention policy?

    A. Regulations require financial transactions to be stored for 7 years.

    B. Employees must remove and lock up all sensitive and confidential documents when not in use.

    C. It describes a formal process of managing configuration changes made to a network.

    D. It is a legal document that describes a mutual agreement between parties.

81. You are attending a meeting with your manager and he wants to validate the cost of a warm site versus a cold site. Which of the following reasons best justify the cost of a warm site? (Choose two.)

    A. Small amount of income loss during long downtime

    B. Large amount of income loss during short downtime

    C. Business contracts enduring no more than 72 hours of downtime

    D. Business contracts enduring no more than 8 hours of downtime

82. Recently, company data that was sent over the Internet was intercepted and read by hackers. This damaged the company's reputation with its customers. You have been asked to implement a policy that will protect against these attacks. Which of the following options would you choose to help protect data that is sent over the Internet? (Choose two.)

    A. Confidentiality

    B. Safety

    C. Availability

    D. Integrity

83. How do you calculate the annual loss expectancy (ALE) that may occur due to a threat?

    A. Exposure Factor (EF) / Single Loss Expectancy (SLE)

    B. Single Loss Expectancy (SLE) × Annual Rate of Occurrence (ARO)

    C. Asset Value (AV) × Exposure Factor (EF)

    D. Single Loss Expectancy (SLE) / Exposure Factor (EF)

84. Which of the following impact scenarios would include severe weather events? (Choose two.)

    A. Life

    B. Reputation

    C. Salary

    D. Property

85. Which of the following outlines a business goal for system restoration and allowable data loss?

    A. RPO

    B. Single point of failure

    C. MTTR

    D. MTBF

86. Which of the following is an example of a preventive control? (Choose two.)

    A. Data backups

    B. Security camera

    C. Door alarm

    D. Cable locks

87. You are a security administrator for your company and you identify a security risk that you do not have in-house skills to address. You decide to acquire contract resources. The contractor will be responsible for handling and managing this security risk. Which of the following type of risk response technique are you demonstrating?

    A. Accept

    B. Mitigate

    C. Transfer

    D. Avoid

88. You are an IT manager and discovered your department had a break-in, and the company's computers were physically damaged. What type of impact best describes this situation?

    A. Life

    B. Reputation

    C. Property

    D. Safety

89. Which of the following would help build informed decisions regarding a specific DRP?

    A. Business impact analysis

    B. ROI analysis

    C. RTO

    D. Life impact

90. Each salesperson who travels has a cable lock to lock down their laptop when they step away from the device. Which of the following controls does this apply?

    A. Administrative

    B. Compensating

    C. Deterrent

    D. Preventive

91. Which of the following secures access to company data in agreement to management policies?

    A. Technical controls

    B. Administrative controls

    C. HTTPS

    D. Integrity

92. You are a server administrator for your company's private cloud. To provide service to employees, you are instructed to use reliable hard disks in the server to host a virtual environment. Which of the following best describes the reliability of hard drives?

    A. MTTR

    B. RPO

    C. MTBF

    D. ALE

93. You are replacing a number of devices with a mobile appliance that combines several functions. Which of the following describes the new implementation?

    A. Cloud computing

    B. Load balancing

    C. Single point of failure

    D. Virtualization

94. Which of the following can help mitigate adware intrusions?

    A. Antivirus

    B. Antispam

    C. Spyware

    D. Pop-up blocker

95. In the initial stages of a forensics investigation, Zack, a security administrator, was given the hard drive of the compromised workstation by the incident manager. Which of the following data acquisition procedures would Zack need to perform in order to begin the analysis? (Choose two.)

    A. Take hashes

    B. Take screenshots

    C. Capture the system image

    D. Start the order of volatility

96. Which of the following best describes a Computer Incident Response Team (CIRT)?

    A. Personnel who participate in exercises to practice incident response procedures

    B. Personnel who promptly and correctly handle incidents so they can be quickly contained, investigated, and recovered from

    C. A team to identify planning flaws before an actual incident occurs

    D. Team members using a walk-through checklist to ensure understanding of roles in a DRP

97. Which of the following decreases the success of brute-force attacks?

    A. Password complexity

    B. Password hints

    C. Account lockout threshold

    D. Enforce password history

98. A warrant has been issued to investigate a file server that is suspected to be part of an organized crime to steal credit card information. You are instructed to follow the order of volatility. Which data would you collect first?

    A. RAM

    B. USB flash drive

    C. Hard disk

    D. Swap files

99. What should human resources personnel be trained in regarding security policies?

    A. Guidelines and enforcement

    B. Order of volatility

    C. Penetration assessment

    D. Vulnerability assessment

100. Which of the following is not a basic concept of computer forensics?

    A. Preserve evidence

    B. Determine if the suspect is guilty based on the findings

    C. Track man-hours and expenses

    D. Interview all witnesses

101. The Chief Information Officer (CIO) wants to set up a redundant server location so that the production server images can be moved within 36 hours and the servers can be restored quickly, should a catastrophic failure occur at the primary location. Which of the following can be implemented?

    A. Hot site

    B. Cold site

    C. Warm site

    D. Load balancing

102. Choose the correct order of volatility when collecting digital evidence.

    A. Hard disk drive, DVD-R, RAM, swap file

    B. Swap file, RAM, DVD-R, hard disk drive

    C. RAM, DVD-R, swap file, hard disk drive

    D. RAM, swap file, hard disk drive, DVD-R

103. Which of the following pieces of information would be summarized in the lessons learned phase of the incident response process? (Choose three.)

    A. When the problem was first detected and by whom

    B. How the problem was contained and eradicated

    C. The work that was performed during the recovery

    D. Preparing a company's team to be ready to handle an incident at a moment's notice

104. You receive a phone call from an employee reporting that their workstation is acting strangely. You gather information from the intrusion detection system and notice unusual network traffic from the workstation, and you determine the event may be an incident. You report the event to your manager, who then begins to collect evidence and prepare for the next steps. Which phase of the incident response process is this?

    A. Preparation

    B. Identification

    C. Containment

    D. Eradication

105. Your manager has asked you to recommend a way to transmit PII via email and maintain its confidentiality. Which of the following options is the best solution?

    A. Hash the information before sending.

    B. Protect the information with a digital signature.

    C. Protect the information by using RAID.

    D. Encrypt the information before sending.

106. Which of the following statements best defines change management?

    A. Responding to, containing, analyzing, and recovering from a computer-related incident

    B. Means used to define which access permissions subjects have for a specific object

    C. Procedures followed when configuration changes are made to a network

    D. Categorizing threats and vulnerabilities and their potential impacts to a network

107. During which step of the incident response process does identification of incidents that can be prevented or mitigated occur?

   A. Containment

   B. Eradication

   C. Preparation

   D. Lessons learned

108. Which of the following best describes the disadvantages of quantitative risk analysis compared to qualitative risk analysis? (Choose two.)

   A. Quantitative risk analysis requires complex calculations.

   B. Quantitative risk analysis is sometimes subjective.

   C. Quantitative risk analysis is generally scenario-based.

   D. Quantitative risk analysis is more time-consuming than qualitative risk analysis.

109. Which of the following are disadvantages of using a cold site? (Choose two.)

   A. Expense

   B. Recovery time

   C. Testing availability

   D. Administration time

110. Which of the following policies should be implemented to minimize data loss or theft?

   A. Password policy

   B. PII handling

   C. Chain of custody

   D. Detective control

111. Which of the following should a comprehensive data policy include?

   A. Wiping, disposing, storage, retention

   B. Disposing, patching, storage, retention

   C. Storage, retention, virtualization

   D. Onboarding, storage, disposing

112. You have revealed a recent intrusion within the company's network and have decided to execute incident response procedures. The incident response team has identified audit logs that hold information about the recent security breach. Prior to the incident, a security consultant firm recommended that your company install a NTP server within the network. Which of the following is a setback the incident response team will likely encounter during the assessment?

   A. Order of volatility

   B. Chain of custody

   C. Eradication

   D. Record time offset

113. You plan to provide a word processing program to the employees in your company. You decide not to install the program on each employee's workstation but rather have a cloud service provider host the application. Which of the following risk response techniques best describes the situation?

    A. Risk mitigation

    B. Risk acceptance

    C. Risk avoidance

    D. Risk transfer

114. Which of the following statements is true about incremental backup?

    A. It backs up all files.

    B. It backs up all files in a compressed format.

    C. It backs up all new files and any files that have changed since the last full backup without resetting the archive bit.

    D. It backs up all new files and any files that have changed since the last full or incremental backup and resets the archive bit.

115. The chief security officer (CSO) has seen four security breaches during the past 2 years. Each breach cost the company $30,000, and a third-party vendor has offered to repair the security weakness in the system for $250,000. The breached system is set to be replaced in 5 years. Which of the following risk response techniques should the CSO use?

    A. Accept the risk.

    B. Transfer the risk.

    C. Avoid the risk.

    D. Mitigate the risk.

116. Which of the following would not be a guideline for performing a BIA?

    A. Identify impact scenarios that put your business operations at risk.

    B. Identify mission-essential functions and the critical systems within each function.

    C. Approve and execute changes in order to ensure maximum security and availability of IT services.

    D. Calculate RPO, RTO, MTTR, and MTBF.

117. You are a network administrator and have purchased two devices that will work as failovers for each other. Which of the following does this best demonstrate?

    A. Integrity

    B. Availability

    C. Authentication

    D. Confidentiality

118. Your company has lost power and the salespeople cannot take orders because the computers and phone systems are unavailable. Which of the following would be the best options to an alternate business practice? (Choose two.)

    A. Tell the salespeople to go home for the day until the power is restored.

    B. Tell the salespeople to use their cell phones until the power is restored.

    C. Have the salespeople use paper and pen to take orders until the power is restored.

    D. Have the salespeople instruct customers to fax their orders until the power is restored.

119. Leigh Ann is the new network administrator for a local community bank. She studies the current file server folder structures and permissions. The previous administrator didn't properly secure customer documents in the folders. Leigh Ann assigns appropriate file and folder permissions to be sure that only the authorized employees can access the data. What security role is Leigh Ann assuming?

    A. Power user

    B. Data owner

    C. User

    D. Custodian

120. Which of the following methods is not recommended for removing data from a storage media that is used to store confidential information?

    A. Formatting

    B. Shredding

    C. Wiping

    D. Degaussing

121. A SQL database server is scheduled for full backups on Sundays at 2:00 a.m. and incremental backups each weeknight at 11:00 p.m. Write verification is enabled, and backup tapes are stored off-site at a bank safety deposit box. Which of the following should be completed to ensure integrity and confidentiality of the backups? (Choose two.)

    A. Use SSL to encrypt the backup data.

    B. Encrypt the backup data before it is stored off-site.

    C. Ensure that an employee other than the backup operator analyzes each day's backup logs.

    D. Ensure that the employee performing the backup is a member of the administrators' group.

122. You are planning to perform a security audit and would like to see what type of network traffic is transmitting within your company's network. Which of the following tools would you use?

    A. Port scanner

    B. Vulnerability scanner

    C. Protocol analyzer

    D. Network intrusion detection system

123. Your company has hired a new administrative assistant to a commercial lender named Leigh Ann. She will be using a web browser on a company computer at the office to access internal documents on a public cloud provider over the Internet. Which type of document should Leigh Ann read and sign?

    A. Internet acceptable use policy

    B. Audit policy

    C. Password policy

    D. Privacy policy

124. During a conversation with another colleague, you suggest there is a single point of failure in the single load balancer in place for the company's SQL server. You suggest implementing two load balancers in place with only one in service at a given time. What type of load balancing configuration have you described?

    A. Active-active

    B. Active directory

    C. Round robin

    D. Active-passive

125. Which of the following policies would you implement to help prevent the company's users from revealing their login credentials for others to view?

    A. Job rotation

    B. Data owner

    C. Clean desk

    D. Separation of duties

126. Which of the following are part of the chain of custody?

    A. Delegating evidence collection to your manager

    B. Capturing the system image to another hard drive

    C. Capturing memory contents before capturing hard disk contents

    D. Preserving, protecting, and documenting evidence

127. Zackary has been assigned the task of performing a penetration test on a server and was given limited information about the inner workings of the server. Which of the following tests will he be performing?

    A. White box

    B. Gray box

    C. Black box

    D. Clear box

128. Which of the following are considered administrative controls? (Choose two.)

    A. Firewall rules

    B. Personnel hiring policy

  C. Separation of duties

  D. Intrusion prevention system

129. Which of the following are examples of alternate business practices? (Choose two.)

  A. The business's point-of-sale terminal goes down, and employees use pen and paper to take orders and a calculator to determine customers' bills.

  B. The network system crashes due to an update, and employees are told to take time off until the company's network system is restored.

  C. Power is lost at a company's site and the manager posts a closed sign until power is restored.

  D. A bank location has lost power, and the employees are sent to another location to resume business.

130. Which of the following require careful handling and special policies for data retention and distribution? (Choose two.)

  A. Personal electronic devices

  B. MOU

  C. PII

  D. NDA

131. Matt is the head of IT security for a university department. He recently read articles about security breaches that involved malware on USB removable devices and is concerned about future incidents within the university. Matt reviews the past incident responses to determine how these occurrences may be prevented and how to improve the past responses. What type of document should Matt prepare?

  A. MOU

  B. SLA

  C. After-action report

  D. Nondisclosure agreement

132. Categorizing residual risk is most important to which of the following risk response techniques?

  A. Risk mitigation

  B. Risk acceptance

  C. Risk avoidance

  D. Risk transfer

133. You are the IT manager and one of your employees asks who assigns data labels. Which of the following assigns data labels?

  A. Owner

  B. Custodian

  C. Privacy officer

  D. System administrator

134. Which of the following is the most pressing security concern related to social media networks?

    A. Other users can view your MAC address.

    B. Other users can view your IP address.

    C. Employees can leak a company's confidential information.

    D. Employees can express their opinion about their company.

135. You are a network administrator looking to test patches quickly and often before pushing them out to the production workstations. Which of the following would be the best way to do this?

    A. Create a full disk image to restore the system after each patch installation.

    B. Create a virtual machine and utilize snapshots.

    C. Create an incremental backup of an unpatched workstation.

    D. Create a differential backup of an unpatched workstation.

136. You have instructed your junior network administrator to test the integrity of the company's backed-up data. Which of the following is the best way to test the integrity of a backup?

    A. Review written procedures.

    B. Use software to recover deleted files.

    C. Restore part of the backup.

    D. Conduct another backup.

137. What concept is being used when user accounts are created by one employee and user permissions are configured by another employee?

    A. Background checks

    B. Job rotation

    C. Separation of duties

    D. Collusion

138. Your company is requesting the installation of a fence around the property and cipher locks on all front entrances. Which of the following concepts is your company concerned about?

    A. Confidentiality

    B. Integrity

    C. Availability

    D. Safety

139. Which of the following is an example of a vulnerability assessment tool?

    A. Ophcrack

    B. John the Ripper

    C. L0phtCrack

    D. Nessus

140. A security analyst is analyzing the cost the company could incur if the customer database was breached. The database contains 2,500 records with PII. Studies show the cost per record would be $300. The likelihood that the database would be breached in the next year is only 5%. Which of the following would be the ALE for a security breach?

    A. $15,000

    B. $37,500

    C. $150,000

    D. $750,000

141. Your team must perform a test of a specific system to be sure the system operates at the alternate site. The results of the test must be compared with the company's live environment. Which test is your team performing?

    A. Cutover test

    B. Walk-through

    C. Parallel test

    D. Simulation

142. Which of the following concepts defines a company goal for system restoration and acceptable data loss?

    A. MTBF

    B. MTTR

    C. RPO

    D. ARO

143. Your IT team has created a disaster recovery plan to be used in case a SQL database server fails. What type of control is this?

    A. Detective

    B. Corrective

    C. Preventive

    D. Deterrent

144. Which of the following is not a step in the incident response process?

    A. Snapshot

    B. Preparation

    C. Recovery

    D. Containment

145. Which of the following threats is mitigated by shredding paper documents?

    A. Shoulder surfing

    B. Physical

    C. Adware

    D. Spyware

146. Your company hires a third-party auditor to analyze the company's data backup and long-term archiving policy. Which type of organization document should you provide to the auditor?

    A. Clean desk policy

    B. Acceptable use policy

    C. Security policy

    D. Data retention policy

147. You are a network administrator and have been given the duty of creating users accounts for new employees the company has hired. These employees are added to the identity and access management system and assigned mobile devices. What process are you performing?

    A. Offboarding

    B. System owner

    C. Onboarding

    D. Executive user

148. Which of the following defines a standard operating procedure (SOP)? (Choose three.)

    A. Standard

    B. Privacy

    C. Procedure

    D. Guideline

149. Computer equipment was suspected to be involved in a computer crime and was seized. The computer equipment was left unattended in a corridor for 10 minutes while officers restrained a potential suspect. The seized equipment is no longer admissible as evidence because of which of the following violations?

    A. Chain of custody

    B. Order of volatility

    C. Preparation

    D. Eradication

150. Which of the following should be performed when conducting a qualitative risk analysis? (Choose two.)

    A. ARO

    B. SLE

    C. Asset estimation

    D. Rating potential threats

Chapter

6

Cryptography and PKI

THE COMPTIA SECURITY+ EXAM SY0-501 TOPICS COVERED IN THIS CHAPTER INCLUDE THE FOLLOWING:

✓ **6.1 Compare and contrast basic concepts of cryptography.**

- Symmetric algorithms
- Modes of operation
- Asymmetric algorithms
- Hashing
- Salt, IV, nonce
- Elliptic curve
- Weak/deprecated algorithms
- Key exchange
- Digital signatures
- Diffusion
- Confusion
- Collision
- Steganography
- Obfuscation
- Stream vs. block
- Key strength
- Session keys
- Ephemeral key
- Secret algorithm
- Data-in-transit
- Data-at-rest
- Data-in-use

- Random/pseudo-random number generation
- Key stretching
- Implementation vs. algorithm selection
  - Crypto service provider
  - Crypto modules
- Perfect forward secrecy
- Security through obscurity
- Common use cases
  - Low power devices
  - Low latency
  - High resiliency
  - Supporting confidentiality
  - Supporting integrity
  - Supporting obfuscation
  - Supporting authentication
  - Supporting non-repudiation
  - Resource vs. security constraints

✓ **6.2 Explain cryptography algorithms and their basic characteristics.**

- Symmetric algorithms
  - AES
  - DES
  - 3DES
  - RC4
  - Blowfish/Twofish
- Cipher modes
  - CBC
  - GCM
  - ECB
  - CTM
  - Stream vs. block

- EAP-TLS
- EAP-TTLS
- IEEE 802.1x
- RADIUS Federation
- Methods
  - PSK vs. Enterprise vs. Open
  - WPS
  - Captive portals

✓ 6.4 **Given a scenario, implement public key infrastructure.**

- Components
  - CA
  - Intermediate CA
  - CRL
  - OCSP
  - CSR
  - Certificate
  - Public key
  - Private key
  - Object identifiers (OID)
- Concepts
  - Online vs. offline CA
  - Stapling
  - Pinning
  - Trust model
  - Key escrow
  - Certificate chaining
- Types of certificates
  - Wildcard
  - SAN
  - Code signing

- Self-signed
- Machine/computer
- Email
- User
- Root
- Domain validation
- Extended validation
- Certificate formats
  - DER
  - PEM
  - PFX
  - CER
  - P12
  - P7B

1. Which of the following would a public key be used for?

   A. To decrypt a hash of a digital signature

   B. To encrypt TLS traffic

   C. To digitally sign messages

   D. To decrypt TLS messages

2. Your company's web server certificate has been revoked and external customers are receiving errors when they connect to the website. Which of following actions must you take?

   A. Renew the certificate.

   B. Create and use a self-signed certificate.

   C. Request a certificate from the key escrow.

   D. Generate a new key pair and new certificate.

3. Mary is concerned about the validity of an email because a coworker denies sending it. How can Mary prove the authenticity of the email?

   A. Symmetric algorithm

   B. Digital signature

   C. CRL

   D. Asymmetric algorithm

4. Wi-Fi Alliance recommends that a passphrase be how many characters in length for WPA2-Personal security?

   A. 6 characters

   B. 8 characters

   C. 12 characters

   D. 16 characters

5. Which of the following digital certificate management practices will ensure that a lost certificate is not compromised?

   A. CRL

   B. Key escrow

   C. Nonrepudiation

   D. Recovery agent

6. Which of the following are restricted to 64-bit block sizes? (Choose two.)

   A. DES

   B. SHA

   C. MD5

   D. 3DES

7. Your company has implemented a RADIUS server and has clients that are capable of using multiple EAP types, including one configured for use on the RADIUS server. Your security manager wants to implement a WPA2-Enterprise system. Since you have the RADIUS server and clients, what piece of the network would you need?

   A. Network access control

   B. Authentication server

   C. Authenticator

   D. Supplicant

8. You are given the task of selecting an asymmetric encryption type that has an appropriate level of encryption strength but uses a smaller key length than is typically required. Which of the following encryption methods will accomplish your requirement?

   A. Blowfish

   B. RSA

   C. DHE

   D. ECC

9. Matt has been told that successful attacks have been taking place and data that has been encrypted by his company's software system has leaked to the company's competitors. Matt, through investigation, has discovered patterns due to the lack of randomness in the seeding values used by the encryption algorithm in the company's software. This discovery has led to successful reverse engineering. What can the company use to ensure patterns are not created during the encryption process?

   A. One-time pad

   B. Initialization vector

   C. Stream cipher

   D. Block cipher

10. You are asked to configure a WLAN that does not require a user to provide any credentials to associate with a wireless AP and access a WLAN. What type of authentication is said to be in use?

   A. IV

   B. WEP

   C. WPA

   D. Open

11. The CIO at your company no longer wants to use asymmetric algorithms because of the cost. Of the following algorithms, which should the CIO discontinue using?

   A. AES

   B. RC4

   C. RSA

   D. Twofish

12. Which of the following would you use to verify certificate status by receiving a response of "good," "revoked," or "unknown"?

   A. CRL

   B. OSCP

   C. RA

   D. PKI

13. Which of the following symmetric key algorithms are block ciphers? (Choose two.)

   A. MD5

   B. 3DES

   C. RC4

   D. Blowfish

14. Which of the following encryption algorithms is the weakest?

   A. Blowfish

   B. AES

   C. DES

   D. SHA

15. What encryption protocol does WEP improperly use?

   A. RC6

   B. RC4

   C. AES

   D. DES

16. James, an IT manager, expresses a concern during a monthly meeting about weak user passwords used on company servers and how they may be susceptible to brute-force password attacks. Which concept can James implement to make the weak passwords stronger?

   A. Key stretching

   B. Key escrow

   C. Key strength

   D. ECC

17. You are installing a network for a small business named Matrix Interior Design that the owner is operating out of their home. There are only four devices that will use the wireless LAN, and you are installing a SOHO wireless router between the wireless LAN clients and the broadband connection. To ensure better security from outside threats connecting to the wireless SOHO router, which of the following would be a good choice for the WPA2-PSK passphrase?

   A. 123456

   B. XXrcERr6Euex9pRCdn3h3

   C. bRtlBv

   D. HomeBusiness

18. You set up your wireless SOHO router to encrypt wireless traffic, and you configure the router to require wireless clients to authenticate against a RADIUS server. What type of security have you configured?

   A. WPA2 Enterprise

   B. WPA2 Personal

   C. TKIP

   D. WEP

19. You must implement a cryptography system that applies encryption to a group of data at a time. Which of the following would you choose?

   A. Stream

   B. Block

   C. Asymmetric

   D. Symmetric

20. Which symmetric block cipher supersedes Blowfish?

   A. RSA

   B. Twofish

   C. MD5

   D. PBKDF2

21. Root CAs can delegate their authority to which of the following to issue certificates to users?

   A. Registered authorities

   B. Intermediate CAs

   C. CRL

   D. CSR

22. Which of the following protocols should be used to authenticate remote access users with smartcards?

   A. PEAP

   B. EAP-TLS

   C. CHAP

   D. MS-CHAPv2

23. Tom is sending Mary a document and wants to show the document came from him. Which of the following should Tom use to digitally sign the document?

   A. TKIP

   B. Intermediate CA

   C. Public key

   D. Private key

24. Which of the following EAP types offers support for legacy authentication protocols such as PAP, CHAP, MS-CHAP, or MS-CHAPv2?

   A. PEAP

   B. EAP-FAST

   C. EAP-TLS

   D. EAP-TTLS

25. You are conducting a training program for new network administrators for your company. You talk about the benefits of asymmetric encryption. Which of the following are considered asymmetric algorithms? (Choose two.)

   A. RC4

   B. DES

   C. RSA

   D. ECC

26. Which of the following is a form of encryption also known as ROT13?

   A. Substitution cipher

   B. Transposition cipher

   C. Diffusion

   D. Confusion

27. Matt needs to calculate the number of keys that must be generated for 480 employees using the company's PKI asymmetric algorithm. How many keys must Matt create?

   A. 114,960

   B. 480

   C. 960

   D. 229,920

28. You are conducting a one-time electronic transaction with another company. The transaction needs to be encrypted, and for efficiency and simplicity, you want to use a single key for encryption and decryption of the data. Which of the following types would you use?

   A. Asymmetric

   B. Symmetric

   C. Hashing

   D. Steganography

29. Which of the following uses two mathematically related keys to secure data during transmission?

   A. Twofish

   B. 3DES

   C. RC4

   D. RSA

30. You have been instructed by the security manager to protect the server's data-at-rest. Which of the following would provide the strongest protection?

  A. Implement a full-disk encryption system.

  B. Implement biometric controls on data entry points.

  C. Implement a host-based intrusion detection system.

  D. Implement a host-based intrusion prevention system.

31. Which of the following EAP types use a three-phase operation?

  A. EAP-FAST

  B. EAP-TLS

  C. EAP-TTLS

  D. PEAP

32. Which of the following is an encryption standard that uses a single 56-bit symmetric key?

  A. DES

  B. 3DES

  C. AES

  D. WPS

33. Which of the following cryptography concepts converts output data into a fixed-length value and cannot be reversed?

  A. Steganography

  B. Hashing

  C. Collision

  D. IV

34. SSL is a protocol used for securing transactions transmitting over an untrusted network such as the Internet. Which of the following best describes the action that occurs during the SSL connection setup process?

  A. The client creates a session key and encrypts it with the server's private key.

  B. The client creates a session key and encrypts it with the server's public key.

  C. The server creates a session key and encrypts it with the client's private key.

  D. The server creates a session key and encrypts it with the client's public key.

35. Which of the following EAP types requires both server and client certificates?

  A. EAP-FAST

  B. PEAP

  C. EAP-TLS

  D. EAP-TTLS

36. You are the network administrator for a small office of 35 users and need to utilize mail encryption that will allow specific users to encrypt outgoing email messages. You are looking for an inexpensive onsite encryption server. Which of the following would you implement?

   A. PGP/GPG

   B. WPA2

   C. CRL

   D. EAP-TLS

37. You have been promoted to security administrator for your company and you need to be aware of all types of hashing algorithms for integrity checks. Which algorithm offers a 160-bit digest?

   A. MD5

   B. RC4

   C. SHA-1

   D. AES

38. You are the security manager for your company, and a system administrator wants to know if there is a way to reduce the cost of certificates by purchasing a certificate to cover all domains and subdomains for the company. Which of the following solutions would you offer?

   A. Wildcards

   B. Object identifiers

   C. Key escrow

   D. OCSP

39. Which of the following are authentication protocols? (Choose two.)

   A. WPS

   B. EAP

   C. IPSec

   D. IEEE 802.1x

40. Your company is looking to accept electronic orders from a vendor and wants to ensure nonauthorized people cannot send orders. Your manager wants a solution that provides nonrepudiation. Which of the following options would meet the requirements?

   A. Digital signatures

   B. Hashes

   C. Steganography

   D. Perfect forward secrecy

41. You are tasked to implement a solution to ensure data that are stored on a removable USB drive hasn't been tampered with. Which of the following would you implement?

   A. Key escrow

   B. File backup

    C. File encryption

    D. File hashing

42. Which of the following is mainly used for remote access into a network?

    A. TACACS+

    B. XTACACS

    C. Kerberos

    D. RADIUS

43. A security manager has asked you to explain why encryption is important and what symmetric encryption offers. Which of the following is the best explanation?

    A. Confidentiality

    B. Nonrepudiation

    C. Steganography

    D. Collision

44. You are a security administrator and have discovered one of the employees has been encoding confidential information into graphic files. Your employee is sharing these pictures on their social media account. What concept was the employee using?

    A. Hashing

    B. Steganography

    C. Symmetric algorithm

    D. Asymmetric algorithm

45. Your company's branch offices connect to the main office through a VPN. You recently discovered the key used on the VPN has been compromised. What should you do to ensure the key isn't compromised in the future?

    A. Enable perfect forward secrecy at the main office and branch office ends of the VPN.

    B. Enable perfect forward secrecy at the main office end of the VPN.

    C. Enable perfect forward secrecy at the branch office end of the VPN.

    D. Disable perfect forward secrecy at the main office and branch office ends of the VPN.

46. You are configuring your friend's new wireless SOHO router and discover a PIN on the back of the router. Which of the following best describes the purpose of the PIN?

    A. This is a WEP PIN.

    B. This is a WPS PIN.

    C. This is a WPA PIN.

    D. This is a Bluetooth PIN.

47. Which of the following benefits do digital signatures provide? (Choose two.)

    A. Nonrepudiation

    B. Authentication

    C. Encryption

    D. Key exchange

48. Your company has asked you to recommend a secure method for password storage. Which of the following would provide the best protection against brute-force attacks? (Choose two.)

    A. ROT13

    B. MD5

    C. PBKDF2

    D. BCRYPT

49. Your IT support center is receiving a high number of calls stating that users trying to access the company's website are receiving certificate errors within their browsers. Which of the following statements best describes what the issue is?

    A. The website certificate has expired.

    B. Users have forgotten their usernames or passwords.

    C. The domain name has expired.

    D. The network is currently unavailable.

50. In asymmetric encryption, what is used to decrypt an encrypted file?

    A. Private key

    B. Public key

    C. Message digest

    D. Ciphertext

51. You are performing a vulnerability assessment on a company's LAN and determine they are using 802.1x for secure access. Which of the following attacks can a threat actor use to bypass the network security?

    A. MAC spoofing

    B. ARP poisoning

    C. Ping of death

    D. Xmas attack

52. Your security manager is looking to implement a one-time pad scheme for the company's salespeople to use when traveling. Which of the following best describes a requirement for this implementation? (Choose three.)

    A. The pad must be distributed securely and protected at its destination.

    B. The pad must always be the same length.

    C. The pad must be used only one time.

    D. The pad must be made up of truly random values.

53. A threat actor has created a man-in-the-middle attack and captured encrypted communication between two users. The threat actor was unable to decrypt the messages. Which of the following is the reason the threat actor is unable to decrypt the messages?

    A. Hashing

    B. Symmetric encryption

C. Asymmetric encryption

D. Key escrow

54. You have implemented a PKI to send signed and encrypted data. The user sending data must have which of the following? (Choose two.)

A. The receiver's private key

B. The sender's private key

C. The sender's public key

D. The receiver's public key

55. Which of the following best describes the drawback of symmetric key systems?

A. You must use different keys for encryption and decryption.

B. The algorithm is more complex.

C. The system works much more slowly than an asymmetric system.

D. The key must be delivered in a secure manner.

56. Your company is looking for a secure backup mechanism for key storage in a PKI. Which of the following would you recommend?

A. CSR

B. Key escrow

C. CRL

D. CA

57. Which cryptography concept uses points on a curve to define public and private key pairs?

A. Obfuscation

B. ECC

C. Stream cipher

D. Block cipher

58. You are a security administrator and have been given instructions to update the access points to provide a more secure connection. The access points are currently set to use WPA TKIP for encryption. Which of the following would you configure to accomplish the task of providing a more secure connection?

A. WEP

B. WPA2 CCMP

C. Enable MAC filtering

D. Disable SSID broadcast

59. Which of the following is an example of a stream cipher?

A. AES

B. DES

C. 3DES

D. RC4

60. Which of the following are negotiation protocols commonly used by TLS? (Choose two.)

   A. DHE

   B. ECDHE

   C. RSA

   D. SHA

61. Which of the following statements is true regarding symmetric key systems?

   A. They use different keys on each end of the transported data.

   B. They use public key cryptography.

   C. They use multiple keys for creating digital signatures.

   D. They use the same key on each end of the transported data.

62. Which of the following ciphers was created from the foundation of the Rijndael algorithm?

   A. TKIP

   B. AES

   C. DES

   D. 3DES

63. Katelyn is sending an important email to Zackary, the manager of human resources. Company policy states messages to human resources must be digitally signed. Which of the following statements is correct?

   A. Katelyn's public key is used to verify the digital signature.

   B. Katelyn's private key is used to verify the digital signature.

   C. Zackary's public key is used to verify the digital signature.

   D. Zackary's private key is used to verify the digital signature.

64. Data integrity is provided by which of the following?

   A. 3DES

   B. MD5

   C. AES

   D. Blowfish

65. Which of the following is a symmetric encryption algorithm that is available in 128-bit, 192-bit, and 256-bit key versions?

   A. AES

   B. DES

   C. RSA

   D. TKIP

66. Which of the following items are found within a digital certificate? (Choose two.)

    A. Serial number

    B. Default gateway

    C. Public key

    D. Session key

67. In an 802.1x implementation, which of the following devices mutually authenticate with each other? (Choose two.)

    A. Authentication server

    B. Certificate authority

    C. Domain controller

    D. Supplicant

68. Which of the following statements is true regarding the confusion encryption method?

    A. It puts one item in the place of another; for example, one letter for another or one letter for a number.

    B. It scrambles data by reordering the plain text in a certain way.

    C. It uses a relationship between the plain text and the key that is so complicated the plain text can't be altered and the key can't be determined.

    D. Change in the plain text will result in multiple changes that are spread throughout the cipher text.

69. Which of the following is required when employing PKI and preserving data is important?

    A. CA

    B. CRL

    C. Key escrow

    D. CER

70. You need to encrypt the signature of an email within a PKI system. Which of the following would you use?

    A. CER

    B. Public key

    C. Shared key

    D. Private key

71. Which of the following standards was developed by the Wi-Fi Alliance and implements the requirements of IEEE 802.11i?

    A. NIC

    B. WPA

    C. WPA2

    D. TKIP

72. You are asked to create a wireless network for your company that implements a wireless protocol that provides maximum security while providing support for older wireless devices. Which protocol should you use?

    A. WPA

    B. WPA2

    C. WEP

    D. IV

73. Bob is a security administrator and needs to encrypt and authenticate messages that are sent and received between two systems. Which of the following would Bob choose to accomplish his task?

    A. Diffie-Hellman

    B. MD5

    C. SHA-256

    D. RSA

74. Which of the following algorithms is generally used in mobile devices?

    A. 3DES

    B. DES

    C. ECC

    D. AES

75. Which of the following statements best describes the difference between public key cryptography and public key infrastructure?

    A. Public key cryptography is another name for an asymmetric algorithm, whereas public key infrastructure is another name for a symmetric algorithm.

    B. Public key cryptography uses one key to encrypt and decrypt the data, and public key infrastructure uses two keys to encrypt and decrypt the data.

    C. Public key cryptography is another name for asymmetric cryptography, whereas public key infrastructure contains the public key cryptographic mechanisms.

    D. Public key cryptography provides authentication and nonrepudiation, whereas public key infrastructure provides confidentiality and integrity.

76. Your company has a public key infrastructure (PKI) in place to issue digital certificates to users. Recently, your company hired temporary contractors for a project that is now complete. Management has requested that all digital certificates issued to the contractors be revoked. Which PKI component would you consult for the management's request?

    A. CA

    B. CRL

    C. RA

    D. CSR

77. Which of the following security setup modes are intended for use in a small office or home office environment? (Choose two.)

   A. WPS

   B. WPA-Enterprise

   C. WPA2-Enterprise

   D. WPA2-Personal

78. Which of the following automatically updates browsers with a list of root certificates from an online source to track which certificates are to be trusted?

   A. Trust model

   B. Key escrow

   C. PKI

   D. RA

79. Which of the following EAP types uses the concepts of public key infrastructure (PKI)?

   A. EAP-TLS

   B. PEAP

   C. EAP-FAST

   D. EAP-TTLS

80. Which of the following use PSK authentication? (Choose two.)

   A. WPA-Enterprise

   B. WPA-Personal

   C. WPA2-Personal

   D. WPA2-Enterprise

81. You are receiving calls from users who are connected to the company's network and are being redirected to a login page with the company's logo after they type a popular social media web address in an Internet browser. Which of the following is causing this to happen?

   A. WEP

   B. Key stretching

   C. MAC filtering

   D. Captive portal

82. Elliptic curve cryptosystem (ECC) is an asymmetric algorithm. Which of the following statements best describe why ECC is different from other asymmetric algorithms? (Choose two.)

   A. It is more efficient.

   B. It provides digital signatures, secure key distribution, and encryption.

   C. It uses more processing power to perform encryption.

   D. It provides fast key generation.

83. WEP's RC4 approach to encryption uses a 24-bit string of characters added to data that are transmitted. The same plain text data frame will not appear as the same WEP-encrypted data frame. What is this string of characters called?

A. Diffusion

B. IV

C. Session key

D. Hashing

84. Your manager has recently purchased a RADIUS server that will be used by remote employees to connect to internal resources. Several client computers need to connect to the RADIUS server in a secure manner. What should your manager deploy?

A. HIDS

B. UTM

C. VLAN

D. 802.1x

85. Katelyn, a network administrator, has deleted the account for a user who left the company last week. The user's files were encrypted with a private key. How can Katelyn view the user's files?

A. The data can be decrypted using the backup user account.

B. The data can be decrypted using the recovery agent.

C. She must re-create the former user's account.

D. The data can be decrypted using a CRL.

86. Your company has recently implemented an encryption system on the network. The system uses a secret key between two parties and must be kept secret. Which system was implemented?

A. Asymmetric algorithm

B. Symmetric algorithm

C. Hashing algorithm

D. Steganography

87. Tim, a wireless administrator, has been tasked with securing the company's WLAN. Which of the following cryptographic protocols would Tim use to provide the most secure environment for the company?

A. WPA2 CCMP

B. WEP

C. WPA

D. WPA2 TKIP

88. Which of the following defines a hashing algorithm creating the same hash value from two different messages?

   A. AES

   B. MD5

   C. Hashing

   D. Collision

89. Matt, a network administrator, is deciding which credential-type authentication to use within the company's planned 802.1x deployment. He is searching for a method that requires a client certificate and a server-side certificate, and that uses tunnels for encryption. Which credential-type authentication method would Matt use?

   A. EAP-TLS

   B. EAP-FAST

   C. PEAP

   D. EAP

90. A coworker is connecting to a secure website using HTTPS. The coworker informs you that before the website loads, their web browser displays an error indicating that the site certificate is invalid and the site is not trusted. Which of the following is most likely the issue?

   A. The web browser is requiring an update.

   B. The server is using a self-signed certificate.

   C. A web proxy is blocking the connection.

   D. The web server is currently unavailable.

91. Zack, an administrator, needs to renew a certificate for the company's web server. Which of the following would you recommend Zack submit to the CA?

   A. CSR

   B. Key escrow

   C. CRL

   D. OCSP

92. Which of the following types of encryption offers easy key exchange and key management?

   A. Obfuscation

   B. Asymmetric

   C. Symmetric

   D. Hashing

93. Which of the following is used to exchange cryptographic keys?

   A. Diffie-Hellman

   B. HMAC

   C. ROT13

   D. RC4

94. Which of the following encryption algorithms is used to encrypt and decrypt data?

   A. MD5

   B. HMAC

   C. Kerberos

   D. RC4

95. Which of the following provides additional encryption strength by repeating the encryption process with additional keys?

   A. 3DES

   B. AES

   C. Twofish

   D. Blowfish

96. Which of the following security mechanisms can be used for the purpose of nonrepudiation?

   A. Encryption

   B. Digital signature

   C. Collision

   D. CA

97. You are a network administrator for your company, and the single AP that allows clients to connect to the wireless LAN is configured with a WPA-PSK preshared key of the company name followed by the number 1. Which of the following statements is correct regarding this implementation?

   A. It is secure because WPA-PSK resolved the problem with WEP.

   B. It is secure because the preshared key is at least five characters long.

   C. It is not secure because the preshared key includes only one number and the company name so it can be easily guessed.

   D. It is not secure because WPA-PSK is as insecure as WEP and should never be used.

98. You are a security technician and have been given the task to implement a PKI on the company's network. When verifying the validity of a certificate, you want to ensure bandwidth isn't consumed. Which of the following can you implement?

   A. CRL

   B. OCSP

   C. Key escrow

   D. CA

99. Which of the following types of device are found in a network that supports Wi-Fi Protected Setup (WPS) protocol? (Choose three.)

   A. Registrar

   B. Supplicant

   C. Enrollee

   D. Access Point

100. You are a network administrator for a distribution company and the manager wants to implement a secure wireless LAN for a BYOD policy. Through research, you determine that the company should implement AES encryption and the 802.1x authentication protocol. You also determine that too many APs and clients will be installed and you will need to configure each one with a preshared key passphrase. Which of the following will meet your needs?

   A. WEP

   B. WPA

   C. WPA2-Personal

   D. WPA2-Enterprise

101. The process of deleting data by sending a single erase or clear instruction to an address of the nonvolatile memory is an example of securing which of the following?

   A. Data-in-transit

   B. Data-over-the-network

   C. Data-in-use

   D. Data-at-rest

102. Which of the following is an authentication service and uses UDP as a transport medium?

   A. TACACS+

   B. RADIUS

   C. LDAP

   D. Kerberos

103. Which of the following is true regarding the importance of encryption of data-at-rest for sensitive information?

   A. It renders the recovery of data more difficult should the user lose their password.

   B. It allows the user to verify the integrity of the data on the stored device.

   C. It prevents the sensitive data from being accessed after a theft of the physical equipment.

   D. It renders the recovery of data easier should the user lose their password.

104. You are a network administrator and your manager has asked you to enable WPA2 CCMP for wireless clients, along with an encryption to protect the data transmitting across the network. Which of the following encryption methods would you use along with WPA2 CCMP?

   A. RC4

   B. DES

   C. AES

   D. 3DES

105. Which of the following is the least secure hashing algorithm?

   A. MD5

   B. RIPEMD

   C. SHA-1

   D. AES

106. Which of the following types of attack sends two different messages using the same hash function, causing a collision?

  A. Xmas attack

  B. DoS

  C. Logic bomb

  D. Birthday attack

107. Which of the following defines a file format commonly used to store private keys with associated public key certificates?

  A. PKCS #1

  B. PKCS #3

  C. PKCS #7

  D. PKCS #12

108. Which of the following statements are true regarding ciphers? (Choose two.)

  A. Stream ciphers encrypt fixed sizes of data.

  B. Stream ciphers encrypt data one bit at a time.

  C. Block ciphers encrypt data one bit at a time.

  D. Block ciphers encrypt fixed sizes of data.

109. How many effective key sizes of bits does 3DES have? (Choose three.)

  A. 56

  B. 112

  C. 128

  D. 168

110. Which of the following statements is true about symmetric algorithms?

  A. They hide data within an image file.

  B. They use one key to encrypt data and another to decrypt data.

  C. They use a single key to encrypt and decrypt data.

  D. They use a single key to create a hashing value.

111. The CA is responsible for revoking certificates when necessary. Which of the following statements best describes the relationship between a CRL and OSCP?

  A. OCSP is a protocol to submit revoked certificates to a CRL.

  B. CRL is a more streamlined approach to OCSP.

  C. CRL validates a certificate in real time and reports it to the OCSP.

  D. OCSP is a protocol to check the CRL during a certificate validation process.

112. Which of the following takes each bit in a character and is XORed with the corresponding bit in the secret key?

  A. ECDHE

  B. PBKDF2

  C. Obfuscation

  D. One-time pad

113. Which of the following works similarly to stream ciphers?

  A. One-time pad

  B. RSA

  C. AES

  D. DES

114. Your manager wants to implement a security measure to protect sensitive company data that reside on the remote salespeople's laptops should they become lost or stolen. Which of the following measures would you implement?

  A. Implement WPS on the laptops.

  B. Set BIOS passwords on the laptops.

  C. Use whole-disk encryption on the laptops.

  D. Use cable locks on the laptops.

115. You want to send confidential messages to a friend through email, but you do not have a way of encrypting the message. Which of the following methods would help you achieve this goal?

  A. AES

  B. Collision

  C. RSA

  D. Steganography

116. Which of the following cipher modes uses a feedback-based encryption method to ensure that repetitive data result in unique cipher text?

  A. ECB

  B. CBC

  C. GCM

  D. CTM

117. Which statement is true regarding the difference between a secure cipher and a secure hash?

  A. A secure hash can be reversed; a secure cipher cannot.

  B. A secure cipher can be reversed; a secure hash cannot.

  C. A secure hash produces a variable output for any input size; a secure cipher does not.

  D. A secure cipher produces the same size output for any input size; a hash does not.

118. Which certificate format is typically used on Windows OS machines to import and export certificates and private keys?

   A. DER

   B. AES

   C. PEM

   D. PFX

119. What is another name for an ephemeral key?

   A. PKI private key

   B. MD5

   C. PKI public key

   D. Session key

120. Why would a threat actor use steganography?

   A. To test integrity

   B. To conceal information

   C. To encrypt information

   D. To create a hashing value

121. The CIO has instructed you to set up a system where credit card data will be encrypted with the most secure symmetric algorithm with the least amount of CPU usage. Which of the following algorithms would you choose?

   A. AES

   B. SHA-1

   C. MD5

   D. 3DES

122. Which of the following encryption methods is used by RADIUS?

   A. Asymmetric

   B. Symmetric

   C. Elliptic curve

   D. RSA

123. When setting up a secure wireless company network, which of the following should you avoid?

   A. WPA

   B. WPA2

   C. EAP-TLS

   D. PEAP

124. You want to authenticate and log connections from wireless users connecting with EAP-TLS. Which of the following should be used?

 A. Kerberos

 B. LDAP

 C. SAML

 D. RADIUS

125. Which of the following would be used to allow certain traffic to traverse from a wireless network to an internal network?

 A. WPA

 B. WEP

 C. Load balancers

 D. 802.1x

126. You are asked to see if several confidential files have changed, and you decide to use an algorithm to create message digests for the confidential files. Which algorithm would you use?

 A. AES

 B. RC4

 C. Blowfish

 D. SHA-1

127. Network data needs to be encrypted, and you are required to select a cipher that will encrypt 128 bits at a time before the data are sent across the network. Which of the following would you choose?

 A. Stream cipher

 B. Hash algorithm

 C. Block cipher

 D. Obfuscation

128. Which of the following are considered cryptographic hash functions? (Choose two.)

 A. AES

 B. MD5

 C. RC4

 D. SHA-256

129. A company's database is beginning to grow, and the data-at-rest are becoming a concern with the security administrator. Which of the following is an option to secure the data-at-rest?

 A. SSL certificate

 B. Encryption

 C. Hashing

 D. TLS certificate

130. Which of the following hardware devices can store keys? (Choose two.)

    A. USB flash drive

    B. Smartcard

    C. PCI expansion card

    D. Cipher lock

131. You are a security manager and have been asked to encrypt database system information that contains employee social security numbers. You are looking for an encryption standard that is fast and secure. Which of the following would you suggest to accomplish the requirements?

    A. SHA-256

    B. AES

    C. RSA

    D. MD5

132. James is a security administrator and wants to ensure the validity of public trusted certificates used by the company's web server, even if there is an Internet outage. Which of the following should James implement?

    A. Key escrow

    B. Recovery agent

    C. OCSP

    D. CSR

133. You are a security administrator looking to implement a two-way trust model. Which of the following would you use?

    A. ROT13

    B. PGP

    C. WPA2

    D. PKI

134. If a threat actor obtains an SSL private key, what type of attack can be performed? (Choose two.)

    A. Eavesdropping

    B. Man-in-the-middle

    C. Social engineering

    D. Brute force

135. Most authentication systems make use of a one-way encryption process. Which of the following is an example of a one-way encryption?

    A. Symmetric algorithm

    B. Hashing

C. Asymmetric algorithm

D. PKI

136. Which of the following transpires in a PKI environment?

A. The CA signs the certificate.

B. The RA signs the certificate.

C. The RA creates the certificate and the CA signs it.

D. The CA creates the certificate and the RA signs it.

137. Which of the following statements best describes how a digital signature is created?

A. The sender encrypts a message digest with the receiver's public key.

B. The sender encrypts a message digest with the receiver's private key.

C. The sender encrypts a message digest with his or her private key.

D. The sender encrypts a message digest with his or her public key.

138. AES is an algorithm used for which of the following?

A. Encrypting a large amount of data

B. Encrypting a small amount of data

C. Key recovery

D. Key revocation

139. PEAP protects authentication transfers by implementing which of the following?

A. TLS tunnels

B. SSL tunnels

C. AES

D. SHA hashes

140. AES-CCMP uses a 128-bit temporal key and encrypts data in what block size?

A. 256

B. 192

C. 128

D. 64

141. Which of the following implement Message Integrity Code (MIC)? (Choose two.)

A. AES

B. DES

C. CCMP

D. TKIP

142. James, a WLAN security engineer, recommends to management that WPA-Personal security should not be deployed within the company's WLAN for their vendors. Which of the following statements best describe James's recommendation? (Choose two.)

    A. Static preshared passphrases are susceptible to social engineering attacks.

    B. WPA-Personal uses public key encryption.

    C. WPA-Personal uses a weak TKIP encryption.

    D. WPA-Personal uses a RADIUS authentication server.

143. Which of the following is correct regarding root certificates?

    A. Root certificates never expire.

    B. A root certificate contains the public key of the CA.

    C. A root certificate contains information about the user.

    D. A root certificate cannot be used to authorize subordinate CAs to issue certificates on its behalf.

144. Which of the following statements are correct about public and private key pairs? (Choose two.)

    A. Public and private keys work in isolation of each other.

    B. Public and private keys work in conjunction with each other as a team.

    C. If the public key encrypts the data using an asymmetric encryption algorithm, the corresponding private key is used to decrypt the data.

    D. If the private key encrypts the data using an asymmetric encryption algorithm, the receiver uses the same private key to decrypt the data.

145. Which of the following are the filename extensions for PKCS #12 files? (Choose two.)

    A. .p12

    B. .KEY

    C. .pfx

    D. .p7b

146. Your company has discovered that several confidential messages have been intercepted. You decide to implement a web of trust to encrypt the files. Which of the following are used in a web of trust concept? (Choose two.)

    A. RC4

    B. AES

    C. PGP

    D. GPG

147. Which of the following algorithms is typically used to encrypt data-at-rest?

    A. Symmetric

    B. Asymmetric

    C. Stream

    D. Hashing

148. Which of the following can assist in the workload of the CA by performing identification and authentication of users requesting certificates?

    A. Root CA

    B. Intermediate CA

    C. Registered authority

    D. OSCP

149. You recently upgraded your wireless network so that your devices will use the 802.11n protocol. You want to ensure all communication on the wireless network is secure with the strongest encryption. Which of the following is the best choice?

    A. WEP

    B. WPA

    C. WPA2

    D. WPS

150. A college wants to move data to a USB flash drive and has asked you to suggest a way to secure the data in a quick manner. Which of the following would you suggest?

    A. 3DES

    B. SHA-256

    C. AES-256

    D. SHA-512

Chapter

7

Practice Test

1. You are asked to separate the Sales and Marketing department's network traffic on a layer 2 device within a LAN. This will reduce broadcast traffic and prevent the departments from seeing each other's resources. Which of the following types of network design would be the best choice?

    A. MAC

    B. NAT

    C. VLAN

    D. DMZ

2. You are a network administrator and your company has asked you to perform a survey of the campus for open Wi-Fi access points. You walk around with your smartphone looking for unsecured access points that you can connect to without a password. What type of penetration testing concept is this called?

    A. Escalation of privilege

    B. Active reconnaissance

    C. Passive reconnaissance

    D. Black-box

3. Which of the following is a certificate-based authentication that allows individuals access to U.S. federal resources and facilities?

    A. Proximity card

    B. TOTP

    C. PIV card

    D. HOTP

4. You attempt to log into your company's network with a laptop. The laptop is quarantined to a restricted VLAN until the laptop's virus definitions are updated. Which of the following best describes this network component?

    A. NAT

    B. HIPS

    C. DMZ

    D. NAC

5. You have been asked to implement a security control that will limit tailgating in high-secured areas. Which of the following security control would you choose?

    A. Mantrap

    B. Faraday cage

    C. Airgap

    D. Cable locks

6. Your company's network administrator is placing an Internet web server in an isolated area of the company's network for security purposes. Which of the following architecture concepts is the network administrator implementing?

    A. Honeynet

    B. DMZ

   C. Proxy

   D. Intranet

7. Your company is offering a new product on its website. You are asked to ensure availability of the web server when it receives a large number of requests. Which of the following would be the best option to fulfill this request?

   A. VPN concentrator

   B. NIPS

   C. SIEM

   D. Load balancer

8. You are a security administrator for a manufacturing company that produces compounded medications. To ensure individuals are not accessing sensitive areas where the medications are created, you want to implement a physical security control. Which of the following would be the best option?

   A. Security guard

   B. Signs

   C. Faraday cage

   D. Cameras

9. An attacker exploited a bug, unknown to the developer, to gain access to a database server. Which of the following best describes this type of attack?

   A. Zero-day

   B. Cross-site scripting

   C. ARP poisoning

   D. Domain hijacking

10. A new employee added network drops to a new section of the company's building. The cables were placed across several fluorescent lights. When users attempted to connect to the data center on the network, they experienced intermittent connectivity. Which of the following environmental controls was the most likely cause of this issue?

   A. DMZ

   B. EMI

   C. BIOS

   D. TPM

11. What method should you choose to authenticate a remote workstation before it gains access to a local LAN?

   A. Router

   B. Proxy server

   C. VPN concentrator

   D. Firewall

12. Which of the following allows a company to store a cryptographic key with a trusted third party and release it only to the sender or receiver with proper authorization?

    A. CRL

    B. Key escrow

    C. Trust model

    D. Intermediate CA

13. Your company recently upgraded the HVAC system for its server room. Which of the following security implications would the company be most concerned about?

    A. Confidentiality

    B. Availability

    C. Integrity

    D. Airgap

14. Your company provides secure wireless Internet access to visitors and vendors working onsite. Some of the vendors are reporting they are unable to view the wireless network. Which of the following best describes the issue?

    A. MAC filtering is enabled on the WAP.

    B. The SSID broadcast is disabled.

    C. The wrong antenna type is being used.

    D. The wrong band selection is being used.

15. Your company's sales team is working late at the end of the month to ensure all sales are reported for the month. The sales members notice they cannot save or print reports after regular hours. Which of the following general concepts is preventing the sales members from performing their job?

    A. Job rotation

    B. Time-of-day restrictions

    C. Least privilege

    D. Location-based policy

16. Which of the following symmetric algorithms are block ciphers? (Choose three.)

    A. 3DES

    B. ECDHE

    C. RSA

    D. RC4

    E. SHA

    F. Twofish

17. A security officer has asked you to use a password cracking tool on the company's computers. Which of the following best describes what the security officer is trying to accomplish?

   A. Looking for strong passwords

   B. Enforcing a minimum password length policy

   C. Enforcing a password complexity policy

   D. Looking for weak passwords

18. Which of the following test gives testers comprehensive network design information?

   A. White box

   B. Black box

   C. Gray box

   D. Purple box

19. You are the network administrator for your company and want to implement a wireless network and prevent unauthorized access. Which of the following would be the best option?

   A. RADIUS

   B. TACACS+

   C. Kerberos

   D. OAUTH

20. Why is input validation important to secure coding techniques? (Choose two.)

   A. It mitigates shoulder surfing.

   B. It mitigates buffer overflow attacks.

   C. It mitigates ARP poisoning.

   D. It mitigates XSS vulnerabilities.

21. To authenticate, a Windows 10 user draws a circle around a picture of a dog's nose and then touches each ear starting with the right ear. Which of the following concepts is this describing?

   A. Something you do

   B. Something you know

   C. Something you have

   D. Somewhere you are

22. Which of the following countermeasures is designed to best protect against a brute-force password attack?

   A. Password complexity

   B. Account disablement

   C. Password length

   D. Account lockout

23. You are a security administrator reviewing the results from a network security audit. You are reviewing options to implement a solution to address the potential poisoning of name resolution server records. Which of the following would be the best choice?

    A. SSL

    B. SSH

    C. DNSSEC

    D. TLS

24. Your manager has implemented a new policy that requires employees to shred all sensitive documents. Which of the following attacks is your manager attempting to prevent?

    A. Tailgating

    B. Dumpster diving

    C. Shoulder surfing

    D. Man-in-the-middle

25. Which of the following cryptography algorithms support multiple bit strengths?

    A. DES

    B. HMAC

    C. MD5

    D. AES

26. A network security auditor will perform various simulated network attacks against your company's network. Which should the security auditor acquire first?

    A. Vulnerability testing authorization

    B. Transfer risk response

    C. Penetration testing authorization

    D. Change management

27. A system administrator is told an application is not able to handle the large amount of traffic the server is receiving on a daily basis. The attack takes the server offline and causes it to drop packets occasionally. The system administrator needs to find another solution while keeping the application secure and available. Which of the following would be the best solution?

    A. Sandboxing

    B. DMZ

    C. Cloud computing

    D. DLP

28. You are a security administrator and are observing unusual behavior in your network from a workstation. The workstation is communicating with a known malicious destination over an encrypted tunnel. You have updated the antivirus definition files and performed a full antivirus scan. The scan doesn't show any clues of infection. Which of the following best describes what has happened on the workstation?

    A. Buffer overflow

    B. Session hijacking

C. Zero-day attack

D. DDoS

29. You are the security engineer and have discovered that communication within your company's encrypted wireless network is being captured with a sniffing program. The data being captured is then being decrypted to obtain the employee's credentials to be used at a later time. Which of the following protocols is most likely being used on the wireless access point? (Choose two.)

A. WPA2 Personal

B. WPA2 Enterprise

C. WPA

D. WEP

30. A network manager has implemented a strategy so that all workstations on the network will receive required security updates regularly. Which of the following best describes what the network manager implemented?

A. Sandboxing

B. Ad hoc

C. Virtualization

D. Patch management

31. Your manager wants to secure the FTP server by using SSL. Which of the following should you configure?

A. FTPS

B. SFTP

C. SSH

D. LDAPS

32. You are an IT security officer and you want to classify and assess privacy risks throughout the development life cycle of a program or system. Which of the following tools would be best to use for this purpose?

A. BIA

B. PIA

C. RTO

D. MTBF

33. Which of the following types of risk analysis makes use of ALE?

A. Qualitative

B. ROI

C. SLE

D. Quantitative

34. Which of the following statements best describes mandatory vacations?

A. Companies ensure their employees can take time off to conduct activities together.

B. Companies use them as a tool to ensure employees are taking the correct amount of days off.

C. Companies ensure their employees are properly recharged to perform their duties.

D. Companies use them as a tool for security protection to detect fraud.

35. Users of your company have been visiting the website www.abccompany.com and a recent increase in virus detection has been noted. Your company has developed a relationship with another company using the web address www.abccompany.com, but not with the site that has been causing the increase of viruses. Which of the following would best describe this attack?

A. Session hijacking

B. Cross-site scripting

C. Replay attack

D. Typo squatting

36. Which of the following would you enable in a laptop's BIOS to provide full disk encryption?

A. RAID

B. USB

C. HSM

D. TPM

37. Your company has hired a third-party auditing firm to conduct a penetration test against your network. The firm wasn't given any information related to the company's network. What type of test is the company performing?

A. White box

B. Red box

C. Black box

D. Gray box

38. Server room access is controlled with proximity cards and records all entries and exits. These records are referred to if missing equipment is discovered, so employees can be identified. Which of the following must be prevented for this policy to become effective?

A. Shoulder surfing

B. Tailgating

C. Vishing

D. Dumpster diving

39. Company users are stating they are unable to access the network file server. A company security administrator checks the router ACL and knows users can access the web server, email server, and printing services. Which of the following is preventing access to the network file server?

   A. Implicit deny

   B. Port security

   C. Flood guard

   D. Signal strength

40. An employee informs you that the Internet connection is slow and they are having difficulty accessing websites to perform their job. You analyze their computer and discover the MAC address of the default gateway in the ARP cache is not correct. What type of attack have you discovered?

   A. DNS poisoning

   B. Injection

   C. Impersonation

   D. ARP poisoning

41. Tony, a college student, downloaded a free word editor program to complete his essay. After downloading and installing the software, Tony noticed his computer was running slow and he was receiving notifications from his antivirus program. Which of the following best describes the malware that he installed?

   A. Keylogger

   B. Worm

   C. Ransomware

   D. Trojan

42. Which of the following measures the amount of time required to return a failed device, component, or network to normal functionality?

   A. RTO

   B. MTTR

   C. MTBF

   D. RPO

43. Natural disasters and intentional man-made attacks can cause the death of employees and customers. What type of impact is this?

   A. Safety

   B. Life

   C. Finance

   D. Reputation

44. A user finds and downloads an exploit that will take advantage of website vulnerabilities. The user isn't knowledgeable about the exploit and runs the exploit against multiple websites to gain access. Which of the following best describes this user?

   A. Man-in-the-middle

   B. Script kiddie

   C. White hat

   D. Hacktivist

45. You are the IT security officer and you plan to develop a general cybersecurity awareness training program for the employees. Which of the following best describes these employees?

   A. Data owners

   B. Users

   C. System administrators

   D. System owners

46. The system administrator needs to secure the company's data-at-rest. Which of the following would provide the strongest protection?

   A. Implement biometrics controls on each workstation.

   B. Implement full-disk encryption.

   C. Implement a host intrusion prevention system.

   D. Implement a host intrusion detection system.

47. Which of the following is a true statement about qualitative risk analysis?

   A. It uses numeric values to measure the impact of risk.

   B. It uses descriptions and words to measure the impact of risk.

   C. It uses industry best practices and records.

   D. It uses statistical theories, testing, and experiments.

48. Which of the following firewalls tracks the operating state and characteristics of network connections traversing it?

   A. Stateful firewall

   B. Stateless firewall

   C. Application firewall

   D. Packet filter firewall

49. Which of the following are examples of PII? (Choose two.)

   A. Fingerprint

   B. MAC address

   C. Home address

   D. Gender

50. An employee informs you they have lost a corporate mobile device. What is the first action you perform?

   A. Enable push notification services.

   B. Remotely wipe the mobile device.

   C. Enable screen lock.

   D. Enable geofencing.

51. You have created a backup routine that includes a full backup each Sunday night and a backup each night of all data that has changed since Sunday's backup. Which of the following best describes this backup schedule?

   A. Full and incremental

   B. Full and differential

   C. Snapshots

   D. Full

52. One of your colleagues attempted to ping a computer name and received the response of fe80::3281:80ea:b72b:0b55. What type of address did the colleague view?

   A. IPv6

   B. IPv4

   C. MAC address

   D. APIPA

53. Which of the following defines the act of sending unsolicited messages to nearby Bluetooth devices?

   A. Jamming

   B. Bluesnarfing

   C. Brute force

   D. Bluejacking

54. You are a system administrator and you are creating a public and private key pair. You have to specify the key strength. Which of the following would be your best choice?

   A. RSA

   B. DES

   C. MD5

   D. SHA

55. You are the security administrator for the sales department and the department needs to email high volumes of sensitive information to clients to help close sales. All emails go through a DLP scanner. Which of the following is the best solution to help the department protect the sensitive information?

   A. Automatically encrypt outgoing emails.

   B. Monitor all outgoing emails.

C. Automatically encrypt incoming emails.

D. Monitor all incoming emails.

56. You are the IT security officer of your company and have established a security policy that requires users to protect all sensitive documents to avoid their being stolen. What policy have you implemented?

A. Separation of duties

B. Clean desk

C. Job rotation

D. Privacy

57. Which of the following options can a security administrator deploy on a mobile device that will deter undesirable people from seeing the data on the device if it is left unattended?

A. Screen lock

B. Push notification services

C. Remote wipe

D. Full device encryption

58. You are a system administrator and are asked to prevent staff members from using each other's credentials to access secured areas of the building. Which of the following will best address this request?

A. Install a biometric reader at the entrance of the secure area.

B. Install a proximity card reader at the entrance of the secure area.

C. Implement least privilege.

D. Implement group policy enforcement.

59. A sales manager has asked for an option for sales reps who travel to have secure remote access to your company's database server. Which of the following should you configure for the sales reps?

A. VPN

B. WLAN

C. NAT

D. Ad hoc

60. An attacker tricks one of your employees into clicking on a malicious link that causes an unwanted action on the website the employee is currently authenticated to. What type of attack is this?

A. Replay

B. Cross-site request forgery

C. Cross-site scripting

D. Buffer overflow

61. Which of the following is considered the strongest access control?

    A. RBAC

    B. DAC

    C. MAC

    D. ABAC

62. Your company wants to expand its data center, but has limited space to store additional hardware. The IT staff needs to continue their operations while expansion is underway. Which of the following would best accomplish this expansion idea?

    A. IaaS

    B. Virtualization

    C. SaaS

    D. Public cloud

63. Which of the following algorithms have known collisions? (Choose two.)

    A. MD5

    B. AES

    C. SHA

    D. SHA-256

    E. RSA

64. Which of the following must a security administrator implement to allow customers, vendors, suppliers, and other businesses to obtain information while preventing access to the company's entire network?

    A. Intranet

    B. Internet

    C. Extranet

    D. Honeynet

65. The head of HR is conducting an exit interview with an IT network administrator named Matt. The interview questions include Matt's view of his manager, why he is leaving his current position, and what he liked most about his job. Which of the following should also be addressed in this exit interview?

    A. Job rotation

    B. NDA

    C. Background checks

    D. Property return form

66. Which of the following is considered the least secure authentication method?

    A. TACACS+

    B. CHAP

    C. NTLM

    D. PAP

67. You are a security administrator for your company and have been asked to recommend a secure method for storing passwords due to recent brute-force attempts. Which of the following will provide the best protection? (Choose two.)

   A. ROT13

   B. BCRYPT

   C. RIPEMD

   D. PBKDF2

68. You installed a WAP for a local coffee shop and have discovered the signal is extending into the parking lot. Which of the following configurations will best correct this issue?

   A. Change the antenna type.

   B. Disable the SSID broadcast.

   C. Reduce the signal strength for indoor coverage only.

   D. Enable MAC filtering to prevent devices from accessing the wireless network.

69. You are a network administrator for a bank. A branch manager discovers that the deskside employees have the ability to delete lending policies found in a folder within the file server. You review the permissions and notice the deskside employees have "modify" permissions to the folder. The employees should have read permissions only. Which of the following security principles has been violated?

   A. Job rotation

   B. Time-of-day restrictions

   C. Separation of duties

   D. Least privilege

70. Which of the following concepts of cryptography ensures integrity of data by the use of digital signatures?

   A. Key stretching

   B. Steganography

   C. Key exchange

   D. Hashing

71. Your manager has asked you to recommend a public key infrastructure component to store certificates that are no longer valid. Which of the following is the best choice?

   A. Intermediate CA

   B. CSR

   C. CRL

   D. Key escrow

72. You are a backup operator and receive a call from a user asking you to send sensitive documents immediately because their manager is going to a meeting with the company's executives. The user states the manager's files are corrupted and he is attending the meeting in the next 5 minutes. Which of the following forms of social engineering best describes this situation?

   A. Scarcity

   B. Consensus

   C. Intimidation

   D. Authority

73. Which of the following controls can you implement together to prevent data loss if a mobile device is lost or stolen? (Choose two.)

   A. Geofencing

   B. Full-device encryption

   C. Screen locks

   D. Push notification services

74. You are asked to find the MAC address on a Linux machine. Which of the following commands can you use to discover it?

   A. `ipconfig`

   B. `ifconfig`

   C. `tracert`

   D. `ping`

75. A chief security officer (CSO) notices that a large number of contractors work for the company. When a contractor leaves the company, the provisioning team is not notified. The CSO wants to ensure the contractors cannot access the network when they leave. Which of the following polices best supports the CSO's plan?

   A. Account disablement

   B. Account lockout policy

   C. Enforce password history

   D. Account expiration policy

76. The CISO wants to strengthen the password policy by adding special characters to users' passwords. Which of the following control best achieves this goal?

   A. Password complexity

   B. Password length

   C. Password history

   D. Group policy

77. Which of the following deployment models allows a business to have more control of the devices given to employees that handle company information?

   A. DLP

   B. COPE

   C. BYOD

   D. CYOD

78. A network administrator uses their fingerprint and enters a PIN to log onto a server. Which of the following best describes this example?

   A. Identification

   B. Single authentication

   C. Multifactor authentication

   D. Transitive trust

79. Your company wants to perform a privacy threshold assessment (PTA) to identify all PII residing in its systems before retiring hardware. Which of the following would be examples of PII? (Choose two.)

   A. Date of birth

   B. Email address

   C. Race

   D. Fingerprint

80. Your HIPS is incorrectly reporting legitimate network traffic as suspicious activity. What is this best known as?

   A. False positive

   B. False negative

   C. Credentialed

   D. Noncredentialed

81. Matt, a network administrator, is asking how to configure the switches and routers to securely monitor their status. Which of the following protocols would he need to implement on the devices?

   A. SSH

   B. SNMP

   C. SMTP

   D. SNMPv3

82. Your company has issued a hardware token-based authentication to administrators to reduce the risk of password compromise. The tokens display a code that automatically changes every 30 seconds. Which of the following best describes this authentication mechanism?

   A. TOTP

   B. HOTP

   C. Smartcard

   D. Proximity card

83. You are the network administrator for your company's Microsoft network. Your CISO is planning the network security and wants a secure protocol that will authenticate all users logging into the network. Which of the following authentication protocols would be the best choice?

   A. RADIUS

   B. TACACS+

   C. Kerberos

   D. SAML

84. Which of the following is not a vulnerability of end-of-life systems?

   A. When systems can't be updated, firewalls and antiviruses are not sufficient protection.

   B. Out-of-date systems can result in fines in regulated industries.

   C. When an out-of-date system reaches the end-of-life, it will automatically shut down.

   D. Operating out-of-date systems can result in poor performance and reliability and can lead to denial of services.

85. Which of the following statements are true regarding viruses and worms? (Choose two.)

   A. A virus is a malware that self-replicates over the network.

   B. A worm is a malware that self-replicates over the network.

   C. A virus is a malware that replicates by attaching itself to a file.

   D. A worm is a malware that replicates by attaching itself to a file.

86. Which of the following wireless attacks would be used to impersonate another WAP to obtain unauthorized information from nearby mobile users?

   A. Rogue access point

   B. Evil twin

   C. Bluejacking

   D. Bluesnarfing

87. Tony, a security administrator, discovered through an audit that all the company's access points are currently configured to use WPA with TKIP for encryption. Tony needs to improve the encryption on the access points. Which of the following would be the best option for Tony?

   A. WPA2 with CCMP

   B. WEP

   C. WPA with CCMP

   D. WPS

88. Your department manager assigns Tony, a network administrator, the job of expressing the business and financial effects that a failed SQL server would cause if it was down for 4 hours. What type of analysis must Tony perform?

- **A.** Security audit
- **B.** Asset identification
- **C.** Business impact analysis
- **D.** Disaster recovery plan

89. You are the security administrator for a local hospital. The doctors want to prevent the data from being altered while working on their mobile devices. Which of the following would most likely accomplish the request?

- **A.** Cloud storage
- **B.** Wiping
- **C.** SIEM
- **D.** SCADA

90. You are a Unix engineer, and on October 29 you discovered that a former employee had planted malicious code that would destroy 4,000 servers at your company. This malicious code would have caused millions of dollars worth of damage and shut down your company for at least a week. The malware was set to detonate at 9:00 a.m. on January 31. What type of malware did you discover?

- **A.** Logic bomb
- **B.** RAT
- **C.** Spyware
- **D.** Ransomware

91. Which of the following is defined as hacking into a computer system for a politically or socially motivated purpose?

- **A.** Hacktivist
- **B.** Insider
- **C.** Script kiddie
- **D.** Evil twin

92. A network administrator with your company has received phone calls from an individual who is requesting information about their personal finances. Which of the following type of attack is occurring?

- **A.** Whaling
- **B.** Phishing
- **C.** Vishing
- **D.** Spear phishing

93. Which of the following can be restricted on a mobile device to prevent security violations? (Choose three.)

  A. Third-party app stores

  B. Biometrics

  C. Content management

  D. Rooting

  E. Sideloading

94. Which of the following does a remote access VPN usually rely on? (Choose two.)

  A. IPSec

  B. DES

  C. SSL

  D. SFTP

95. Matt, a security administrator, wants to use a two-way trust model for the owner of a certificate and the entity relying on the certificate. Which of the following is the best option to use?

  A. WPA

  B. Object identifiers

  C. PFX

  D. PKI

96. If domain A trusts domain B, and domain B trusts domain C, then domain A trusts domain C. Which concept does this describe?

  A. Multifactor authentication

  B. Federation

  C. Single sign-on

  D. Transitive trust

97. A user entered a username and password to log into the company's network. Which of the following best describes the username?

  A. Authorization

  B. Authentication

  C. Identification

  D. Accounting

98. Which of the following tools can be used to hide messages within a file?

  A. Data sanitization

  B. Steganography

  C. Tracert

  D. Network mapping

99. Which of the following is best used to prevent ARP poisoning on a local network? (Choose two.)

   A. Antivirus

   B. Static ARP entries

   C. Patching management

   D. Port security

100. Which of the following is the best practice to place at the end of an ACL?

   A. USB blocking

   B. Time synchronization

   C. MAC filtering

   D. Implicit deny

Appendix

Answers to Practice Tests

Chapter 1: Threats, Attacks, and Vulnerabilities

1. B. The correct answer is a boot sector virus, which is one that will affect the boot sector of the hard drive. Thus, what operating system you boot to is irrelevant.

Option A is incorrect. There is no element of ransom in the description of this attack.

Option C is incorrect. A rootkit can sometimes also affect the boot sector, but in this case the boot sector virus is the most accurate description.

Option D is incorrect. Nothing in this description indicates key logging.

2. C. The correct answer is spear phishing. Spear phishing is targeted to a specific group, in this case insurance professionals. Attackers can find individuals from public sources to target. This is known as open source intelligence.

Option A is incorrect because that is too broad a category.

Option B is incorrect because, though social engineering is a part of every phishing attack, this is more than just social engineering.

Option D is incorrect because this is not a Trojan horse. In fact, malware is not even part of the attack.

3. B. A logic bomb is malware that performs its malicious activity when some condition is met.

Option A is incorrect because a worm is malware that self-propagates.

Option C is incorrect because a Trojan horse is malware attached to a legitimate program.

Option D is incorrect because a rootkit is malware that gets root or administrative privileges.

4. C. The text shown is the classic example of a basic SQL injection to log in to a site.

Option A is incorrect. Cross-site scripting would have JavaScript in the text field.

Option B is incorrect. Cross-site request forgery would not involve any text being entered in the web page.

Option D is incorrect. ARP poisoning is altering the ARP table in a switch; it is not related to website hacking.

5. B. Half-open connections are the hallmark of a SYN flood.

Option A is incorrect. We know from the question that this is a denial of service, but nothing indicates that it is (or is not) a distributed denial of service.

Option C is incorrect. Buffer overflow involves putting too much data into a variable or array.

Option D is incorrect. ARP poisoning is altering the ARP table in a switch; it is not related to website hacking.

6. B. The primary and best way to defend against the attacks mentioned is filtering user input.

Option A is incorrect. Encrypting the web traffic will not have any effect on these two attacks.

Option C is incorrect. A web application firewall (WAF) might mitigate these attacks, but it would be secondary to filtering user input.

Option D is incorrect. An IDS will simply detect the attack—it won't stop it.

7. C. If users have been connecting but the WAP does not show them connecting, then they have been connecting to a rogue access point. This could be the cause of an architecture and design weakness such as a network without segmentation and control of devices connecting to the network.

Option A is incorrect. Session hijacking involves taking over an already authenticated session. Most session hijacking attacks involve impersonation. The attacker attempts to gain access to another user's session by posing as that user.

Option B is incorrect. Clickjacking involves causing visitors to a website to click on the wrong item.

Option D is incorrect. Bluejacking is a Bluetooth attack.

8. C. Cross-site scripting involves entering a script into text areas that other users will view.

Option A is incorrect. SQL injection is not about entering scripts, but rather SQL commands.

Option B is incorrect. Clickjacking is about tricking users into clicking on the wrong thing.

Option D is incorrect. Bluejacking is a Bluetooth attack.

9. B. A Trojan horse wraps a malicious program to a legitimate program. When the user downloads and installs the legitimate program, they get the malware.

Option A is incorrect. A logic bomb is malware that does its misdeeds when some condition is met.

Option C is incorrect. A rootkit is malware that gets administrative, or root access.

Option D is incorrect. A macro virus is a virus that is embedded in a document as a macro.

10. C. A backdoor is a method for bypassing normal security and directly accessing the system.

Option A is incorrect. A logic bomb is malware that performs its misdeeds when some condition is met.

Option B is incorrect. A Trojan horse wraps a malicious program to a legitimate program. When the user downloads and installs the legitimate program, they get the malware.

Option D is incorrect. A rootkit is malware that gets root or administrative privileges.

11. C. The machines in her network are being used as bots, and the users are not aware that they are part of a DDoS attack.

Option A is incorrect. Social engineering is when someone tries to manipulate you into giving information. Techniques involved in social engineering attacks include consensus, scarcity, and familiarity.

Option B is incorrect. There is a slight chance that all computers could have a backdoor, but that is very unlikely, and attackers normally don't manually log into each machine to do a distributed denial of service (DDoS)—it would be automated, as through a bot.

Option D is incorrect. Crypto-viruses are not related to DDoS attacks.

12. B. This is a classic example of ransomware.

Option A is incorrect. A rootkit provides access to administrator/root privileges.

Option C is incorrect. A logic bomb executes its malicious activity when some condition is met.

Option D is incorrect. This scenario does not describe whaling.

13. D. The primary method for stopping both cross-site scripting and SQL injection is to check or filter user input.

Option A is incorrect. A web application firewall might help, but a basic SPI firewall won't prevent this.

Option B is incorrect. Most IDSs/IPSs won't detect cross-site scripting, and even if one will, option A is still the best way to prevent cross-site scripting.

Option C is incorrect. This is not a buffer overflow, and checking buffer boundaries won't help.

14. B. This is the description of a buffer overflow.

Option A is incorrect. Bluesnarfing is a Bluetooth attack.

Option C is incorrect. Bluejacking is a Bluetooth attack.

Option D is incorrect. This is not a distributed denial of service.

15. A. Vulnerability scan uses automated tools such as Nessus and Microsoft Baseline Security Analyzer to find known vulnerabilities.

Option B is incorrect. Penetration tests seek to actually exploit the vulnerabilities and break into systems.

Option C is incorrect. Security audits usually focus on checking policies, incident reports, and other documents.

Option D is incorrect. Security test is a generic term for any sort of test.

16. A. Credentials the WAP shipped with are an example of default configuration.

Option B is incorrect. Race conditions involve multithreaded applications accessing shared variables.

Option C is incorrect. Patches won't change the default password.

Option D is incorrect. Encryption does not affect logging into the administrative screen.

17. C. Social engineering can only be countered by user training and education.

Options A and B are incorrect. No technology can prevent social engineering.

Option D is incorrect. Strong policies can only help if users are well trained in the policies.

18. C. ARP poisoning is used to change the ARP tables routing data to a different MAC address, which would explain why there were no entries.

Option A is incorrect. A backdoor would not explain that the log entries were sent, but not received.

Option B is incorrect. A buffer overflow would not explain that the log entries were sent but not received.

Option D is incorrect. An IDS would not stop log entries even if it was malfunctioning.

19. A. From the description it appears that they are not logging into the real web server but rather a fake server. That indicates typosquatting: have a URL that is named very similarly to a real site so that when users mistype the real site's URL they will go to the fake site.

Options B, C, and D are all incorrect. These are all methods of attacking a website, but in this case, the actual website was not attacked. Instead, some users are visiting a fake site.

20. D. The term for low-skilled hackers is *script kiddie*.

Option A is incorrect. Nothing indicates this is being done for ideological reasons.

Option B is incorrect. "Amateur" may be an appropriate description, but the correct term is *script kiddie*.

Option C is incorrect. Nothing in this scenario indicates an insider threat.

21. B. The term for this is *botnet*, usually spelled as one word.

Options A, C, and D are all incorrect. Although these terms might sound the same, they are simply not the terms used in the industry.

22. B. Passive reconnaissance is any reconnaissance that is done without actually connecting to the target.

Option A is incorrect. Active reconnaissance involves communicating with the target network, such as doing a port scan.

Option C is incorrect. The initial exploitation is not information gathering; it is actually breaking into the target network.

Option D is incorrect. A pivot is when you have breached one system and use that to move to another system.

23. C. Some spyware takes screen captures of the system, and it is common for such spyware to hide them in the temp folder.

Option A is incorrect. There is no evidence of any corporate data, just screenshots from the salesperson's own machine. And if he was stealing data, he would not draw attention to his computer by reporting a problem.

Option B is incorrect. Nothing in this scenario indicates a backdoor.

Option D is incorrect. Updates won't affect this.

24. A. This is an exact description of DNS poisoning or domain hijacking.

Option B is incorrect. ARP poisoning involves altering the MAC-IP tables in a switch.

Options C and D are incorrect. These are both Bluetooth attacks.

25. C. A black-box test involves absolutely minimal information.

Option A is incorrect. A white-box test involves very complete information being given to the tester.

Option B is incorrect. This scenario is probably done from outside the network, but external test is not the correct terminology.

Option D is incorrect. Threat test is not a term used in penetration testing.

26. D. A pivot occurs when you exploit one machine and use that as a basis to attack other systems.

Option A is incorrect. Pivots can be done from internal or external tests.

Options B and C are incorrect. These describe how much information the tester is given in advance, not how the tester performs the test.

27. A. Shimming is when the attacker places some malware between an application and some other file, and intercepts the communication to that file (usually to a library or system API).

Option B is incorrect. A Trojan horse might be used to get the shim onto the system, but that is not described in this scenario.

Option C is incorrect. A backdoor is a means to circumvent system authorization and get direct access to the system.

Option D is incorrect. Refactoring is the process of changing names of variables, functions, etc. in a program.

28. A. A white-box test involves providing extensive information, as described in this scenario.

Option B is incorrect. A white-box test could be internal or external.

Option C is incorrect. This is the opposite of a black-box test.

Option D is incorrect. Threat test is not a term used in penetration testing.

29. B. His machines are part of a distributed denial-of-service attack.

Option A is incorrect. This scenario describes a generic DDoS, not a specific one like SYN flood.

Option C is incorrect. These machines could be part of a botnet, or just have a trigger that causes them to launch the attack at a specific time. The real key in this scenario is the DDoS attack.

Option D is incorrect. A backdoor gives an attacker access to the target system.

30. D. This is a textbook example of how ransomware works.

Option A is incorrect. A rootkit gives administrative, or root, access.

Option B is incorrect. A logic bomb executes its malicious activity when some specific condition is met.

Option C is incorrect. A boot sector virus, as the name suggests, infects the boot sector of the target computer.

31. D. Whaling is targeting a specific individual.

Option A is incorrect. Spear phishing targets a small group.

Option B is incorrect. Targeted phishing is not a term used in the industry.

Option C is incorrect. Phishing is the generic term for a wide range of related attacks.

32. C. You are concerned about buffer overflows, and thus checking buffer boundaries is the best defense.

Options A and B are incorrect. While these technological solutions can always be a benefit for security, they are unlikely to address buffer overflow attacks effectively.

Option D is incorrect. Checking user input helps defend against SQL injection and cross-site scripting.

33. C. Security audits typically focus on checking policies, documents, and so forth.

Option A is incorrect. Vulnerability scans use automated and semiautomated processes to check for known vulnerabilities.

Option B is incorrect. Penetration tests attempt to actually exploit vulnerabilities and breach systems.

Option D is incorrect. Security test is too general a term.

34. A. Although many things could explain what she is experiencing, the scenario most closely matches connecting to a rogue access point where her login credentials were stolen.

Options B and C are incorrect. Both involve malware, and the scenario states no sign of malware was found.

Option D is incorrect. This does not match the symptoms of a buffer overflow attack.

35. D. This is a classic example of an attacker using social engineering on the accountant, in order to gain access to his system.

Options A and B are incorrect. This scenario does not describe either IP or MAC spoofing.

Option C is incorrect. A man-in-the-middle attack would require an attacker to get in between a source and destination for some sort of electronic communication. That is not described in this scenario.

36. D. An intrusion detection system will simply report issues, and not block the traffic.

Option A is incorrect. An intrusion prevention system will stop suspected traffic, and in the event of a false positive, will shut down legitimate traffic.

Option B is incorrect. A web application firewall (WAF), as the name suggests, primarily protects a web server against external attacks.

Option C is incorrect. SIEMs aggregate logs for analysis.

37. A. A rainbow table is a table of precomputed hashes, used to retrieve passwords.

Option B is incorrect. A backdoor is used to gain access to a system, not recover passwords.

Options C and D are incorrect. While both of these can be used to gain access to passwords, they are not tables of precomputed hashes.

38. A. Bluejacking involves sending unsolicited messages to Bluetooth devices when they are in range.

Option B is incorrect. Bluesnarfing involves getting data from the Bluetooth device.

Options C and D are incorrect. Evil twin uses a rogue access point whose name is similar or identical to that of a legitimate access point.

39. A. This is the term for rummaging through the waste/trash.

Options B and D are incorrect. These terms, though grammatically correct, are simply not the terms used in the industry.

Option C is incorrect. Nothing in this scenario describes social engineering.

40. B. Bluesnarfing involves accessing data from a Bluetooth device when it is in range.

Option A is incorrect. Bluejacking involves sending unsolicited messages to Bluetooth devices when they are in range.

Option C is incorrect. Evil twin uses a rogue access point whose name is similar or identical to that of a legitimate access point.

Option D is incorrect. A RAT is a remote-access Trojan. Nothing in this scenario points to a RAT being the cause of the stolen data.

41. A. This is a remote-access Trojan (RAT), malware that opens access for someone to remotely access the system.

Option B is incorrect. A backdoor does provide access but it is usually in the system due to programmers putting it there, not due to malware on the system.

Option C is incorrect. A logic bomb executes its misdeeds when some logical condition is met.

Option D is incorrect. A rootkit provides root or administrative access to the system.

42. D. The term used in the industry is *excessive privileges*, and it is the opposite of good security practice, which states that each user should have *least privileges* (i.e., just enough privileges to do his or her job).

Options A through C are incorrect. While these are grammatically correct, they are not the terms used in the industry.

43. Option B is correct; zero-day exploits are new, and they are not in the virus definitions for the antivirus programs. This makes them difficult to detect, except by their behavior.

Options A, C, and D are incorrect. These are all forms of malware, but should be picked up by at least one of the antivirus programs.

44. Option B is correct. When using products the vendor no longer supports, also known as end-of-life, one major concern is that there won't be patches available for any issues or vulnerabilities.

Option A is incorrect; this is certainly not normal.

Option C is incorrect. SIEMs aggregate logs and are operating system agnostic.

Option D is incorrect. An older system is not necessarily more susceptible to denial-of-service (DoS) attacks.

45. D. WiFi protected setup (WPS) uses a PIN to connect to the wireless access point (WAP). The WPS attack attempts to intercept that PIN in transmission, connect to the WAP, and then steal the WPA2 password.

Options A and B are incorrect. Nothing in this scenario requires or describes a rogue access point/evil twin.

Option C is incorrect. An IV attack is an obscure cryptographic attack.

46. C. Initialization vectors are used with stream ciphers. An IV attack attempts to exploit a flaw to use the IV to expose encrypted data.

Options A and B are incorrect. Nothing in this scenario requires or describes a rogue access point/evil twin.

Option D is incorrect. WiFi protected setup (WPS) uses a PIN to connect to the wireless access point (WAP). The WPS attack attempts to intercept that PIN in transmission, connect to the WAP, and then steal the WPA2 password.

47. A. Any of these systems could help with detecting malicious activity by an insider, but the intrusion prevention system will block such activity, if detected.

Option B is incorrect. SIEMs simply aggregate logs.

Option C is incorrect. A honeypot can be useful in trapping a malicious actor but not in stopping data exfiltration.

Option D is incorrect. Firewalls can block traffic, but normally data exfiltration looks like normal traffic and is hard for a firewall to block.

48. D. This appears to be a situation where your network's DNS server is compromised and sending people to a fake site.

    Option A is incorrect. A Trojan horse is malware tied to a legitimate program.

    Option B is incorrect. IP spoofing would be using a fake IP address, but that is not described in this scenario. In fact, the users are not even typing in IP addresses—they are typing in URLs.

    Option C is incorrect. Clickjacking involves tricking users into clicking something other than what they intended.

49. B. This is a classic description of jamming.

    Option A is incorrect. IV attacks are obscure cryptographic attacks on stream ciphers.

    Option C is incorrect. WiFi protected setup (WPS) uses a PIN to connect to the wireless access point (WAP). The WPS attack attempts to intercept that PIN in transmission, connect to the WAP, and then steal the WPA2 password.

    Option D is incorrect. A botnet is a group of machines that are being used, without their consent, as part of an attack.

50. A. This is the classic description of clickjacking.

    Options B and C are incorrect. These are Bluetooth attacks.

    Option D is incorrect. Nothing in this scenario requires or describes an evil twin.

51. B. Cross-site request forgery sends fake requests to a website that purport to be from a trusted, authenticated user.

    Option A is incorrect. Cross-site scripting exploits the trust the user has for the website and embeds scripts into that website.

    Option C is incorrect. Bluejacking is a Bluetooth attack.

    Option D is incorrect. Nothing in this scenario requires or describes an evil twin.

52. C. This is a classic example of typosquatting. The website is off by only one or two letters, hoping that when users to the real website mistype the URL they will go to the fake website.

    Option A is incorrect. Session hijacking is taking over an authenticated session.

    Option B is incorrect. Cross-site request forgery sends fake requests to a website that purport to be from a trusted, authenticated user.

    Option D is incorrect. Clickjacking attempts to trick users into clicking on something other than what they intended.

53. A. Bluesnarfing uses Bluetooth to extract data from a Bluetooth device.

Option B is incorrect. Session hijacking is taking over an authenticated session.

Option C is incorrect. Backdoors are built-in methods to circumvent authentication.

Option D is incorrect. Cross-site request forgery sends fake requests to a website that purport to be from a trusted, authenticated user.

54. B. This is a classic example of a disassociation attack. The attacker tricks users into disassociating from the device.

Option A is incorrect. Misconfiguration won't cause authenticated users to de-authenticate.

Option C is incorrect. Session hijacking involves taking over an authenticated session.

Option D is incorrect. Backdoors are built-in methods to circumvent authentication.

55. A. This is an example of a dictionary attack. The attacker uses a list of words that are believed to be likely passwords.

Option B is incorrect. A rainbow table is a precomputed table of hashes.

Option C is incorrect. Brute force tries every possible random combination. If attacker has the original plaintext and ciphertext for a message, they can determine the key space used through brute force attempts targeting the keyspace.

Option D is incorrect. Session hijacking is when the attacker takes over an authenticated session.

56. B. This is a classic example of a downgrade attack.

Option A is incorrect. In a disassociation attack, the attacker attempts to force the victim into disassociating from a resource.

Option C is incorrect. Session hijacking is when the attacker takes over an authenticated session.

Option D is incorrect. Brute force attempts every possible random combination to get the password or encryption key.

57. D. A collision is when two different inputs produce the same hash.

Option A is incorrect. A rainbow table is a table of precomputed hashes.

Option B is incorrect. Brute force attempts every possible random combination to get the password or encryption key.

Option C is incorrect. Session hijacking is when the attacker takes over an authenticated session.

58. C. An advanced persistent threat (APT) involves sophisticated (i.e., advanced) attacks over a period of time (i.e., persistent)

Option A is incorrect. A distributed denial of service could be a part of an APT, but in and of itself is unlikely to be an APT.

Option B is incorrect. Brute force attempts every possible random combination to get the password or encryption key.

Option D is incorrect. In a disassociation attack, the attacker attempts to force the victim into disassociating from a resource.

59. D. Whether the attacker is an organized criminal, hacktivist, nation-state attacker, or script kiddie, the amount of data stolen could be large or small.

Options A, B, and C are all incorrect. These are exactly the attributes of an attack you do examine to determine the most likely attacker.

60. A. When an IDS or antivirus mistakes legitimate traffic for an attack, this is called a false positive.

Option B is incorrect. A false negative is when the IDS mistakes an attack for legitimate traffic. It is the opposite of a false positive.

Options C and D are both incorrect. While these may be grammatically correct, these are not the terms used in the industry.

61. A. The term for attempting to gain any privileges beyond what you have is *privilege escalation.*

Option B is incorrect. Session hijacking is taking over an authenticated session.

Options C and D are incorrect. These are not terms used in the industry.

62. C. This is a classic definition of a race condition: when multiple threads in an application are using the same variable and the situation is not properly handled.

Option A is incorrect. A buffer overflow is attempting to put more data in a buffer than it is designed to hold.

Option B is incorrect. A logic bomb is malware that performs its misdeed when some logical condition is met.

Option D is incorrect. As the name suggests, improper error handling is the lack of adequate or appropriate error handling mechanisms within software.

63. B. This is a classic example of a Trojan horse.

Option A is incorrect. A rootkit gives root or administrative access.

Option C is incorrect. Spyware is malware that records user activities.

Option D is incorrect. A boot sector virus is a virus that infects the boot sector of the hard drive.

64. A. If a certificate is revoked, it can be used until the new certificate revocation list is published.

Options B, C, and D are all incorrect. They do not accurately describe the scenario given.

65. C. A buffer overflow is possible when boundaries are not checked and the attacker tries to put in more data than the variable can hold.

Option A is incorrect. Cross-site scripting is a web page attack.

Option B is incorrect. Cross-site request forgery is a web page attack.

Option D is incorrect. A logic bomb is malware that performs its misdeed when some condition is met.

66. B. This is the definition of a logic bomb.

    Option A is incorrect. A boot sector virus infects the boot sector of the hard drive.

    Option C is incorrect. A buffer overflow occurs when the attacker attempts to put more data in a variable than it can hold.

    Option D is incorrect. A sparse infector virus performs its malicious activity intermittently to make it harder to detect.

67. D. A polymorphic virus changes from time to time, and that would explain the different behavior on different computers.

    Option A is incorrect. The scenario is about malware.

    Option B is incorrect. A boot sector virus infects the boot sector of the hard drive.

    Option C is incorrect. A macro virus is embedded into a document as a macro.

68. A. This is the definition of a Smurf attack.

    Option B is incorrect. The scenario does not state if this attack is coming from multiple sources, thus being distributed (i.e., distributed denial of service).

    Option C is incorrect. A hijacking attack attempts to take over an authenticated session.

    Option D is incorrect. The signature of a SYN flood is multiple half-open connections.

69. C. Polymorphic viruses periodically change their signature or even their code.

    Option A is incorrect. A boot sector virus infects the boot sector of the hard drive.

    Option B is incorrect. This is not a hoax—it is an actual virus.

    Option D is incorrect. The category of stealth virus is very broad and might include polymorphic as well as armored and sparse infectors, but the scenario is more specific, pointing to polymorphic.

70. A. This is the definition of a macro virus.

    Option B is incorrect. A boot sector virus infects the boot sector of the hard drive.

    Option C is incorrect. A Trojan horse is malware that is tied to a legitimate program. In this scenario, the malware is actually embedded in an Office document. The two are similar, but not the same.

    Option D is incorrect. A remote access Trojan (RAT) is a Trojan horse that gives the attacker remote access to the machine.

71. C. The intermittent burst of malicious activity is the definition of a sparse infector virus.

    Option A is incorrect. A macro virus is embedded in a document as a macro.

    Option B is incorrect. A logic bomb executes its misdeeds when a specific condition is met.

    Option D is incorrect. A polymorphic virus changes its signature, or even its code, periodically.

72. B. Multipartite viruses combine boot sector with file infection.

    Option A is incorrect. Polymorphic viruses periodically change their signature or even their code.

Option C is incorrect. Stealth viruses use one or more techniques to make them harder to find.

Option D is incorrect. This is not an industry term for any sort of virus.

73. C. By giving the tester logins, you are allowing him to conduct a privileged scan (i.e., a scan with some privileges).

Options A and B are incorrect. These describe the level of knowledge the tester is given of the network. A privilege scan cannot be a black-box test, but it could be either white-box or gray-box.

Option D is incorrect. While this is grammatically correct, it is not the term used in the industry.

74. C. Botnets are often used to launch DDoS attacks, with the attack coming from all the computers in the botnet simultaneously.

Option A is incorrect. Phishing attacks attempt to get the user to give up information, click on a link, or open an attachment.

Option B is incorrect. Adware consists of unwanted pop-up ads.

Option D is incorrect. A Trojan horse attaches malware to a legitimate program.

75. A. Accounts should be configured to expire. If this had occurred, then the account would no longer be active.

Option B is incorrect. While properly trained users are important, that is not what caused this issue.

Options C and D are incorrect. These are unrelated to an old account still being active.

76. C. This is a classic example of the problem with default configurations.

Option A is incorrect. Configuring the accounts is not the issue; changing default passwords and settings is.

Option B is incorrect. Yes, training users is important, but that's not the issue in this scenario.

Option D is incorrect. Patching systems is important, but that won't change default settings.

77. D. In a DLL injection, the malware attempts to inject code into the process of some library. This is a rather advanced attack.

Option A is incorrect. A logic bomb executes its misdeed when some condition is met.

Option B is incorrect. Session hijacking is taking over an authenticated session.

Option C is incorrect. Buffer overflows are done by sending more data to a variable than it can hold.

78. D. This is the definition of pointer dereferencing. It is a somewhat obscure and sophisticated attack on a target program.

Option A is incorrect. In a DLL injection, the malware tries to inject code into the memory process space of a library.

Option B is incorrect. In a buffer overflow, the attacker sends more data to a variable than it can hold.

Option C is incorrect. A memory leak occurs when memory is allocated in some programming function but not deallocated. Each time the function is called, more system memory is used up.

79. B. System sprawl occurs when a system grows and there are devices on the system that are not documented.

Options A, C, and D are all incorrect. While these are all serious security issues, they are unrelated to the scenario presented.

80. C. An intrusive scan could possibly cause some disruption of operations. For this reason, it should be conducted outside normal business hours.

Option A is incorrect. A penetration test actually attempts to breach the network by exploiting vulnerabilities.

Option B is incorrect. An audit is primarily a document check.

Option D is incorrect. Both intrusive and nonintrusive vulnerability scans can be effective at finding vulnerabilities.

81. D. The fact that the website is defaced in a manner related to the company's public policies is the definition of hacktivism.

Options A, B, and C are incorrect. None of these account for the statements adverse to the company's policies, which is why hacktivism is the real cause.

82. C. While you might suppose that a nation-state attacker (the usual attacker behind an advanced persistent threat) would attack from a foreign IP address, they often use a compromised address in the target country as a base for attacks.

Options A, B, and D are all incorrect. These are actually signs of an advanced persistent threat.

83. A. The terms evil twin and rogue access point both refer to fake access points that broadcast what appear to be legitimate SSIDs.

Options B, C, and D are incorrect. They do not adequately explain this attack.

84. A. The fact that the IP addresses are within your country might make you discard the nation-state attacker, but it is common for nation-state attackers to use compromised IP addresses in the target country from which to attack. The other symptoms—a sophisticated attack, over time—are hallmarks of nation-state attackers.

Option B is incorrect. Nothing in the scenario indicates an ideological motive.

Option C is incorrect. In fact, this attack is the antithesis of the simple attack of a script kiddie.

Option D is incorrect. A lone attacker, no matter how skilled, would have difficulty maintaining sustained attacks over a year.

85. A. This is the definition of a zero-day attack.

Options B, C, and D are incorrect. These do not adequately describe a zero-day attack.

86. C. This is the definition of DNS poisoning.

Option A is incorrect. A backdoor provides access to the system by circumventing normal authentication.

Option B is incorrect. An APT is an advanced persistent threat.

Option D is incorrect. A Trojan horse ties a malicious program to a legitimate program.

87. B. This is, in fact, the definition of a Trojan horse.

Options A, C, and D are incorrect. These are all possible attacks, but do not match what is described in the question scenario.

88. A. A remote access Trojan (RAT) is malware that gives the attacker remote access to the victim machine.

Option B is incorrect. While a backdoor will give access, it is usually something in the system put there by programmers, not introduced by malware.

Option C is incorrect. A RAT is a type of Trojan horse, but Trojan horse is more general than what is described in the scenario.

Option D is incorrect. A macro virus is a virus embedded in a document.

89. B. Cross-site request forgery sends forged requests to a website, supposedly from a trusted user.

Option A is incorrect. Cross-site scripting is the injection of scripts into a website to exploit the users.

Option C is incorrect. A buffer overflow tries to put more data in a variable than the variable can hold.

Option D is incorrect. A remote-access Trojan (RAT) is malware that gives the attacker access to the system.

90. C. Sparse infector viruses perform their malicious activity sporadically.

Option A is incorrect. This does not describe an advanced persistent threat.

Option B is incorrect. A boot sector virus infects the boot sector of the hard drive.

Option D is incorrect. A keylogger is spyware that records keystrokes.

91. D. This is a classic example of whaling, phishing that targets a specific individual.

Option A is incorrect. Clickjacking is an attack that tries to trick users into clicking on something other than what they believe they are clicking on.

Option B is incorrect. While all phishing uses some social engineering, whaling is the most accurate description of this attack.

Option C is incorrect. Spear phishing targets a group, not a single individual.

92. B. Large, half-open connections are the hallmark of a SYN flood.

Option A is incorrect. These are all coming from a single IP address, so they cannot be a distributed denial-of-service attack.

Option C is incorrect. A buffer overflow seeks to put more data in a variable than it is designed to hold.

Option D is incorrect. ARP poisoning poisons the address resolution table of a switch.

93. A. SQL injection places malformed SQL into text boxes.

Option B is incorrect. Clickjacking attempts to trick the user into clicking on something other than what he or she intended.

Option C is incorrect. Cross-site scripting puts scripts into text fields that will be viewed by other users.

Option D is incorrect. Bluejacking is a Bluetooth attack.

94. C. The user-selected password is always a weak link in hard drive encryption.

Option A is incorrect. Yes, it is good system, but there is a weakness.

Option B is incorrect. 128-bit AES is more than adequate for corporate purposes.

Option D is incorrect. DES is outdated, and AES should be used.

95. A. If an attacker can induce the web application to generate the memory leak, then eventually the web application will consume all memory on the web server and the web server will freeze up.

Option B is incorrect. Backdoors are not caused by memory leaks.

Option C is incorrect. SQL injection places malformed SQL into text boxes.

Option D is incorrect. A buffer overflow attempts to put more data in a variable than it can hold.

96. D. This is the definition of a race condition.

Option A is incorrect. Memory leaks occur when memory is allocated, but not deallocated.

Option B is incorrect. A buffer overflow is when more data is put into a variable than it can hold.

Option C is incorrect. An integer overflow occurs when an attempt is made to put an integer that is too large into a variable, such as trying to put a 64-bit integer into a 32-bit variable.

97. B. Near-field communication (NFC) is susceptible to an attacker eavesdropping on the signal.

Option A is incorrect. Tailgating is a physical attack and not affected by NFC technology.

Options C and D are incorrect. These are both unrelated to NFC technology.

98. B. Tailgating involves simply following a legitimate user through the door once he or she has opened it.

Option A is incorrect. This is unrelated to physical security.

Option C is incorrect. It is possible to generate a fake smartcard, but that is a very uncommon attack.

Option D is incorrect. Again, this is possible but is very uncommon.

99. D. This is the definition of shimming.

Option A is incorrect. Application spoofing is not a term used in the industry.

Options B and C are incorrect. These are both wireless attacks.

100. D. This scenario is the definition of passing the hash.

Option A is incorrect. A real hash was provided; it was not spoofed.

Option B is incorrect. Evil twin is a wireless attack.

Option C is incorrect. Shimming is inserting malicious code between an application and a library.

101. B. Claiming to be from tech support is claiming authority, and the story the caller gave indicates urgency.

Option A is incorrect. Yes, this caller used urgency (the virus spread) but did not attempt intimidation.

Option C is incorrect. Authority and trust are closely related, and in this case urgency was the second major factor.

Option D is incorrect. This caller used urgency but not intimidation.

102. A. This is the definition of ARP poisoning.

Option B is incorrect. In DNS poisoning domain name to IP address entries in a DNS server are altered.

Option C is incorrect. This attack did not involve a man-in-the-middle.

Option D is incorrect. A backdoor provides access to the attacker, which circumvents normal authentication.

103. A. This is a classic multipartite virus. It infects the boot sector, as well as an operating system file.

Option B is incorrect. This infects the boot sector, but also infects an operating system file as well.

Option C is incorrect. A macro virus is embedded, as a macro, into a document.

Option D is incorrect. A polymorphic virus changes periodically.

104. C. Bluesnarfing accesses data on the cell phone.

Option A is incorrect. Phonejacking is not a term used in the industry.

Option B is incorrect. Bluejacking sends unwanted text messages to the phone.

Option D is incorrect. Evil twin is a WiFi attack.

105. D. A rainbow table is a table of precomputed hashes.

Option A is incorrect. A dictionary attack is a table of common words used to guess the password.

Option B is incorrect. Brute force involves trying every random possibility.

Option C is incorrect. In pass the hash, the attacker has the hash and bypasses the application, passing the hash directly to the backend service.

106. C. The fact that the attack is coming from multiple sources makes this a distributed denial of service.

Option A is incorrect. A Smurf attack involves sending spoofed broadcast packets to the target network's router.

Option B is incorrect. Yes, this is a denial-of-service attack, but it is distributed.

Option D is incorrect. A SYN flood involves lots of half-open connections.

107. A. A downgrade attack is often used against secure communications such as TLS in an attempt to get the user to shift to less secure modes.

Option B is incorrect. A brute-force attack tries either all possible passwords or all possible cryptography keys to gain access.

Option C is incorrect. A rainbow table is a table of precomputed hashes used to retrieve passwords.

Option D is incorrect. Bluesnarfing is a Bluetooth attack on cell phones.

108. A. In a white-box test, the tester is given extensive knowledge of the target network.

Option B is incorrect. This is not a term used to describe testing.

Option C is incorrect. Black-box testing involves only very minimal information being given to the tester.

Option D is incorrect. A red team test simulates a particular type of attacker, such as a nation-state attacker, an insider, or other type of attacker.

109. C. Social engineering is about using people skills to get information you would not otherwise have access to.

Option A is incorrect. Despite the word *engineering*, this has nothing to do with technical means.

Option B is incorrect. This would be dumpster diving.

Option D is incorrect. Yes, phishing emails use some social engineering, but that is one example of social engineering, not a definition.

110. C. Shoulder surfing involves literally looking over someone's shoulder in a public place and gathering information, perhaps login passwords.

Option A is incorrect. ARP poisoning alters the address resolution protocol tables in the switch.

Option B is incorrect. Phishing is an attempt to gather information, often via email, or to convince a user to click a link to, and/or download, an attachment.

Option D is incorrect. Smurf is a type of denial-of-service attack.

111. D. The sending of spoofed broadcast messages to the target network router is a Smurf attack.

Option A is incorrect. In a SYN flood, a large number of SYN packets are sent but not responded to. This leads to a large number of half-open connections.

Option B is incorrect. An ICMP flood is a large amount of ICMP (such as ping) packets sent to the target.

Option C is incorrect. In a buffer overflow attack, more data is sent to a variable than it was designed to hold.

112. C. Cross-site scripting involves entering code (script) into a text field that will be displayed to other users.

Option A is incorrect. In SQL injection, malformed SQL statements are entered into a text box in an attempt to circumvent the website's security.

Option B is incorrect. A logic bomb is software that performs its malicious activity when some condition is met.

Option D is incorrect. Session hijacking involves taking over an authenticated session.

113. A. Putting false entries into the DNS records of a DNS server is DNS poisoning.

Option B is incorrect. A denial-of-service attack attempts to overwhelm a server or service and render it inaccessible to legitimate users.

Option C is incorrect. DNS caching is a method of normal DNS operations.

Option D is incorrect. A Smurf attack is a type of denial of service.

114. D. IP addresses in the range of 169.254 are automatic private IP addresses (APIPA) and indicate the system could not get a dynamic IP address from the DHCP server. This is a typical symptom of DHCP starvation.

Option A is incorrect. Smurf attacks involve sending spoofed broadcast messages to the target network's router.

Option B is incorrect. Nothing in this scenario describes a man-in-the-middle attack.

Option C is incorrect. Nothing in this scenario indicates a distributed denial-of-service attack.

115. B. Distributed denial-of-service (DDoS) attacks often use bots in a botnet to perform the attack.

Option A is incorrect. Denial of service (DoS) is too broad a category and does not adequately match the scenario description.

Option C is incorrect. A buffer overflow attempts to put more data into a variable than it is designed to accept.

Option D is incorrect. A Trojan horse links a malware program to a legitimate program.

116. B. A logic bomb will perform its malicious activity when some condition is met, often a date or time. This is commonly done by disgruntled exiting employees.

Options A, C, and D are all incorrect. It is certainly possible that any of these could be left by an exiting employee, but logic bombs are far more common. The reason is that the other three would execute their malicious activity immediately, making an obvious connection to the exiting employee.

117. C. A correct three-way handshake involves the client sending a SYN packet, the server responding with SYN and ACK, and the client completing the handshake with an ACK. If you see a large number SYN packets without the corresponding ACK, that is likely to be a SYN flood.

Options A and B are incorrect. Address and port numbers have nothing to do with SYN flood attacks.

Option D is incorrect. RST is not the appropriate response to a SYN, and you should not expect to see RSTs in response to a SYN.

118. A. In a white-box test, the tester has full or very nearly full knowledge of the system.

Option B is incorrect. No knowledge is a black-box test.

Options C and D are incorrect. In any test, the tester should have permission to access the system.

119. A. Passive information gathering involves using methods other than directly accessing the network to gather information. Social media and newsgroups are commonly used.

Option B is incorrect. Active information gathering involves tasks such as port scanning that actually do connect to the target network.

Option C is incorrect. The initial exploit is when the tester tries to gain some access to some aspect of the system.

Option D is incorrect. Vulnerability scanning involves automated and semiautomated processes to find known vulnerabilities in a system.

120. B. This is the definition of session hijacking.

Option A is incorrect. Man-in-the-middle involves having some process between the two ends of communication in order to compromise passwords or cryptography keys.

Option C is incorrect. A backdoor is some means for accessing a system that circumvents normal authentication.

Option D is incorrect. A Smurf attack is a specific type of denial-of-service attack.

121. B. Vulnerability scans use automated and semiautomated processes to identify known vulnerabilities.

Option A is incorrect. Audits usually involve document checks.

Options C and D are incorrect. These are both types of penetration tests.

122. A. Near-field communication (NFC) can be susceptible to eavesdropping. Smartphones with NFC can be used as payment methods and should utilize biometric/pin to avoid information being stolen.

Option B is incorrect. Man-in-the-middle involves having some process between the two ends of communication in order to compromise passwords or cryptography keys.

Option C is incorrect. A buffer overflow attack attempts to put more data in a variable than the variable is designed to hold. This is improper input handling is the root cause to many buffer overflow.

Option D is incorrect. A Smurf attack is a type of denial of service.

123. A. A gray-box test involves the tester being given partial information about the network.

Option B is incorrect. A white-box test involves the tester being given full or nearly full information about the target network.

Options C and D are incorrect. Neither of these is a testing term.

124. D. In the man-in-the-middle attack, the attacker is between the client and the server, and to either end, the attacker appears like the legitimate other end.

Option A is incorrect. This does not describe any denial-of-service attack.

Option B is incorrect. A replay attack involves resending login information.

Option C is incorrect. Although a man-in-the-middle can be used to perform eavesdropping, in this scenario the best answer is man-in-the-middle.

125. A. In a man-in-the-browser attack, the malware intercepts calls from the browser to the system, such as system libraries.

Option B is incorrect. Man-in-the-middle involves having some process between the two ends of communication in order to compromise passwords or cryptography keys.

Option C is incorrect. In a buffer overflow attack, more data is put into a variable than the variable was intended to hold.

Option D is incorrect. Session hijacking involves taking over an authenticated session.

126. B. This is the initial exploit, which involves getting initial access to the system.

Option A is incorrect. Vulnerability scanning is an automated process that checks for the presence of known vulnerabilities.

Options C and D are incorrect. These both refer to how much information about the network the tester is given. In both black-box and white-box tests, there will still be an initial exploit.

127. C. When a vendor no longer supports software, there won't be patches for vulnerabilities or other issues.

Option A is incorrect. Although this may be true, it is not a security issue.

Option B is incorrect. Again, this may be true, but this is not the primary risk.

Option D is incorrect. This may or may not be true.

128. D. Placing a larger integer value into a smaller integer variable is an integer overflow.

Option A is incorrect. Memory overflow is not a term used, and memory leak is about allocating memory and not deallocating it.

Option B is incorrect. Buffer overflows usually involve arrays.

Option C is incorrect. Variable overflow is not a term used in the industry.

129. C. Armoring can be as simple as very trivial encryption, but any process that makes it difficult to reverse-engineer a virus is armoring.

Option A is incorrect. A polymorphic virus periodically changes itself.

Option B is incorrect. A macro virus is embedded, as a macro, into a document.

Option D is incorrect. A boot sector virus infects the boot sector of a hard drive.

130. A. Deauthorizing users from a resource is called disassociation.

Option B is incorrect. Session hijacking involves taking over an authenticated session.

Option C is incorrect. In the man-in-the-middle attack, the attacker is between the client and the server, and to either end, the attacker appears like the legitimate other end.

Option D is incorrect. Smurf is a type of denial-of-service attack where the attacker attempts to exhaust the resources and prevent users from accessing necessary systems.

131. A. Sending fake DNS requests that are overly large is called an amplification attack. It is a highly specialized type of denial of service.

Option B is incorrect. DNS poisoning seeks to put fake DNS records in a DNS server.

Option C is incorrect. DNS spoofing is using fake DNS information.

Option D is incorrect. The Smurf attack is a denial of service.

132. B. In this scenario, no technical issues are mentioned—just people seeing information. So shoulder surfing best fits the scenario.

Option A is incorrect. No social engineering is involved in this scenario.

Option C is incorrect. Although a man-in-the-middle attack on the wireless access point (WAP) could compromise data, that's not what is described in this scenario.

Option D is incorrect. Cross-site request forgery is a website attack.

133. A. Cross-site scripting is an attack on the user that is based on the user trusting the website.

Options B, C, and D are incorrect.

134. A. Targeting a specific group is the definition of spear phishing.

Option B is incorrect. In the man-in-the-middle attack, the attacker is between the client and the server, and to either end, the attacker appears like the legitimate other end.

Option C is incorrect. Target phishing is not an industry term.

Option D is incorrect. Vishing is phishing via voice over IP (VoIP).

135. A. Encryption is one method for armored viruses.

Option B is incorrect. Ransomware encrypts files but is not encrypted itself.

Option C is incorrect. A polymorphic virus periodically changes itself.

Option D is incorrect. A Trojan horse combines malware with a legitimate program.

136. D. This is the definition of a rootkit.

Option A is incorrect. A Trojan horse combines malware with a legitimate program.

Option B is incorrect. A logic bomb performs its malicious activity when some condition is met.

Option C is incorrect. A multipartite virus infects the boot sector and a file.

137. B. This is vishing, or using voice calls for phishing.

Option A is incorrect. Spear phishing is targeting a small, specific group.

Option C is incorrect. War dialing is dialing numbers hoping a computer modem answers.

Option D is incorrect. Robocalling is used to place unsolicited telemarketing calls.

138. A. Cross-site request forgery is an attack on the website that is based on the website trusting the user.

Options B, C, and D are all incorrect.

139. A. This is the definition of a multipartite virus.

Option B is incorrect. A rootkit gets admin or root privileges.

Option C is incorrect. Ransomware encrypts files and demands a ransom.

Option D is incorrect. A worm is a fast-spreading virus.

140. A. This is the definition of a worm.

Option B is incorrect. A virus is software that self-replicates.

Option C is incorrect. A logic bomb executes its malicious activity when some condition is met.

Option D is incorrect. A Trojan horse combines malware with a legitimate program.

141. B. Dumpster diving is the process of going through the trash to find documents.

Option A is incorrect. Phishing is often done via email or phone, and is an attempt to elicit information or convince a user to click a link or open an attachment.

Option C is incorrect. Shoulder surfing is literally looking over someone's shoulder.

Option D is incorrect. In the man-in-the-middle attack the attacker is between the client and the server, and to either end, the attacker appears like the legitimate other end.

142. D. This is the definition of a macro virus.

Option A is incorrect. A logic bomb executes its malicious activity when some condition is met.

Option B is incorrect. A rootkit obtains administrative or root access.

Option C is incorrect. A Trojan horse connects malware to a legitimate program.

143. A. URL hijacking or typosquatting is done by naming a phishing URL very similar to an actual URL.

Option B is incorrect. DNS poisoning would be entering fake entries into a DNS server.

Option C is incorrect. Cross-site scripting would show as a breach of the website.

Option D is incorrect. In the man-in-the-middle attack, the attacker is between the client and the server, and to either end, the attacker appears like the legitimate other end.

144. C. The dictionary attack uses common passwords.

Option A is incorrect. Rainbow tables are tables of precomputed hashes.

Option B is incorrect. The birthday attack is a method for generating collisions of hashes.

Option D is incorrect. No spoofing is indicated in this scenario.

145. A. This is the definition of a replay attack.

Option B is incorrect. IP spoofing is the process of faking an IP address.

Option C is incorrect. This is not a term used in the industry.

Option D is incorrect. Session hijacking is done by taking over an authenticated session.

146. D. Active reconnaissance actually connects to the network using techniques such as port scanning.

Option A is incorrect. Either can be done manually or with tools.

Option B is incorrect. Black-box and white-box refer to the amount of information the tester is given.

Option C is incorrect. Attackers and testers use both types of reconnaissance.

147. C. Vulnerability scans identify known vulnerabilities. Penetration tests actually exploit those vulnerabilities in order to breach the system.

Option A is incorrect. Either insiders or outsiders can do both vulnerability scans and penetration tests.

Option B is incorrect. Both vulnerability scans and penetration tests can use automated tools and manual techniques.

Option D is incorrect. Black-box and white-box refer to the amount of information the tester is given.

148. B. This is the definition of a pivot.

Option A is incorrect. In the man-in-the-middle attack, the attacker is between the client and the server, and to either end, the attacker appears like the legitimate other end.

Option C is incorrect. Shimming involves inserting code between a program and a library.

Option D is incorrect. Vishing is phishing over the phone line, often VoIP.

149. C. Active scanning actually connects to the target network.

Option A is incorrect. Passive scanning does not actually connect to the target network.

Options B and D are incorrect. Black-box and white-box refer to the amount of information the tester is given.

150. D. A firewall not running is not a configuration issue.

Options A, B, and C are all incorrect. These are all common security misconfiguration issues.

Chapter 2: Technologies and Tools

1. D. The correct answer is stateful packet inspection (SPI). SPI looks at the entire context of the conversation and will stop SYN floods.

Option A is incorrect. A packet filter examines each packet in isolation and won't stop the SYN flood. A packet filter is stateless and won't deter the SYN flood.

Option B is incorrect. An application gateway may have SPI functionality, but its primary benefit is to protect against a specific application attack, such as web attacks.

Option C is incorrect. Bastion is another name for a border firewall and does not indicate the process it uses.

2. A. The correct answer is NAC, or Network Access Control. NAC is a network management solution that defines and implements a policy that enables only compliant and trusted endpoint devices to access network resources.

Option B is incorrect. Stateful packet inspection (SPI) is a type of firewall.

Option C is incorrect. IDS stands for intrusion detection system.

Option D is incorrect. BYOD, or Bring Your Own Device, is the problem, but the solution described is Network Access Control (NAC).

3. D. Transport mode is the mode wherein IPSec encrypts the data, but not the packet header.

Option A is incorrect. Tunneling mode does encrypt the header as well as the packet data.

Option B is incorrect. Internet Key Exchange (IKE) is used in setting up security associations in IPSec.

Option C is incorrect. Encapsulating Security Payload (ESP) is used for authentication and encryption in IPSec, whether tunneling or transport mode is used.

4. D. When an IDS (or any security device) labels legitimate traffic as an attack, that is called a false positive.

Option A is incorrect. A false negative is when an attack is mislabeled as legitimate.

Option B is incorrect. Passive refers to how the IDS responds to suspicious activity. The question does not tell you if this is passive or active.

Option C is incorrect. Active refers to how the IDS responds to suspicious activity. The question does not tell you if this is passive or active.

5. D. Security Information and Event Management (SIEM) systems are designed specifically for log aggregation and analysis.

Option A is incorrect. Network Access Control (NAC) scans devices to ensure they meet minimum network security requirements.

Option B is incorrect. Port forwarding could be used, in conjunction with other steps, to aggregate logs, but it would not be the best approach.

Option C is incorrect. An intrusion detection system (IDS) won't aggregate other systems logs.

6. C. A web application firewall (WAF) is designed to provide firewall protection that also will protect against specific web attacks.

Option A is incorrect. An access control list (ACL) is an important security measure but will not provide protection against web attacks.

Option B is incorrect. A stateful packet inspector (SPI) is a robust firewall and will stop attacks such as SYN floods, but it won't provide the best protection against web attacks.

Option D is incorrect. An IDS is a good security measure, but it won't provide the best protection against web attacks.

7. C. A site-to-site VPN is a permanent VPN connection between sites. Connecting remote offices is a typical site-to-site VPN implementation.

Option A is incorrect. L2TP is a protocol for VPN and could be used for either site-to-site or remote-access VPNs.

Option B is incorrect. IPSec is a protocol for VPN and could be used for either site-to-site or remote-access VPNs.

Option D is incorrect. A remote-access VPN is used by an individual to remotely access the corporate network.

8. D. By mapping network jacks to specific MAC addresses of machines, you can prevent a rogue machine from being connected.

Option A is incorrect. Access control lists won't prevent a rogue device from being connected to a port.

Option B is incorrect. Intrusion detection systems won't prevent a rogue device from being connected to a port.

Option C is incorrect. If that specific jack is part of a VLAN, it would limit the attacker to only that VLAN, but that is certainly not as reliable or as robust a security measure as port security.

9. A. An active-active cluster has all servers working, rather than keeping a duplicate server in reserve.

Option B is incorrect. An active-passive cluster has, for each pair of servers, one not functioning. It simply is used in case the primary server should fail.

Options C and D are incorrect. These are means for a cluster deciding how to route traffic in the cluster.

10. A. Round-robin load balancing simply sends each new connection to the next server in the cluster.

Option B is incorrect. Affinity load balancing ties specific users to specific servers in the cluster.

Option C is incorrect. Weighted load balancing examines the bandwidth utilization for each server and sends the next connection to the server with the least current bandwidth utilization.

Option D is incorrect. Rotating is not a term used in load balancing.

11. D. The term for this is *thin wireless access point*.

Option A is incorrect. Fat wireless access points have all the functionality and features the wireless network needs.

Option B is incorrect. A repeater resends a signal.

Option C is incorrect. Thick is another term for fat access point.

12. B. Controller-based wireless access points have minimal functionality, with most functions centrally controlled.

Option A is incorrect. A fat wireless access point has all necessary functionality contained in the WAP.

Option C is incorrect. Stand-alone is synonymous with fat WAP.

Option D is incorrect. 802.11i is the wireless security standard.

13. B. Encapsulating Security Payload provides both integrity and encryption.

Option A is incorrect. Authentication Header only provides integrity, not encryption.

Option C is incorrect. Internet Key Exchange is used during the setup of IPSec to establish security associations.

Option D is incorrect. The Internet Security Association and Key Management Protocol provides a framework for authentication and key exchange.

14. C. ESP provides encryption and AH provides complete authentication, including the header, so both are needed to meet the requirements.

Option A is incorrect. Authentication Header will provide complete packet authentication, including the header, but it won't provide encryption.

Option B is incorrect. Encapsulating Security Payload provides both integrity and encryption but only authenticates the data, not the header.

Option D is incorrect. Internet Key Exchange is used during the setup of IPSec to establish security associations.

15. D. USB blocking will prevent anyone from plugging in a USB and taking out data.

Option A is incorrect. An IPS would only stop exfiltration of data if it was sent over the network and appeared as an attack. It would not stop hand carrying out of data.

Option B is incorrect. This is a more time-consuming option and would not be the first thing you implement.

Option C is incorrect. Virtual local area networks (VLANs) won't help with this issue.

16. B. Secure Multipurpose Internet Mail Extensions (S/MIME) encrypts email using X.509 certificates that are created and authenticated by a trusted third party.

Option A is incorrect. The Internet Message Access Protocol is used for receiving email. It does not send email and is not natively encrypted.

Option C is incorrect. PGP (Pretty Good Privacy) can be used to encrypt email, but it uses self-generated certificates that are not authenticated by a third party.

Option D is incorrect. Simple Mail Transfer Protocol Secure is encrypted, but it is only for sending email, not receiving. It can also be done with S/MIME or PGP.

17. D. Secure Shell gives a remote command-line interface that is encrypted.

Option A is incorrect. HyperText Transport Protocol Secure is for encrypting web traffic.

Option B is incorrect. Windows Remote Desktop Protocol is not encrypted.

Option C is incorrect. Telnet is not encrypted.

18. D. Earlier versions of SNMP sent all traffic in clear text. SNMP v3 sends all data encrypted.

Options A, B, and C are incorrect. They are not features of SNMP v3.

19. B. Choose Your Own Device (CYOD) allows employees to bring their own devices to work, but only if they are chosen from a list of approved models.

Option A is incorrect. Bring Your Own Device (BYOD) allows employees to bring whatever model device they happen to have.

Option C is incorrect. Company-Owned Personally Enabled (COPE) equipment is provided by and owned by the company.

Option D is incorrect. BYOE is not a term used in the industry.

20. C. Virtual Desktop Infrastructure does have all patch management centrally controlled.

Option A is incorrect. This is a benefit of VDI but not a security benefit.

Option B is incorrect. VDI is no more or less resistant to malware than physical desktops.

Option D is incorrect. Some vendors claim VDI is less susceptible to man-in-the-middle attacks, but no one claims it is immune to them.

21. C. Satellite communications are most resistant to disasters that disrupt communications.

Option A is incorrect. While cellular is effective and reasonably resilient, it is not as resilient as SATCOM.

Option B is incorrect. WiFi can fail for any number of reasons, and a disaster is very likely to affect it.

Option D is incorrect. If there is any disruption to the network, then VoIP will not function.

22. A. The most effective protection against data loss is the ability to remotely wipe the phone.

Option B is incorrect. Geolocation will allow you to locate the phone, but data may have already been exfiltrated.

Option C is incorrect. A strong PIN is a good idea, but not as effective as remote wiping.

Option D is incorrect. This only limits how much data could be on the device to be stolen.

23. B. Geofencing sets up geographic boundaries, beyond which a device won't work.

Option A is incorrect. Geolocation provides geographic location, not geofencing.

Options C and D are incorrect because geofencing is not related to WiFi.

24. B. Content management for a mobile device involves limiting what content can be placed on the phone.

Option A is incorrect. Content management is not involved in limiting the amount of data.

Option C is incorrect. In the context of a mobile device, this is not content management.

Option D is incorrect. Digitally signing authorized content could be used in some content management systems, but this is not the best definition of content management.

25. C. The `ipconfig /renew` command will request a new IP from the DHCP server.

Option A is incorrect. There is no `/request` flag for `ipconfig`.

Options B and D are incorrect. Netstat has nothing to do with getting a dynamic IP address. Also `/request` and `-renew` are not `NETSTAT` flags.

26. D. ANT is a proprietary wireless network technology that provides low-power modes and is used in WiFi settings. It has been used in sports-related technologies.

Option A is incorrect. WiFi uses power constantly, whether users connect or not.

Option B is incorrect. Cellular consumes too much power.

Option C is incorrect. The range of Bluetooth is too short.

27. A. Date Execution Prevention (DEP) requires the user to authorize any executable to execute. It should be noted that this is the definition Microsoft used for its functionality. A more technical definition is that Data Execution Prevention is preventing software from accessing restricted memory such as the operating system's memory.

Option B is incorrect. Data Loss Prevention (DLP) is related to preventing exfiltration of data. Most DLP solutions have the capability to control removable medias such as USB devices.

Option C is incorrect. Unified Threat Management (UTM) is the combining of security services such as antivirus, HIDS, log monitoring, firewall, and so forth in a single device.

Option D is incorrect. ANT is a networking technology.

28. D. Transport Layer Security (TLS) is used to encrypt and secure web traffic.

Options A and B are incorrect. L2TP and IPSec are VPN technologies and not appropriate for securing web traffic.

Option C is incorrect. Secure Sockets Layer was the appropriate choice a long time ago, but TLS is the successor to SSL and was released in 1999.

29. A. Heuristic scanning involves scanning for anomalous behavior that might indicate an attack, even if there is no known attack signature.

Option B is incorrect. Signature scanning can only detect known signatures, and that appears to be what the college is using now.

Options C and D are incorrect. Neither is an IDS term.

30. D. Lightweight Directory Access Protocol Secure (LDAPS) would at least mitigate the risk. LDAP is a directory of the network (computers, users, etc.). Securing that would help mitigate network enumeration.

Option A is incorrect. HTTPS is for secure web pages.

Option B is incorrect. TLS will help only if applied to a directory protocol, as it is in LDAPS.

Option C is incorrect. A VPN won't solve this issue.

31. C. FTPS is File Transfer Protocol with SSL/TLS and uses digital certificates to secure file transfer.

Option A is incorrect. File Transfer Protocol is not secure.

Option B is incorrect. SFTP is secure, but it uses SSH for security and does not use digital certificates.

Option D is incorrect. Secure Copy is secure, but it uses SSH for security and does not use digital certificates.

32. C. Secure Real-Time Transport Protocol (SRTP) is used to encrypt and secure RTP. RTP is the protocol for transmitting VoIP.

Option A is incorrect. Session Initiation Protocol is used to initiate a VoIP call but not to send the VoIP data.

Option B is incorrect. TLS is used to secure data, but by itself it cannot secure VoIP.

Option D is incorrect. Secure Shell SSH is for remote terminal connection and is not used in VoIP.

33. B. A screen lock limits access to users who know the code.

Option A is incorrect. While device encryption is common, the screen lock code does not encrypt the device.

Option C is incorrect. Unlike desktop operating systems, mobile devices are not designed to be used by multiple users.

Option D is incorrect. The lock codes for screen locks have no relationship to connecting to WiFi.

34. A. Context-aware authentication does still require a username and password, but in addition to those criteria, it examines the user's location, time of day they are logging in, computer they are logging in from, what they are trying to do, and so forth.

Option B is incorrect. Context-aware authentication still requires a username and password.

Options C and D are incorrect. Context-aware authentication is not about digital certificates or tokens.

35. C. Application management is primarily concerned with ensuring only authorized and approved applications are installed on mobile devices.

Option A is incorrect. Not every app in the iTunes store is appropriate for business use, and the iTunes store only affects Apple devices.

Option B is incorrect. Simply knowing what is installed is not the same thing as ensuring only authorized apps are installed.

Option D is incorrect. Patch management can be a part of application management, but the primary goal is controlling what apps get installed on a device.

36. D. An inline IDS is actually in the traffic line (i.e., on the network segment where traffic is).

Option A is incorrect. An active IDS refers to one that takes action against suspected attack traffic—it has nothing to do with where it is placed.

Option B is incorrect. IPS is another name for active IDS.

Option C is incorrect. Passive refers to whether or not the system acts against suspected traffic, not the location of the IDS.

37. A. Split tunneling allows a mobile user to access dissimilar security domains like a public network (e.g., the Internet) and a local LAN or WAN at the same time.

Option B is incorrect. IPSec is the protocol for establishing and securing a VPN, rather than connecting to different resources. You can use IPSec in either a split or full tunnel.

Option C is incorrect. A full tunnel is a dedicated tunnel to one single target.

Option D is incorrect. TLS is a protocol that can be used for establishing and securing a VPN, rather than connecting to different resources. You can use TLS in either a split or full tunnel.

38. A. A forward proxy is a single location that provides access to a wide range of web sources.

Option B is incorrect. A reverse proxy is usually an internal-facing proxy used as a front end to control and protect access to a server on a private network.

Option C is incorrect. Stateful packet inspection is a type of firewall.

Option D is incorrect. Open proxies are usable by anyone on the Internet.

39. A. This is the term for rummaging through the waste/trash.

Options B and D are incorrect. These terms, while grammatically correct, are simply not the terms used in the industry.

Option C is incorrect. Nothing in this scenario describes social engineering.

40. A. Affinity load balancing ties certain users or groups of users to a specific server so they will be routed to that server if possible.

Option B is incorrect. Binding is not a term used in load balancing.

Option C is incorrect. Yes, load balancing is needed, but the question asks what type of load balancing.

Option D is incorrect. Round-robin simply goes to the next available server.

41. D. Placing the WAPs carefully so as to provide the best coverage for the company, with minimum overlap outside the company, will be the best way to keep those in adjacent offices from attempting to breach the WiFi. When placing WAPs for the best coverage, one needs to focus on signal strength to ensure there is no gaps between WPAs.

Option A is incorrect. Thin versus fat WAP refers to the functionality in the WAP and won't have any effect on the ability of nearby people to breach the WAP.

Option B is incorrect. Geofencing is used to limit the area in which a mobile device can be used.

Option C is incorrect. Securing the admin screen is a great idea and should be done, but it won't address the issue of nearby tenants attempting to breach the WiFi.

42. D. Correlating the events from the servers related to the breach would be the most important issue to address for the SIEM manager.

Option A is incorrect. Event duplication is an issue that needs to be addressed, but it is far less important than correlation.

Option B is incorrect. Time synchronization will be important, but it is either done before an incident, during setup and maintenance of the servers, or after correlation, when correlated events need to have their time synchronized.

Option C is incorrect. Impact assessment is important, but is not part of SIEM management.

43. B. The total number of erroneous reports (i.e., false positives and false negatives) is the biggest concern because this determines effectiveness of the system.

Option A is incorrect. Yes, cost is an issue, but effectiveness is the most important issue.

Option C is incorrect. Yes, cost is an issue, but effectiveness is the most important issue and power consumption is a much less important concern.

Option D is incorrect. Both the management interface and the cost are important but less important than efficacy.

44. A. Access control lists are Cisco's primary recommendation to prevent spoofing on routers. ACLs limit access to the router and its functionality.

Option B is incorrect. A login for accessing a router is often not practical because the router access may be needed when a user is not present to log on.

Option C is incorrect. A network intrusion prevention system is a good idea, but it won't prevent spoofing.

Option D is incorrect. A network intrusion detection system is a good idea, but it won't prevent spoofing.

45. A. A SYN attack is a type of flooding attack that is a denial of service. Flood guards are either stand-alone or, more often, part of a firewall, and they prevent flooding attacks.

Option B is incorrect. DNS poisoning involves inserting fake entries into a DNS server; a flood guard will do nothing to prevent that.

Option C is incorrect. Spoofing a MAC address does not involve any flooding.

Option D is incorrect. Spoofing Address Resolution Protocol is a type of MAC spoofing and does not involve any flooding.

46. A. An application proxy server is often used when the client and the server are incompatible for direct connection with the server.

Option B is incorrect. Network address translation involves translating a private IP address to a public IP address.

Option C is incorrect. Changing the server is a drastic measure. It is assumed that this server is being used for some valid reason.

Option D is incorrect. A protocol analyzer is essentially a packet sniffer.

47. C. Virtual IP load balancing does not take the load of each interface into account and assumes all loads are essentially similar.

Option A is incorrect. This load balancing is not resource intensive.

Option B is incorrect. Most servers do support virtual IP load-balancing.

Option D is incorrect. Windows will also support virtual IP load-balancing.

48. A. If Network Time Protocol (NTP) is disrupted, then the various servers that forward logs to the SIEM might not have the same time. This could lead to events that actually took place at the same time appearing to have occurred at different times.

Option B is incorrect. Event correlation is related to time synchronization, but that is a secondary effect.

Option C is incorrect. NTP issues should not lead to any event duplication.

Option D is incorrect. NTP issues should not lead to events failing to be logged.

49. A. The -n command is used to set the number of ping packets to send—in this case, 6—and -l sets the size—in this case, 100 bytes.

Option A is incorrect. IV attacks are obscure cryptographic attacks on stream ciphers.

Options B, C, and D are all incorrect. This is a ping command, but these options have incorrect flags.

50. B. An insider could send out data as an email attachment.

Option A is incorrect. Portable devices usually connect via USB, which is blocked, and if they don't, they will likely be found on the exit search.

Option C is incorrect. The range of Bluetooth is 10 meters. That makes it ineffective for data exfiltration.

Option D is incorrect. Optical media is a type of portable media.

51. D. Phishing emails are often sent out to masses of people and a spam filter would block at least some of that, thus reducing the phishing email attacks.

Option A is incorrect. Although email encryption is a good idea, it will do nothing to stop phishing.

Option B is incorrect. Hardening all servers is a good security practice, but it has no impact on phishing emails.

Option C is incorrect. Although digitally signing email is a good idea, it cannot stop phishing or even reduce it significantly. It might mitigate phishing emails that claim to come from a company employee, but it won't impact other phishing emails.

52. C. A TLS accelerator is a processor that handles processing, specifically processor-intensive public-key encryption for Transport Layer Security (TLS). This should significantly improve server responsiveness.

Option A is incorrect. Increasing RAM will have only a minimal effect on network responsiveness.

Option B is incorrect. From the question, there is no indication that the servers were not performing fine before TLS implementation, so addressing the TLS issues is the best solution.

Option D is incorrect. Setting up clustering is a rather significant step, and not the first thing that should be considered. Implementation of TLS accelerators is a better option.

53. B. An employee could hide sensitive data in files using steganography and then exfiltrate that data.

Option A is incorrect. Password crackers are a separate type of tool than steganography tools.

Option C is incorrect. Very few steganography tools and methods allow you to hide network traffic.

Option D is incorrect. Although it is possible to hide malware in a file via steganography, this is not the greatest or most common concern.

54. B. The `netstat` command displays all connections, and the -o flag shows the process that owns that connection.

Option A is incorrect. The `netstat -a` command will show listening ports.

Option C is incorrect. The `arp -a` command shows the current address routing protocol entries.

Option D is incorrect. The `arp -g` command is identical to `arp -a`.

55. A. This is an example of a dictionary attack. The attacker uses a list of words that are believed to be likely passwords.

Option B is incorrect. A rainbow table is a precomputed table of hashes.

Option C is incorrect. Brute force tries every possible random combination.

Option D is incorrect. Session hijacking is when the attacker takes over an authenticated session.

56. C. Netcat is a tool widely used by network administrators to establish communication between two machines. Having netcat on a machine could indicate an intruder has compromised that machine and installed netcat as a backdoor, or that the employee is setting up covert communication channels.

Option A is incorrect. Netcat is not a password cracker.

Option B is incorrect. Netcat is not a packet sniffer.

Option D is incorrect. Netcat is not a denial-of-service tool.

57. A. The certificate revocation list designates certificates that have been revoked for some reason. Those certificates should no longer be used. But if the CRL is published only once per week, then a revoked certificate could potentially be used for up to a week after being revoked.

Option B is incorrect. CRLs are not part of the certificate issuing process.

Option C is incorrect. Yes, it would present a possible security issue.

Option D is incorrect. Key generation for certificates is completely separate from CRLs.

58. C. A clear security policy must be created that explains software licensing and the company processes for software licensing. Without clear policies, any other countermeasures will be less effective.

Option A is incorrect. Although software audits are a good idea, meaningful audits can take place only after good policies are in place.

Option B is incorrect. Scanning the network to see what is installed is a good idea, but policies must be established first.

Option D is incorrect. This may, or may not, be a step the company wishes to take. But policies must be established first.

59. B. The false rejection rate (FRR) is the rate at which authentication attempts are rejected when they should have succeeded. When you are getting a high number of authorized individuals being denied access, that is due to an FRR that is too high.

Option A is incorrect. The false acceptance rate (FAR) is the rate at which people who should not be authenticated are. This is certainly a concern but a different concern.

Option C is incorrect. The crossover error rate (CER) is the rate at which FAR and FRR are equal.

Option D is incorrect. Equal error rate (ERR) is another name for CER.

60. D. Unified threat management (UTM) combines multiple security services into one device. It is common for a UTM to have firewall, antivirus, and IDS services all in one device.

Options A, B, and C are incorrect. These are all good devices, but the UTM is a better choice.

61. C. The security concept of implicit deny states that any new access account will by default be denied all access. When a request is made for specific privileges for that account, then the privileges are explicitly applied. This means that by default all privileges are implicitly denied.

Option A is incorrect. Least privileges are what every account should have, but in this scenario the accounts were all given default privileges. The concept of implicit deny is a better answer.

Option B is incorrect. Separation of duties is used to prevent any one person from executing any action that might have significant security ramifications for the company.

Option D is incorrect. It is true that your network is only as secure as its weakest link, but that is not the best description of this scenario.

62. C. Write once, read many (WORM) storage is a type of high-capacity storage wherein once the data is written to the storage, it cannot be edited. It provides both high-capacity storage and secure storage, since the backups cannot be tampered with.

Option A is incorrect. Large-capacity external drives would need to be stored in a secure place, and they can be edited and are thus not secure. You could secure one with encryption, but the question does not mention encrypted drives.

Option B is incorrect. Backup tapes are older technology. Tapes frequently have issues, and data can become irretrievable.

Answer D is incorrect. Backup media should always be stored off-site, but there is the issue that tapes can easily be damaged or corrupted, which is unacceptable for long-term storage.

63. A. An SIEM aggregates logs from multiple servers and devices. It is difficult to review so many logs, and of course issues could occur when Elizabeth is away from the SIEM management console. Having automatic alerts is the best way to be made aware of issues that require Elizabeth's attention.

Option B is incorrect. Logs and events anomalies can be quite large, and having them forwarded to her email is unwieldy and does not solve the problem. Elizabeth will still need to read through them to be aware of any issues that require her attention.

Option C is incorrect. This situation is not optimal.

Option D is incorrect. Reviewing SIEM logs is one way that administrators become aware of issues. So reviewing them only when you are already aware of an issue is not a good use of SIEM.

64. D. Tethering is usually inexpensive, and simply tethering a portable device to a desk makes it difficult to steal the device. No antitheft method is foolproof, but tethering is simple, cost effective, and reasonably effective.

Option A is incorrect. Full-disk encryption (FDE) can be a good idea and will protect the data on the laptop. However, the laptop can still be stolen, the drive wiped, and the laptop reused or sold.

Option B is incorrect. GPS tagging may allow you to locate a stolen laptop, but it is usually more expensive than tethering.

Option C is incorrect. Geofencing just limits where the device will work—it does not prevent theft of the device.

65. A. Full-disk encryption (FDE) is the best way to protect data on any device. In this scenario, the sensitive data on the tablets is the most important concern; therefore, securing that data with FDE is the most important security measure to take.

Option B is incorrect. GPS tagging might be a good idea—it would help locate lost or stolen devices. However, it is less important than FDE.

Option C is incorrect. Geofencing limits where a device can be used, and it does not address the issues presented in this scenario.

Option D is incorrect. Content management is always a good idea. But in this case, it won't address the most important security concern.

66. A. HIDSs/HIPSs and NIDSs/NIPSs each have output that the vendor specifies. But all such devices will output what protocol the traffic was, the source and destination IP addresses, as well as the source and destination port. More information may be provided, but this is the essential basic information all IDSs/IPSs display.

Option B is incorrect. Many of these devices won't display the suspected attack type. The person operating the device should recognize that a flood of SYN packets on a given port is a SYN flood.

Option C is incorrect. Usernames and machine names may or may not be included, but IP addresses will be.

Option D is incorrect. Usernames and machine names may or may not be included, but IP addresses will be.

67. A. The standard items in any firewall log are the source and destination IP address and port of all traffic, the protocol the traffic is using, and whether that traffic was allowed or denied.

Option B is incorrect. Firewall logs record both traffic that is allowed and traffic that is denied.

Option C is incorrect. Many firewalls don't record a reason the traffic was denied, but all record the protocol used.

Option D is incorrect. Firewall logs record both traffic that is allowed and traffic that is denied.

68. A. Since 20 servers send logs to the SIEM, de-duplicating events will be important.

Option B is incorrect. An SIEM is a log aggregation and analysis tool. Log forwarding was established before the incident.

Option C is incorrect. This is certainly something to do at some point, but it won't be the first action.

Option D is incorrect. This is certainly something to do at some point, but it won't be the first action.

69. A. In any IDS (HIDS/HIPS; NIDS/NIPS), the sensors collect data from the network segment they are on and forward that information to the analyzer.

Option B is incorrect. A data source is any source of information for the IDS.

Option C is incorrect. The manager is the interface that a human operator uses to interact with the NIDS/NIPS or HIDS/HIPS.

Option D is incorrect. The analyzer takes data sent to it from the sensors and analyzes the data looking for indicators of an attack.

70. A. An access control list (ACL) has a list of which requestors are allowed access to which resources. Using an IP address to block or allow requests is a common technique.

Option B is incorrect. A network intrusion prevention system (NIPS) is not part of access control.

Option C is incorrect. A network intrusion detection system (HIPS) is not part of access control.

Option D is incorrect. Port blocking can be used to block a port on a router or switch, but it is not part of access control.

71. D. Secure Shell (SSH) uses port 22 and provides a secure, encrypted command-line interface. Telnet uses port 23 and is not secure.

Option A is incorrect. Telnet uses port 23 and is not secure, but ports 20 and 21 are for File Transfer Protocol (FTP).

Option B is incorrect. Ports 20 and 21 are for File Transfer Protocol (FTP). Port 22, SSH, is what you should open.

Option C is incorrect. This is the opposite of the correct answer. You should block 23 and allow port 22.

72. B. A reverse proxy is a type of proxy server that retrieves resources on behalf of a client from one or more servers. The sources appear to the client as if they came from the proxy server. In other words, the entire outside world appears as the proxy server to the client.

Option A is incorrect. A forward proxy server acts as an intermediary for requests from clients seeking resources from other servers.

Option C is incorrect. A transparent proxy is between clients and the Internet, and as the name suggests, the clients are unaware. Often these are co-located with the gateway.

Option D is incorrect. Although firewalls and proxy servers can be co-located, they are two different technologies.

73. C. By giving the tester logins, you are allowing him to conduct a privilege scan (i.e., a scan with some privileges).

Options A and B are incorrect. They describe the level of knowledge the tester is given of the network. A privilege scan cannot be a black-box test, but it could be either white box or gray box.

Option D is incorrect. Although this is grammatically correct, it is not the term used in the industry.

74. C. A network intrusion detection system (NIDS) will detect suspected attacks on a given network segment and notify the administrator. For example, in an anomaly detection, the administrator will be notified if there are any deviation from an expected pattern or behavior.

Option A is incorrect. A host intrusion detection system (HIDS) only detects intrusions for a single host.

Option B is incorrect. A host intrusion prevention system (HIPS) only detects intrusions on a single host, and it blocks suspected intrusions.

Option D is incorrect. A network intrusion prevention system (NIPS) will check the entire network segment, but rather than simply notify the administrator for him or her to take action, the NIPS will block the suspected traffic.

75. C. A network intrusion detection system (NIDS) will detect intrusions across a network segment, but it won't block the possible attacks, thus not disrupting work due to false positives.

Option A is incorrect. A host intrusion detection system (HIDS) will only detect intrusions for a specific host.

Option B is incorrect. A host intrusion prevention system (HIPS) will only detect intrusions for a specific host, and will block them, so it would disrupt work due to false positives.

Option D is incorrect. A network intrusion prevention system (NIPS) will detect intrusions across a network segment, but it will also block them, possibly disrupting workflow.

76. A. Company-Provided Equipment provides the most security because the company owns and provides the equipment to employees. This allows the company to fully control security, such as preventing carrier unlocking, disable recording microphone, prevent WiFi direct and WiFi ad-hoc.

Option B is incorrect. Choose Your Own Device (CYOD) would have the employees choose any device they wish from a set of options selected by the company. But these would still be employee-owned and -controlled devices.

Option C is incorrect. Geotagging simply allows you to locate a device.

Option D is incorrect. Bring Your Own Device (BYOD) allows employees to bring whatever device they have to work. This is a security concern.

77. A. A tunneling mode is the mode wherein IPSec encrypts the entire packet, header, and data. This prevents someone sniffing traffic from gathering metadata about the traffic.

Option B is incorrect. Authentication Header (AH) provides authentication and integrity but no encryption, so it cannot be the most secure mode.

Option C is incorrect. Internet Key Exchange (IKE) is used in setting up security associations in IPSec.

Option D is incorrect. Transport mode encrypts only the data, not the header. This allows metadata about traffic to be sniffed by an attacker. Therefore, this cannot be the most secure mode.

78. D. An active-passive cluster has backup servers that are not handling any workload. They are brought into action if the primary server fails. This means the backup server will not have been subjected to any workload and is effectively a new machine.

Option A is incorrect. An active-active cluster has all servers working, with the load balanced between them. Should a primary server fail, there is some chance the backup might fail in the near future.

Options B and C are incorrect. Round-robin and affinity describe how connections are routed in the cluster, not how failover functions.

79. A. A fat wireless access point (WAP) is one that has all the functionality needed, such as; ability to traffic forwarded between wired interfaces like a layer 2 or layer 3 switch and MAC filtering, and no other servers or devices are required. In this case, since each WAP might have completely different needs, a fat WAP is preferred.

Option B is incorrect. Thin WAPs require some server or device to offload some functionality to. Since each WAP has different needs, this would be difficult to implement with thin WAPs.

Option C is incorrect. A repeater resends a signal.

Option D is incorrect. Full is not a term used in the industry.

80. D. Pretty Good Privacy (PGP) is very appropriate for email security. It provides self-signed certificates for email signing and encrypting. It is also very low cost.

Option A is incorrect. Simple Mail Transfer Protocol Secure (SMTPS) is encrypted, but it is only for sending email, not receiving. It also can be done with S/MIME or PGP.

Option B is incorrect. Secure/Multi-Purpose Internet Mail Extensions (S/MIME) uses X.509 certificates, which are issued by a third party, and this has a cost associated with it.

Option C is incorrect. Internet Message Access Protocol (IMAP) is for receiving email. It does not send email; therefore, IMAP would not provide a full solution.

81. A. Date Execution Prevention (DEP) specifically monitors programs accessing system memory and prevents that. Note that the Microsoft implementation of DEP simply requires the end user to authorize all program execution.

Option B is incorrect. Full-disk encryption (FDE) is a good idea, but it will not prevent running programs from accessing system memory.

Option C is incorrect. Unified threat management (UTM) is the combining of security services such as antivirus, HIDS, log monitoring, firewall, and so forth in a single device.

Option D is incorrect. An intrusion detection system (IDS) monitors traffic on the network, not running programs on a machine.

82. B. Real-time Transport Protocol (RTP) is used to transport VoIP and video signals, but it is not encrypted. Secure Real-time Transport Protocol (SRTP) should be used.

   Option A is incorrect. Session Initiation Protocol (SIP) is used to initiate a VoIP call but not to send the VoIP data.

   Option C is incorrect. The speed is not the issue.

   Option D is incorrect. The speed is not the issue.

83. A. The output shown is from `nslookup`, which is used to interact with the DNS server for your domain.

   Option A is incorrect. The `ipconfig` command will show the network configuration for your network cards.

   Option C is incorrect. The `netstat -a` command will show listening ports.

   Option D is incorrect. The `dig` command is a DNS-related utility, but the output shown is not from `dig`.

84. A. Online Certificate Status Protocol (OCSP) checks the status of a certificate in real time. So when the browser is about to download a certificate, it first gets a real-time update if the certificate is valid or not.

   Option B is incorrect. X.509 is the standard for certificates and does not determine when they are checked for status.

   Option C is incorrect. A certificate revocation list (CRL) does show the status of certificates, but they are not updated in real time.

   Option D is incorrect. The public key infrastructure (PKI) does not determine when certificate status is checked.

85. D. While most people think of content filtering in regard to filtering content you view, it can also be thought of in terms of content that is sent out. Implementing content filtering ensures that the problem of data exfiltration via email will be mitigated.

   Option A is incorrect. Email encryption would actually make it easier to exfiltrate data, since the data would be hidden from any analysis.

   Option B is incorrect. USB blocking won't affect email filtration.

   Option C is incorrect. A network-based intrusion prevention system (NIPS) cannot stop email attachments.

86. D. Encrypting a mobile device is the best way to ensure the data on the device is secure. If the device is stolen or simply misplaced, then the data cannot be retrieved.

   Option A is incorrect. Geofencing limits the operational area of a device. But even a device that is not operating can have data accessed.

   Option B is incorrect. A screen lock is always a good idea; however, that is not as effective as device encryption.

   Option C is incorrect. GPS tagging could be used to locate the device, but it won't prevent data from being copied off the device.

87. A. The `nmap -O` flag indicates that you want to guess the operating system. The `-PT` scan means do a ping with TCP. The `-T1` is a very slow scan.

   Options B, C, and D are all incorrect. The ping scan variations all start with `-P` (`-PT` TCP ping, `-TS SYN` ping, etc.), the `-T` is timing, and the options are T1 (slowest) to T5 (fastest).

88. D. Tcpdump is a widely used packet sniffer, made for Linux but ported to Windows. It works from the shell in Linux (the command line in Windows) and allows the user to dump current network traffic.

Option A is incorrect. Ophcrack is a Windows password-cracking tool.

Option B is incorrect. Nmap is a port scanner, rogue system detection, and network mapping tool.

Option C is incorrect. Wireshark is a network traffic scanner, and wireless scanner but it is for Windows or Macintosh.

89. A. The tracert command is used to trace the route to a target (the equivalent command in Linux is traceroute). The -h command sets the maximum number of hops before giving up.

Option B is incorrect. The image shows a maximum of 10 hops. Without specifying the maximum, tracert will perform 30 hops.

Option C is incorrect. This is not the output of netstat.

Option D is incorrect. This is not the output of nmap.

90. A. Transport Layer Security (TLS) can be used to secure any network communication (HTTP, LDAP, SMTP, etc.) and it uses digital certificates.

Option B is incorrect. Secure Sockets Layer (SSL) is a much older technology that has been replaced by TLS. TLS was first released in 1999.

Option C is incorrect. You could set up an IPSec VPN, but that would have more overhead than TLS, and it would not leverage the existing digital certificate infrastructure.

Option D is incorrect. WPA2 is for security WiFi transmissions.

91. C. Using cloud storage means that data is placed in the cloud, and can be accessed from outside the network. This presents a problem for data loss prevention (DLP) since it provides a convenient way to exfiltrate data from the network.

Option A is incorrect. There is a security hazard for DLP.

Option B is incorrect. Malware is unlikely from a cloud server, but it also is not a DLP concern.

Option D is incorrect. Company security policies apply to any company asset, including cloud storage.

92. D. The DMZ is the best location for a honeypot, if the concern is outside intruders. An intruder is likely to first breach the outer firewall of the DMZ. A honeypot could conceivably catch the intruder there and prevent him or her from going further into the network.

Options A, B, and C are incorrect. Certainly, you can put a honeypot anywhere, but the most important area is in the DMZ.

93. A. When backing up data, if you do not encrypt the data, then it would be possible for anyone to restore the backup and have access to all data you have backed up. Not all backup utilities include data encryption.

Options B and D are incorrect. Both of these are very good ideas and ensure data integrity, but they were not mentioned as one of Sheila's concerns.

Option C is incorrect. Although this is important, it is a feature that exists in all backup utilities.

94. C. Banner grabbing is a process whereby someone connects to a target web server and attempts to gather information, literally grabbing the web services "banner." This is often done by telnetting into the web server. It can also be done with netcat, using an HTTP request.

Option A is incorrect. Passive reconnaissance would not involve active connections to the server.

Option B is incorrect. Although this is active reconnaissance, it is more accurately described as banner grabbing.

Option D is incorrect. This scenario is not describing vulnerability scanning.

95. B. Exploit frameworks are tools that provide a framework for finding vulnerabilities and then attempting to exploit those vulnerabilities. These tools are an important part of network security testing.

Option A is incorrect. A vulnerability scanner would only identify the vulnerabilities; it would not provide a means to use the vulnerability.

Option C is incorrect. Metasploit is a popular exploit framework, but the question asked about the class of tools, not about identifying a specific tool.

Option D is incorrect. Nessus is a well-known vulnerability scanner.

96. D. US DoD data sanitization standard DoD 5220.22-M recommends an average of 7 complete wipes to wipe data. The standard has a matrix wherein you match the sensitivity of the data to a specific number of wipes, but the general rule is 7.

Options A, B, and C are all incorrect. Less than 7 wipes are considered inadequate to prevent data recovery tools from recovering the data.

97. C. Firewalls do block inbound traffic and can be configured to fine-tune that blocking. However, they can and should also be configured to handle outbound traffic. This can prevent data exfiltration and other breaches.

Option A is incorrect. This configuration is missing outbound rules.

Option B is incorrect. It is often a good idea to encrypt some traffic, but not all traffic can or should be encrypted. DNS requests, for example, are not usually encrypted.

Option D is incorrect. Digital certificates can be a very good mechanism for authentication. However, not all traffic can be authenticated with a digital certificate.

98. C. X.509 is the most common standard for digital certificates. It is relatively easy to create your own self-signed certificate. However, if you use a self-signed certificate on a public website, everyone visiting the website will receive a security error message from their browser.

Option A is incorrect. You can encrypt all web traffic, and it is usually done with TLS and X.509 certificates.

Option B is incorrect. PGP certificates are usually for email and not used for websites.

Option D is incorrect. This is not appropriate—he should not be using self-signed certificates.

99. C. Port 442 is used for HTTPS, HTTP encrypted via TLS. Port 22 is used for secure shell (SSH), which is a secure, encrypted command-line interface often used by administrators. Port 80 is for unencrypted HTTP traffic. Port 23 is for telnet, an insecure command-line interface.

Options A, B, and D are incorrect. These are not the proper ports to block or to open.

100. B. Steganography allows you to embed data, messages, or entire files in other files. It is common to use this to embed some identifying mark that would track the owner of the document and perhaps its originating location. Steganography can track confidential documents.

Options A and D are incorrect. Encryption of any type can be used to secure a document but won't help identify a document should it be leaked.

Option C is incorrect. Hashes can be useful in detecting changes to a document but are less useful in identifying documents and their origin.

101. B. Port 465 is for Simple Mail Transfer Protocol Secure (SMTPS). Port 993 is for Internet Message Access Protocol Secure (IMAPS). Port 995 is for Post Office Protocol Secure (POP3S). By allowing these ports you allow encrypted email. Port 25 is for SMTP, unencrypted. Port 110 is for POP3 unencrypted. Ports 143 (or 220) can be used for IMAP unencrypted. By blocking these ports, you prevent unencrypted email traffic.

Options A, C, and D are incorrect. All of these have the wrong port configurations. In fact, option A is the exact opposite of what you would want to implement.

102. A. Each of these firewalls is logging all activity, but the logs are not centralized. This makes it quite difficult to monitor all logs. By integrating with an SIEM, all logs are centralized and Mark can get alerts for issues.

Options B and D are incorrect. A honeypot or honeynet might be a good idea, but neither is the next logical step or part of firewall configuration.

Option C is incorrect. Integrating with Active Directory (AD) may or may not be a good choice for Mark, but it won't improve his firewall configuration.

103. C. In IPSec, tunneling mode encrypts not only the packet data but the header as well. This prevents someone from determining what protocol the traffic is using, the packet sequence number, or other metadata.

Option D is incorrect. Transport mode is the mode wherein IPSec encrypts the data but not the packet header.

Option A is incorrect. Authentication Header is used for integrity and authentication.

Option B is incorrect. ESP (Encapsulating Security Payload) is used for authentication and encryption in IPSec, whether tunneling or transport mode is used.

104. A. If an intrusion detection system is missing attacks (whether it is a NIDS or HIDS) this is a false negative. The IDS is incorrectly identifying traffic as not an attack. John needs to reconfigure to reduce false negatives.

Option B is incorrect. Port blocking is a firewall function.

Option C is incorrect. Stateful packet inspection (SPI) is a method of firewall operations.

Option D is incorrect. When an IDS (or any security device) labels legitimate traffic as an attack, that is called a false positive.

105. D. Remote-access VPNs are used to allow users at diverse locations to remotely access the network via a secure connection. Traveling employees is a typical scenario in which a remote-access VPN would be used.

Option A is incorrect. L2TP is a protocol for VPN and could be used for either site-to-site or remote-access VPNs.

Option B is incorrect. IPSec is a protocol for VPN and could be used for either site-to-site or remote-access VPNs.

Option C is incorrect. A site-to-site VPN is a permanent VPN connection between sites.

106. A. Since employees use the Company-Owned Personally Enabled (COPE) device for personal use, the devices will have the employee's personal information. This can lead to personal and private data being exposed to the company.

Option B is incorrect. Any portable device has the chance of being used for data exfiltration, but COPE is no more susceptible than other configurations such as BYOD.

Option C is incorrect. In fact, the opposite is true. It is less likely that devices will be improperly configured because the company controls configuration.

Option D is incorrect. There are issues with this option.

107. B. Application management is primarily concerned with ensuring only authorized and approved applications are installed on mobile devices. This would be the next logical step to perform. Control of which applications are allowed on the device is central to basic security.

Option A is incorrect. Geofencing may or may not even be appropriate for every company.

Option C is incorrect. Geolocation is useful to locating stolen devices, but it is not the next step to take in security.

Option D is incorrect. Remote wipe can be useful should a device be lost or stolen, but it is not the next step to take in security.

108. A. Containerization establishes a secure, isolated area of the device that is also encrypted. It separates data and applications in the container from the rest of the phone. This would be the best way to segregate company data from personal data on BYOD.

Option B is incorrect. Screen locks are fundamental to mobile device security, but they won't address this concern.

Option C is incorrect. SQL FDE is a good idea, but it does not segregate company from personal data.

Option D is incorrect. Biometrics is an excellent idea for authentication but will do nothing to address the issue in this scenario.

109. A. The term *sideloading* in general means to transfer data between two devices—more specifically, with mobile devices. It most often is associated with using the sideloading to install Android apps from places other than Google Play.

Option B is incorrect. The loading is done via some device, not via WiFi.

Option C is incorrect. The process of sideloading does not bypass the screen lock.

Option D is incorrect. Sideloading could get malware on the device, but the process of sideloading involves active participation from the user.

110. C. Whether the device is Company-Owned and Personally Enabled (COPE) or Bring Your Own Device (BYOD), any mobile device can be a USB On-the-Go (OTG) device. This means the device itself serves as a mass storage USB drive, and data can be exfiltrated on the device. This is a concern for data loss prevention (DLP).

Options A and B are incorrect. Any device can be USB OTG.

Option D is incorrect. You need not jailbreak a phone or tablet in order to use it as USB OTG.

111. B. Domain Name System Security Extensions (DNSSEC) is a suite of extensions that add security to the DNS protocol by enabling DNS responses to be validated. With DNSSEC, the DNS protocol is much less susceptible to certain types of attacks, particularly DNS spoofing attacks.

Option A is incorrect. IPSec is used for VPNs and will not mitigate DNS poisoning.

Option C is incorrect. L2TP is used for VPNs and will not mitigate DNS poisoning.

Option D is incorrect. TLS can be used to encrypt transmissions over the Internet, but it is not helpful in mitigating DNS poisoning.

112. D. Kerberos uses encrypted tickets with a time limit. Service tickets are usually limited to less than 5 minutes. The Key Distribution Center, client, and services all need to have time synchronized. If Network Time Protocol (NTP) is not functioning, it is possible that legitimate tickets may appear to have expired.

Options A, B, and C are incorrect. None of these require time synchronization.

113. C. Network Address Allocation is the process of allocating network addresses. In a DHCP environment, this can be done to limit how many IP addresses are requested from a single network segment. For example, if a network segment has only 30 nodes, then no more than 30 addresses can be allocated to that segment. This would mitigate DHCP starvation.

Option A is incorrect. Encrypting communications is often a good idea, but it won't mitigate this issue.

Option B is incorrect. Full-disk encryption (FDE) is often a good idea but won't mitigate this issue.

Option D is incorrect. Just like TLS, IPSec can often be a good answer for securing communications. But securing the transmission is not the issue in this case.

114. D. This is really about network address allocation. Classless Inter-Domain Routing (CIDR) notation provides the number of bits that are masked for the network. Remaining bits are used for nodes. To determine the size of a subnet based in CIDR notation (/N), the formula is simple: $[2 \wedge (32 - N)] - 2$. In this case, that is $[2 \wedge (32 - 26)] - 2$ or $(2 \wedge 6) - 2$, or $64 - 2$, or 62 nodes.

Options A, B, and C are all incorrect. They all yield subnets that are too small (/27 and /29) or are needlessly large (/24)>.

115. B. Infrastructure as a Service (IaaS) uses a third-party service and templates to provide the network infrastructure in a virtualized manner, but the client company still administers the network. By moving to a virtualized solution, administration is very centralized. By using IaaS, Lydia will reduce costs, but she will still maintain direct control.

Option A is incorrect. Outsourcing will remove control of the network to a third party.

Option C is incorrect. Platform as a Service (PaaS) can only provide operating systems.

Option D is incorrect. Open source won't help centralized administration, and the total cost of ownership may not actually be less.

116. C. Terminal Access Controller Access Control System+ (TACACS+) is a remote access protocol. It uses TCP, which is a reliable transport protocol, and it fully encrypts the messages. TACACS+ also supports a range of network protocols.

Option A is incorrect. Remote Authentication Dial-In User Service (RADIUS) uses UDP, which is not a reliable transport protocol and does not support many networking protocols.

Option B is incorrect. Diameter (not an acronym) does support TCP, but it does not fully encrypt the messages.

Option D is incorrect. IPSec is a VPN protocol, not a remote access and authentication protocol.

117. C. Voice over IP (VoIP) is accomplished with at least two protocols. Session Initiation Protocol (SIP) is used to establish the call. Real-time Transport Protocol (RTP) is used to send the actual data. These two, at a minimum, must be allowed through the firewall. If there are secure calls, the Secure Real-time Transport Protocol (SRTP) would also need to be allowed.

Option A is incorrect. RADIUS is a remote authentication protocol and Simple Network Management Protocol (SNMP) is used to manage the network.

Option B is incorrect. TCP and UDP are types of protocol; all network protocols are either TCP or UDP.

Option D is incorrect. SIP is needed, but RADIUS is a remote authentication protocol.

118. D. Classless Inter-Domain Routing (CIDR) notation provides the number of bits that are masked for the network. Remaining bits are used for nodes. To determine the size of a subnet based in CIDR notation (/N), the formula is simple: $[2 \wedge (32 - N)] - 2$. In this case, that is $[2 \wedge (32 - 29)] - 2$, or $(2 \wedge 3) - 2$, or $8 - 2$, or 6 nodes.

Options A, B, and C are incorrect. The most common wrong answer is C, which would be the result if you forgot to subtract 2 at the end of the calculation.

119. C. With application blacklisting, any application that is not on the blacklist is allowed. Since it is impossible to know all the malicious applications that exist in the world, this means that at least some malicious applications would not be blocked. A better approach is application whitelisting. In whitelisting, only those applications on the list can be installed.

Option A is incorrect. Blacklisting will block only a finite number of malicious applications.

Option B is incorrect. This approach won't block any legitimate applications. In fact, it won't block all malicious applications.

Option D is incorrect. This should not have a deleterious effect on productivity.

120. A. Patch management software is used to roll out patches to the network. Such software will also provide reports as to what machines are patched, which ones still have not been patched, and any issues with applying a patch.

Option B is incorrect. Automatic updates should not be used on corporate networks. It is always possible that a particular update will interfere with some mission-critical application in the corporation. Instead patches are tested and then rolled out to the network.

Option C is incorrect. The issue is to get the unpatched systems patched.

Option D is incorrect. Scanning is possible but not as good a solution as patch management.

121. C. Unified Threat Management (UTM) combines multiple security services into one device. In this example, we have blocking (firewall), detection (IDS), and anti-malware all in one device.

Option A is incorrect. An IDS would only detect possible intrusions. It would not accomplish all the goals of the question.

Option B is incorrect. A firewall would block incoming traffic, but would not accomplish the other goals in the question.

Option D is incorrect. An SIEM is used for log aggregation and would not accomplish any of the goals of the question.

122. B. Data loss prevention (DLP) is a broad term encapsulating a family of technologies and policies designed to prevent data from being lost. Limiting the use of unapproved USB devices is one example of DLP.

Option A is incorrect. An intrusion detection system (IDS) would not address this issue.

Option C is incorrect. Content filtering limits content users can access, such as via a web browser. This won't stop them from copying documents to unapproved USB devices.

Option D is incorrect. A network intrusion prevention system (NIPS) won't stop the copying of documents to a USB.

123.

Firewall	C
HIDS	A
SIEM	B
NIDS	D

124. C. When a device is jailbroken—particularly an iOS device—the device owner can then install any application they wish onto the device. This can lead to unauthorized, and potentially malicious, applications being installed.

Option A is incorrect. Jailbroken devices can still be patched.

Option B is incorrect. Full disk encryption will still function on jailbroken devices.

Option D is incorrect. Data can be exfiltrated on mobile devices, whether or not the device is jailbroken.

125. B. Over-the-air (OTA) updates are accomplished wirelessly. This can be done over a cellular network, wherever the device is. Using OTA updates for the mobile devices is the most efficient solution.

Option A is incorrect. This would work but would interrupt the employees' normal work schedules and be inefficient.

Option C is incorrect. Moving from Company-Owned and Personally Enabled to Bring Your Own Device (BYOD) would actually make the situation worse, but doing so would absolve the company of the responsibility of managing updates.

Option D is incorrect. Policies require a mechanism for implementation. OTA is such a mechanism.

126. A. Remote Authentication Dial-In User Service (RADIUS) is an older authentication and access control protocol, but it uses UDP. The other options mentioned do not use UDP.

Options B and C are incorrect. Both Diameter and TACACS+ are newer protocols, but both use TCP.

Option D is incorrect. IPSec is a VPN protocol, not a remote authentication and access control protocol.

127. C. Employees using tethering can be a significant security issue. However, none of the technological solutions listed would solve it. Therefore, implementing (and enforcing) a clear policy against tethering is the only viable option.

Option A is incorrect. She is not using the company wireless; she is making her phone into a WAP (wireless access point).

Option B is incorrect. A web application firewall (WAF) protects the web server; it does nothing to limit outgoing web traffic.

Option D is incorrect. A host intrusion prevention system (HIPS) would have a chance of addressing this issue only if it was installed on the machine being tethered.

128. A. Many banks already implement a policy of sending a customer an SMS message with an authentication code anytime someone tries to log into the bank website from an unknown location. This provides a second communications channel for authenticating the customer.

Option B is incorrect. All bank websites are already encrypted with TLS, and that does not address this issue.

Option C is incorrect. Strong passwords are an excellent idea, but it won't address this issue.

Option D is incorrect. This sort of restriction would seriously impede usability of the bank website.

129. A. Although many things can occur from running custom firmware on a device, the most likely issue is that unauthorized software can be installed. This software could be malicious software.

Options B and C are incorrect. It is certainly possible that these could occur, but they are not the primary issues.

Option D is incorrect. It is a security issue.

130. B. Network Access Control (NAC) allows the network to enforce a level of host health checks on devices before allowing it to connect. With agent NAC, a software agent is installed on any device that wishes to connect to the network. That agent can do a much more thorough systems health check of the BYOD.

Option A is incorrect. Agentless NAC can be useful but is less effective than agent NAC.

Options C and D are incorrect. Stronger authentication is a good security measure but won't address the issue of scanning BYOD to ensure compliance with security rules.

131. C. Network Access Control (NAC) performs a systems health check on devise and validates that the device meets minimum security standards before allowing it to connect. An agent-based NAC is more thorough in scanning the device. However, that leaves an agent on the visitor's device. A dissolvable agent will delete after a period of time.

Option A is incorrect. A permanent NAC would have an impact on visitors' devices.

Option B is incorrect. Agentless NAC would have less impact, and would also be less thorough and thus less secure.

Option D is incorrect. Company-Owned Personally Enabled (COPE) devices are not possible for guests.

132. C. File integrity checkers work by storing hashes of various files. At any time, the administrator can use the file integrity checker to compare the stored hash to the hash of the "live" file on the network. This will detect whether any changes have been made to the file.

Option A is incorrect. Network Access Control (NAC) is used to ensure devices connecting to the network meet minimum security standards.

Option B is incorrect. A network intrusion detection system (NIDS) won't be able to tell you whether files have been altered.

Option D is incorrect. A vulnerability scanner only scans for known vulnerabilities.

133. B. An out-of-band network intrusion detection system (NIDS) places the management portion on a different network segment, making detection of the NIDS more difficult.

Option A is incorrect. A hybrid NIDS combines a network node IDS with a host IDS.

Option C is incorrect. A network intrusion prevention system (NIPS) is usually quite detectable, by its very nature. By blocking offending traffic, it will absolutely be noticed.

Option D is incorrect. A network node IDS (NNIDS) uses a network approach, but it delegates the IDS functions to individual hosts.

134. B. An SSL decryptor is used to decrypt SSL/TLS transmission. The decryptor must have the appropriate encryption keys and certificate to accomplish this. It is a good way for a company to monitor outbound SSL/TLS traffic. The traffic is first decrypted before the network gateway, and then re-encrypted to leave the network. This allows outbound traffic to be analyzed.

Options A and C are incorrect. NIDS and NIPS cannot see the content of encrypted traffic.

Option D is incorrect. An SSL accelerator is used to offload some of the processing for establishing an SSL/TLS tunnel.

135. A, C. One for the gateway and one for the call agent. From the call agent to the gateway is using UDP port 2427, and if it's from the gateway to the call agent, it uses UDP port 2727.

Options B and D are incorrect. 1707 is L2TP, and 1727 is PPTP.

136. IPSec   C

      WPA2   A

      SSH   D

      SIP   B

137. C. When you must support machines that cannot connect to newer, more secure WiFi protocols, then put those machines on a separate WiFi network. That won't prevent them from being breached, but it will prevent that breach from exposing your entire network.

Option A is incorrect. A VLAN is not applicable to this scenario.

Option B is incorrect. Denying wireless access is not necessary.

Option D is incorrect. Although encrypting network traffic is often a good idea, it won't solve this problem.

138. A. Secure File Transfer Protocol (SFTP) is a protocol based on Secure Shell, and it provides directory listing, remote file deletion, and other file management abilities. It is also secure.

Option B is incorrect. Secure Shell (SSH) provides a secure terminal connection.

Option C is incorrect. Secure Copy (SCP) is based on SSH and does allow file transfer. But it does not support other file management capabilities.

Option D is incorrect. IPSec is a VPN protocol.

139. A. Third-party app stores are stores run by someone other than the vendor. They don't have restrictions on what apps can be placed in them. This can lead to malicious apps being in the store. By only using vendor stores (iTunes, Google Play, etc.), you can be assured that the apps have been scanned for malware.

Option B is incorrect. Vulnerability scanning is an automated process that checks for the presence of known vulnerabilities.

Options C and D are incorrect. These both refer to how much information about the network the tester is given. In both black-box and white-box tests, there will still be an initial exploit.

140. C. The best way to see if passwords are crackable is to attempt to crack them. This is done by using one or more well-known and reliable password crackers. If you are able to crack your passwords, that demonstrates they are not adequate.

Option A is incorrect. Many vulnerability scanners don't check passwords, and those that do only check rudimentary requirements.

Option B is incorrect. The concern is that the policies may not be adequate. So, an audit will only show if people are complying with the policy, not whether the policy itself is adequate.

Option D is incorrect. Passwords are usually stored as a hash. This does not prevent tools, like rainbow tables, from cracking passwords.

141. B. Port 25 is for Simple Mail Transfer Protocol (SMTP), which is used to send email. Port 110 is for Post Office Protocol (POP) version 3, which is used to receive email. These two ports are used for the unencrypted versions of these email protocols. So if these are being used, then you will see unencrypted email credentials. The username and password will be sent in clear text.

Option A is incorrect. Ports 80 and 443 are for website traffic.

Option C is incorrect. Ports 20 and 21 are for FTP traffic.

Option D is incorrect. Digital certificates would indicate encrypted data, and ports 25 and 110 are not encrypted.

142. B. Secure Shell (SSH) uses port 22. If there was a breach that allowed external access to the SSH server, there will be traffic on port 22.

Option A is incorrect. Port 23 is for telnet, not SSH.

Option C is incorrect. SSH is encrypted, so you would not see clear-text credentials.

Option D is incorrect. This breach would not cause malformed credentials.

143. B. Push notifications are used to send out updates when they are ready. With push notifications, you do not wait for the user to check for an update; the update is sent as soon as it is ready.

Option A is incorrect. Firmware Over-the-Air (OTA) updates are a good idea, but this question is about custom apps, not firmware.

Option C is incorrect. This issue in this question is not if updates are being scheduled but if they are being applied.

Option D is incorrect. A policy against custom firmware is a good security policy. However, this question is about custom apps, not firmware.

144. D. Rooting is a process that allows you to attain root access to the Android operating system code. Rooting allows the user to do virtually anything, including modify the software code on the device or install other software that normally would be blocked.

Option A is incorrect. Blocking third-party apps is a good idea but does not address the administrative access issue.

Option B is incorrect. Jailbreaking is the term used for iOS devices, not Android.

Option C is incorrect. You would first need to get administrative access in order to install custom firmware.

145. A. Biometrics, type III authentication, are very robust. Biometrics are based on a biological part of the authorized user, so they are very difficult to fake and impossible for the user to lose.

Option B is incorrect. Screen locks are necessary, but they are only a rudimentary security measure.

Option C is incorrect. In combination with the username and password, context-aware authentication examines the user's location, the time of day the user is logging in, the computer that the user is logging in from, what the user is trying to do, the context, and so forth. This is a very good authentication method, but biometrics can still be more effective and more user-friendly.

Option D is incorrect. Storage segmentation is very good for separating user personal data from company data, but it won't address unauthorized access.

146. C. Infrared uses a wavelength of light that is not visible to humans. Since it is light, it is not susceptible to EMI. It can be used over most distances, provided there is a line of sight. The disadvantage is that any break in the line of sight breaks communication.

Option A is incorrect. Bluetooth has a range of only 10 meters.

Option B is incorrect. WiFi is susceptible to EMI.

Option D is incorrect. RF is susceptible to EMI.

147. D. The -sW flag for Windows is a Windows scan. The -sT is a TCP full-connect scan. Those are not at all stealthy, but they are very accurate. The -s0 is a protocol scan that will check all protocols. The -T determines timing. Since stealth is not important, simply scan as fast as you wish using -T5.

Option A is incorrect. The -sL just lists targets, and the /24 would scan the entire subnet, not just the target.

Option B is incorrect. The -T1 would be very slow but stealthy. And this command lacks the -s0 protocol scan.

Option C is incorrect. This scan lacks the -s0 protocol scan and scans the entire subnet needlessly.

148. B. The arp -a command displays the Address Resolution Protocol routing table. That is what is shown in the figure.

Options A and D are incorrect. The netstat command lists the current network connections.

Option C is incorrect. The arp -s command adds a host to the Address Resolution Protocol routing table.

149. A. Blacklisting blocks any sites or content specifically on the blacklist. However, it is impossible to list every inappropriate site on the Internet, so some are not going to be listed and thus are accessible.

Option B is incorrect. You could argue that this issue is due to misconfiguration, but that is most likely cause.

Option C is incorrect. The proxy server as a whole is not the issue. It is the content filtering that is at issue.

Option D is incorrect. While this is possible, it is not the most likely explanation.

150. C. Metasploit is a widely used exploit framework. It provides a complete suite of tools that allow you to scan targets, locate vulnerabilities, and then attempt to exploit those vulnerabilities.

Options A, B, and D are incorrect. Although each of these describes aspects of Metasploit, they are incomplete definitions.

151. B. Configuration compliance scanning solutions take the configuration settings that the administrator provides and scans targeted devices and computers to see whether they comply. This is an effective method for checking compliance.

Options A, C, and D are all incorrect. Each of these would uncover at least some configuration compliance issues but would be less effective and/or more cumbersome than configuration compliance scanning.

Chapter 3: Architecture and Design

1. **A.** The correct answer is ISO 27002. ISO 27002 is an international standard for implementing and maintaining information security systems.

   Option B is incorrect. ISO 27017 is an international standard for cloud security.

   Option C is incorrect. NIST 800-12 is a general security standard and it is a U.S. standard, not an international one.

   Option D is incorrect. NIST 800-14 is a standard for policy development, and it is a U.S. standard, not an international one.

2. **A.** The correct answer is the Open Web Application Security Project. It is the de facto standard for web application security.

   Option B is incorrect. The North American Electric Reliability Corporation is concerned with electrical power plant security.

   Option C is incorrect. The National Institute of Standards does not, as of this writing, publish web application standards.

   Option D is incorrect. ISA/IEC standards are for securing industrial automation and control systems (IACSs).

3. **B.** Vendor diversity gives two security benefits. The first is that there is not a single point of failure should one vendor cease operations. The second benefit is that each vendor has a specific methodology and algorithms used for detecting malware. If you use the same vendor at all points where you need malware detection, any flaw or weakness in that vendor's methodology will persist across the network.

   Option A is incorrect. Using a single vendor means that any weakness in that vendor's methodology permeates the entire network.

   Option C is incorrect. Vendor forking is not a term in the industry.

   Option D is incorrect. This is not a neutral act. Vendor diversity improves security.

4. **D.** Control diversity means utilizing different controls to mitigate the same threat. For malware, the use of technical controls, such as anti-malware, is critical. But it is also important to have administrative controls, such as good policies, and to ensure employees are properly trained.

   Option A is incorrect. This approach ignores training employees. Policies are only useful if employees are properly trained.

   Option B is incorrect. This approach uses only one type of control: technical controls.

   Option C is incorrect. This approach ignores training employees. Policies are useful only if employees are properly trained. Furthermore, website whitelisting can be beneficial but leaves many websites unchecked, each of which could be hosting malware.

5. A. The demilitarized zone (DMZ) is a zone between an outer firewall and an inner firewall. It is specifically designed as a place to locate public-facing servers. The outer firewall is more permissive, thus allowing public access to the servers in the DMZ. However, the inner firewall is more secure, thus preventing outside access to the corporate network.

Option B is incorrect. An intranet is for internal web pages.

Option C is incorrect. Guest networks provide network access, often wireless, to guests. This is not an appropriate place for any server.

Option D is incorrect. An extranet is a scenario wherein external partners are allowed access to limited portions of the company network.

6. B. Air gapping refers to the server not being on a network. This means literally that there is "air" between the server and the network. This prevents malware from infecting the backup server.

Options A and C are incorrect. A separate VLAN or physical network segment can enhance security but is not as effective as air gapping.

Option D is incorrect. A honeynet is a good security measure, but it won't provide the best protection against malware.

7. C. The first step in security is hardening the operating system, and one of the most elementary aspects of that is turning off unneeded services. This is true regardless of the operating system.

Options A, B, and D are incorrect. Each of these is a good security measure and should be implemented. However, none of these are as fundamental as turning off unneeded services and therefore would not be done first.

8. C. Administrative controls are policies and processes designed to mitigate some threat. The use of policies that govern the opening of email attachments and the downloading of files is an administrative control for malware.

Options A, B, and D are incorrect. Each of these are good steps to take, but they are all technical controls, not administrative ones.

9. A. A guest network is separate from your production network; therefore, even if there is some breach of that network, it won't affect your production network. It is a common security practice to establish a guest network so that guests can access the Internet, without providing them with access to the corporate network resources.

Option B is incorrect. A DMZ is used to locate public-facing servers such as web servers.

Option C is incorrect. An intranet consists of internal web-based resources for employees.

Option D is incorrect. This would provide nonemployees with access to the corporate network.

10. A. Full disk encryption fully encrypts the hard drive on a computer. This is an effective method for ensuring the security of data on a computer.

Option B is incorrect. Trusted platform modules are crypto-processors and won't affect this problem.

Option C is incorrect. Software-defined networking is virtualized networking and won't affect this problem.

Option D is incorrect. Demilitarized zones are used to segment a network and won't affect this problem.

11. A. A VPN concentrator is a hardware device used to create remote access VPNs. The concentrator creates encrypted tunnel sessions between hosts, and many use two-factor authentication for additional security.

Option B is incorrect. SSL accelerators are a method of offloading processor-intensive public-key encryption for Transport Layer Security (TLS) and Secure Sockets Layer (SSL) to a hardware accelerator.

Option C is incorrect. A demilitarized zone is a place to locate public-facing servers.

Option D is incorrect. Guest networks provide nonemployees with Internet access.

12. B. If a system is infected with malware, the malware will operate with the privileges of the current user. If you use nonadministrative accounts, with least privileges, then the malware won't be able to access administrative functionality.

Options A, C, and D are all incorrect. These are all good security measures, but they won't address the issue of malware accessing administrative functionality.

13. B. The network operating system is determined by the operating system running on a domain controller. A network could be mostly Windows, but as long as the domain controller is Unix, the network operating system is Unix.

Options A, C, and D are all correct. These items do not determine the network operating system.

14. A. A Type I hypervisor is also known as a bare-metal hypervisor. It installs directly onto hardware and does not require an operating system to be installed first.

Options B, C, and D are all incorrect. Type I hypervisors do not require a preinstalled operating system.

15. D. ISO 27017 is an international standard for cloud security.

Option A is incorrect. NIST 800-14 describes common security principles that should be addressed within security policies.

Option B is incorrect. NIST 800-53 organizes security measures into families of controls, such as risk assessment, access control, incident response, and others.

Option D is incorrect. ISO 27002 recommends best practices for initiating, implementing, and maintaining information security management systems (ISMSs).

16. B. A kiosk computer must be limited to only those functions that are required. It is important to remove or disable any unnecessary functions, and to have the system logged in with the least privileges necessary for the kiosk functionality.

Option A is incorrect. Although this is always a good idea, it is not the most important issue for a kiosk computer.

Option C is incorrect. Yes, antivirus is important. However, if this machine is locked down so that it only performs the specified functions, it is unlikely to get a virus.

Option D is incorrect. A host-based firewall is not even absolutely necessary in this scenario, and it is certainly less important that limiting the computer's functionality.

17. A. The correct answer is to disable WiFi if it is not absolutely needed. Many peripheral devices are WiFi enabled. If you don't require this functionality, then disabling it is a very basic and essential security measure you can take. For example, WiFi enabled MiroSD cards is vulnerable to attacks.

Option B is incorrect. Very few peripheral devices will even have a BIOS.

Option C is incorrect. Encryption may be warranted for some specific peripherals, but many don't have storage that can be encrypted, and this would not be the first step one takes.

Option D is incorrect. Many peripherals don't have a hard drive to install antivirus on.

18. A. A DMZ provides limited access to public facing servers, for outside users, but blocks outside users from accessing systems inside the LAN. It is a common practice to place web servers in the DMZ.

Option B is incorrect. A VLAN is most often used to segment the internal network.

Option C is incorrect. Routers direct traffic based on IP address.

Option D is incorrect. A guest network allows internal users who are not employees to get access to the Internet.

19. B. Physically portioning your network is the physical equivalent of a VLAN. A VLAN is designed to emulate physical partitioning.

Option A is incorrect. Perimeter security does not segment the network.

Option C is incorrect. Security zones are useful, but don't, by themselves, segment a network. Often a network is segmented, using physical partitions or VLAN, to create security zones.

Option D is incorrect. A firewall is meant to block certain traffic, not to segment the network.

20. D. Honeypots are designed to attract a hacker by appearing to be security holes that are ripe and ready for exploitation. A honeynet is a network honeypot. This security technique is used to observe hackers in action while not exposing vital network resources.

Option A is incorrect. Active detection is not a term used in the industry.

Option B is incorrect. False subnet is not a term used in the industry.

Option C is incorrect. An intrusion detection system is used to detect activity that could indicate an intrusion or attack.

21. A. Nonessential protocols provide additional areas for attack. The fact that all protocols have weaknesses would be sufficient to eliminate nonessential protocols. Those nonessential protocols' ports provide possible avenues of attack. You should always follow the principle of least privilege.

Option B is incorrect. Any port can be secured. This is an example of security control.

Option C is incorrect. It is not the case that specific ports are less secure. But every port that is open provides a possible mode of entry into a system.

Option D is incorrect. There is no additional effort to secure a port that is nonessential.

22. B. A stateful inspection firewall examines the content and context of each packet it encounters. This means that an SPI firewall understands the preceding packets that came from the same IP address. This makes certain attacks, like a SYN flood, almost impossible.

Option A is incorrect. Packet filtering firewalls examine each packet, but not the context.

Option C is incorrect. Application layer firewalls can use SPI or simple packet filtering, but their primary role is to examine application-specific issues. A classic example is a web application firewall.

Option D is incorrect. A gateway firewall is simply a firewall at the network gateway. This does not tell us whether it is packet filtering or SPI.

23. A. Whitelists are lists of approved software. Only if software appears on the whitelist can it be installed.

Option B is incorrect. Blacklisting blocks specific applications, but it cannot account for every possible malicious application.

Option C is incorrect. Access control lists determine who can access a resource.

Option D is incorrect. A host intrusion detection system (HIDS) does not prevent software from being installed.

24. B. A demilitarized zone (DMZ) is a separate subnet coming off the separate router interface. Public traffic may be allowed to pass from the external public interface to the DMZ, but it won't be allowed to pass to the interface that connects to the internal private network.

Option A is incorrect. A guest network provides visitors with internet access.

Option C is incorrect. An intranet consists of internal web resources. Frequently companies put up web pages that are accessible only from within the network for items like human resources notifications, requesting vacation, and so forth.

Option D is incorrect. A VLAN is used to segment your internal network.

25. A. Filters prevent unauthorized packets from entering or leaving a network. Packet filters are a type of firewall that blocks specified port traffic.

Options B and C are incorrect. A packet filter will allow some packets to enter and will block others. The same goes for exiting packets: some will be allowed and others will be blocked, based on the rules implemented in the firewall.

Option D is incorrect. Packet filtering does nothing to eliminate collisions in the network.

26. C. WiFi Protected Access 2 (WPA2) was intended to provide security that's equivalent to that on a wired network, and it implements elements of the 802.11i standard.

Option A is incorrect. A WAP is a wireless access point.

Option B is incorrect. A WPA is not as secure as WPA2.

Option D is incorrect. WEP is the oldest, and least secure, wireless security protocol.

27. A. An IV attack is usually associated with the WEP wireless protocol. This is because WEP uses the RC4 stream cipher with an initialization vector. However, WEP improperly implements RC4 and reuses its IVs (an IV should only be used once, then discarded), making it vulnerable to IV attacks.

Option B is incorrect. A WAP is a wireless access point, not a protocol.

Option C is incorrect. WPA does not use an IV; it uses TKIP.

Option D is incorrect. WPA2 does not use an IV; it uses AES with CBC and a MAC.

28. C. A test server should be identical to the production server. This can be used for functional testing as well as security testing, prior to deploying the application.

Option A is incorrect. The production server is the live server.

Option B is incorrect. A development server would be one the programmers use during development of a web application.

Option D is incorrect. Predeployment server is not a term used in the industry.

29. B. Kernel integrity subsystems are a form of integrity measurement used to detect whether files have been accidentally or maliciously altered, both remotely and locally; to appraise a file's measurement against a "good" value stored as an extended attribute; and to enforce local file integrity. These goals are complementary to Mandatory Access Control (MAC) protections provided by Linux Security Modules.

Option A is incorrect. Antivirus software is used to detect malware.

Option C is incorrect. Kernel integrity subsystems cannot detect what programs have been installed.

Option D is incorrect. Kernel integrity systems don't detect changes to user accounts.

30. C. BIOS password management is the most basic security measure for the BIOS. Without this fundamental step, any other steps will be far less effective.

Options A and B are incorrect. NIST 800-155 does list both of these as BIOS integrity measures, but they are not the most fundamental measures—passwords are.

Option D is incorrect. Backing up the BIOS is not a common security measure, and it certainly would not be the most fundamental step.

31. A. The correct answer is NIST 800-82. Special Publication 800-82, Revision 2, "Guide to Industrial Control System (ICS) Security," is specific to industrial control systems. Industrial systems include SCADA (Supervisor Control And Data Acquisition) and PLCs (primary logic controllers).

Option B is incorrect. PCI-DSS is a standard for credit card security.

Option C is incorrect. NIST 800-30 is the U.S. standard for conducting risk assessments.

Option D is incorrect. This standard recommends best practices for initiating, implementing, and maintaining information security management systems (ISMSs).

32. B. Wearable devices have storage and thus can be used to bring in files to a network, or to exfiltrate data from the network.

Option A is incorrect. Distractions are not a security concern, though they may be a management issue.

Options C and D are incorrect. Although either of these might be appropriate security concerns to mitigate, they are not the most significant concern.

33. B. A heating, ventilation, and air conditioning system will affect availability. By maintaining temperature and humidity, the servers in the datacenter are less likely to crash and thus be more available.

    Option A is incorrect. HVACs have no effect on data confidentiality.

    Option C is incorrect. HVACs are not fire suppression systems.

    Option D is incorrect. HVACs are not monitoring systems.

34. B. Maria should implement ongoing auditing of the account usage on the SCADA system. This will provide a warning that someone's account is being used when they are not actually using it.

    Option A is incorrect. Host based antivirus is almost never a bad idea. But this scenario did not indicate that the compromise was due to malware, so anti-malware may not address the threat.

    Option C is incorrect. Since the engineer has access to the SCADA system, a NIPS is unlikely to block him from accessing the system.

    Option D is incorrect. Full disk encryption will not mitigate this threat.

35. B. The correct answer is virtualization. By virtualizing the servers Lucy can administer them all in a single location, and it is very easy to set up a new virtual server, should it be needed.

    Option A is incorrect. A cluster won't make installing a new server any more streamlined.

    Options C and D are incorrect. Segmenting the servers, such as with a VLAN or subnet, won't address the issues presented in this question.

36. A. A hardware security module (HSM) is the most secure way to store private keys for the e-commerce server. An HSM is a physical device that safeguards and manages digital keys.

    Option B is incorrect. Full disk encryption will protect the data on the e-commerce server, but it won't help store the key. It is also difficult to fully encrypt the e-commerce server drive, since the drive will need to be in use for the e-commerce to function.

    Option C is incorrect. A self-encrypting drive (SED) is just an automatic full disk encryption.

    Option D is incorrect. Software-defined networking won't address the issues in this scenario.

37. B. The correct answer is to use a sandboxed environment to test the malware and determine its complete functionality. A sandboxed system could be an isolated virtual machine or an actual physical machine that is entirely isolated from the network.

    Option A is incorrect. Leaving the malware on a production system is never the correct approach.

    Option C is incorrect. You should test the malware to determine exactly what damage it causes.

    Option D is incorrect. A honeypot is used for trapping attackers, not for testing malware.

38. C. You should implement a staging server so that code can be deployed to an intermediate staging environment. This will allow testing of security features, as well as checking to see that the code integrates with the entire system. Using third-party libraries and SDKs can help reduce errors and vulnerabilities in the code.

Option A is incorrect. Sandboxing is used to isolate a particular environment.

Option B is incorrect. Virtualization will not mitigate this risk. Even if the production server is virtualized, the risks are the same.

Option D is incorrect. Deployment policies are a good idea, but they are not the most effective way to mitigate this particular risk.

39. A. A real-time operating system is a secure system used for embedded devices. RTOSs were originally developed for military applications but were not available to the public.

Option B is incorrect. Although SCADA systems can sometimes be embedded systems, this won't address the security concerns.

Option C is incorrect. Full drive encryption won't address issues with the security of the operating system.

Option D is incorrect. A trusted platform module can be very useful for cryptographic applications, but it will not address the security of the operating system.

40. C. The WPA2 standard fully implements the 802.11i security standard.

Options A, B, and D are incorrect. These standards are concerning bandwidth and frequency, not security.

41. A. The encryption technology associated with WPA is TKIP.

Option B is incorrect. CCMP is the technology used in WPA2. It combines AES in cipher-block chaining mode with a message authentication code.

Option C is incorrect. WEP uses RC4.

Option D is incorrect. WPA2 uses CCMP.

42. C. Disabling the SSID broadcast keeps it from being seen in the list of available networks, but it is still possible to connect to it and use the wireless network.

Options A, B, and D are all incorrect. These are not accurate descriptions of what happens when you disable SSID broadcast.

43. B. In the Platform as a Service (PaaS) model, the consumer has access to the infrastructure to create applications and host them.

Option A is incorrect. Software as a Service simply supplies a particular application.

Option C is incorrect. Infrastructure as a Service provides entire network infrastructure.

Option D is incorrect. Cloud as a Service provides access to cloud storage.

44. A. With the Software as a Service (SaaS) model, the consumer has the ability to use applications provided by the cloud provider over the Internet. SaaS is a subscription service where software is licensed on a subscription basis.

Answer B is incorrect. Platform as a Service provides an operating system.

Option C is incorrect. Infrastructure as a Service provides entire network infrastructure.

Option D is incorrect. Cloud as a Service provides access to cloud storage.

45. B. Elasticity is a feature of cloud computing that involves dynamically provisioning (or deprovisioning) resources as needed.

Option A is incorrect. Multitenancy refers to the ability to host multiple different virtualized environments.

Option C is incorrect. A configuration management database is used to store configuration information.

Option D is incorrect. Sandboxing refers to the ability to isolate an environment.

46. A. Type I hypervisor implementations are known as "bare metal."

Option B is incorrect. Type II hypervisors have to be installed on an underlying operating system.

Options C and D are incorrect. These are not valid hypervisor types.

47. C. A snapshot is an image of the virtual machine at some point in time. It is standard practice to periodically take a snapshot of a virtual system so that you can return that system to a last known good state.

Option A is incorrect. Sandboxing is the process of isolating a system.

Option B is incorrect. The hypervisor is the mechanism whereby the virtual environment interacts with the hardware.

Option D is incorrect. Elasticity is the ability for the system to scale.

48. D. RAID level 5 is disk striping with distributed parity. It can withstand the loss of any single disk.

Option A is incorrect. RAID 0 is disk striping; it does not provide any fault tolerance.

Option B is incorrect. RAID 1 is mirroring. It does protect against the loss of a single disk but not with distributed parity.

Option C is incorrect. RAID 3 is disk striping with dedicated parity. This means a dedicated drive containing all the parity bits.

49. D. A Faraday cage, named after the famous physicist Michael Faraday, involves placing wire mesh around an area or device to block electromagnetic signals.

Option A is incorrect. A VLAN can segment a network but won't block EMI.

Option B is incorrect. Software-defined networking virtualizes a network but does not protect against EMI.

Option C is incorrect. A trusted platform module is used for cryptographic applications.

50. B. The correct answer is bollards. These are large objects, often made of concrete or similar material, designed specifically to prevent a vehicle getting past them.

Option A is incorrect. Most gates can be breached with a vehicle.

Option C is incorrect. A security guard is a good idea, but he or she would not be able to stop a vehicle from ramming the building.

Option D is incorrect. Security cameras will provide evidence of a crime that was committed, but won't prevent the crime.

51. A. The correct answer is to attach cable locks to the computers that lock them to the table. This makes it more difficult for someone to steal a computer.

Option B is incorrect. Full disk encryption won't stop someone from stealing the computer.

Option C is incorrect. Strong passwords won't stop someone from stealing a computer.

Option D is incorrect. A sign-in sheet is a good idea and may deter some thefts. But it is not the best approach to stopping theft.

52. B. The correct answer is to incorporate two-factor authentication with a mantrap. By having a smartcard at one door (type II authentication) and a pin number (type I authentication) at the other door, Joanne will combine strong two-factor authentication with physical security.

Option A is incorrect. Smartcards by themselves are single-factor authentication.

Option C is incorrect. Video surveillance, though often a good idea, won't help with two-factor authentication.

Option D is incorrect. Again, the smartcard by itself is a single-factor authentication.

53. A. Baselining is the process of establishing a standard for security. A change from the original baseline value is referred to as baseline deviation.

Option B is incorrect. Security evaluations or audits check security but don't establish security standards.

Option C is incorrect. Hardening is the process of securing a given system, but it does not establish security standards.

Option D is incorrect. Normalization is the process of removing redundant entries from a database.

54. B. Hardening is the process of improving the security of an operating system or application. One of the primary methods of hardening an trusted OS is to eliminate unneeded protocols. This is also known as creating a secure baseline that allows the OS to run safely and securely.

Option A is incorrect. FDE is full disk encryption.

Option C is incorrect. SED is self-encrypting drive.

Option D is incorrect. Baselining is the process of establishing security standards.

55. A. RAID 1+0 is a mirrored data set (RAID 1), which is then striped (RAID 0): a "stripe of mirrors."

Option B is incorrect. RAID 6 is disk striping with dual parity (distributed).

Option C is incorrect. RAID 0 is just striping.

Option D is incorrect. RAID 1 is just mirroring.

56. D. Normalization is the process of removing duplication or redundant data from a database. There are typically four levels of normalization ranging from 1N at the lowest (i.e., the most duplication) to 4N at the highest (i.e., the least duplication).

Option A is incorrect. Although database integrity is important, that is not what is described in the question. Furthermore, integrity checking usually refers to checking the integrity of files.

Option B is incorrect. Deprovisioning is a virtualization term for removing a virtual system (server, workstation, etc.) and reclaiming those resources.

Option C is incorrect. Baselining involves setting security standards.

57. C. "Whitelists" are lists of those items that are allowed (as opposed to a blacklist—things that are prohibited).

Answer A is incorrect. Blacklists are lists of blocked items (applications or websites).

Options B and D are incorrect. These are not terms used in the industry.

58. C. The correct answer is to only allow signed components to be loaded in the browser. Code signing verifies the originator of the component (such as an ActiveX component) and thus makes malware far less likely.

Option A is incorrect. Although host-based anti-malware is a good idea, it is not the best remedy for this specific threat.

Option B is incorrect. Blacklists cannot cover all sites that are infected, just the sites you know about. And given that users on Hans's network visit a lot of websites, blacklisting is likely to be ineffective.

Option D is incorrect. If you block all active content, many websites will be completely unusable.

59. D. Agile development works in cycles, each cycle producing specific deliverables. This means that phases like design and development are repeated.

Options A and B are incorrect. The issue is not how many phases; it is the fact that in waterfall when a phase is finished, there is no returning to that phase.

Option C is incorrect. Neither method is inherently more secure.

60. D. Security should be addressed at every stage of development. This means requirements, design, implementation, verification/testing, and maintenance.

Options A, B, and C are incorrect. These are all only partially correct.

61. D. Stored procedures are the best way to have standardized SQL. Rather than programmers writing their own SQL commands, they simply call the stored procedures that the database administrator creates.

Options A and B are both incorrect. Although these are good ideas, they are not as effective as stored procedures in addressing concerns about bad SQL commands.

Option C is incorrect. Agile programming is a method for developing applications rapidly and won't determine how SQL commands are created.

62. A. Proper error handling is the most fundamental item to address in application development. Robust and thorough error handling will mitigate many security risks.

Options B, C, and D are all incorrect. Each of these is a good security measure but not the most important step for Mary to take.

63. B. When virtualization reaches the point that IT can no longer effectively manage it, the condition is known as VM sprawl.

Options A and C are incorrect. These are not the terms used in industry.

Option D is incorrect. VM zombie is a term for a virtual machine that is running and consuming resources but no longer has a purpose.

64. A. VM escape is a situation wherein an attacker is able to go through the VM to interact directly with the hypervisor, and potentially the host operating system. The best way to prevent this is to limit the ability of the host and the VM to share resources. If possible, they should not share any resources.

Option B is incorrect. This is one method that might mitigate the situation, but it is not the most effective.

Options C and D are incorrect. Both of these are good security practices but would have minimal effect on mitigating VM escape.

65. A. The correct answer is to implement a virtual desktop environment. If all the desktops are virtualized, then from a single central location you can manage patches, configuration, and software installation. This single implementation will solve all the issues mentioned in the question.

Option B is incorrect. Strong policies are a good idea but are often difficult to enforce.

Option C is incorrect. Imaging workstations affects only their original configuration. It won't keep them patched or prevent rogue software from being installed.

Option D is incorrect. Strong patch management will address only one of the three concerns.

66. C. Pre-action fire suppression is ideal for computers. The pipes have no water in them during normal operations. When the temperature rises to a certain level, water fills the pipes. Then if the temperature continues to rise, the fire suppression system activates. This provides time to stop the fire before the servers are soaked with water.

Option A is incorrect. Wet pipes have water in them at all times. If a pipe freezes and/or bursts, then the servers will be damaged.

Option B is incorrect. Deluge fire suppression, as the name suggests, uses a very large amount of water. This is not appropriate for computers.

Option D is incorrect. Halon is now banned.

67. A. The correct answer is to have a motion-activated camera that records everyone who enters the server room.

Options B, C, and D are all incorrect. These are all good security measures but won't detect theft.

68. B. Session tokens are used to authenticate sessions. These can be effective against replay attacks and session hijacking.

Options A, C, and D are all incorrect. Session tokens will not be effective in mitigating these attacks.

69. C. Hot aisle/cold aisle is a layout design for server racks and other computing equipment in a data center. The goal of a hot aisle/cold aisle configuration is to conserve energy and lower cooling costs by managing airflow. An infrared camera will detect heat levels on the aisles.

Options A, B, and D are all incorrect. Although these are issues to be concerned about in a data center, the infrared camera is not an appropriate way to monitor them.

70. D. A security guard is the most effective way to prevent unauthorized access to a building.

Options A, B, and C are all incorrect. These are all good physical security measures, but they are not the most effective ways to prevent entry into a building.

71. B. Software-defined networking makes the network very scalable. It is relatively easy to add on new resources or remove unneeded resources.

Options A, C, and D are all incorrect. SDN does not accomplish these goals.

72. A. The correct answer is to use an application container to isolate that application from the host operating system. Applications containers provide a virtualized environment in which to run an application.

Option B is incorrect. Moving to software-defined networking is a very involved process and does not provide an efficient solution.

Option C is incorrect. Not only will this not separate the application from the host operating system; it might not solve the problem.

Option D is incorrect. This is not an option in this question. Mark must support the legacy application.

73. D. The fence should reach within 2 inches of hard surfaces like pavement or concrete. For soft dirt it should actually go into the ground.

Options A and B are incorrect. These are not the correct measurements.

Option C is incorrect. Per the standard, chain-link fence should reach within 2 inches of hard surfaces like pavement or concrete. For soft dirt, it should actually go into the ground.

74. A. An immutable server's configuration cannot be changed.

Option B is incorrect. A virtual machine won't stop the application or the OS from being altered.

Option C is incorrect. This won't prevent the OS from being altered.

Option D is incorrect. Segregating the application on a separate VLAN won't address the issues.

75. B. The correct answer is to have the source code for the application stored with a third-party source code escrow. Should the vendor go out of business, or otherwise be unable to continue to support the application, the source code escrow will supply you with the source code you can then maintain yourself (or hire a new company).

Option A is incorrect. Detailed credit checks of vendors are a good idea, but are no guarantee against the vendor failing.

Option C is incorrect. If the vendor goes out of business, contractual penalties will be ineffective.

Option D is incorrect. Even if another vendor is willing to be a backup for you, they cannot effectively support the application without the source code.

76. C. The correct answer is to implement IaC. Infrastructure as Code (IaC) is the process of managing and provisioning computer datacenters through machine-readable definition files, rather than physical hardware configuration or interactive configuration tools. Whether the data center(s) use physical machines or virtual machines, this is an effective way to manage the data centers.

Option A is incorrect. Although data center managers may be needed, that won't necessarily provide consistent management across the enterprise.

Option B is incorrect. Software-defined networking will not fix this problem.

Option D is incorrect. The issue is not just provisioning; it is management.

77. C. These particular web application attacks are best mitigated with proper input validation. Any user input should be checked for indicators of XSS or SQL injection.

Option A is incorrect. Error handling is always important, but it won't mitigate these particular issues.

Option B is incorrect. Stored procedures can be a good way of ensuring SQL commands are standardized, but that won't prevent these attacks.

Option D is incorrect. Code signing is used for code that is downloaded from a web application to the client computer. It is used to protect the client, not the web application.

78. B. Fuzzing is a technique whereby the tester intentionally enters incorrect values into input fields to see how the application will handle it.

Option A is incorrect. Static code analysis tools simply scan the code for known issues.

Option C is incorrect. Baselining is the process of establishing security standards.

Option D is incorrect. Version control simply tracks changes in the code; it does not test the code.

79. A. The waterfall method has the steps of requirements gathering, design, implementation (also called coding), testing (also called verification), deployment, and maintenance.

Options B, C, and D are all incorrect. These are not the proper steps for the waterfall method.

80. D. Both client-side and server-side validation are important, so both should be used for a complete validation solution.

Options A and B are both incorrect since they are both incomplete.

Option C is incorrect. This is not a validation method.

81. A. The correct answer is to assign digital certificates to the authorized users and to use these to authenticate them when logging in. This is an effective way to ensure that only authorized users can access the application.

Options B, C, and D are all incorrect. These are each good security measures but not the best way to authenticate the client and prevent unauthorized access to the application.

82. D. The correct answer is to first test patches. It is always possible that a patch might cause issues for one or more current applications. This is particularly a concern with applications that have a lot of interaction with the host operating system. An operating system patch can prevent the application from executing properly. But as soon as the patches are tested, a phased rollout to the company should begin.

Option A is incorrect. Automatic patching is not recommended in corporate environments because a patch could possibly interfere with one or more applications.

Option B is incorrect. This is a very bad idea and will lead to inconsistent patching and the application of untested patches.

Option C is incorrect. This is only slightly better than having end users handle their own patching.

83. B. In a code reuse attack, the attacker executes code that is meant for some other purposes. In many cases this can be old code that is no longer even used (dead code), even if that code is in a third-party library.

Option A is incorrect. A buffer overflow occurs when too much data is sent to a buffer. For example, say a buffer is designed to hold 10 bytes, and it is sent 100 bytes.

Option C is incorrect. A denial-of-service attack is meant to make a service unavailable to legitimate users.

Option D is incorrect. Session hijacking involves taking over an existing authenticated session.

84. B. The correct answer is to turn off any remote access to such devices that is not absolutely needed. Many peripheral devices come with SSH, telnet, or similar services. If you are not using them, turn them off.

Option A is incorrect. Full disk encryption will improve peripheral security, and many peripherals don't have a disk to encrypt.

Option C is incorrect. Fuzzy testing is for applications.

Option D is incorrect. Not all devices are even capable of having a digital certificate assigned to them.

85. C. The correct answer is to use static code analysis. Memory leaks are usually caused by failure to deallocate memory that has been allocated. A static code analyzer can check to see if all memory allocation commands (`malloc`, `alloc`, etc.) have a matching deallocation command.

Option A is incorrect. Fuzzing involves entering data that is outside expected values to see how the application handles it.

Option B is incorrect. Stress testing involves testing how a system handles extreme workloads.

Option D is incorrect. Normalization is a technique for deduplicating a database.

86. A. The correct answer is to use Secure Shell. This protocol is encrypted. SSH also authenticates the user with public key cryptography.

Option B is incorrect. Telnet is insecure. It does not encrypt data.

Option C is incorrect. Remote Shell sends at least some data unencrypted and is thus insecure.

Option D is incorrect. Simple Network Management Protocol is used to manage a network and is not used for remote communications.

87. B. Software attestation is often done with digital certificates and digital signing. The software proves that it is the legitimate program before being allowed to execute.

Option A is incorrect. Secure boot involves the system booting into a trusted configuration.

Option C is incorrect. Sandboxing is used to isolate an application.

Option D is incorrect. Trusted platform module is a cryptoprocessor, often used for key management.

88. D. When two or more components are tested together, this is referred to as integration testing.

Option A is incorrect. Unit testing is testing a single unit of code.

Option B is incorrect. Regression testing is testing a system after a change to ensure that the change did not cause any other problems.

Option C is incorrect. Stress testing involves subjecting a system to extensive loads to determine if it can handle them.

89. B. Intrusion prevention systems are critical for a system that needs high availability. Depending on the nature of the system, it may require an HIPS, NIPS, or both.

Option A is incorrect. Security information and event management consolidates logs. Although this can be a valuable security feature, it is not the most important in this situation.

Option C is incorrect. Automated patch control is usually a good idea; however, it is not the most important in this situation.

Option D is incorrect. Honeypots can be a valuable security control, but they are far less important than IPS or patch control.

90. B. System on a Chip devices are complete self-contained systems on a single chip. Therefore, having their own unique cryptographic keys is the best way to implement authentication and security.

Option A is incorrect. A system on a chip is self-contained, so a TPM would not be an appropriate solution.

Option C is incorrect. A self-encrypting drive is not relevant to system on a chip, since that system does not have a "drive."

Option D is incorrect. Many SoC technologies don't use a BIOS.

91. A. Such systems need to have all communications encrypted. As of the current date, breaches of portable network devices have all involved unencrypted communications.

Option B is incorrect. Full disk encryption may or may not even be appropriate for such devices. Many don't have a disk to encrypt.

Option C is incorrect. It may not be possible to install anti-malware on many such devices.

Option D is incorrect. Fuzz testing is used for applications.

92. D. The more vehicles utilize computers and have network communication capabilities, the more they will be vulnerable to cyberattacks.

Options A, B, and C are all incorrect. These are incomplete.

93. B. DevOps is a compound term: software DEVelopment and information technology OPerationS. The term refers to collaboration between software developers and IT professionals to align software development with infrastructure issues.

Option A is incorrect. Integration testing refers to testing two or more components.

Options C and D are both incorrect. Although clear policies and employee training are usually a good idea, they won't be the best way to address Ariel's concerns.

94. A. All software changes must go through proper change management. That includes a request for changes (RFC) that will be evaluated.

Option B is incorrect. Greg cannot know what effect the change might have on other aspects of the system. This fix could cause additional problems.

Option C is incorrect. This is a better answer than B but still does not follow change control procedures.

Option D is incorrect. Simply documenting the issue does nothing to correct it.

95. C. Model verification must be completed before you can rely on the models used. It is important to verify that all aspects of a simulation model are accurate. If the model has any inaccurate data or settings, then the results will not be accurate.

Option A is incorrect. Change approval boards (CABs) are part of the change control process.

Option B is incorrect. Although it is always a good idea to thoroughly read documentation, this is not the most critical issue in this scenario.

Option D is incorrect. Integration testing involves testing two or more components to ensure they function together.

96. D. Any change to a system requires regression testing. Regression testing ensures that the change made does not cause any new issues.

Option A is incorrect. Full disk encryption may or may not even be appropriate for such devices. Many don't have a disk to encrypt.

Option B is incorrect. You should have received approval from the change approval board prior to making the change.

Option C is incorrect. Stress testing is designed to see what loads the system can handle.

97. A. Compiled code runs faster. This is because runtime code, such as Java, is compiled at runtime (thus the name) and thus performance is slower.

Option B is incorrect. In fact, the opposite is true. Runtime code can be platform independent, as with Java. Compiled code is compiled for a specific operating system.

Option C is incorrect. Security is not directly related to whether the code is compiled or runtime. This issue has minimal impact on security.

Option D is incorrect. Development time is not impacted by whether the code will be compiled or runtime code.

98. C. A community cloud presents a compromise solution. Community clouds are semi-private. They are not accessible to the general public but only to a small community of specific entities.

Option A is incorrect. This would not be true.

Option B is incorrect. The cost of a private cloud is beyond many small companies.

Option D is incorrect. This is not a good answer. It ignores the company's desire to find a cloud solution.

99. B. Platform as a Service is a good solution to this problem. The programmer can access a virtualized Linux machine with PaaS.

Options A and C are both incorrect. Although these would work, they are less efficient than using PaaS.

Option D is incorrect. Infrastructure as a Service is used to provide networking infrastructure via virtualization. In this scenario, you only need an operating system.

100. A. A cloud access security broker (CASB) is a software tool or service that sits between an organization's on-premises network and a cloud provider's infrastructure. A CASB acts as a gatekeeper, allowing the organization to extend the reach of their security policies into the cloud.

Option B is incorrect. Integration testing is used to test two or more components to ensure they integrate.

Option C is incorrect. Although security policies are a good idea, just having policies in your company won't affect the cloud solution.

Option D is incorrect. Security as a Service is a process of outsourcing certain security functions.

101. B. Stress testing is designed to test an application under workloads that are larger than normal. Although this may not be adequate to test for DoS response, it is the most relevant software test.

Option A is incorrect. Regression testing is done after a change to ensure the change did not cause any other issues.

Option C is incorrect. Integration testing is done to see whether two or more components function together.

Option D is incorrect. Fuzz testing is testing an application by entering nonstandard/unexpected values.

102. C. The correct answer is a public cloud. Public clouds are usually less expensive. The cloud provider has a number of customers and costs are dispersed. Even individuals can afford to use cloud storage with services like iCloud and Amazon Cloud.

Option A is incorrect. A community cloud is usually private for a small group of partners. Each of the partners must share a greater part of the expense than they would with a public cloud. But they retain more control over the cloud than they would with a public cloud.

Option B is incorrect. Private clouds are the most expensive. The company must completely develop and maintain the cloud resources.

Option D is incorrect. A hybrid deployment model is a good compromise for many situations, but it will be more expensive than a public cloud.

103. D. The correct answer is continuous monitoring. There are technologies that perform continuous monitoring of a network. These systems can identify any issue as it is occurring, or very soon thereafter.

Option A is incorrect. Monthly audits won't give notice of an issue until they are conducted, as much as a month after the issue.

Options B and C are incorrect. A network intrusion detection system or network intrusion prevention system could certainly be part of the solution. But such systems would only detect breaches, not policy violations, login issues, and so forth.

104. B. The correct answer is to use an SSL accelerator. SSL accelerators are a method of offloading processor-intensive public-key encryption for Transport Layer Security (TLS) and Secure Sockets Layer (SSL) to a hardware accelerator.

Option A is incorrect. A VPN concentrator is a hardware device used to create remote access VPNs. The concentrator creates encrypted tunnel sessions between hosts, and many use two-factor authentication for additional security.

Option C is incorrect. Returning to smaller encryption keys would have a deleterious effect on security.

Option D is incorrect. This may, or may not, correct the problem, but it would entail a significantly greater cost and difficulty than implementing and SSL accelerator.

105. C. Only using code that is digitally signed verifies the creator of the software. For example, if a printer/MFD driver is digitally signed, this gives you confidence that it really is a printer driver from the vendor it purports to be from, and not malware masquerading as a printer driver.

Option A is incorrect. Signed software gives you a high degree of confidence that it is not malware but does not provide a guarantee. For example, the infamous Flame virus was signed with a compromised Microsoft digital certificate.

Option B is incorrect. Digital signing of software has no effect on patch management.

Option D is incorrect. Digitally signed software will not execute faster or slower than non-signed software.

106. B. VM sprawl refers to a situation in which the network has more virtual machines than the IT staff can effectively manage.

Options A, C, and D are incorrect. These descriptions have nothing to do with the term VM sprawl.

107. C. Stored procedures are commonly used in many database management systems to contain SQL statements. The database administrator, or someone designated by the DBA, creates the various SQL statements that are needed in that business, and then programmers can simply call the stored procedures.

Option A is incorrect. Stored procedures are not related to dynamic linked libraries.

Option B is incorrect. This is close but inaccurate, because stored procedures can be called by other stored procedures that are also on the server.

Option D is incorrect. Stored procedures are not related to middleware.

108. D. Bollards are large barriers that are often made of strong substances like concrete. They are effective in preventing a vehicle from being driven into a building.

Options A, B, and C are incorrect. These do not describe the purpose of a bollard.

109. A. Electromagnetic interference could cause damage to circuitry, including the RAM or CPU chips. At a minimum, it could wipe data from memory and drives.

Options A, B, and C are incorrect. These do not describe the effects of electromagnetic inference.

110. A. The correct answer is VM escape attacks are attacks that find some method for moving from the VM to the hypervisor and then the host. The most effective way to prevent this is to completely isolate the VM.

Option B is incorrect. Antivirus is always a good idea and may even stop some malware-based VM escape attacks. But isolating the VM is more effective.

Option C is incorrect. Full disk encryption will have no effect since the disk must be unencrypted during operation.

Option D is incorrect. A trusted platform module is used for storing cryptographic keys.

111. C. Security as a Service uses an outside company to handle security tasks. Some or even all security tasks can be outsourced, including IDS/IPS management, SIEM integration, and other security controls.

Option A is incorrect. Software-defined networking would make managing security somewhat easier but would itself be difficult to implement.

Option B is incorrect. Automating as much security activity as is practical would help alleviate the problem but would not be as effective as Security as a Service.

Option D is incorrect. This would mean intentionally not implementing some security controls.

112. B. Cryptographic hashes are used for integrity checking of files, network packets, and a variety of other applications. Storing a cryptographic hash of the application and comparing the application on the network to that hash will confirm (or refute) whether the application has been altered in any way.

Options A and D are both incorrect. Network intrusion detection or network intrusion prevention systems are useful, but they won't prevent an application from being altered.

Option C is incorrect. Sandboxing is used to isolate an application, but it won't detect whether it has been tampered with.

113. C. Separating the SCADA system from the main network makes it less likely that the SCADA system can be affected from the main network. This includes malware as well human action.

Option A is incorrect. Software-defined networking would make isolating the SCADA system easier but would not actually isolate it.

Option B is incorrect. Patch management is always important, but in this case it would not have prevented the issue.

Option D is incorrect. Encrypted data transmissions, such as TLS, would have no effect on this situation.

114. C. Authentication headers provide complete packet integrity, authenticating the packet and the header.

Options A and B are incorrect. Authentication headers do not provide any encryption at all.

Option D is incorrect. Authentication headers authenticate the entire packet, not just the header.

115. D. Transport Layer Security provides a reliable method of encrypting web traffic. It supports mutual authentication and is considered secure.

Option A is incorrect. Although SSL can encrypt web traffic, TLS was created in 1999 as its successor. Although many network administrators still use the term *SSL*, in most cases today what you are using is actually TLS, not the outdated SSL.

Options B and C are incorrect. These are protocols for establishing a VPN, not for encrypting web traffic.

116. A. Network taps are analogous to phone taps. They are completely passive methods of getting network traffic to a central location.

Option B is incorrect. Port mirroring would get all the traffic to the NIPS but is not completely passive. It requires the use of resources on switches to route a copy of the traffic. Incorrect switch configurations can cause looping. Configuring loop detection can prevent looped ports.

Option C is incorrect. It is not clear that this answer would even work.

Option D is incorrect. This is not the assignment. Setting up an NIPS on each segment would also dramatically increase administrative efforts.

117. B. Internet key exchange is used to set up security associations on each end of the tunnel. The security associations have all the settings (i.e., cryptographic algorithms, hashes, etc.) for the tunnel.

Options A and C are incorrect. IKE is not directly involved in encrypting or authenticating.

Option D is incorrect. One might argue that by establishing the security associations, IKE is establishing the tunnel. However, answer B is a more accurate answer.

118. A. A DDoS mitigator is a tool or service designed specifically to respond to distributed denial-of-service attacks. Such tools can both inhibit the attacking traffic and temporarily increase bandwidth to prevent legitimate users from being adversely affected by the attack.

Option B is incorrect. Certainly, a web application firewall with stateful packet inspection would help, but it is not the most effective means of addressing this threat.

Option C is incorrect. A network intrusion prevention system would be a good idea and would mitigate this threat. However, it is not the most effective means of mitigating this threat.

Option D is incorrect. This would probably not help in a DDoS with attacks coming from multiple sources.

119. D. Link aggregation switches allow you to combine the bandwidth of multiple links into one connection. This would allow Doug to improve bandwidth to the e-commerce server.

Option A is incorrect. This would reduce the impact on the rest of the network but would not address the bandwidth needs of the e-commerce server.

Options B and C are both incorrect. Each of these would most likely address the problem, but neither is cost effective.

120. C. A correlation engine is software that is used to aggregate events and to seek out correlations. In some cases, this is done with advanced analytic algorithms, including fuzzy logic.

Option A is incorrect. A network intrusion detection system would be helpful but will not (by itself) necessarily correlate events.

Option B is incorrect. A security information event manager will certainly aggregate log information but may not correlate the events.

Option D is incorrect. An aggregation switch simply combines bandwidth.

121. A. The NIPS is not seeing the traffic on that network segment. By implementing port mirroring, the traffic from that segment can be copied to the segment where the NIPS is installed.

Option B is incorrect. This would work but is not the most efficient approach.

Option C is incorrect. Nothing in this scenario suggests that the NIPS is inadequate. It just is not seeing all the traffic.

Option D is incorrect. This would isolate that network segment but would still not allow the NIPS to analyze the traffic from that segment.

122. C. Layer 2 Tunneling Protocol is a VPN technology that supports a wide range of remote access methods, including TACACS+. L2TP also supports a range of protocols, including ATM and X.25.

Option A is incorrect. Point-to-Point Tunneling Protocol is a VPN protocol but won't support TACACS+.

Option B is incorrect. Remote Authentication Dial-In User Service is a remote access protocol, not a VPN protocol. It is an early predecessor to TACACS+.

Option D is incorrect. Challenge Handshake Authentication Protocol is an authentication protocol, not a VPN protocol.

123. C. Whenever any part of your business process is outsourced, you need to ensure that the vendor meets or exceeds all of your security policies and procedures. Supply chain assessment security is a critical issue.

Options A, B, and D are all incorrect. Each of these is something that needs to be addressed, but the most important issue is the supply chain assessment security.

124. B. Infrared can still detect at night. A burglar is likely to be in the building at dark, so detecting via infrared is important.

Options A and C are both incorrect. It does not matter how the camera is activated (motion or sound) if the area is dark the camera will not record adequate imagery.

Option D is incorrect. High definition is a good choice if the area is well lit.

125. D. A Faraday cage is a metal wire mesh designed to block electromagnetic interference.

Options A, B, and C are all incorrect. These are not functions of a Faraday cage.

126. B. Smartcards can be used to allow entrance into a building. The smartcard can also store information about the user, and thus the system can log who enters the building.

Option A is incorrect. A security guard with a sign-in sheet would function, but there are many ways to subvert a sign-in sheet, and a guard can be distracted or become inattentive. This makes smartcard access a better solution.

Option C is incorrect. Yes, a camera would record who enters but would not control access. A nonemployee could enter the building.

Option D is incorrect. An uncontrolled/supervised sign-in sheet would not be secure.

127. C. Certificate revocation lists are designed specifically for revoking certificates. Since public keys are distributed via certificates, this is the most effective way to deauthorize a public key.

Option A is incorrect. Simply notifying users that a key/certificate is no longer valid is not effective.

Option B is incorrect. Deleting a certificate is not always possible and ignores the possibility of a duplicate of that certificate existing.

Option D is incorrect. The registration authority is used in creating new certificates, not in revoking them.

128. C. Type C fire extinguishers are used for electrical fires, including computer equipment fires.

Option A is incorrect. Type A fire extinguishers are for paper and wood fires.

Option B is incorrect. Type B fire extinguishers are for fuel fires such as gasoline.

Option D is incorrect. Type D fire extinguishers are for chemical fires.

129. C. Of the locks listed here, deadbolts are the most secure. The locking bolt goes into the door frame, making it more secure.

Option A is incorrect. Whether a lock uses a key or combination does not change how secure it is.

Option B is incorrect. Key-in-knob is a very common, and fairly insecure, solution.

Option D is incorrect. Padlocks can be cut off with common bolt cutters.

130. B. Forty percent to 60 percent is considered ideal humidity. High humidity can cause corrosion, and low humidity can cause electrostatic discharge.

Options A, C, and D are all incorrect. These are not the proper humidity values.

131. A. False acceptance rate is the rate at which the system incorrectly allows in someone it should not. This is clearly a significant concern.

Option B is incorrect. Any error is a concern, but the false rejection rate is less troublesome than the false acceptance rate.

Option C is incorrect. The cross-over error rate is when the FAR and FRR become equal. This actually indicates a consistent operation of the biometric system.

Option D is incorrect. The equal error rate is another name for cross-over error rate.

132. C. Physical locks must always fail open, which is also called fail safe. The safety of employees must take precedence over the safety of property. If the lock does not fail open, then employees could be trapped in the building.

Options A, B, and D are incorrect. Fail secure is the usual term, but it also means fail closed or fail locked. This puts lives at danger. In the case of fire, power will fail, and then the doors would fail locked, trapping people in the building.

133. B. Protected cabling will secure the cable and prevent anyone from eavesdropping. These systems, also called protected distribution systems, use a variety of safeguards so that classified information can be sent unencrypted.

Option A is incorrect. Cat 7 will improve bandwidth, not security.

Option C is incorrect. This is not even a practical solution. To place a Faraday cage around all cable would require extensive rework of the building(s).

Option D is incorrect. That is not a viable option. The scenario indicates that Donald needs to send classified data.

134. A. A secure cabinet is tamper proof and provides a good place to store anything you are trying to physically protect.

Option B is incorrect. This would then require you to store the key used to encrypt the thumb drive, thus continuing the problem.

Option C is incorrect. It is actually a good practice to store BitLocker keys on removable media, provided that media is safeguarded.

Option D is incorrect. Desk drawers are not secure and can easily be broken into.

135. D. RAID 6, disk striping with dual parity, uses a minimum of four disks with distributed parity bits. RAID 6 can handle up to two disks failing.

Option A is incorrect. RAID 1+0 is disk striping with mirroring.

Option B is incorrect. RAID 3, disk striping with dedicated parity, can only handle one disk failing.

Option C is incorrect. RAID 5, disk striping with distributed parity, can only handle one disk failing.

136. D. The correct answer is to use a master image that is properly configured and to create all workstations from that image. This is a standard way large corporations configure systems.

Option A is incorrect. Many things cannot be configured by a single configuration file, so this option simply would not work.

Option B is incorrect. Policies are always a good idea, but this would not ensure that all systems are properly configured.

Option C is incorrect. The operating system and applications are only a part of configuration. This solution would not fully configure the workstations.

137. B. There is now a serious security issue on the web server. The primary concern must be to correct this. Rolling back to the last known good state will immediately correct the problem; then Mike can investigate to find the cause.

Option A is incorrect. This would be too slow, and in the interim the flaw would be on the live website.

Options C and D are both incorrect. These would be the slowest solutions and thus leave the security flaw in place for an unacceptable amount of time.

138. D. A firewall has two types of rules. One type is to allow specific traffic on a given port. The other type of rule is to deny traffic. What is shown here is a typical firewall rule.

Options A, B, and C are incorrect. The rule shown is clearly a firewall rule.

139. A. A web proxy can be used to block certain websites. It is common practice for network administrators to block either individual sites or general classes of sites (like job-hunting sites).

Option B is incorrect. Network address translation is used to translate the private IP addresses of internal computers to public IP addresses.

Option C is incorrect. A firewall can block traffic on a given port or using a particular protocol, but generally they are not able to block specific websites.

Option D is incorrect. Network intrusion prevention systems identify and block attacks. They cannot prevent users from visiting specific websites.

140. D. Load balancing the cluster will prevent any single server from being overloaded. And if a given server is offline, other servers can take on its workload.

Option A is incorrect. A VPN concentrator, as the name suggests, is used to initiate VPNs.

Option B is incorrect. Aggregate switching can shunt more bandwidth to the servers but won't mitigate the threat of one or more servers being offline.

Option C is incorrect. SSL accelerators are a method of offloading processor-intensive public-key encryption for Transport Layer Security (TLS) and Secure Sockets Layer (SSL) to a hardware accelerator.

141. D. Failure to release memory you have allocated can lead to a memory leak. Therefore, if you are using a programming language like C++ that allows you to allocate memory, make certain you deallocate that memory as soon as you are finished using it.

Options A and C are incorrect. Both of these are good programming practices. However, failure to follow them just leads to wasteful use of memory; it does not lead to a security problem like a memory leak.

Option B is incorrect. Although this is a good idea to prevent buffer overflows, it is not a memory management issue.

142. A. Off-premises clouds are always less expensive and require less changes to the existing infrastructure. That is true for public, private, or community clouds.

Option B is incorrect. An on-premises cloud is always the most expensive solution and has a tremendous impact on the existing IT infrastructure. Few companies opt for this approach.

Option C is incorrect. A hybrid solution is better than on-premises but not as good as off-premises.

Option D is incorrect. It need not be a community cloud. An off-premises public cloud or even a private cloud would fulfill the requirements.

143. B. The correct answer is to encrypt all the web traffic to this application using Transport Layer Security (TLS). This is one of the most fundamental security steps to take with any website.

Option A is incorrect. A web application firewall is probably a good idea, but it is not the most important thing for Ryan to implement.

Options C and D are incorrect. Either a network intrusion detection service or network intrusion prevent service may be a good idea, but those should be considered after TLS is configured.

144. C. This is commonly called obfuscation. Many years ago (i.e., late 1990s) it was thought of as a weak security measure. Today it can only be thought of as a possible security flaw and should not be used.

Options A, B, and D are all incorrect. These are not accurate descriptions of what is being done in this scenario.

145. A. Agile programming was developed specifically to speed up development time. Although it is not appropriate for all projects, it has become quite popular.

Option B is incorrect. Usually the opposite occurs, and Agile programming leads to less documentation.

Option C is incorrect. You could argue that if done properly, the many cycles of Agile programming, each with repeated design, lead to more focus on design. But this is not always the case, and it is not the reason companies consider Agile.

Option D is incorrect. You could argue that if done properly, that the many cycles of Agile programming, each with repeated testing, lead to more focus on testing. But this is not always the case, and it is not the reason companies consider Agile.

146. D. The most important issue is that the camera itself is tamper proof and that the data stored is tamper proof. Wireless security cameras are an example of home automation and is one of the driving factors behind the IoT movement.

Options A, B, and C are all incorrect. These are important considerations, and you should consider all three of these. But the most important issue is the security of the camera and the video storage.

147. A. A monitor displays data, and it is possible others can see that data. For example, traveling employees with laptops may inadvertently disclose data on their monitor that someone else can see. For this reason, screen filters are recommended for laptops.

Option B is incorrect. This may be theoretically possible but has not been reported to have actually ever occurred. And even if it should be encountered, it is not the primary security issue.

Option C is incorrect. Although the monitor displays login screens, it is not where the actual authentication processing occurs.

Option D is incorrect. Old CRT monitors were very susceptible to this issue. For modern monitors, screen burn is very unlikely to occur. If it is a concern, it is certainly not the primary concern.

148. B. Just like desktops, laptops, and servers, patch management is a fundamental security issue and must be addressed. Many malware outbreaks and other breaches can be prevented by simply having good patch management.

Options A, C, and D are all incorrect. Each of these is a good idea and should at least be considered. However, they apply only to specific security issues, primarily how to handle lost or stolen mobile devices. Patch management affects all mobile devices, even if the device is never lost or stolen, and is thus more important.

149. A. Phishing depends on deceiving the user. The only true protection against that is proper user training. There are some technologies that can reduce the chance of phishing emails getting through, but none can stop all phishing emails. The best protection is user training

Option B is incorrect. Network intrusion prevention systems are usually not effective against phishing emails.

Options C and D are incorrect. Both of these should block at least some phishing emails. But no filter can block all phishing emails; therefore, user training is the most important security measure against phishing.

150. D. Regulatory requirements are enforced by law. You must implement these; therefore, they are the most important.

Options A, B, and C are incorrect. Each is very important, and you should implement all three. But they are less important than regulatory requirements.

Chapter 4: Identity and Access Management

1. B. Type II authentication is something you have. A smartcard is a physical item that you have. Though more sophisticated than a key, ultimately it is still just something you have.

Option A is incorrect. Type I is something you know, such as a password or pin.

Option C is incorrect. Type III is something you are, such as biometrics.

Option D is incorrect. Strong authentication uses at least two different types, such as Type I and Type II.

2. A. The correct answer is that Kerberos uses various tickets, each with a time limit. The service tickets are typically only good for 5 minutes or less. This means that if NTP is failing, valid tickets may appear to be expired.

Options B, C, and D are incorrect. None of these are likely to have any significant effect due to NTP failure.

3. C. The correct answer is that Challenge Handshake Authentication Protocol (CHAP) periodically has the client reauthenticate. This is transparent to the user, but specifically is done to prevent session hijacking.

Option A is incorrect. Password Authentication Protocol is actually quite old and does not reauthenticate. In fact, it even sends the password in clear text, so it should not be used any longer.

Option B is incorrect. SPAP (Shiva Password Authentication Protocol) adds password encryption to PAP but does not reauthenticate.

Option D is incorrect. OAUTH is used in web authentication and does not reauthenticate.

4. C. Type III authentication is biometrics. Anything based on biology, or "something you are," is type III.

Option A is incorrect. Type I is something you know, such as a password or pin.

Option B is incorrect. Type II is something you have, such as a card or key.

Option D is incorrect. Strong authentication uses at least two different types, such as Type I and Type II.

5. D. A service account is the most appropriate in this scenario. Service accounts are given the least privileges the service needs and are used by the service, without the need for a human user.

Option A is incorrect. You could assign a user account, but that is not as good a solution as using a service account.

Option B is incorrect. A guest account would never be a good idea for a service. Guest accounts are typically too limited. It's common practice to disable default accounts such as the Guest account.

Option C is incorrect. An admin account would give too many privileges to the service and violate the principle of least privileges.

6. A. Shibboleth is a middleware solution for authentication and identity management that uses SAML (Security Assertions Markup Language) and works over the Internet.

Option B is incorrect. OAUTH (Open Authorization) allows an end user's account information to be used by third-party services, without exposing the user's password.

Option C is incorrect. Shiva Password Authentication Protocol (SPAP) is an older authentication method that simply encrypted the username and password in transit.

Option D is incorrect. Challenge Handshake Authentication Protocol (CHAP) periodically re-authenticates the user.

7. D. NTLM (NT Lan Manager) was the method used in Windows for many years. It was eventually replaced by NTLM v2 for many years, and Microsoft networks now use Kerberos.

Option A is incorrect. Password Authentication Protocol (PAP) is a very old authentication protocol that sent username and password in clear text.

Option B is incorrect. Challenge Handshake Authentication Protocol (CHAP) periodically re-authenticates the user.

Answer C is incorrect. Open Authorization (OAUTH) allows an end user's account information to be used by third-party services, without exposing the user's password.

8. **A.** Mandatory Access Control (MAC) is the correct solution. It will not allow lower privilege users to even see the data at a higher privilege level.

Option B is incorrect. Discretionary Access Control (DAC) has each data owner configure his or her own security.

Option C is incorrect. Role- Based Access Control (RBAC) could be configured to meet the needs, but is not the best solution for these requirements.

Answer D is incorrect. Security Assertions Markup Language (SAML) is not an access control model.

9. **D.** Lightweight Directory Access Protocol Secure (LDAPS) will use TLS to protect the LDAP information, thus mitigating the risk of an attacker gathering information about network resources.

Option A is incorrect. LDAP (Lightweight Directory Access Protocol) contains information about network resources, which is what Clarice is trying to protect.

Option B is incorrect. Transport Layer Security (TLS) is used to secure data, but TLS alone can secure any transmission. Therefore, it needs to be combined with the data you are securing.

Option C is incorrect. Simple Network Management Protocol (SNMP) does have information about network resources, but not as much information as LDAP. Also, all networks have LDAP, but not all networks have SNMP.

10. **B.** Kerberos does not send the users password across the network. When the user's name is sent to the authentication service, the service retrieves the hash of the user's password from the database, and then uses that as a key to encrypt data to be sent back to the user. The user's machine takes the password that the user entered, hashes it, and then uses that as a key to decrypt what was sent back by the server.

Option A is incorrect. CHAP sends the user's password encrypted.

Option C is incorrect. RBAC is an access control model, not an authentication protocol.

Option D is incorrect. Type II authentication is something you have, such as a key or card.

11. **C.** OAUTH (Open Authorization) is an open standard for token-based authentication and authorization on the Internet and allows an end user's account information to be used by third-party services, without exposing the user's password.

Option B is incorrect. Kerberos is a network authentication protocol and not used for cross domain/service authentication.

Option B is incorrect. Security Assertion Markup Language (SAML) is an XML-based, open-standard data format for exchanging authentication and authorization data between parties.

Option D is incorrect. OpenID is an authentication service often done by a third party, and it can be used to sign into any website that accepts OpenID. It would be possible for this to work, but only with websites that support OpenID, so it is not as good a solution as OAUTH.

12. A. Remote Authentication Dial-In User Service (RADIUS) is a protocol specifically designed for remotely accessing a network.

Option B is incorrect. Kerberos could be used to authenticate these users, but by itself cannot connect them.

Option C is incorrect. CHAP could be used to authenticate these users, but by itself cannot connect them.

Option D is incorrect. OpenID is an authentication service often done by a third party, and it can be used to sign into any website that accepts OpenID. It is not used for remotely accessing a network.

13. B. NTLM is an older Windows authentication protocol. Microsoft no longer recommends it except for certain specific situations. One of those is attempting to authenticate to a server that is not part of the domain.

Option A is incorrect. Kerberos is used in Windows domains, but cannot be used to authenticate to a server not in the domain. Microsoft, recommends using NTLM for this purpose.

Option C is incorrect. OpenID is an authentication service often done by a third party, and it can be used to sign into any website that accepts OpenID.

Option D is incorrect. CHAP is not specifically used for Windows, and while it might be used in this scenario, NTLM is the recommendation of Microsoft.

14. A. The correct answer is that OpenID is an authentication service often done by a third party, and it can be used to sign into any website that accepts OpenID.

Option B is incorrect. Kerberos is a network authentication protocol for use within a domain.

Option C is incorrect. NTLM is an older Windows authentication protocol.

Option D is incorrect. Shibboleth is a single sign-on system, but it works with federated systems.

15. A. Cross-over Error Rate (CER), also sometimes called Equal Error Rate (EER), is the point at which false rejection and false acceptance are the same.

Options B, C, and D are incorrect. These are not correct terms for this situation.

16. D. A Time-based One-time Password (TOTP), can only be used once and is only valid for a brief period of time after issues. Users can request a password reset and a TOTP can be sent to some alternate communications, such as a text message to their phone.

Option A is incorrect. Many users won't have the equipment to support facial recognition.

Option B is incorrect. Not all users will have Digital certificates.

Option C is incorrect. Role Based Access Control won't solve this problem.

17. C. IEEE 802.1x port-based network access control (PNAC) is a network authentication protocol that can integrate with RADIUS for remote access, and can use digital certificates to authenticate clients.

Option A is incorrect. CHAP does not use digital certificates.

Option B is incorrect. 802.11i is the IEEE wireless security standard.

Option D is incorrect. OAuth (Open Authorization) is an open standard for token-based authentication and authorization on the Internet and allows an end user's account information to be used by third-party services, without exposing the user's password.

18. D. A Database Activity Monitoring and Prevention (DAMP) system would be the most effective of the choices given. These systems work like an IPS, but specifically for databases.

    Option A is incorrect. Attribute-Based Access Control (ABAC) can be a powerful way to control access in any system. However, DAMP is specifically designed for databases, so it would be the best choice in this scenario.

    Option B is incorrect. A Time-based One-time Password (TOTP) is not for regular use, as each user would need a new password each time they need to access the database.

    Option C is incorrect. A Host-Based Intrusion Detection System (HIDS) doesn't prevent access; it simply records anomalous behavior.

19. A. Attribute Based Access Control (ABAC) looks at a group of attributes, in addition to the login username and password, to make decisions about whether or not to grant access. One of the attributes examined is the location of the person. Since the users in this company travel frequently, they will often be at new locations, and that might cause ABAC to reject their logins.

    Option B is incorrect. Wrong passwords can certainly prevent login, but are not specific to ABAC.

    Option C is incorrect. ABAC does not prevent remote access.

    Option D is incorrect. A firewall can be configured to allow, or prohibit, any traffic you wish.

20. B. Personal Identity Verification is a standardized FIPS 201 (Federal Information Processing Standard Publication 201) for use with federal employees.

    Option A is incorrect. Common Access Cards (CACs) are for U.S. Military personnel.

    Option C is incorrect. Near Field Communication (NFC) cards might be used, but PIV cards are more appropriate for DoD contractors.

    Answer D is incorrect. Smartcard is a generic term. Both PIV and CAC are smartcards.

21. B. Single Sign-On (SSO) is designed specifically to address this risk. Users have only a single logon to remember; thus, they have no need to write down the password.

    Option A is incorrect. OAuth (Open Authorization) is an open standard for token-based authentication and authorization on the Internet. It does not eliminate the use or need for multiple passwords.

    Option C is incorrect. OpenID is a third-party authentication service but does not eliminate the use or need for multiple passwords.

    Option D is incorrect. Kerberos is an authentication service but does not eliminate the use or need for multiple passwords.

22. D. Rule-Based Access Control applies a set of rules to an access request. Based on the application of the rules, the user may be given access to a specific resource that they were not explicitly granted permission to.

Options A, B, and C are all incorrect. None of these could give a user access unless that user has already been explicitly given said access.

23. A. The False Acceptance Rate (FAR) indicates how often the system will accept an invalid login. This is a measure of the mistakes a biometric system makes, and the lower the rate, the better.

Options B, C, and D are all incorrect. These are all inaccurate.

24. B. Tokens are physical devices that often contain cryptographic data for authentication. They can store digital certificates for use with authentication.

Option A is incorrect. OAuth (Open Authorization) is an open standard for token-based authentication and authorization on the Internet. The user still must remember a password.

Option C is incorrect. OpenID is a third-party authentication service; the user still must remember a password.

Option D is incorrect. Role-Based Access Control and Rule-Based Access Control (which both use the acronym RBAC) are access control models.

25. D. Least privileges is the most fundamental concept in establishing accounts. Each user should only have just enough privileges to do his or her job. This also applies to service accounts.

Options A, B, and C are all incorrect. Each of these is something you would consider, but none are as important as least privileges.

26. A. Restricting each faculty account so that it is only usable when that particular faculty member is typically on campus will prevent someone from logging in with that account after hours, even if he or she has the password.

Option B is incorrect. Usage auditing may detect misuse of accounts, but will not prevent it.

Option C is incorrect. Longer passwords are effective security, but they are not the most effective answer to this question.

Answer D is incorrect. Credential management is always a good idea, but won't address this specific issue.

27. A. A permissions audit will find what permissions each user has and compare that to his or her job requirements. Permission audits should be conducted periodically.

Option B is incorrect. Job rotation, while beneficial for other security reasons, will actually exacerbate this problem.

Option C is incorrect. It is impractical to forbid anyone from ever changing job roles.

Option D is incorrect. Separation of duties would have no impact on this issue.

28. C. Password complexity requires that passwords have a mixture of uppercase letters, lowercase letters, numbers, and special characters. This would be the best approach to correct the problem described in the question.

Option A is incorrect. Longer passwords are a good security measure, but will not correct the issue presented here.

Option B is incorrect. Changing passwords is a good security measure, but won't make those passwords any stronger.

Option D is incorrect. Single Sign-On (SSO) will have no effect on the strength of passwords.

29. B. TACACS+ (Terminal Access Controller Access Control System plus) uses TCP rather than UDP, and is therefore more reliable. It also supports a wide range of protocols.

Option A is incorrect. RADIUS uses UDP, an unreliable protocol, and does not support many protocols.

Option C is incorrect. NTLM is the Windows authentication protocol.

Option D is incorrect. CHAP is an authentication protocol, not a remote access protocol.

30. C. HMAC-based One-Time Password (HOTP) is a one-time password that is used by the Initiative for Open Authentication.

Option A is incorrect. CHAP is an authentication protocol but is not a one-time password.

Option B is incorrect. A Time-based One-time Password (TOTP) algorithm does work with Initiative for Open Authentication, but it is time limited. The password must be used within a short time of being issued.

Option D is incorrect. Attribute-Based Access Control (ABAC) is a method for controlling access to your system.

31. D. The original TACACS defined in RFC 1492 can use either UDP or TCP.

Option A is incorrect. RADIUS uses only UDP.

Option B is incorrect. DIAMETER uses only TCP.

Option C is incorrect. TACACS+ uses only TCP.

32. B. Voice recognition systems have to be trained to recognize the voices of authorized users, and that training takes time.

Option A is incorrect. Minor and normal changes to a person's voice will not prevent voice recognition from recognizing the user.

Options C and D are incorrect. Voice recognition does not have a false negative or false positive rate that is particularly higher than other biometrics.

33. A. The correct answer is that facial recognition is among the most expensive biometrics to implement.

Option B is incorrect. They cannot be fooled easily. Adding glasses, changing hair color, or even gaining or losing some weight, will not prevent most facial recognition systems from functioning properly.

Option C is incorrect. Facial recognition systems actually have very low false positive rates.

Option D is incorrect. Most of these systems only need a few seconds.

34. D. Rainbow table attacks are best mitigated by longer passwords. Generating rainbow tables are computationally intensive, and longer passwords (over 14 characters) cannot be cracked by most rainbow tables.

Options A, B, and C are incorrect. These are all password issues that should be addressed, but they have no impact on rainbow tables.

35. A. Disabling the account will leave all resources intact, including history and logs, but will render the account unusable.

Option B is incorrect. At some point, the account will be deleted, but not immediately. Deleting the account could render some resources inaccessible.

Option C is incorrect. Changing the account password is effective, but not as effective as disabling the account. It is always possible for any password to be compromised.

Option D is incorrect. This is a very significant security violation.

36. C. Biometric security is any security based on a user's physical characteristics.

Option A is incorrect. CHAP is an authentication protocol.

Option B is incorrect. Multi-factor authentication is authentication using at least one of two categories of authentication. That might include biometrics, but might not.

Option D is incorrect. A token is a physical item you have that is used for authentication.

37. B. TACACS uses TCP and UDP 49.

Option A is incorrect. IMAP4 uses TCP 143.

Option C is incorrect. SSL uses port TCP 443 for web communications.

Option D is incorrect. DNS queries use UDP 53.

38. B. Mandatory access control (MAC) is based on documented security levels associated with the information being accessed.

Option A is incorrect. Role-Based Access Control (RBAC) is based on the role the user is placed in.

Option C is incorrect. Discretionary Access Control (DAC) lets the data owner set access control.

Option D is incorrect. BBC is not an access control model.

39. B. All accounts should have just enough privileges to execute their job functions. This is referred to as least privileges.

Option A is incorrect. Separation of duties means that no one person can perform all the steps of a critical task.

Option C is incorrect. Transitive trust is when party A trusts party B and B trusts party C; therefore, A trusts C.

Option D is incorrect. Account management is a general set of guidelines for managing accounts.

40. A. Discretionary Access Control (DAC) allows data owners to assign permissions.

Option B is incorrect. Role-Based Access Control (RBAC) assigns access based on the role the user is in.

Option C is incorrect. Mandatory Access Control (MAC) is stricter.

Option D is incorrect. Attribute-Based Access Control (ABAC) considers various attributes such as location, time, computer, etc. in addition to username and password.

41. D. Secure lightweight directory access protocol uses port 636 by default.

Option A is incorrect. DNS uses port 53.

Option B is incorrect. LDAP (without security) uses 389.

Option C is incorrect. Secure HTTP uses port 443.

42. B. Role-Based Access Control (RBAC) grants permissions on the user's position within the organization.

Option A is incorrect. Mandatory Access Control uses security classifications to grant permissions.

Option D is incorrect. Discretionary Access Control (DAC) allows data owners to set permissions.

Option D is incorrect. Attribute-Based Access Control (ABAC) considers various attributes such as location, time, computer, etc. in addition to username and password.

43. D. Dual-factor authentication requires at least one authentication method from at least two categories. The categories are: Type I, which is something you know; Type II, which is something you have; and Type III, which is something you are. Option D is correct because it names authentication methods from two different categories: Type III (iris scan) and Type I (password).

Option A is incorrect. Both of these are type I.

Option B is incorrect. These are not authentication methods.

Option C is incorrect. These are not authentication methods.

44. D. The Key Distribution Center (KDC) issues tickets. The tickets are generated by the ticket-granting service, which is usually part of the KDC.

Option A is incorrect. The authentication service simply authenticates the user.

Option B is incorrect. X.509 certificates and certificate authorities are not part of Kerberos.

Option C is incorrect. The ticket-granting service does generate the ticket, but the KDC issues it.

45. B. Two-factor authentication requires at least one authentication method from at least two categories. The categories are: Type I, which is something you know; Type II, which is something you have; and Type III, which is something you are. The question has two types: Type III (something you are) and Type I (something you know).

Option A is incorrect. A token is something you have (type II).

Option C is incorrect. Kerberos is not related to this question.

Option D is incorrect. Biometrics is something you are (type III).

46. **A.** Digital certificates use the X.509 standard (or the PGP standard) and allow the user to digitally sign authentication requests.

Option B is incorrect. OAUTH allows an end user's account information to be used by third-party services, without exposing the user's password. It does not use digital certificates or support digital signing.

Option C is incorrect. Kerberos does not use digital certificates nor does it support digitally signing.

Option D is incorrect. Smartcards can contain digital certificates, but don't necessarily have them.

47. **C.** SAML (Security Assertion Markup Language) is an Extensible Markup Language (XML) framework for creating and exchanging security information between partners online. The integrity of users is the weakness in the SAML identity chain. To mitigate this risk, SAML systems need to use timed sessions, HTTPS, and SSL/TLS.

Option A is incorrect. LDAP (Lightweight Directory Access Protocol) is a protocol that enables a user to locate individuals and other resources such as files and devices in a network.

Option B is incorrect. TACACS+ is a protocol that is used to control access into networks. TACACS+ provides authentication and authorization in addition to accounting of access requests against a central database.

Option D is incorrect. Transitive trust is a two-way relationship that is automatically created between a parent and a child domain in a Microsoft Active Directory forest. It shares resources with its parent domain by default and enables an authenticated user to access resources in both the child and parent domain.

48. **C.** A permissions audit will tell Greg exactly what the current situation is. He must know what is occurring now, in order to address any weaknesses.

Option A is incorrect. Minimum password length is a good idea, but he first needs to know the current situation.

Option B is incorrect. Password lockout is a good idea, but he first needs to know the current situation.

Option D is incorrect. It's important to ensure least privileges, but Greg must first conduct a permissions audit in order to determine if this principle is being adhered to or not.

49. **D.** An essential part of account maintenance is checking all accounts to ensure there are no active accounts for employees who are no longer with the company.

Option A is incorrect. Two-factor authentication is always preferred, but is not part of account maintenance.

Option B is incorrect. Time-of-day restrictions are optional. If they are implemented, then that would be a part of account maintenance, but option D is a better answer because it is always a part of account maintenance.

Option C is incorrect. Onboarding is critical (as is offboarding), but is not generally considered a part of account maintenance.

50. **C.** Location-based policies can be used to prevent any login that is not from within the physical network. In this scenario, since no employees work remotely, such a policy would be practical. And it would prevent an attacker from using an employee's login from outside the network.

Option A is incorrect. Kerberos is an effective authentication protocol, but if the attacker has the user's login credentials, Kerberos cannot prevent them from logging in.

Option B is incorrect. Time-based One-Time Passwords (TOTPs) are not practical for daily use.

Option D is incorrect. Group-based access control would do nothing to prevent an attacker who had the credentials of a legitimate user.

51. B. If the system maintains a password history, that would prevent any user from reusing an old password. Common password histories can be up to 24 passwords.

Option A is incorrect. Password complexity is always preferred, but is not part of account maintenance.

Options A and C are incorrect. Password length and complexity are very important but would not mitigate this issue.

Option D is incorrect. The password age indicates how frequently a password must be changed, and does not affect password reuse.

52. A. Auditing and reviewing how users actually utilize their account permissions would be the best way to determine if there is any inappropriate use. A classic example would be a bank loan officer. By the nature of their job, they have access to loan documents. But they should not be accessing loan documents for loans they are not servicing.

Option B is incorrect. The issue in this case is not permissions, because the users require permission to access the data. The issue is how the users are using their permissions.

Option C is incorrect. Usage auditing and permissions auditing are both part of account maintenance, but answer A is directly addressing the issue in this question.

Option D is incorrect. This is not a policy issue.

53. B. A scenario such as guest WiFi access does not provide the logins with any access to corporate resources. The people logging in merely get to access the Internet. This poses very limited security risk to the corporate network, and thus is often done with a common or shared account.

Option A is incorrect. Tech support personnel generally have significant access to corporate network resources.

Option C is incorrect. While this is a relatively low access scenario, it is still important to know which specific student is logging on and accessing what resources.

Option D is incorrect. Any level of access to corporate resources should have its own individual login account.

54. B. While password length is important, it is not part of password complexity.

Options A, C, and D are all incorrect. These are all part of password complexity. Password complexity means passwords contain uppercase letters, lowercase letters, numbers, and symbols.

55. A. Credential management is expressly designed for this, and it is explicitly for federated identities. In fact, Microsoft has a credential management API that programmers can use to implement this.

Option B is incorrect. OAUTH allows an end user's account information to be used by third-party services, without exposing the user's password and is used for services, not federated identities. Even the service being logged onto won't know the password.

Option C is incorrect. Kerberos is a network/domain authentication protocol.

Option D is incorrect. Shibboleth is a middleware solution for authentication and identity management that uses SAML (Security Assertion Mark-up Language) and works over the Internet.

56. B. A formal password recovery process is needed. This allows users the possibility of recovering forgotten passwords.

Option A is incorrect. This might work (or it may not) but would have a negative impact on security.

Option C is incorrect. This might work (or it may not) but would have a negative impact on security.

Option D is incorrect. This might work (or it may not) but would have a negative impact on security.

57. D. Password expiration would mean that even if the exiting employee's login is not disabled, the password will simply expire without anyone having to take any action.

Option A is incorrect. Password complexity won't address this issue. That would simply make a password harder to guess.

Option B is incorrect. Offboarding would help in this situation and should be implemented. But password expiration would occur automatically, even if offboarding procedures are not followed. That is why password expiration is a better answer.

Option C is incorrect. Onboarding involves bringing a new employee into the team, not the process of exiting an employee.

58. D. 802.1x is the IEEE standard for port-based Network Access Control. This protocol is frequently used to authenticate devices.

Option A is incorrect. Challenge handshake authentication protocol is an authentication protocol, but not the best choice for device authentication.

Option B is incorrect. Kerberos is an authentication protocol, but not the best choice for device authentication.

Option C is incorrect. 802.11i is the WiFi security standard, and is fully implemented in WPA2. It is not a device authentication procedure.

59. C. Multi-factor authentication uses at least one authentication method from at least two of the three categories. For example, a password (Type I: something you know) and a swipe card (Type II: something you have). Multi-factor authentication is the strongest authentication.

Options A, B, and D are all incorrect. Each of these is a good method of authentication, but they all are simply one single factor.

60. B. Lightweight Directory Access Protocol (LDAP) is often described as a phone book for your network. It lists all the network resources. Various attacks on LDAP can give the attacker a very thorough inventory of your network. Furthermore, an attacker can remove an item from LDAP and thus render it inaccessible. LDAP can be secured with TLS, and thus become LDAPS (LDAP Secure).

Option A is incorrect. Simple Network Management Protocol (SNMP) would give an attacker a great deal of information about your network, but not all. Also, it would not allow the attacker to make resources unavailable.

Option C is incorrect. Hyper Text Transfer Protocol (HTTP) is used for web pages.

Option D is incorrect. Dynamic Host Configuration Protocol (DHCP) is used to dynamically assign IP addresses.

61. C. Password Authentication Protocol (PAP) is a very old protocol that sent username and password in clear text. This should no longer be used.

Options A, B, and D are all correct; however, these are not the most significant issues with PAP.

62. A. With larger organizations, group-based is usually the most effective. Users are placed in groups (student, faculty, IT staff, support staff, administration, etc.), and permissions are managed for the group.

Option B is incorrect. Location-based would not help manage the large number of users.

Option C is incorrect. MAC is very secure, but requires granular account management that is impractical with such a large group.

Option D is incorrect. DAC would simply not be secure enough for most situations.

63. A. Periodic recertification of accounts is critical. The recertification process verifies that the account holder still requires the permissions they have been granted.

Option B is incorrect. Usage auditing could be done to support recertification, but is not as important as the recertification process.

Option C is incorrect. Standard naming conventions would not help.

Option D is incorrect. Account recovery won't help in managing permissions.

64. D. While you should use standard naming conventions, the names of accounts should not reflect the actual account role.

Options A, B, and C are all incorrect. Each of these clearly indicates the role of the account holder.

65. B. Access control to files and directories is the most fundamental aspect of file system security. This includes selecting the correct access control methodology (MAC, DAC, RBAC).

Option A is incorrect. Encryption is a very good technique for file system security, but is not the most fundamental.

Option C is incorrect. Auditing is definitely recommended for file system security, but is not the most fundamental activity.

Option D is incorrect. RAID provides fault tolerance, which is certainly necessary for servers, but is not the most fundamental form of file system security.

66. B. While there are multiple issues with this account, the password length is the most significant. Shorter passwords are inherently insecure.

Option A is incorrect. Even for a low security account, these parameters are too insecure.

Options C and D are both incorrect. Both of these are issues, but the short password length is the most significant. If the password were complex and long (perhaps over 14 characters), then the lack of password history and the password age would be less serious issues.

67. C. Disabling all accounts for the exiting user should happen immediately.

Options A and B are both incorrect. While each of these might be done, they would not be done before disabling of accounts.

Option D is incorrect. You should not delete the accounts. That might render some data (logs, files, etc.) inaccessible. Simply disable the account.

68. D. TACACS+ can use TCP or UDP, though it is more common to use TCP. It should also be noted that TACACS+ is not backward compatible.

Options A, B, and C are all incorrect. These do not accurately describe TACACS v TACACS+.

69. D. CHAP uses a hash, often MD5 for authentication, as does MS-CHAPv2. However, MS-CHAPv2 provides for mutual authentication, whereas CHAP only provides authenticating the client to the server.

Options A and C are incorrect. Neither one of these uses AES.

Option B is incorrect. CHAP does not provide mutual authentication, MS-CHAPv2 does.

70. B. With a challenge response token, the system will encrypt some value (often a random number) with the user's public key. If the user's token has the correct private key, it can decrypt the value that the system sent, and confirm that.

Option A is incorrect. An asynchronous password token generates a one-time password without the use of a clock.

Option C is incorrect. TOTP is a time synchronized one-time password.

Option D is incorrect. A static password token simply contains a password.

71. D. Discretionary Access Control (DAC) is based on the Trusted Computer System Evaluation Criteria (TCSEC). The data owner has control over the access control.

Options A, B, and C are all incorrect. These models are not based on TCSEC.

72. B. While all of these features are important to security, the Encrypted File System (EFS) allows a person to easily encrypt any file or folder. This is important to file systems security.

Option A is incorrect. Password policies are important, but not as important to file system security as being able to encrypt files and folders.

Option C is incorrect. Account lockout, like password policies, is important. But EFS is more central to file system security.

Option D is incorrect. User account control prevents unauthorized applications from running, which is important. But it's not as central to file system security as EFS.

73. D. Access control is the most important issue for database security. It is critical that the principle of least privileges is adhered to and that each database user only has access to the data necessary to do his or her job.

Option A is incorrect. Password policies are important, but are less important than access control.

Option B is incorrect. Anti-virus is always important. But database servers are not usually used for web surfing or email, thus two common means of getting a virus removed. This means anti-virus is less important than access control.

Option C is incorrect. Encrypting files is not as important to database security as access control. The files must be decrypted for access; therefore, access control is more important.

74. C. Recertification is a means for checking permissions. It essentially involves conducting certification of accounts, as if they were new. This can be done to audit permissions.

Option A is incorrect. While usage auditing is related to permissions auditing, they are not the same topic.

Option B is incorrect. Recertification is not part of onboarding.

Option D is incorrect. Credential management is important, but is not part of re-certification.

75. A. While there are security concerns with password managers, they can provide a method for storing large numbers of passwords so that users don't have to remember them all.

Option B is incorrect. Using shorter passwords would compromise security.

Option C is incorrect. OAUTH allows an end user's account information to be used by third-party services, without exposing the user's password. It won't reduce the number of passwords one has to remember.

Option D is incorrect. Kerberos is an excellent authentication protocol, but will not reduce the number of passwords one must remember.

76. C. Accounts should lock out after a small number of login attempts. Three is a common number of attempts before the account is locked out. This prevents someone from just attempting random guesses.

Option A is incorrect. Password aging will force users to change their passwords, but won't affect password guessing.

Option B is incorrect. Longer passwords would be harder to guess, but this is not as effective as account lockout policies.

Option D is incorrect. Account usage auditing won't have any effect on this issue.

77. A. Security Assertion Markup Language (SAML) is an XML-based, open-standard format for exchanging authentication and authorization data between parties.

Option B is incorrect. OAUTH allows an end user's account information to be used by third-party services, without exposing the user's password.

Option C is incorrect. RADIUS is a remote access protocol.

Option D is incorrect. NTLM is how Windows hashes passwords.

78. B. Authentication is the process that validates an identity. When a user provides their credentials (username and password), it is compared to those on file in a database on a local operating system or within an authentication server.

Option A is incorrect. Identification is the process of presenting information such as username that claims an identity.

Option C is incorrect. Authorization is the process of granting a user permission to do something.

Option D is incorrect. Accounting is the process of logging session and usage information. This can include the amount of time a user has used a resource or the amount of data the user has sent or received during their session.

79. B. Mandatory Access Control (MAC) is a type of access control that enforces authorization rules by the operating system. Users cannot override authentication or access control policies.

Option A is incorrect. Discretionary Access Control (DAC) does not have centralized control of authorization, and users can override authentication and access control policies.

Option C is incorrect. Role-Based Access Control (RBAC) provides access control based on the group the user is placed in.

Option D is incorrect. Attribute-Based Access Control (ABAC) looks at a set of environmental attributes to determine access.

80. D. The cross-over error rate or (CER) is also sometimes called the equal error rate (EER) and is the point at which the false acceptance and false rejection rates are the same.

Options A, B, and C are all incorrect. None of these accurately describes the CER.

81. A. Challenge Handshake Authentication Protocol (CHAP) was designed specifically for this purpose. It periodically reauthenticates, thus preventing session hijacking.

Options B and C are incorrect. Neither of these prevents session hijacking.

Option D is incorrect. RADIUS is a protocol for remote access, not authentication.

82. C. OpenID connect works with the Oauth 2.0 protocol and supports multiple clients including web-based and mobile clients. OpenID connect also supports REST.

Option A is incorrect. Shibboleth is a middleware solution for authentication and identity management that uses SAML (Security Assertion Mark-up Language) and works over the internet.

Option C is incorrect. RADIUS is a remote access protocol.

Option D is incorrect. OAUTH allows an end user's account information to be used by third-party services, without exposing the user's password.

83. B. Proximity cards only need to be very close to the card reader to work properly.

Option A is incorrect. Smartcards can include proximity cards, but don't have to. Put another way, there are smartcards that don't work based on proximity and have to be inserted or swiped.

Option C is incorrect. Tokens don't have a hands-free option.

Option D is incorrect. Clearly a fingerprint scanner is not hands free.

84. D. Federated identities introduce transitive trust. A login account can be used across multiple business entities, thus creating an implied trust relationship between them. The security of any of the federated identities is impacted by the security of the others.

Option A is incorrect. Kerberos can be configured to work with federated identities via remote ticket granting servers.

Options B and C are incorrect. The use of federated identities has no impact on whether or not least privileges is being obeyed or if good password management is being practiced.

85. C. Type II authentication is something you have. A smartcard is an item that the person has.

Option A is incorrect. Passwords are something you know, type I.

Option C is incorrect. Retinal scans, and all biometrics, are something you are, type III.

Option D is incorrect. These are still passwords, and thus type I.

86. A. A TPM (Trusted Platform Module) can be used in authentication. These are computer chips, and thus hardware-based access control.

Option B is incorrect. While one could argue that all hardware has at least firmware operating it, software-based access control is not a good description of this scenario.

Option C is incorrect. TPMs may use digital certificates, but this question did not specify that this particular TPM did or did not use digital certificates.

Option D is incorrect. While grammatically correct, this is not a term used in the industry.

Chapter 5: Risk Management

1. C. Adverse actions are administrative actions that are placed against employees. These actions include letters of reprimand, leave with or without pay, or termination. Along with these actions the policy should include actions such as disabling user accounts and revoking privileges, such as access to facilities to prevent data from being compromised. When an employee has been placed with administrative actions, the company shouldn't worry about vindictive actions they will take against the company.

Option A is incorrect. Mandatory vacation policy is used by companies to detect fraud by having a second person, familiar with the duties, help discover any illicit activities.

Option B is incorrect. Exit interviews give the company an opportunity to find problems within departments. They also allow HR to identify any knowledge that is about to be lost, such as information the employee knows that is not written down anywhere.

Option D is incorrect. Onboarding is the process of adding an employee to a company's identity and access management system.

2. C. Change management is the process of documenting all changes made to a company's network and computers. Avoiding making changes at the same time makes tracking any problems that can occur much simpler.

Option A is incorrect. Due diligence is the process of investigation and verification of the accuracy of a particular act.

Option B is incorrect. Acceptable use is a policy stating what a user may or may not have access to on a company's network or the Internet.

Option D is incorrect. Due care is the effort made by a reasonable party to avoid harm to another. It is the level of judgment, care, determination, and activity a person would reasonably expect to do under certain conditions.

3. A. The main reason to avoid penetration tests is answer A. It's advised to perform vulnerability test often rather than penetration tests. Pentests can cause disruption to businesses. This is the main focus of the question.

Options B, C, and D are incorrect. These options are positive reasons why penetration testing should be performed.

4. A. Acceptable use policy is a document stating what a user may or may not have access to on a company's network or the Internet.

Option B is incorrect. Clean desk policy ensures that all sensitive/confidential documents are removed from an end-user workstation and locked up when the documents are not in use.

Option C is incorrect. Mandatory vacation policy is used by companies to detect fraud by having a second person, familiar with the duties, help discover any illicit activities.

Option D is incorrect. Job rotation is a policy that describes the practice of moving employees between different tasks to promote experience and variety.

5. D. Encrypting the backup data before storing it off-site ensures data confidentiality.

Option A is incorrect. Generating file hashes will ensure integrity; files have not changed or been tampered with.

Option B is incorrect. Scanning the backup data for viruses is a task that's performed before the data is restored.

Option C is incorrect. Chain of custody refers to the chronological documentation showing the custody, control, transfer, analysis, and disposition of physical or electronic evidence.

6. C. A hot site contains all of the alternate computer and telecommunication equipment needed in a disaster. Testing this environment is simple.

Option A is incorrect. A warm site is harder to test because it contains the equipment but no employees and company data.

Option B is incorrect. A cold site is the hardest to test because it includes a basic room with limited equipment.

Option D is incorrect. A medium site is not something referred to as a recovery site.

7. B. Switches forwards data only to the devices that need to receive it, so when capturing network traffic the computer will see only broadcast and multicast packets along with traffic being sent and received to the connected computer.

Option A is incorrect. Ethernet switches in an isolated broadcast domain will send broadcast packets to all computers that are part of the domain. The entire switch can be a broadcast domain or a certain number of ports can be grouped into a VLAN (virtual local area network).

Option C is incorrect. Promiscuous mode enabled on the NIC will capture all traffic within the network, but this was not the problem in this scenario.

Option D is incorrect. Promiscuous mode disabled on the NIC will not capture all traffic within the network but will only broadcast and multicast packets along with traffic being sent and received from the computer. The scenario focused on the Ethernet switch, not the laptop's NIC.

8. A. A snapshot is the state of a system at a particular point in time. It's also known as a system image and is not a step in the incident response process.

Options B, C, and D are incorrect. Preparation, recovery, and containment are steps of the incident response process.

9. B. Technical controls are used to restrict data access and operating system components, security applications, network devices, and encryption techniques. Logical controls use authentication mechanisms.

Option A is incorrect. Access controls can be part of technical controls; however, it is not a term that is synonymous with technical controls.

Option C is incorrect. Detective controls detect intrusion as it happens and uncovers a violation.

Option D is incorrect. Preventive controls avoid a security breach or an interruption of critical services before they can happen.

10. A. Companies will use mandatory vacations policies to detect fraud by having a second person, familiar with the duties, help discover any illicit activities.

Option B is incorrect. Clean desk policy ensures that all sensitive/confidential documents are removed from an end user workstation and locked up when the documents are not in use.

Option C is incorrect. A nondisclosure agreement (NDA) protects sensitive and intellectual data from getting into the wrong hands.

Option D is incorrect. Continuing education is the process of training adult learners in a broad list of post-secondary learning activities and programs. Companies will use continuing education in training their employees on the new threats and also reiterating current policies and their importance.

11. A. Privacy impact assessment (PIA) is a measurement of how a company can keep private information safe while the company is in possession of PII.

Option B is incorrect. Business impact analysis (BIA) determines the potential effects of an interruption to a company's operations as a result of a disaster or emergency.

Option C is incorrect. Recovery time objective (RTO) is the duration of time in which a company's process must be restored after a disaster.

Option D is incorrect. A single point-of-failure (SPF) is a component that will stop the entire operations of a system to work if it fails.

12. B. A business continuity plan is a policy that describes and approves the company's overall business continuity strategy. This also includes identifying critical systems to protect.

Option A is incorrect. A disaster recovery plan (DRP) is a policy that describes and approves the company's disaster recovery strategy. This plan will help the company recover from an incident with minimal loss of time and money.

Option C is incorrect. An IT contingency plan is a component of the BCP. It specifies alternate IT procedures for a company to switch over to when it's faced with a disruption of service leading to a disaster for the company.

Option D is incorrect. A succession plan ensures all key company personnel have at least one designated backup who can perform the critical functions when required.

13. B. Locking cabinets and drawers is the best solution because the employee would be the only one with a key.

Option A is incorrect. Multiple people may have keys to a department door lock.

Option C is incorrect. A proximity card is a contactless smartcard that is held near an electronic reader to grant access to a particular area.

Option D is incorrect. Onboarding is the process of adding an employee to a company's identity and access management system.

14. D. The tabletop exercise test is considered a cost-effective and efficient way to identify areas of overlaps in a plan before implementing a test.

Option A is incorrect. An after-action report examines a response to an incident or exercise and identifies its strengths that will be maintained and built on. Also, it helps recognize potential areas of improvement.

Option B is incorrect. Failover is the continuous ability to automatically and flawlessly switch to a highly reliable backup. This can be activated in a redundant manner or in a standby operating mode should the primary server fail. The main purpose of failover is to provide availability of data or service to a user.

Option C is incorrect. The eradication process involves removing and restoring affected systems by reimaging the system's hard drive and installing patches.

15. C. Fingerprints are considered PHI (Protected Health Information), according to HIPPA rules.

Options A, B, and D are incorrect. These are classified as PII (Personally Identifiable Information), according to the NIST.

16. D. Quantitative risk assessment is the process of assigning numerical values to the probability an event will occur and what the impact of the event will have.

Option A is incorrect. Change management is the process of managing configuration changes made to a network.

Option B is incorrect. Vulnerability assessment attempts to identify, quantify, and rank the weaknesses in a system.

Option C is incorrect. Qualitative risk assessment is the process of ranking which risk poses the most danger such as low, medium, and high.

17. B. Risk avoidance is a strategy to deflect threats in order to avoid the costly and disruptive consequences of a damaging event. It also attempts to minimize vulnerabilities that can pose a threat.

Option A is incorrect. Risk transfer is the act of moving the risk to hosted providers who assume the responsibility for recovery and restoration or by acquiring insurance to cover the costs emerging from a risk.

Option C is incorrect. Risk acceptance is a strategy of recognizing, identifying, and accepting a risk that is sufficiently unlikely or has limited impact that a corrective control is not warranted.

Option D is incorrect. Risk mitigation is when a company implements controls to reduce vulnerabilities or weaknesses in a system. It can also reduce the impact of a threat.

18. D. A memorandum of understanding (MOU) is a type of agreement that is usually not legally binding. This agreement is intended to be mutually beneficial without involving courts or money.

Option A is incorrect. A SLA (service level agreement) defines the level of service the customer expects from the service provider. The level of service definitions should be specific and measurable in each area.

Option B is incorrect. A BPA (business partnership agreement) is a legal agreement between partners. It establishes the terms, conditions, and expectations of the relationship between the partners.

Option C is incorrect. An ISA (interconnection security agreement) is an agreement that specifies the technical and security requirements of the interconnection between organizations.

19. B. A SLA (service level agreement) defines the level of service the customer expects from the service provider. The level of service definitions should be specific and measurable in each area.

Option A is incorrect. A MOU (memorandum of understanding) is a legal document that describes a mutual agreement between parties.

Option C is incorrect. An ISA (interconnection security agreement) is an agreement that specifies the technical and security requirements of the interconnection between organizations.

Option D is incorrect. A BPA (business partnership agreement) is a legal agreement between partners. It establishes the terms, conditions, and expectations of the relationship between the partners.

20. A. The single loss expectancy (SLE) is the product of the value ($16,000) and the exposure factor (.35), or $5,600.

Options B, C, and D are incorrect. These values do not represent the single loss expectancy.

21. C. Antivirus is an example of a corrective control. A corrective control is designed to correct a situation.

Option A is incorrect. An IDS (intrusion detection system) is a detective control because it detects security breaches.

Option B is incorrect. An audit log is a detective control because it detects security breaches.

Option D is incorrect. A router is a preventive control because it prevents security breaches with access control lists.

22. A, C. A deterrent control is used to warn a potential attacker not to attack. Lighting added to the perimeter and warning signs such as a "no trespassing" sign are deterrent controls.

Options B and D are incorrect. These are examples of detective controls. A detective control is designed to uncover a violation.

23. D. Testing and training are preventative administrative controls. Administrative controls dictate how security policies should be executed to accomplish the company's security goals.

Option A is incorrect. Detective technical control uncovers a violation through technology.

Option B is incorrect. Preventive technical control attempts to stop a violation through technology.

Option C is incorrect. Detective administrative control uncovers a violation through policies, procedures, and guidelines.

24. D. Eradication is the next step after containment.

Options A, B, and C are incorrect. The correct steps of the incident response process are preparation, identification, containment, eradication, recovery, and lessons learned.

25. A. Risk acceptance is a strategy of recognizing, identifying, and accepting a risk that is sufficiently unlikely or has limited impact that a corrective control is not warranted.

Option B is incorrect. Risk transfer is the act of moving the risk to hosted providers who assume the responsibility for recovery and restoration or by acquiring insurance to cover the costs emerging from a risk.

Option C is incorrect. Risk avoidance is the removal of the vulnerability that can increase a particular risk so that it is avoided altogether.

Option D is incorrect. Risk mitigation is when a company implements controls to reduce vulnerabilities or weaknesses in a system. It can also reduce the impact of a threat.

26. A. Taking screenshots gives an investigator a useful way to collect information on a computer screen. Screenshots can be acquired in many ways and allow the investigator to reproduce what happened on the screen.

Option B is incorrect. The identification phase is part of an incident response process and deals with the discovery and determination of whether a deviation from normal operations within a company was an incident.

Option C is incorrect. The tabletop exercise test is considered a cost-effective and efficient way to identify areas of overlaps in a plan before implementing a test.

Option D is incorrect. Generating file hashes will ensure integrity and ensure that files have not changed or been tampered with.

27. B. Storing backup data at an alternate site in another city will help protect the data if there were a complete disaster at the primary location. Storing backups outside of the original location is known as off-site backups. Also, the distance associated with an off-site backup can be a logistics challenge.

Option A is incorrect. Storing backup data at an alternate location within the city may not be good if the area has to be evacuated.

Option C is incorrect. Storing backup data in a safe at the company's site may not be good should the primary location become completely destroyed.

Option D is incorrect. Storing backup data at an employee's home is never a good idea.

28. C. Identifying systems that are considered a single point of failure is not a purpose of PTA.

Options A, B, and D are incorrect. Privacy threshold analysis (PTA) can determine whether a program or system has privacy implications and whether additional privacy compliance documentation is required such as a privacy impact assessment (PIA).

29. C. Purging removes all the data from a hard drive and the data cannot be rebuilt.

Option A is incorrect. Destruction wouldn't help the company sell the hard drive at the computer sale.

Option B is incorrect. Shredding wouldn't help the company sell the hard drive at the computer sale because it physically destroys the hard drive.

Option D is incorrect. Formatting isn't good enough to remove data because it can be recovered by third-party software. Formatting moves the pointer to the location the data resides.

30. B. An acceptable use policy describes the limits and guidelines for users to make use of an organization's physical and intellectual resources. This includes allowing or limiting the use of personal email during work hours.

Option A is incorrect. A service level agreement (SLA) defines the level of service the customer expects from the service provider. The level of service definitions should be specific and measurable in each area.

Option C is incorrect. An incident response plan provides instructions for detecting, responding to, and limiting the effects of an information security event.

Option D is incorrect. Chain of custody refers to the chronological documentation showing the custody, control, transfer, analysis, and disposition of physical or electronic evidence.

31. C. After identifying the malware incident, the next step you would perform based on the incident response process is to contain the malware to further study the incident and prevent it from spreading across the network.

Option A is incorrect. Recovery is performed after eradicating the malware.

Option B is incorrect. Eradicating the malware is performed after you have contained the malware.

Option D is incorrect. Identification has been performed when you discovered the malware.

32. A. Onboarding is the process of adding an employee to a company's identity and access management system.

Option B is incorrect. Offboarding is the process of removing an employee from the company's identity and access management system.

Option C is incorrect. Adverse action is an official personnel action that is taken for disciplinary reasons.

Option D is incorrect. Job rotation gives individuals the ability to see various parts of the organization and how it operates. It also eliminates the need for a company to rely on one individual for security expertise should the employee become disgruntled and decide to harm the company. Recovering from a disgruntled employee's attack is easier when multiple employees understand the company's security posture.

33. D. An interconnection security agreement (ISA) is an agreement that specifies technical and security requirements for planning, establishing, maintaining, and disconnecting a secure connection between at least two companies.

Option A is incorrect. A business partners agreement (BPA) is a written agreement that details what the relationship will be between business partners. This agreement will include the partner's obligations toward the partnership. A BPA can help settle conflicts that arise within the partnership.

Option B is incorrect. A memorandum of understanding (MOU) is an agreement of understanding between two or more parties signifying their purpose to work together toward a common goal. A MOU is less formal than an SLA and will not include monetary penalties.

Option C is incorrect. A service level agreement (SLA) is an agreement between a company and a vendor that specifies performance expectations. Minimum uptime and maximum downtime levels are included in an SLA. Also included is a monetary penalty should the vendor not be able to meet the agreed expectations.

34. A. A clean desk policy ensures that all sensitive/confidential documents are removed from an end-user workstation and locked up when the documents are not in use.

Option B is incorrect. Background checks are performed when a potential employee is considered for hire.

Option C is incorrect. Continuing education is the process of training adult learners in a broad list of postsecondary learning activities and programs. Companies will use continuing education in training their employees on the new threats and also reiterating current policies and their importance.

Option D is incorrect. Job rotation policy is the practice of moving employees between different tasks to promote experience and variety.

35. A. As users register for an account, they enter letters and numbers they are given on the web page before they can register. This is an example of a deterrent control as it prevents bots from registering and proves this is a real person.

Option B is incorrect. Detective controls detect intrusion as it happens and uncovers a violation.

Option C is incorrect. A compensating control is used to satisfy a requirement for a security measure that is too difficult or impractical to implement at the current time.

Option D is incorrect. Degaussing is a method of removing data from a magnetic storage media by changing the magnetic field.

36. D. Parking policy generally outlines parking provisions for employees and visitors. This includes the criteria and procedures for allocating parking spaces for employees.

Option A is incorrect. An acceptable use policy describes the limits and guidelines for users to make use of an organization's physical and intellectual resources. This includes allowing or limiting the use of personal email during work hours.

Option B is incorrect. Social media policy defines how employees should use social media networks and applications such as Facebook, Twitter, LinkedIn, and others. It can adversely affect a company's reputation.

Option C is incorrect. Password policy defines the complexity of creating passwords. It should also define weak passwords and how users should protect password safety.

37. C. Proprietary data is a form of confidential information, and if the information is revealed, it can have severe effects on the company's competitive edge.

Option A is incorrect. High is a generic label assigned to data internally that represents the amount of risk being exposed outside the company.

Option B is incorrect. The top-secret label is often used within governmental systems where data and access may be granted or denied based on assigned categories.

Option D is incorrect. Low is a generic label assigned to data internally that represents the amount of risk being exposed outside the company.

38. B. Provide security user awareness training to all employees regarding the risk of using personal email through company computers. The ability to access personal email is a security risk because the company is unable to filter emails through the company's Exchange server.

Option A is incorrect. The company is unable to encrypt user's email messages through services such as Yahoo Mail and Gmail. The encryption is performed by the company providing the email service.

Option C is incorrect. Providing every user with their own device to access their personal email is not the best option as the next step. While employees use these devices within the company's network, the company doesn't have full control of what emails are entering the network.

Option D is incorrect. The company may have some control of personal emails routing through the company's Exchange server, but this is not the best next step after creating and approving the email use policy. The purpose of the email use policy is to limit the use of personal email because the company doesn't have full control of what emails the employees are allowing into the network.

39. C. Antivirus software is used to protect computer systems from malware and is not a physical security control.

Options A, B, and D are incorrect. Physical controls are security measures put in place to reduce the risk of harm coming to a physical property. This includes protection of personnel, hardware, software, networks, and data from physical actions and events that could cause damage or loss.

40. B. A disaster recovery plan (DRP) is a plan that helps a company recover from an incident with minimal loss of time and money. It prioritizes critical computer systems.

Option A is incorrect. A single point of failure is a weakness in the design, or configuration of a system in which one fault or malfunction will cause the whole system to halt operating and would not be found within a DRP.

Option C is incorrect. Exposure factor would be found within a risk assessment.

Option D is incorrect. Asset value would be found within a risk assessment.

41. A. Quantitative risk assessment is the process of assigning numerical values to the probability an event will occur and what the impact of the event will have.

Option B is incorrect. Qualitative risk assessment is the process of ranking which risk poses the most danger such as low, medium, and high.

Option C is incorrect. Business impact analysis is used to evaluate the possible effect a business can suffer should an interruption to critical system operations occur. This interruption could be as a result of an accident, emergency, or disaster.

Option D is incorrect. Threat assessment is a process of identifying and categorizing different threats such as, environmental and manmade. It also attempts to identify the potential impact from the threats.

42. D. A nondisclosure agreement (NDA) protects sensitive and intellectual data from getting into the wrong hands.

Options A, B, and C are incorrect. An NDA is a legal contract between the company and third-party vendor to not disclose information per the agreement. Sending encrypted data can still be decrypted by the third-party vendor if they have the appropriate certificate but does not restrict access to the data. Violating an NDA would constitute unauthorized data sharing, and a violation of privileged user role-based awareness training has nothing to do with sharing proprietary information.

43. A and C. FTP (File Transport Protocol) uses port 21 and Telnet uses port 23. These protocols are considered weak and are not recommended for use. They are susceptible to eavesdropping.

Option B is incorrect. SMTP (Simple Mail Transport Protocol) uses port 25.

Option D is incorrect. DNS (Domain Name System) uses port 53.

44. A. Incremental backups are the quickest backup method but the slowest method to restore. Incremental backup backs up all new files and any files that have changed since the last full backup or incremental backup. To restore from incremental backups, you will need the full backup and every incremental backup in order.

Option B is incorrect. Differential backup backs up all new files and any files that have changed since the last full backup. To restore from differential backups, you will need the full backup and the most recent differential backup.

Option C is incorrect. Full backup backs up all the files each time the backup runs.

Option D is incorrect. A snapshot is the state of a system at a particular point in time. It's also known as a system image.

45. C. Data labeling policy includes how data is labeled such as confidential, private, or public. It should also include how the data is handled and disposed of for all classifications of data. Before data can be disposed of, you will need to destroy it with a data sanitization tool.

Option A is incorrect. Degaussing is a method of removing data from a magnetic storage media by changing the magnetic field.

Option B is incorrect. An acceptable use policy describes the limits and guidelines for users to make use of an organization's physical and intellectual resources. This includes allowing or limiting the use of personal email during work hours.

Option D is incorrect. Wiping, also known as overwriting, will replace the data with all zeros to prevent data from being recovered by third-party software.

46. D. A single point of failure is a weakness in the design or configuration of a system in which one fault or malfunction will cause the whole system to halt operating.

Option A is incorrect. Failover is the continuous ability to automatically and flawlessly switch to a highly reliable backup.

Option B is incorrect. A cluster ensures the availability of critical services by using a group of computers instead of a single computer.

Option C is incorrect. Load-balancing divides the amount of work a computer can do between two or more computers. This allows more work to be completed in the same amount of time.

47. A. Detective controls detect intrusion as it happens and uncovers a violation.

Option B is incorrect. A guard is an example of a preventive control. Preventive controls stop an action from happening.

Option C is incorrect. A firewall is an example of a technical control. Technical controls are applied through technology and may be deterrent, preventive, detective, or compensating.

Option D is incorrect. An IPS (intrusion prevention system) is an example of a technical control. Technical controls are applied through technology and may be a deterrent, preventive, detective, or compensating.

48. D. An ISA (interconnection security agreement) is an agreement that specifies the technical and security requirements of the interconnection between organizations.

Option A is incorrect. A memorandum of understanding (MOU) is a type of agreement that is usually not legally binding. This agreement is intended to be mutually beneficial without involving courts or money.

Option B is incorrect. A BPA (business partnership agreement) is a legal agreement between partners. It establishes the terms, conditions, and expectations of the relationship between the partners.

Option C is incorrect. An SLA (service level agreement) defines the level of service the customer expects from the service provider. The level of service definitions should be specific and measurable in each area.

49. C. Sharing of profits and losses and the addition or removal of a partner are typically included in a BPA (business partner agreement). Also included are the responsibilities of each partner.

Option A is incorrect. Expectations between parties such as a company and an Internet service provider are typically found in a service level agreement. Expectations include the level of performance given during the contractual service.

Option B is incorrect. A service level agreement will provide a clear means of determining whether a specific function or service has been provided according to the agreed-upon level of performance.

Option D is incorrect. Security requirements associated with interconnecting IT systems are typically found in an interconnection security agreement.

50. C. A continuity of operations plan focuses on restoring critical business functions after an outage to an alternate site. The plan will determine if a company can continue its operations during the outage.

Option A is incorrect. BIA (business impact analysis) is performed before the creation of business continuity plans, and BIAs are not tested.

Option B is incorrect. A succession plan ensures all key company personnel have at least one designated backup who can perform the critical functions when required.

Option D is incorrect. A service level agreement (SLA) defines the level of service the customer expects from the service provider. The level of service definitions should be specific and measurable in each area.

51. D. System owner is a type of employee who would receive role-based training on how best to manage a particular system.

Option A is incorrect. Users are generally the front-line employees and would receive general security awareness training.

Option B is incorrect. Privileged users would receive training on how best to handle additional network and system access.

Option C is incorrect. Executive users would receive training on how to spot targeted attacks.

52. A. A vulnerability scanner attempts to identify weaknesses in a system.

Option B is incorrect. A protocol analyzer used with a promiscuous mode NIC can capture all network traffic.

Option C is incorrect. A port scanner identifies open ports on a server or host.

Option D is incorrect. Password crackers can be used to check for easily crackable passwords. Vulnerability scanners can provide more data about computer security such as open ports and weak passwords.

53. C. Recovery process brings affected systems back into the company's production environment carefully to avoid leading to another incident.

Option A is incorrect. The lessons learned process is the most critical phase because it is the phase in which you complete any documentation that may be beneficial in future incidents. Documentation should include information such as when the problem was first detected and by whom, how the problem was contained and eradicated, the work that was performed during the recovery, and areas that may need improvement.

Option B is incorrect. The preparation process prepares a company's team to be ready to handle an incident at a moment's notice.

Option D is incorrect. The containment process is designed to minimize the damage and prevent any further damage from happening.

54. D. Chain of custody refers to the chronological documentation showing the custody, control, transfer, analysis, and disposition of physical or electronic evidence.

Option A is incorrect. Incident handling is a guide that explains the process and procedures of how to handle particular incidents.

Option B is incorrect. Legal hold is a written directive issued by attorneys ordering clients to preserve pertinent evidence in an anticipated litigation, audit, or government investigation. This evidence can include paper documents and electronically stored information.

Option C is incorrect. Order of volatility represents the order in which you should collect evidence. In general terms, evidence should be collected starting with the most volatile and moving to the least volatile. Volatile means data is not permanent.

55. D. The first response from the incident response should be identification. The malware needs to be identified as well as the computers.

Option A is incorrect. The containment process is designed to minimize the damage and prevent any further damage from happening.

Option B is incorrect. The eradication process involves removing and restoring affected systems by reimaging the system's hard drive and installing patches.

Option C is incorrect. The lessons learned process is the most critical phase because it is the phase in which you complete any documentation that may be beneficial in future incidents. Documentation should include information such as when the problem was first detected and by whom, how the problem was contained and eradicated, the work that was performed during the recovery, and areas that may need improvement.

56. A, D. Custodians maintain access to data as well as the integrity.

Options B and C are incorrect. CEO and sales executives are not normally responsible for maintaining access to and integrity of the data.

57. D. A backup generator is a compensating control—an alternate control that replaces the original control when it cannot be used due to limitations of the environment.

Option A is incorrect. A firewall is considered a preventive control.

Option B is incorrect. A security guard is considered a physical control.

Option C is incorrect. An IDS (intrusion detection system) is considered a detective control.

58. A. Preventive controls stop an action from happening—in this scenario, preventing an unauthorized user from gaining access to the network when the user steps away.

Option B is incorrect. A corrective control is designed to correct a situation.

Option C is incorrect. A deterrent control is used to deter a security breach.

Option D is incorrect. A detective control is designed to uncover a violation.

59. B. PHI (protected health information) is any data that refers to health status, delivery of health care, or payment for health care that is gathered by a health care provider and can be linked to an individual according to U.S. law.

Option A is incorrect. AES (Advanced Encryption Standard) is a symmetrical 128-bit block encryption system.

Option C is incorrect. PII (Personally Identifiable Information) is information that can be used on its own or with other information to identify an individual.

Option D is incorrect. TLS (Transport Layer Security) is a protocol that encrypts data over a computer network.

60. C. Job rotation allows individuals to see various parts of the organization and how it operates. It also eliminates the need for a company to rely on one individual for security expertise should the employee become disgruntled and decide to harm the company. Recovering from a disgruntled employee's attack is easier when multiple employees understand the company's security posture.

Option A is incorrect. Separation of duties is the concept of having more than one person required to complete a task.

Option B is incorrect. Mandatory vacation policy is used by companies to detect fraud by having a second person, familiar with the duties, help discover any illicit activities.

Option D is incorrect. Onboarding is the process of adding an employee to a company's identity and access management system.

61. B and C. Backup tapes should not be stored near power sources such as CRT monitors and speakers. These devices can cause the tapes to be degaussed.

Option A is incorrect. A workstation has no chance of degaussing backup tapes.

Option D is incorrect. An LCD screen has no chance of degaussing backup tapes.

62. A. The eradication process involves removing and restoring affected systems by reimaging the system's hard drive and installing patches.

Option B is incorrect. The preparation process prepares a company's team to be ready to handle an incident at a moment's notice.

Option C is incorrect. The purpose of the containment process is to minimize the damage and prevent any further damage from happening.

Option D is incorrect. The recovery process brings affected systems back into the company's production environment carefully to avoid leading to another incident.

63. D. A unified threat management (UTM) appliance is a single console a security administrator can monitor and manage easily. This could create a single point of failure.

Options A, B, and C are incorrect. With a UTM, each protection can be performed simultaneously. This UTM can centralize various security techniques into a single appliance. It is also tied to one vendor and allows for a single, streamlined function.

64. C. Unauthorized access of a network through a firewall by a threat actor is considered an external threat.

Options A, B, and D are incorrect. Each of the threats are considered internal because they can compromise a company's network from within.

65. A and B. ALE (annual loss expectancy) is the product of the ARO (annual rate of occurrence) and the SLE (single loss expectancy) and is mathematically expressed as ALE = ARO × SLE. Single loss expectancy is the cost of any single loss and it is mathematically expressed as SLE = AV (asset value) × EF (exposure factor).

Options C and D are incorrect. Training expenses and man-hour expenses are valid IT forensic budget items.

66. C. Capturing the system image involves making an exact image of the drive so that it can be referenced later in the investigation.

Option A is incorrect. Chain of custody offers assurances that evidence has been preserved, protected, and handled correctly after it has been collected. Documents show who handled the evidence and when they handled it.

Option B is incorrect. Order of volatility represents the order in which you should collect evidence. In general terms, evidence should be collected starting with the most volatile and moving to the least volatile. Volatile means data is not permanent.

Option D is incorrect. Taking screenshots gives an investigator a useful way to collect information on a computer screen. This will allow the investigator to reproduce what happened on the screen.

67. A. Risk is defined as the likelihood of occurrence of a threat and the corresponding loss potential. Risk is the probability of a threat actor to exploit vulnerability. The purpose of system hardening is to remove as many security risks as possible. Hardening is typically performed by disabling all nonessential software programs and utilities from the workstation.

Option B is incorrect. The threat agent is the component that exploits a vulnerability.

Option C is incorrect. The exposure factor is the percentage or portion of the asset that will be lost or destroyed when exposed to a threat.

Option D is incorrect. Risk mitigation is when a company implements controls to reduce vulnerabilities or weaknesses in a system. It can also reduce the impact of a threat.

68. B. Lessons learned documentation is a phase of the incident response process.

Options A, C, and D are incorrect. These elements should be included in the preparation phase.

69. C. Nondisclosure agreements (NDAs) are signed by an employee at the time of hiring, and they impose a contractual obligation on employees to maintain the confidentiality of information. Disclosure of information can lead to legal ramifications and penalties. NDAs cannot ensure a decrease in security breaches.

Option A is incorrect. Job rotation policy is the practice of moving employees between different tasks to promote experience and variety.

Option B is incorrect. Separation of duties is the concept of having more than one person required to complete a task.

Option D is incorrect. Mandatory vacation policy is used by companies to detect fraud by having a second person, familiar with the duties, help discover any illicit activities.

70. C. Security policy defines how to secure physical and information technology assets. This document should be continuously updated as technology and employee requirements change.

Option A is incorrect. Account policy enforcement regulates the security parameters of who can and cannot access a system.

Option B is incorrect. Change management is the process of managing configuration changes made to a network.

Option D is incorrect. Risk assessment identifies the dangers that could negatively impact a company's ability to conduct business.

71. C. A differential backup copies files that have changed since the last full backup.

Option A is incorrect. A partial backup is when only portions of files changed are backed up.

Option B is incorrect. A full backup is when all files are copied to a storage media.

Option D is incorrect. Backing up only the files that have changed since the last full or incremental backup is considered an incremental backup.

72. B. Lessons learned process is the most critical phase because it is the phase to complete any documentation that may be beneficial in future incidents. Documentation should include information such as when the problem was first detected and by whom, how the problem was contained and eradicated, the work that was performed during the recovery, and areas that may need improvement.

Option A is incorrect. The preparation process prepares a company's team to be ready to handle an incident at a moment's notice.

Option C is incorrect. The containment process is designed to minimize the damage and prevent any further damage from happening.

Option D is incorrect. The recovery process brings affected systems back into the company's production environment carefully to avoid leading to another incident.

73. B and C. Penetration and vulnerability testing can help identify risk. Before a tester performs these tests, they should receive written authorization.

Option A is incorrect. Quantitative risk assessment is the process of assigning numerical values to the probability an event will occur and what the impact of the event will have.

Option D is incorrect. Qualitative risk assessment is the process of ranking which risk poses the most danger using measures such as low, medium, and high.

74. C. Shredding is the process of reducing the size of objects so the information is no longer usable. Other practices includes burning, pulping, and pulverizing.

Option A is incorrect. Degaussing is a method of removing data from a magnetic storage media by changing the magnetic field.

Option B is incorrect. Capturing the system image involves making an exact image of the drive so that it can be referenced later in the investigation.

Option D is incorrect. Wiping, also known as overwriting, will replace the data with all zeros to prevent data from being recovered by third-party software.

75. C. SFTP (secure FTP) encrypts data that is transmitted over the network.

Option A is incorrect. Telnet is a command-line utility for accessing remote computers and does not provide any security features.

Option B is incorrect. FTP (File Transport Protocol) sends data in clear text and can easily be viewed over the network.

Option D is incorrect. SMTP (Simple Mail Transfer Protocol) sends and receives emails and does not provide any security features.

76. C. Zackary will need four backups to restore the server if it crashes on Thursday afternoon. The four backups are Sunday evening full backup, Monday evening incremental backup, Tuesday evening incremental backup, and Wednesday evening incremental backup. Incremental backups require the full backup and all the incremental backups in order.

Options A, B, and D are incorrect. Incremental backups require the full backup and all the incremental backups in order.

77. A. Risk avoidance is a strategy to deflect threats in order to avoid the costly and disruptive consequences of a damaging event. It also attempts to minimize vulnerabilities that can pose a threat.

Option B is incorrect. The risk register is a document, also known as a risk log, created at the beginning of a project to track issues and address any problems as they arise.

Option C is incorrect. Risk acceptance is a strategy of recognizing, identifying, and accepting a risk that is sufficiently unlikely or has limited impact that a corrective control is not warranted.

Option D is incorrect. Risk mitigation is when a company implements controls to reduce vulnerabilities or weaknesses in a system. It can also reduce the impact of a threat.

78. C. A hot site, also known as an alternate processing site, contains all of the alternate computer and telecommunication equipment needed in a disaster. Testing this environment is simple.

Option A is incorrect. A cold site is the hardest to test because it includes a basic room with limited equipment.

Option B is incorrect. A warm site is harder to test because it contains only the equipment and no employees or company data.

Option D is incorrect. A differential site is not a valid term.

79. D. Systems should be restored within four hours with a minimum loss of one day's worth of data. RTO is the amount of time within which a process must be restored after a disaster to meet business continuity. It defines how much time it takes to recover after notification of process disruption. RPO specifies the allowable data loss. It is the amount of time that can pass during an interruption before the quantity of data lost during that period surpasses business continuity planning's maximum acceptable threshold.

Options A, B, and C are incorrect. These restorations do not fall within the description of the plan.

80. A. This statement refers to the data retention policy.

Option B is incorrect. This statement refers to the clean desk policy.

Option C is incorrect. This statement refers to the change management policy.

Option D is incorrect. This statement refers to the memorandum of understanding (MOU) policy.

81. B and D. Companies can lose a large amount of income in a short period of downtime. Companies can have business contracts that state a minimum amount of downtime can occur if a disaster occurs. These reasons can be used to support the reason for a warm site because the warm site relies on backups to recover from a disaster.

Option A is incorrect. A company losing a small amount of income during a long period of downtime may not support the cost of a warm site.

Option C is incorrect. A company can bring a cold site online within 72 hours and resume business services. This would not support the cost of a warm site.

82. A and D. Confidentiality allows authorized users to gain access to sensitive and protected data. Integrity ensures that the data hasn't been altered and is protected from unauthorized modification.

Option B is incorrect. Safety is a common goal of security that includes providing protection to personnel and other assets.

Option C is incorrect. Availability means information is always going to be something a user can access.

83. B. ALE (annual loss expectancy) is the product of the ARO (annual rate of occurrence) and the SLE (single loss expectancy) and is mathematically expressed as ALE = ARO × SLE. Single loss expectancy is the cost of any single loss and it is mathematically expressed as SLE = AV (asset value) × EF (exposure factor).

84. A and D. The correct answer is life and property. Both of these impact scenarios include examples of severe weather events.

Option B is incorrect. A reputation impact scenario includes price gouging during natural disasters and response time for addressing information disclosure.

Option C is incorrect. Salary is not an impact scenario.

85. A. RPO (recovery point objective) specifies the allowable data loss. It is the amount of time that can pass during an interruption before the quantity of data lost during that period surpasses business continuity planning's maximum acceptable threshold.

Option B is incorrect. A single point of failure is a weakness in the design, or configuration of a system in which one fault or malfunction will cause the whole system to stop operating.

Option C is incorrect. MTTR (mean time to repair) is the average time it takes for a failed device or component to be repaired or replaced.

Option D is incorrect. MTBF (mean time between failures) is a measurement to show how reliable a hardware component is.

86. A and D. Preventive controls are proactive and are used to avoid a security breach or an interruption of critical services before they can happen.

Options B and C are incorrect. Security cameras and door alarms are examples of detective control. Detective controls detect intrusion as it happens and uncovers a violation.

87. C. Risk transfer is the act of moving the risk to hosted providers who assume the responsibility for recovery and restoration or by acquiring insurance to cover the costs emerging from a risk.

Option A is incorrect. Risk acceptance is a strategy of recognizing, identifying, and accepting a risk that is sufficiently unlikely or has such limited impact that a corrective control is not warranted.

Option B is incorrect. Risk mitigation is when a company implements controls to reduce vulnerabilities or weaknesses in a system. It can also reduce the impact of a threat.

Option D is incorrect. Risk avoidance is the removal of the vulnerability that can increase a particular risk so that it is avoided altogether.

88. C. The correct answer is property. Physical damage to a building and the company's computer equipment can be caused by intentional man-made attacks.

Option A is incorrect. Life impact endangers the lives of employees and customers.

Option B is incorrect. Reputation impact could impact the image the company has in its community.

Option D is incorrect. Safety impact jeopardizes the safety of employees and customers.

89. A. A business impact analysis (BIA) helps identify the risks that would affect business operations such as finance impact. The will help a company recover from a disaster.

Option B is incorrect. Return on investment (ROI) is used to assess the efficiency of an investment. ROI measures the amount of return on an investment to the investment's cost.

Option C is incorrect. Recovery time objective (RTO) is the duration of time in which a company's process must be restored after a disaster.

Option D is incorrect. Life impact endangers the lives of employees and customers.

90. D. A preventive control is used to avoid a security breach or an interruption of critical services before they can happen.

Option A is incorrect. Administrative controls are defined through policies, procedures, and guidelines.

Option B is incorrect. A compensating control is used to satisfy a requirement for a security measure that is too difficult or impractical to implement at the current time.

Option C is incorrect. A deterrent control is used to deter a security breach.

91. A. Technical controls are applied through technology and may be deterrent, preventive, detective, or compensating. They include hardware or software solutions using access control in accordance with established security policies.

Option B is incorrect. Administrative controls are defined through policies, procedures, and guidelines.

Option C is incorrect. HTTPS is a communications protocol used to secure communication over a computer network used on the Internet.

Option D is incorrect. Integrity ensures that the data hasn't been altered and is protected from unauthorized modification.

92. C. Mean time between failures (MTBF) is a measurement to show how reliable a hardware component is.

Option A is incorrect. MTTR (mean time to repair) is the average time it takes for a failed device or component to be repaired or replaced.

Option B is incorrect. RPO (recovery point objective) is the period of time a company can tolerate lost data being unrecoverable between backups.

Option D is incorrect. ALE (annual loss expectancy) is the sum of the annual rate of occurrence and the single loss expectancy.

93. C. Single point of failure is a single weakness that can bring an entire system down and prevent it from working.

Option A is incorrect. Cloud computing allows the delivery of hosted service over the Internet.

Option B is incorrect. Load-balancing divides the amount of work a computer can do between two or more computers. This allows more work to be completed in the same amount of time.

Option D is incorrect. Virtualization allows the creation of virtual resources such as a server operating system. Multiple operating systems can run on one machine by sharing the resources such as RAM, hard drive, and CPU.

94. D. A pop-up blocker program can help prevent pop-ups from displaying in a user's web browser. Pop-ups can contain adware or spyware.

Option A is incorrect. Antivirus software can help prevent the spreading of malware such as worms and Trojans.

Option B is incorrect. Antispam software can help reduce the amount of junk email in a user's inbox.

Option C is incorrect. Spyware gathers personal information and computer usage habits without the user's knowledge.

95. A and C. Taking hashes of the hard drive will preserve the evidence. If the hash has not been changed, the data hasn't changed. Capturing the system image involves making an exact image of the drive so that it can be referenced later in the investigation.

Option B is incorrect. Taking screenshots gives an investigator a useful way to collect information on a computer screen. This will allow the investigator to reproduce what happened on the screen.

Option D is incorrect. Order of volatility represents the order in which you should collect evidence. In general terms, evidence should be collected starting with the most volatile and moving to the least volatile. Volatile means data is not permanent.

96. B. A Computer Incident Response Team (CIRT) includes personnel who promptly and correctly handle incidents so that they can be quickly contained, investigated, and recovered from.

Options A, C, and D are incorrect. These statements are not considered a CIRT.

97. C. The account lockout threshold setting defines the number of failed sign-in attempts that will cause a user account to be locked. This policy best mitigates brute-force password attacks.

Option A is incorrect. Password complexity is a series of guidelines that a password adheres to three of the four categories: uppercase letter, lowercase letter, numbers, and symbols.

Option B is incorrect. Password hints help users remember their passwords.

Option D is incorrect. Password history determines the number of unique new passwords a user can use before an old password can be reused.

98. A. Random access memory (RAM) data is lost when the device is powered off. Therefore, RAM must be properly collected first.

Option B is incorrect. A USB flash drive will maintain its data when the power is removed.

Option C is incorrect. A hard disk will maintain its data when the power is removed.

Option D is incorrect. A swap file is an extension of memory and is stored on the hard disk, so it is less volatile than RAM.

99. A. A standard operating procedure (SOP) is a document that details the processes that a company will have in place to ensure that routine operations are delivered consistently every time. Guidelines and enforcement are items that are included in a SOP.

Option B is incorrect. Order of volatility represents the order in which you should collect evidence. In general terms, evidence should be collected starting with the most volatile and moving to the least volatile. Volatile means data is not permanent.

Option C is incorrect. Penetration assessment is a simulated attack authorized on a network system that searches for security weaknesses that may potentially gain access to the network's features and data.

Option D is incorrect. A vulnerability assessment identifies, quantifies, and prioritizes vulnerabilities in a network system.

100. B. Determining if the suspect is guilty is determined by the legal system and is not part of the basic concept of computer forensics.

Options A, C, and D are incorrect. Other valid basic concepts include capture video and active logging. These options are valid basic concepts of computer forensics.

101. C. A warm site is harder to test because it contains only the equipment and no employees or company data.

Option A is incorrect. A hot site contains all of the alternate computer and telecommunication equipment needed in a disaster. Testing this environment is simple.

Option B is incorrect. A cold site is the hardest to test because it includes a basic room with limited equipment.

Option D is incorrect. Load-balancing divides the amount of work a computer can do between two or more computers. This allows more work to be completed in the same amount of time. Distributive allocation handles the assignment of jobs across the servers.

102. D. Digital evidence for forensic review must first be collected from the most volatile (not permanent) locations such as RAM and swap files. A swap file is a location on a hard disk drive used as the virtual memory extension of a computer's RAM. A hard disk drive is the next least volatile, then DVD-R. Some digital evidence can be gathered by using a live boot media.

Options A, B, and C are incorrect. RAM is more volatile than swap files and hard disk drives. Swap files are more volatile than DVD-R.

103. A, B, and C. The lessons learned process is the most critical phase because it is the phase in which you complete any documentation that may be beneficial in future incidents. Documentation should include information such as when the problem was first detected and by whom, how the problem was contained and eradicated, the work that was performed during the recovery, and areas that may need improvement.

Option D is incorrect. The preparation process prepares a company's team to be ready to handle an incident at a moment's notice.

104. B. The identification phase deals with the discovery and determination of whether a deviation from normal operations within a company is an incident. This phase requires a person to collect events from various sources and report the incident as soon as possible.

Option A is incorrect. The preparation process prepares a company's team to be ready to handle an incident at a moment's notice.

Option C is incorrect. The containment process is designed to minimize the damage and prevent any further damage from happening.

Option D is incorrect. Eradication is a phase of the incident response process that removes and restores affected systems by reimaging the system's hard drive and installing patches.

105. D. Encrypting PII ensures confidentiality.

Option A is incorrect. Hashing PII only ensures integrity.

Option B is incorrect. A digital signature provides nonrepudiation.

Option C is incorrect. RAID (redundant array of independent disks) ensures higher availability for a disk subsystem.

106. C. Change management ensures that proper procedures are followed when configuration changes are made to a network.

Options A, B, and D are incorrect. These statements do not define change management.

107. C. The preparation phase of the incident response process prepares a company's team to be ready to handle an incident at a moment's notice. During this step, a company may identify incidents that can be prevented or mitigated.

Option A is incorrect. The containment process is designed to minimize the damage and avoid any further damage from happening.

Option B is incorrect. The eradication phase involves removing and restoring affected systems by reimaging the system's hard drive and installing patches.

Option D is incorrect. The lessons learned process is the most critical phase because it is the phase in which you complete any documentation that may be beneficial in future incidents. Documentation should include information such as when the problem was first detected and by whom, how the problem was contained and eradicated, the work that was performed during the recovery, and areas that may need improvement.

108. A and D. Quantitative risk analysis requires complex calculations and is more time-consuming.

Options B and C are incorrect. These statements describe qualitative risk analysis, not quantitative risk analysis.

109. B and C. Cold sites require a large amount of time to bring online after a disaster. They are not easily available for testing as other alternatives.

Option A is incorrect. Cold sites are inexpensive and require no daily administration time. This is an advantage to using a cold site.

Option D is incorrect. Cold sites do not require daily administration time to ensure the site is ready within a maximum tolerable downtime. This is an advantage to using a cold site.

110. B. Personally identifiable information (PII) is personal information that can be used to identify an individual. Protecting PII is important because if an attacker gains PII, they can use it for financial gain at the expense of the individual.

Option A is incorrect. Password policy defines the complexity of creating passwords. It should also define weak passwords and how users should protect password safety.

Option C is incorrect. Chain of custody refers to the chronological documentation showing the custody, control, transfer, analysis, and disposition of physical or electronic evidence.

Option D is incorrect. Detective controls detect intrusion as it happens and uncover a violation.

111. A. Wiping a drive can remove sensitive data. Disposal of hard drives can be done with shredding. Storage includes types of devices and configurations of data safety. Retention can be required for legal and compliance reasons.

Options B, C, and D are incorrect. Virtualization and onboarding do not apply to data policies.

112. D. Record time offset is used to validate the date and time stamps of digital forensic evidence.

Option A is incorrect. Order of volatility represents the order in which you should collect evidence. In general terms, evidence should be collected starting with the most volatile and moving to the least volatile. Volatile means data is not permanent.

Option B is incorrect. Chain of custody refers to the chronological documentation showing the custody, control, transfer, analysis, and disposition of physical or electronic evidence.

Option C is incorrect. Eradication is the process of removing and restoring affected systems by reimaging the system's hard drive and installing patches.

113. D. Risk transfer is the act of moving the risk to hosted providers who assume the responsibility for recovery and restoration or by acquiring insurance to cover the costs emerging from a risk.

Option A is incorrect. Risk mitigation is when a company implements controls to reduce vulnerabilities or weaknesses in a system. It can also reduce the impact of a threat.

Option B is incorrect. Risk acceptance is a strategy of recognizing, identifying, and accepting a risk that is sufficiently unlikely or has such limited impact that a corrective control is not warranted.

Option C is incorrect. Risk avoidance is the removal of the vulnerability that can increase a particular risk so that it is avoided altogether.

114. D. An incremental backup backs up all new files and any files that have changed since the last full backup or incremental backup. Incremental backups clear the archive bit.

Option A is incorrect. A full backup backs up all the files each time the backup runs.

Option B is incorrect. A compressed full backup backs up all the files in a compressed format.

Option C is incorrect. A differential backup backs up all new files and any files that have changed since the last full backup. Differential backups do not clear the archive bit.

115. B. Each breach cost the company $60,000 per year and over the course of 5 years, the total amount will total $300,000. Transferring the risk will help save money for the company because the third-party vendor's solution will cost $250,000.

Option A is incorrect. Accepting the risk will cost the company $50,000.

Option C is incorrect. Avoiding the risk is not engaging in the service at all, which may be the effective solution but often not possible due to the company's requirements.

Option D is incorrect. Mitigating the risk is reducing the engagement of the service, and the company may not be able to reduce the system.

116. C. Approving and executing changes to ensure maximum security and availability of a company's IT services is considered change management. A business impact analysis (BIA) identifies a company's risk and determines the effect on ongoing, mission-critical operations and processes.

Options A, B, and D are incorrect. These are considered guidelines when performing a BIA.

117. B. Failover is the continuous ability to automatically and flawlessly switch to a highly reliable backup. This can be activated in a redundant manner or in a standby operating mode should the primary server fail. The main purpose of failover is to provide availability of data or service to a user.

Option A is incorrect. Integrity ensures the data hasn't been altered and is protected from unauthorized modification.

Option C is incorrect. Authentication is the process of certifying and confirming a user's identity.

Option D is incorrect. Confidentiality allows authorized users to gain access to sensitive and protected data.

118. B and C. An alternate business practice is a temporary substitute for normal business activities. When the power is out, the salespeople can use their cell phones to continue to sell and write the orders on a sheet of paper. Once the power is restored, the salespeople can enter the orders into the system without compromising business activities.

Option A is incorrect. Having the salespeople go home until the power is restored is not an example of an alternate business practice. The company may not know how long the power will be out, and this could lead to lost business opportunities.

Option D is incorrect. The company's fax machine will not operate if the company's power is out.

119. D. A custodian configures data protection based on security policies.

Option A is incorrect. The local community bank is the data owner, not Leigh Ann.

Option B is incorrect. Leigh Ann is a network administrator, not a user.

Option C is incorrect. Power user is not a standard security role in the industry.

120. A. Formatting is not a recommended method. Formatting removes the pointer to the location of the data on the storage media but does not ensure the data is removed.

Option B is incorrect. Shredding physically destroys the storage media in a way data cannot be retrieved.

Option C is incorrect. Wiping, also known as overwriting, will replace the data with all zeros to prevent data from being recovered by third-party software.

Option D is incorrect. Degaussing is a method of removing data from a magnetic storage media by changing the magnetic field.

121. B and C. Encrypting the backup data before it is stored off-site ensures confidentiality. To avoid data tampering and ensure data integrity, a different employee should review the backup logs.

Option A is incorrect. Using SSL (Secure Socket Layer) encrypts the data transmitting across the network, not the data that is stored off-site.

Option D is incorrect. The employee performing the backup doesn't need to be a member of the Administrators group. The employee should be a member of the Backup Operators group.

122. C. A protocol analyzer used with a promiscuous mode NIC can capture all network traffic.

Option A is incorrect. A port scanner identifies open ports on a server or host.

Option B is incorrect. A vulnerability scanner attempts to identify weaknesses in a system.

Option D is incorrect. A network intrusion detection system (NIDS) analyzes incoming network traffic.

123. A. The correct answer is an Internet acceptable use policy. Leigh Ann will be using the company's equipment to access the Internet, so she should read and sign this policy.

Option B is incorrect. An audit policy defines the requirements and parameters for risk assessment and audits of the organization's information and resources.

Option C is incorrect. A password policy defines the standards for creating complex passwords such as an uppercase letter, lowercase letter, number, and symbol.

Option D is incorrect. A privacy policy defines what information will be shared with third parties. This information includes company and customer information.

124. D. Active-passive is a configuration that involves two load-balancers. Traffic is sent to the primary node, and the secondary node will be in listening mode. When too much traffic is sent to the main server, the second server will handle some of the requests. This will prevent a single point of failure.

Option A is incorrect. In an active-active configuration, each server will handle the service requested by the user. This will distribute the load to each server.

Option B is incorrect. Active Directory is a directory service Microsoft developed for the Windows domain network. It stores information about network components.

Option C is incorrect. Round-robin configuration sends traffic to the first node, then the second node, then the third node, and then back to the first node. This configuration is not related to fault tolerance.

125. C. A clean desk policy ensures that all sensitive/confidential documents are removed from an end-user workstation and locked up when the documents are not in use.

Option A is incorrect. Job rotation is the practice of rotating employees that are assigned jobs within their employment to promote flexibility and keep employees interested in their jobs.

Option B is incorrect. A data owner has administrative control and can be designated as accountable and responsible for a particular set of data.

Option D is incorrect. Separation of duties is the concept of having more than one person required to complete a task.

126. D. Chain of custody offers assurances that evidence has been preserved, protected, and handled correctly after it has been collected. Documents show who handled the evidence and when they handled it.

Option A is incorrect. Delegating evidence to your manager is a task performed when gathering forensic evidence. Chain of custody is preserving evidence, also referred to as legal hold.

Option B is incorrect. Capturing system image is making an exact copy of the hard disk to further investigate. This does not define chain of custody.

Option C is incorrect. Capturing memory contents is defined as order of volatility.

127. B. Gray-box testing uncovers any application vulnerabilities within the internal structure, devices, and components of a software application. During gray-box testing, limited information regarding the internal devices and structure is given to the testing team.

Option A is incorrect. During white-box testing, complete information regarding the internal devices and structure is given to the testing team.

Option C is incorrect. During black-box testing, very little or no information regarding the internal devices and structure is given to the testing team.

Option D is incorrect. Clear-box testing is also known as white-box testing.

128. B and C. A personnel hiring policy and separation of duties are administrative controls. Administrative controls are defined through policies, procedures, and guidelines.

Options A and D are incorrect. Firewall rules and IPSs are considered technical controls.

129. A and D. An alternate business practice is a temporary substitute for normal business activities. Having employees write down customers' orders is a substitute for the point-of-sale system. Having employees work from another bank location means that the employees can continue using the computer system and phones to assist customers.

Options B and C are incorrect. These are not examples of substitutes for normal business activities.

130. A and C. Personally identifiable information (PII) is personal information that can be used to identify an individual. PII must be carefully handled and distributed to prevent ID theft and fraud. Personal electronic devices, in a BYOD environment, should be protected and secured because these devices can be used for personal and business purposes.

Option B is incorrect. A MOU (memorandum of understanding) is a legal document that describes a mutual agreement between parties.

Option D is incorrect. A nondisclosure agreement (NDA) protects sensitive and intellectual data from getting into the wrong hands.

131. C. An after-action report examines a response to an incident or exercise and identifies its strengths that will be maintained and built on. Also, it helps recognize potential areas of improvement.

Option A is incorrect. An MOU (memorandum of understanding) is a legal document that describes a mutual agreement between parties.

Option B is incorrect. An SLA (service level agreement) defines the level of service the customer expects from the service provider. The level of service definitions should be specific and measurable in each area.

Option D is incorrect. A nondisclosure agreement (NDA) protects sensitive and intellectual data from getting into the wrong hands.

132. B. Risk acceptance is a strategy of recognizing, identifying, and accepting a risk that is sufficiently unlikely or has such limited impact that a corrective control is not warranted.

Option A is incorrect. Risk mitigation is when a company implements controls to reduce vulnerabilities or weaknesses in a system. It can also reduce the impact of a threat.

Option C is incorrect. Risk avoidance is the removal of the vulnerability that can increase a particular risk so that it is avoided altogether.

Option D is incorrect. Risk transfer is the act of moving the risk to hosted providers who assume the responsibility for recovery and restoration or by acquiring insurance to cover the costs emerging from a risk.

133. A. Data owners assign labels such as top secret to data.

Option B is incorrect. Custodians assign security controls to data.

Option C is incorrect. A privacy officer ensures that companies comply with privacy laws and regulations.

Option D is incorrect. System administrators are responsible for the overall functioning of the IT system.

134. C. Employees can leak a company's confidential information. Exposing a company's information could put the company's security position at risk because hackers can use this information to gain unauthorized access to the company.

Option A is incorrect. Gaining access to a computer's MAC address is not relevant to social media network risk.

Option B is incorrect. Gaining access to a computer's IP address is not relevant to social media network risk.

Option D is incorrect. Employees can easily express their concerns about a company in general. This is not relevant to social media network risk as long as the employee doesn't reveal any confidential information.

135. B. A snapshot is the state of a system at a particular point in time. Snapshots offer considerably easier and faster backups than any traditional backup system can.

Options A, C, D and are incorrect. Each of these backup concepts will take longer to restore the original OS settings should a problem occur with the installed patches.

136. C. To test the integrity of backed-up data, restore part of the backup.

Option A is incorrect. Reviewing written procedures will not ensure that the data has been backed up properly. The procedures only show you how and when the backup should occur.

Option B is incorrect. You use software to recover deleted files after you restore from a backup.

Option D is incorrect. Conducting another backup only ensures that the backup procedures are correct and properly working.

137. C. Separation of duties is the concept of having more than one person required to complete a task.

Option A is incorrect. A background check is a process that is performed when a potential employee is considered for hire.

Option B is incorrect. Job rotation allows individuals to see various parts of the organization and how it operates. It also eliminates the need for a company to rely on one individual for security expertise should the employee become disgruntled and decide to harm the company. Recovering from a disgruntled employee's attack is easier when multiple employees understand the company's security posture.

Option D is incorrect. Collusion is an agreement between two or more parties to defraud a person of his or her rights or to obtain something that is prohibited by law.

138. D. Safety is a common goal of security that includes providing protection for personnel and other assets.

Option A is incorrect. Confidentiality allows authorized users to gain access to sensitive and protected data.

Option B is incorrect. Integrity ensures that the data hasn't been altered and is protected from unauthorized modification.

Option C is incorrect. Availability means that information is always going to be something a user can access.

139. D. Nessus is considered a vulnerability scanner. It attempts to identify weaknesses in a system.

Options A, B, and C are incorrect. These tools are used for cracking passwords.

140. B. ALE (annual loss expectancy) = SLE (single loss expectancy) × ARO (annualized rate of occurrence). SLE equals $750,000 (2,500 records × $300), and ARO equals 5%, so $750,000 times 5% equals $37,500.

Options A, C, and D are incorrect. Based on the calculation of ALE, the answer is $37,500.

141. C. A parallel test can test certain systems to confirm their operation at alternate sites. Compare the results of the test to the results of the original system to confirm that the alternate site operates as close to normal as possible.

Option A is incorrect. A cutover test will shut down the main system and everything will fail over to the backup systems.

Option B is incorrect. A walkthrough test reviews the plan to confirm that all the steps are included.

Option D is incorrect. A simulation test performs a practice run of the disaster recovery plan for a given scenario.

142. C. RPO (recovery point objective) specifies the allowable data loss. It is the amount of time that can pass during an interruption before the quantity of data lost during that period surpasses business continuity planning's maximum acceptable threshold.

Option A is incorrect. MTBF (mean time between failures) is the rating on a device or component that predicts the expected time between failures.

Option B is incorrect. MTTR (mean time to repair) is the average time it takes for a failed device or component to be repaired or replaced.

Option D is incorrect. ARO (annual rate of occurrence) is the ratio of an estimated possibility that a threat will take place within a one-year time frame.

143. B. A corrective control is designed to correct a situation.

Option A is incorrect. Detective controls detect intrusion as it happens and uncover a violation.

Option C is incorrect. A preventive control is used to avoid a security breach or an interruption of critical services before they can happen.

Option D is incorrect. A deterrent control is used to deter a security breach.

144. A. A snapshot is the state of a system at a particular point in time. It's also known as a system image and is not a step in the incident response process.

Options B, C, and D are incorrect. Preparation, recovery, and containment are steps of the incident response process.

145. B. Shredding documents can prevent physical threats such as theft of the documents or obtaining information from the documents.

Option A is incorrect. Shoulder surfing is using direct observation techniques, such as looking over someone's shoulder, to obtain information.

Option C is incorrect. Adware are ads that are delivered through pop-up windows or bars that appear on the program's user interface.

Option D is incorrect. Spyware is software that is installed on a system without the end user's knowledge and is used for innocuous reasons. It is sometimes referred to as tracking software.

146. D. A data retention policy states how data should be stored based on various types; such as storage location, amount of time the data should be retained, and the type of storage medium should be used.

Option A is incorrect. A clean desk policy ensures that all sensitive/confidential documents are removed from an end-user workstation and locked up when the documents are not in use.

Option B is incorrect. An acceptable use policy describes the limits and guidelines for users to make use of an organization's physical and intellectual resources. This includes allowing or limiting the use of personal email during work hours.

Option C is incorrect. A security policy defines how to secure physical and information technology assets. This document should be continuously updated as technology and employee requirements change.

147. C. Onboarding is the process of adding an employee to a company's identity and access management system.

Option A is incorrect. Offboarding is the process of removing an employee from the company's identity and access management system.

Option B is incorrect. A system owner is an individual who is in charge of physically securing one or more systems and can include patching and updating operating systems.

Option D is incorrect. An Executive User is a group that users are assigned to along with the least privilege policy.

148. A, C, and D. The correct answer is standard, procedure, and guideline. A standard defines how to measure the level of adherence to the policy. A procedure contains the step-by-step instructions for implementing components of the policy. A guideline is a suggestion, recommendation, or best practices for how to meet the policy standard.

Option B is incorrect. Privacy is a policy that defines standards for disclosing company information to third parties.

149. A. Chain of custody refers to the chronological documentation showing the custody, control, transfer, analysis, and disposition of physical or electronic evidence.

Option B is incorrect. Order of volatility represents the order in which you should collect evidence. In general terms, evidence should be collected starting with the most volatile and moving to the least volatile. Volatile means data is not permanent.

Option C is incorrect. Preparation is a phase of the incident response process that prepares a company's team to be ready to handle an incident at a moment's notice.

Option D is incorrect. Eradication is a phase of the incident response process that removes and restores affected systems by reimaging the system's hard drive and installing patches.

150. C and D. The correct answers are asset estimation and rating potential threats. Qualitative risk analysis measures the probability of risks that will hinder normal business operations and rate them relative to one another. Assets that are protected from risks must have assigned value to determine whether the cost of risk mitigation is justified.

Options A and B are incorrect. ARO (annual rate of occurrence) and SLE (single loss expectancy) are used to calculate the ALE (annual loss expectancy) by multiplying ARO by SLE.

Chapter 6: Cryptography and PKI

1. **A.** A digital signature is a one-way hash and encrypted with the private key. The public key is used to decrypt the hash and validate the integrity of the digital signature. Digital signatures supports non-repudiation; where the sender can not refute sending the message.

   Option B is incorrect. TLS (Transport Layer Security) creates a secure connection by using symmetric cryptography based on a shared secret. The same key encrypts and decrypts the data.

   Option C is incorrect. Digital signatures are created with the private key.

   Option D is incorrect. TLS creates a secure connection by using symmetric cryptography based on a shared secret. The same key encrypts and decrypts the data.

2. **D.** A revoked certificate is no longer valid for the intended purpose, and a new key pair and certificate will need to be generated.

   Option A is incorrect. The certificate cannot be renewed after its expiration date.

   Option B is incorrect. A self-signed certificate will generate errors within the client's web browser and should not be used as a replacement since the self-signed certificate is not from a trusted certificate authority.

   Option C is incorrect. Key escrow is a cryptographic key exchange process in which a key is stored by a third party. Should the original user's key be lost or compromised, the stored key can be used to decrypt encrypted material, allowing restoration of the original material to its unencrypted state. This scenario didn't state the key was lost but rather that the certificate had expired.

3. **B.** Digital signatures are created by using the user's or computer's private key that is accessible only to that user or computer. Nonrepudiation is the assurance that someone cannot deny something.

   Option A is incorrect. A symmetric algorithm, also known as a secret key algorithm, uses the same key to encrypt and decrypt data.

   Option C is incorrect. A CRL (certificate revocation list) is a list of digital certificates that have been revoked by the issuing certificate authority (CA) before their scheduled expiration date and should not be trusted.

   Option D is incorrect. An asymmetric algorithm, also known as public key cryptography, uses public and private keys to encrypt and decrypt data.

4. **B.** WiFi Alliance, a nonprofit organization that promotes WiFi technology, recommends a passphrase be at least eight characters long and include a mixture of upper- and lowercase letters and symbols.

   Options A, C, and D are incorrect.

5. **A.** A CRL (certificate revocation list) is a list of digital certificates that have been revoked by the issuing certificate authority (CA) before their scheduled expiration date and should not be trusted.

   Option B is incorrect. Key escrow is a cryptographic key exchange process in which a key is stored by a third party. Should the original user's key be lost or compromised, the stored key can be used to decrypt encrypted material, allowing restoration of the original material to its unencrypted state.

Option C is incorrect. Nonrepudiation is a method of guaranteeing a message transmission between parties by a digital signature.

Option D is incorrect. A recovery agent is a user who is permitted to decrypt another user's data in case of emergency or in special situations.

6. A and D. DES and 3DES are symmetric-key block ciphers using a 64-bit block size.

Option B is incorrect. SHA is a hashing algorithm and is used for integrity.

Option C is incorrect. MD5 is a hashing algorithm and is used for integrity.

7. D. You would need the supplicant. The authenticator, an AP or wireless controller, sends authentication messages between the supplicant and authentication server.

Option A is incorrect. Network access control (NAC) increases the security of a proprietary network by restricting access to devices that do not comply with a defined security policy.

Option B is incorrect. The authentication server is the RADIUS server and is responsible for authenticating users wanting to connect to the network.

Option C is incorrect. The authenticator is the client that authenticates against the RADIUS server using an EAP method configured on the RADIUS server.

8. D. ECC (elliptic curve cryptography) is an asymmetric algorithm that uses smaller keys and has the same level of strength compared to longer key length asymmetric algorithm.

Option A is incorrect. Blowfish is a symmetric algorithm that uses the same key to encrypt and decrypt data.

Option B is incorrect. RSA uses a longer key length than ECC.

Option C is incorrect. DHE uses a longer key length than ECC.

9. B. Initialization vectors (IVs) are random values that are used with algorithms to ensure patterns are not created during the encryption process. IVs are used with keys and are not encrypted when being sent to the destination.

Option A is incorrect. A one-time pad is an encryption method and uses a pad with random values that are XORed against the message to produce ciphertext. One-time pad is at least as long as the message itself and is used once and then discarded. This technology is not addressed in this scenario.

Option C is incorrect. Stream ciphers encrypt data one bit at a time. This concept is not addressed in this scenario.

Option D is incorrect. Block ciphers encrypts data one block, or fixed block, at a time. This concept is not addressed in this scenario.

10. D. An open wireless network does not require a user to enter credentials for access.

Option A is incorrect. An IV (initialization vector) is an arbitrary number that is used with a secret key for data encryption.

Option B is incorrect. WEP (Wired Equivalent Privacy) is a security standard for 802.11b. It is designed to provide a level of security for a WLAN.

Option C is incorrect. WPA (WiFi Protected Access) is a security standard that replaced and improved on WEP.

11. C. RSA is an asymmetric algorithm and should be discontinued.

Options A, B, and D are incorrect. AES, RC4, and Twofish are symmetric algorithms.

12. B. OCSP (Online Certificate Status Protocol) is a protocol that can be used to query a certificate authority about the revocation status of a given certificate. It validates certificates by returning responses such as "good," "revoked," and "unknown."

Option A is incorrect. A CRL (certificate revocation list) is a list of digital certificates that have been revoked by the issuing certificate authority (CA) before their scheduled expiration date and should not be trusted.

Option C is incorrect. An RA (registered authority) is used to verify requests for certificates and forwards responses to the CA.

Option D is incorrect. PKI (public key infrastructure) is an entire system of hardware, software, policies and procedures, and people. PKI creates, distributes, manages, stores, and revokes certificates. OCSP is part of the PKI.

13. B and D. 3DES and Blowfish are a symmetric-key block cipher. 3DES and Blowfish use a block size of 64 bits.

Option A is incorrect. MD5 is a hashing algorithm and is used for integrity.

Option C is incorrect. RC4 is a stream cipher and uses key sizes of 40 to 2048 bits.

14. C. DES (Data Encryption Standard) is a 56-bit key and is superseded by 3DES. DES is considered to be insurance for many applications.

Option A is incorrect. Blowfish has a 64-bit block size and a variable key length up to 448 bits.

Option B is incorrect. AES (Advanced Encryption Standard) is a newer and stronger encryption standard and is capable of using 128-bit, 192-bit, and 256-bit keys.

Option D is incorrect. SHA is a hashing algorithm.

15. B. WEP uses the encryption protocol RC4 and is considered insecure.

Options A, C, and D are incorrect. WEP does not use the RC6, AES, or DES encryption protocol.

16. A. Key stretching increases the strength of stored passwords and protects passwords from brute-force attacks and rainbow table attacks.

Option B is incorrect. Key escrow is a cryptographic key exchange process in which a key is stored by a third party. Should the original user's key be lost or compromised, the stored key can be used to decrypt encrypted material, allowing restoration of the original material to its unencrypted state.

Option C is incorrect. Key strength is the length of the key that is being used to encrypt the data. According to NIST guidance, the use of keys that provide less than 112 bits of security strength for key agreement is disallowed.

Option D is incorrect. ECC (elliptic curve cryptography) is an asymmetric algorithm that uses smaller keys and has the same level of strength compared to longer key length asymmetric algorithm.

17. B. Complex passwords of 16 or more ASCII characters are considered strong. Passwords should follow the complexity rule of having three of the four following items: lowercase letter, uppercase letter, number, and special character.

Option A is incorrect. This password is too common and can be easily guessed.

Option C is incorrect. This password isn't following the complexity rule and it has only six ASCII characters, which can easily be guessed through the use of brute force.

Option D is incorrect. This password is commonly found in the dictionary and can be susceptible to a dictionary attack.

18. A. WPA2 Enterprise uses an authentication server such as a RADIUS server to control access to a WLAN.

Option B is incorrect. WPA2 Personal does not use an authentication server. It uses a passphrase that is entered into the SOHO router.

Option C is incorrect. TKIP is a wrapper that wraps around existing WEP encryption and is used in WPA. TKIP replaced WEP in WLAN devices.

Option D is incorrect. WEP does not use an authentication server. Users enter a passphrase to connect to the SOHO router.

19. B. Block ciphers encrypt data one block, or fixed block, at a time. Cryptographic service provider, a cryptographic module, performs block and stream cryptography algorithms.

Option A is incorrect. Stream ciphers encrypt data one bit at a time.

Option C is incorrect. An asymmetric algorithm, also known as public key cryptography, uses public and private keys to encrypt and decrypt data.

Option D is incorrect. A symmetric algorithm, also known as a secret key algorithm, uses the same key to encrypt and decrypt data.

20. B. Twofish is a symmetric block cipher that replaced Blowfish.

Option A is incorrect. RSA is an asymmetric algorithm.

Option C is incorrect. MD5 is a hashing algorithm.

Option D is incorrect. PBKDF2 is a key stretching algorithm.

21. B. In a certification hierarchy, the root CA certifies the intermediate CA and can issue certificates to users, computers, or services.

Option A is incorrect. A registered authority (RA) is used to verify requests for certificates and forwards responses to the CA.

Option C is incorrect. A CRL (certificate revocation list) is a list of digital certificates that have been revoked by the issuing certificate authority (CA) before their scheduled expiration date and should not be trusted.

Option D is incorrect. A CSR (certificate signing request) is a request an applicant sends to a CA for the purpose of applying for a digital identity certificate.

22. B. EAP-TLS is a remote access authentication protocol that supports the use of smartcards.

Option A is incorrect. PEAP is an encapsulating protocol that uses a certificate on the authentication server and a certificate on the client. It supports password-based authentication.

Option C is incorrect. CHAP authenticates by using PPP servers to validate the identity of remote clients. It supports password-based authentication.

Option D is incorrect. MS-CHAPv2 is Microsoft's version of CHAP and is used as an authentication option with RADIUS. It supports password-based authentication.

23. D. Digital signatures are created by using the user's or computer's private key that is accessible only to that user or computer. Nonrepudiation is the assurance that someone cannot deny something.

Option A is incorrect. TKIP is a wrapper that wraps around existing WEP encryption and is used in WPA. TKIP replaced WEP in WLAN devices.

Option B is incorrect. An intermediate certificate authority sits between the root certificate authority and the end entity to better secure the root certificate authority. Intermediate certificate authorities can also help a large organization handle large requests for certifications.

Option C is incorrect. A public key is held by the certificate authority and is available for anyone to use to encrypt data or verify a user's digital signature.

24. D. EAP-TTLS determines how user authentication will perform during phase 2. The user authentication may be a legacy protocol such as PAP, CHAP, MS-CHAP, or MS-CHAPV2.

Options A, B, and C are incorrect. PEAP, EAP-FAST, and EAP-TLS create a TLS tunnel to protect the supplicant credentials but do not support legacy authentication protocols.

25. C and D. RSA is an asymmetric algorithm (also known as public key cryptography) that uses a public and a private key to encrypt and decrypt data during transmissions. ECC (elliptical curve cryptography) is based on elliptic curve theory that uses points on a curve to define more efficient public and private keys.

Option A is incorrect. RC4 is a symmetric algorithm and uses one key to encrypt and decrypt data.

Option B is incorrect. DES is a symmetric algorithm and uses one key to encrypt and decrypt data.

26. A. Substitution ROT13 replaces a letter with the 13th letter after it in the alphabet.

Option B is incorrect. Transposition scrambles data by reordering the plain text in some certain way.

Option C is incorrect. Diffusion is a change in the plain text resulting in multiple changes that are spread out throughout the ciphertext.

Option D is incorrect. Confusion encryption is a method that uses a relationship between the plain text and the key that is so complicated the plain text can't be altered and the key can't be determined by a threat actor.

27. C. With asymmetric algorithms, every user must have at least one pair of keys (private and public). The two keys are mathematically related. If a message is encrypted with one key, the other key is required to decrypt the message. The formula to determine the number of keys needed is $N \times 2$, where N is the number of people.

Option A is incorrect. This is the number of keys needed in a symmetric key cryptosystem. Each pair of users who are exchanging data must have two instances of the same key. The formula for calculating the number of symmetric keys needed is: $N (N-1) / 2$ = number of keys.

Option B is incorrect. Each user in a public key infrastructure requires at least one pair of keys (private and public). The formula for determining the number of keys that are needed is $N \times 2$.

Option D is incorrect. This total is derived from $N (N-1)$, which is part of the formula for calculating the number of symmetric keys needed.

28. B. A symmetric algorithm, also known as a secret key algorithm, uses the same key to encrypt and decrypt data.

Option A is incorrect. An asymmetric algorithm, also known as public key cryptography, uses public and private keys to encrypt and decrypt data.

Option C is incorrect. Hashing is a one-way encryption that transforms a string of characters into a fixed-length value or key also known as a hash value. Hashes ensure the integrity of data or messages.

Option D is incorrect. Steganography is a process of hiding data within data. This technique can be applied to images, video files, or audio files.

29. D. RSA is an asymmetric algorithm (also known as public key cryptography) that uses a public and a private key to encrypt and decrypt data during transmissions.

Options A, B, and C are incorrect. Twofish, 3DES, and RC4 are symmetric algorithms. Also known as a secret key algorithm, a symmetric algorithm uses the same key to encrypt and decrypt data.

30. A. Full-disk encryption on data-at-rest will help protect the inactive data should the storage device be stolen. The thief would not be able to read the data.

Option B is incorrect. Implementing biometrics will control who enters the location. An unauthorized user can tailgate and obtain the storage device and read the data-at-rest.

Option C is incorrect. Implementing a host-based intrusion detection system is designed to alert you when an attack occurs on a network but does not protect the data-at-rest if the storage device is stolen.

Option D is incorrect. Implementing a host-based intrusion prevention system is designed to prevent an attack on a network but does not protect the data-at-rest if the storage device is stolen.

31. A. EAP-FAST is for situations where strong password policy cannot be enforced and certificates are not used. EAP-FAST consists of three phases: EAP-FAST authentication, establishment of a secure tunnel, and client authentication.

Options B, C, and D are incorrect. These EAP types do not use a three-phase phase.

32. A. DES is a symmetric encryption standard that uses a key length of 56 bits.

Option B is incorrect.

Option C is incorrect. AES uses a block length of 128 bits and key lengths of 128, 192, or 256 bits.

Option D is incorrect. WPS is a network security standard that allows home users to easily add new devices to an existing wireless network without entering long passphrases.

33. B. Hashing is a one-way encryption that transforms a string of characters into a fixed-length value or key, also known as a hash value. Hashes ensure the integrity of data or messages.

Option A is incorrect. Steganography is a process of hiding data within data, also known as security through obscurity. This technique can be applied to images, video files, or audio files.

Option C is incorrect. A collision occurs when a hashing algorithm creates the same hash from two different messages.

Option D is incorrect. An IV (initialization vector) is an arbitrary number that is used with a secret key for data encryption. IV makes it more difficult for hackers to break a cipher.

34. B. SSL (Secure Socket Layer) uses public key encryption. When a client accesses a secured website, it will generate a session key and encrypt it with the server's public key. The session key is decrypted with the server's private key, and the session key is used to encrypt and decrypt data sent back and forth.

Option A is incorrect. The server's private key is held privately by the server and is used only to decrypt data the client encrypted with the server's public key.

Option C is incorrect. The server doesn't create the session key as the client is accessing the secured website.

Option D is incorrect. The server doesn't create the session key as the client is accessing the secured website. The server's public key is used to encrypt the session key created by the client.

35. C. EAP-TLS requires both client and server to have certificates. The authentication is mutual where the server authenticates to the client and the client authenticates to the server.

Options A, B, and D are incorrect. The other EAP types may use client certificates but they are not required.

36. A. PGP (Pretty Good Privacy) or GPG (GNU Privacy Guard) provides a low-cost or open source alternative solution that allows users to encrypt their outgoing emails.

Option B is incorrect. WPA2 is a security standard that secures computers connected to a WiFi network.

Option C is incorrect. A CRL (certificate revocation list) is a list of digital certificates that have been revoked by the issuing certificate authority (CA) before their scheduled expiration date and should not be trusted.

Option D is incorrect. EAP-TLS is a remote access authentication protocol that supports the use of smartcards.

37. C. SHA-1 is a hashing algorithm that produces a 160-bit digest.

Option A is incorrect. MD5 is a hashing algorithm that produces a 128-bit digest.

Option B is incorrect. RC4 is a symmetric algorithm and encrypts data.

Option D is incorrect. AES is a symmetric algorithm and encrypts data.

38. A. Wildcard certificates allow the company to secure an unlimited number of subdomain certificates on a domain name from a third party.

Option B is incorrect. Object identifiers (OIDs) identify an object or entity. OIDs are used in X.509 certificates to name almost every object type.

Option C is incorrect. Key escrow is a cryptographic key exchange process in which a key is stored by a third party. Should the original user's key be lost or compromised, the stored key can be used to decrypt encrypted material, allowing restoration of the original material to its unencrypted state.

Option D is incorrect. OCSP (Online Certificate Status Protocol) is a protocol that can be used to query a certificate authority about the revocation status of a given certificate. An OCSP response contains signed assertions that a certificate is not revoked.

39. B and D. EAP and IEEE 802.1x are authentication protocols that transfer authentication data between two devices.

Option A is incorrect. WPS (WiFi Protected Setup) is a network security standard that allows home users to easily add new devices to an existing wireless network without entering long passphrases.

Option C is incorrect. IPSec is a framework of open standards that ensures communications are private and secure over IP networks.

40. A. Digital signatures are created by using the user's or computer's private key that is accessible only to that user or computer. Nonrepudiation is the assurance that someone cannot deny something.

Option B is incorrect. Hashing is a one-way encryption that transforms a string of characters into a fixed-length value or key, also known as a hash value. Hashes ensure the integrity of data or messages.

Option C is incorrect. Steganography is a process of hiding data within data. This technique can be applied to images, video files, or audio files.

Option D is incorrect. Perfect forward secrecy is a way to ensure the safety of session keys from future abuse by threat actors.

41. D. Hashing is a one-way encryption that transforms a string of characters into a fixed-length value or key, also known as a hash value. Hashes ensure the integrity of data or messages.

Option A is incorrect. Key escrow is a cryptographic key exchange process in which a key is stored by a third party. Should the original user's key be lost or compromised, the stored key can be used to decrypt encrypted material, allowing restoration of the original material to its unencrypted state.

Option B is incorrect. File backup allows the data to be available in case the original files are deleted or become corrupted.

Option C is incorrect. Encryption is the process of using an algorithm to change plain text data into unreadable information to protect it from unauthorized users. The main purpose of encryption is to protect the confidentiality of digital data stored on a computer system or transmitted via a network.

42. D. RADIUS is a client-server protocol that enables remote access servers to communicate with a central server to authenticate users. RADIUS uses symmetric encryption for security.

Option A is incorrect. TACACS+ is a Cisco proprietary authentication protocol and is used to securely access Cisco devices.

Option B is incorrect. XTACACS is a Cisco proprietary authentication protocol that replaced TACACS and was used to securely access Cisco devices.

Option C is incorrect. Kerberos is a protocol for authenticating service requests between trusted hosts across an untrusted network such as the Internet.

43. A. Encryption provides confidentiality because the data is scrambled and cannot be read by an unauthorized user. Symmetric encryption uses one key to encrypt, and decrypting data with one key is considered fast.

Option B is incorrect. Nonrepudiation is a method of guaranteeing a message transmission between parties by a digital signature.

Option C is incorrect. Steganography is a process of hiding data within data. This technique can be applied to images, video files, or audio files.

Option D is incorrect. A collision occurs when a hashing algorithm creates the same hash from two different messages.

44. B. Steganography is a process of hiding data within data. This technique can be applied to images, video files, or audio files.

Option A is incorrect. Hashing is a one-way encryption that transforms a string of characters into a fixed-length value or key, also known as a hash value. Hashes ensure the integrity of data or messages.

Option C is incorrect. A symmetric algorithm, also known as a secret key algorithm, uses the same key to encrypt and decrypt data.

Option D is incorrect. An asymmetric algorithm, also known as public key cryptography, uses public and private keys to encrypt and decrypt data.

45. A. Enable perfect forward secrecy (PFS) at the main office and branch office end of the VPN. Perfect forward secrecy is a way to ensure the safety of session keys from future abuse by threat actors.

Options B, C, and D are incorrect. You should enable PFS at both ends of the VPN since PFS depends on asymmetric encryption and ensures the session key created from the public and private keys will not be compromised if one of the private keys is compromised.

46. B. WPS is a network security standard that allows home users to easily add new devices to an existing wireless network without entering long passphrases. Users enter a PIN to allow the device to connect after pressing the WPS button on the SOHO router.

Options A, C, and D are incorrect. WEP and WPA have passphrases, not PINs, that are entered. Bluetooth PINs are used to set up devices to communicate via Bluetooth, not with a SOHO router.

47. A and B. Digital signatures provide three core benefits: authentication, integrity, and non-repudiation.

Option C is incorrect. A digital signature is a one-way hash and encrypted with the private key. A digital signature does not encrypt data.

Option D is incorrect. A digital signature is used for authentication, integrity, and nonrepudiation—not to securely exchange keys.

48. C and D. PBKDF2 applies a pseudo-random function such as a HMAC to the password along with a salt value and produces a derived key. PBKDF2 is designed to protect against brute-force attacks. BCRYPT is a password-hashing function derived from the Blowfish cipher. It adds a salt value to protect against rainbow table attacks.

Option A is incorrect. ROT13 is a substitution cipher, also known as a Caesar cipher, that replaces a letter with the 13th letter after it in the alphabet. ROT13 is not recommended in this scenario due to patterns it creates.

Option B is incorrect. MD5 is a hashing algorithm that transforms a string of characters into a fixed-length value or key, also known as a hash value. Hashes ensure the integrity of data or messages. MD5 is considered weak and is not recommended.

49. A. Users are receiving the error because the website certificate has expired. The user can continue accessing the website, but the error will state the user could be accessing an untrusted site.

Option B is incorrect. The scenario states that users are receiving an error when they access the company's website. Users are not logging into the company's website, so any username and password issue would not fit in this scenario.

Option C is incorrect. If the domain had expired, the users would receive a page stating that the website domain is unavailable. Domain name expiration does not relate to this scenario.

Option D is incorrect. If the network was unavailable, the users would not be able to access the company's website whether or not the certificate was expired. The users would possibly not be able to access other resources.

50. A. In asymmetric encryption, sometimes referred to as public key encryption, the private key is used to decrypt an encrypted file.

Option B is incorrect. A public key is used to encrypt a file.

Option C is incorrect. A message digest is created to check the integrity of a file to ensure it hasn't changed.

Option D is incorrect. Ciphertext is plain text that has been encrypted.

51. A. A threat actor can spoof a device's MAC address and bypass 802.1x authentication. Using 802.1x with client certificates or tunneled authentication can help prevent this attack.

Option B is incorrect. ARP poisoning is an attack where a threat actor sends spoofed ARP messages over a LAN.

Option C is incorrect. Ping of death is a denial-of-service attack in which a threat actor sends a larger IP packet than allowed by the IP protocol. The IP packet is broken down into smaller segments, which would cause the system to crash.

Option D is incorrect. The Xmas attack is a specifically crafted TCP packet that turns on flags to scan the system and determine what operating system it's using.

52. A, C, and D. A one-time pad must be delivered by a secure method and properly guarded at each destination. The pad must be used one time only to avoid introducing patterns, and it must be made up of truly random values. Today's computer systems have pseudo-random-number generators, which are seeded by an initial value from some component within the computer system.

    Option B is incorrect. The one-time pad must be at least as long as the message. If the pad is not as long as the message, it will need to be reused to be the same length as the message. This could introduce patterns and make it easy to crack.

53. C. In asymmetric encryption, sometimes referred to as public key encryption, the private key is used to decrypt an encrypted file.

    Option A is incorrect. Hashing is a one-way encryption that transforms a string of characters into a fixed-length value or key, also known as a hash value. Hashes ensure the integrity of data or messages.

    Option B is incorrect. Symmetric encryption uses the same key to encrypt and decrypt the data.

    Option D is incorrect. Key escrow is a cryptographic key exchange process in which a key is stored by a third party. Should the original user's key be lost or compromised, the stored key can be used to decrypt encrypted material, allowing restoration of the original material to its unencrypted state.

54. B and D. To sign the data for nonrepudiation purposes, the sender uses their private key and when encrypting the data, the sender uses the receiver's public key.

    Option A is incorrect. The receiver's private key is kept private by the receiver.

    Option C is incorrect. The sender's public key is used to encrypt data that is being sent to the sender and decrypted by its private key.

55. D. Symmetric encryption uses the same key to encrypt and decrypt data, so the key must be sent to the receiver in a secure manner. If a person were to get the key somewhere in the middle, they would be able to decrypt the information and read the data or inject it with malware.

    Options A, B, C are incorrect. These statements describe asymmetric encryption.

56. B. Key escrow is a security measure where cryptographic keys are held in escrow by a third party and under normal circumstances, the key should not be released to someone other than the sender or receiver without proper authorization.

    Option A is incorrect. A CSR (certificate signing request) is a request an applicant sends to a CA for the purpose of applying for a digital identity certificate.

    Option C is incorrect. A CRL (certificate revocation list) is a list of digital certificates that have been revoked by the issuing certificate authority (CA) before their scheduled expiration date and should not be trusted.

    Option D is incorrect. A CA (certificate authority) is a trusted entity that issues electronic documents that verify a digital entity's identity on the Internet or computer network.

57. B. ECC (elliptical curve cryptography) is based on elliptic curve theory that uses points on a curve to define more efficient public and private keys.

Option A is incorrect. Obfuscation is the action of making something difficult to read and understand.

Option C is incorrect. Stream ciphers encrypt data one bit at a time.

Option D is incorrect. Block ciphers encrypt data one block, or fixed block, at a time.

58. B. WPA2 CCMP replaced TKIP and is a more advanced encryption standard. CCMP provides data confidentiality and authentication.

Option A is incorrect. WEP is a security standard for wireless networks and devices but is not as secure as WPA.

Option C is incorrect. Enabling MAC filtering by allowing or prohibiting a MAC address is not a secure option since threat actors can spoof MAC addresses.

Option D is incorrect. Disabling SSID broadcast will not help better secure the network since threat actors can use tools to sniff hidden SSIDs.

59. D. RC4 is an example of a stream cipher that encrypts data one bit at a time.

Options A, B, and C are incorrect. AES, DES, and 3DES are examples of block ciphers that encrypt data one fixed block of data at a time.

60. A and B. DHE (Diffie-Hellman Ephemeral) and ECDHE (Elliptic Curve Diffie-Hellman Ephemeral) are commonly used with TLS to provide perfect forward secrecy.

Option C is incorrect. RSA is an asymmetric algorithm (also known as public key cryptography) that uses a public and a private key to encrypt and decrypt data during transmissions.

Option D is incorrect. SHA is a hashing algorithm and is used for integrity.

61. D. A symmetric key system uses the same key to encrypt and decrypt data during the transport.

Options A, B, and C are incorrect. These statements refer to an asymmetric key system, where it uses two keys to encrypt and decrypt data and creates digital signatures for non-repudiation purposes.

62. B. AES is a subset of the Rijndael cipher developed by Vincent Rijmen and Joan Daemen. Rijndael is a family of ciphers with different key and block sizes.

Option A is incorrect. TKIP uses RC4. RC4 was designed by Ron Rivest of RSA Security.

Option C is incorrect. DES is a block cipher and is unrelated to Rijndael.

Option D is incorrect. 3DES is a block cipher and is unrelated to Rijndael.

63. A. Digital signatures are created with the sender's private key and verified by the sender's public key.

Answers B, C, and D are incorrect. Katelyn is sending the digital signature created by her private key and Zackary verifies the digital signature by obtaining Katelyn's public key.

64. B. MD5 is a hashing algorithm that transforms a string of characters into a fixed-length value or key, also known as a hash value. Hashes ensure the integrity of data or messages.

Options A, C, and D are incorrect. 3DES, AES, and Blowfish are symmetric algorithms. Also known as a secret key algorithm, a symmetric algorithm uses the same key to encrypt and decrypt data.

65. A. AES is a symmetric encryption that supports key sizes of 128, 192, and 256 bits.

Option B is incorrect. DES is a symmetric encryption that supports a key size of 56 bits.

Option C is incorrect. RSA is an asymmetric encryption.

Option D is incorrect. TKIP is a wrapper that wraps around existing WEP encryption and supports a key size of 128 bits.

66. A and C. The structure of an X.509 digital signature includes a serial number and public key of the user or device.

Option B is incorrect. A default gateway is an access point that a device uses to send data to a device in another network or to the Internet.

Option D is incorrect. A session key is a symmetric key that uses the same key for encryption and decryption.

67. A and D. The authentication server and supplicant mutually authenticate with each other. This helps prevent rogue devices from connecting to the network.

Option B is incorrect. A certificate authority (CA) is a trusted entity that issues electronic documents that verify a digital entity's identity on the Internet or computer network.

Option C is incorrect. A domain controller (DC) is a server computer within a Windows domain that responds to requests such as logging in or checking permissions.

68. C. Confusion encryption is a method that uses a relationship between the plain text and the key that is so complicated the plain text can't be altered and the key can't be determined by a threat actor.

Option A is incorrect. This method defines substitution.

Option B is incorrect. This method defines transposition.

Option D is incorrect. This method defines diffusion.

69. C. Key escrow is a database of stored keys that can be retrieved should the original user's key be lost or compromised. The stored key can be used to decrypt encrypted material, allowing restoration of the original material to its unencrypted state.

Option A is incorrect. A certificate authority (CA) is a trusted entity that issues electronic documents that verify a digital entity's identity on the Internet or computer network.

Option B is incorrect. A certificate revocation list (CRL) is a list of digital certificates that have been revoked by the issuing certificate authority (CA) before their scheduled expiration date and should not be trusted.

Option D is incorrect. CER is a certificate file extension for an SSL certificate and is used by web servers to help confirm the identity and security of the site a user is visiting.

70. D. The private key is used to encrypt the signature of an email, and the sender's public key is used to decrypt the signature and verify the hash value.

Option A is incorrect. CER is a certificate file extension for an SSL certificate and is used by web servers to help confirm the identity and security of the site a user is visiting.

Option B is incorrect. The public key is used to decrypt the signature to verify the sender.

Option C is incorrect. The shared key is used in a symmetric algorithm and should not be used to encrypt and decrypt a signature of an email.

71. C. 802.11i is an amendment to the original IEEE 802.11 and is implemented as WPA2. The amendment deprecated WEP.

Option A is incorrect. A NIC (network interface card) enables a device to network with other devices.

Option B is incorrect. WPA (WiFi Protected Access) is a security standard that replaced and improved on WEP.

Option D is incorrect. TKIP is a wrapper that wraps around existing WEP encryption and is used in WPA. TKIP replaced WEP in WLAN devices.

72. A. WPA (WiFi Protected Access) is a security standard that replaced and improved on WEP and is designed to work with older wireless clients.

Option B is incorrect. WPA2 implements the 802.11i standard completely but does not support the use of older wireless cards.

Option C is incorrect. WEP is a security standard for wireless networks and devices but is not as secure as WPA.

Option D is incorrect. An IV (initialization vector) is an arbitrary number that is used with a secret key for data encryption.

73. D. RSA is a public key encryption algorithm that can both encrypt and authenticate messages.

Option A is incorrect. Diffie-Hellman encrypts data only and is used to exchange keys.

Option B is incorrect. MD5 is a cryptography hashing function that transforms a string of characters into a fixed-length value.

Option C is incorrect. SHA is a cryptography hashing function that transforms a string of characters into a fixed-length value.

74. C. ECC (elliptical curve cryptography) uses less processing power and works best in devices such as wireless devices and cellular phones. ECC generates keys faster than other asymmetric algorithms. Determining the correct set of security and resource constraints is an important beginning step when planning a cryptographic implementation.

Options A, B, and D are incorrect. 3DES, DES, and AES are not used in mobile devices because they use more computing power to generate cryptographic keys than ECC. It's important that there be high resiliency in cryptography, or the ability to resume normal operations after an external disruption.

75. C. Public key cryptography is also known as asymmetric cryptography. Public key cryptography is one piece of the PKI (public key infrastructure).

Option A is incorrect. Public key cryptography is also known as asymmetric cryptography and PKI (public key infrastructure) is an entire system of hardware, software, policies and procedures, and people. PKI creates, distributes, manages, stores, and revokes certificates.

Option B is incorrect. Public key cryptography uses two keys to encrypt and decrypt the data, also known as asymmetric encryption. PKI (public key infrastructure) is not known as an asymmetric encryption (using two keys to encrypt and decrypt data) but rather as an entire system that creates, distributes, manages, stores, and revokes certificates.

Option D is incorrect. Public key cryptography can provide authentication and nonrepudiation, but PKI (public key infrastructure) cannot provide confidentiality and integrity. PKI can use algorithms that can provide these security services.

76. B. A CRL (certificate revocation list) is a list of digital certificates that have been revoked by the issuing certificate authority (CA) before their scheduled expiration date and should not be trusted.

Option A is incorrect. A certificate authority (CA) is a trusted entity that issues electronic documents that verify a digital entity's identity on the Internet or computer network.

Option C is incorrect. A registered authority (RA) is used to verify requests for certificates and forwards responses to the CA.

Option D is incorrect. A certificate signing request (CSR) is a request an applicant sends to a CA for the purpose of applying for a digital identity certificate.

77. A and D. Most small office, home office (SOHO) networks use WPS and WPA2-Personal. WPS is a network security standard that allows home users to easily add new devices to an existing wireless network without entering long passphrases. WPA2-Personal uses a passphrase that is entered into the SOHO router.

Options B and C are incorrect. WPA-Enterprise and WPA2-Enterprise, also known as 802.1x, use a RADIUS server for authentication purposes.

78. A. A trust model is a collection of rules that informs applications as to how to decide the validity of a digital certificate.

Option B is incorrect. Key escrow is a security measure where cryptographic keys are held in escrow by a third party, and under normal circumstances, the key should not be released to someone other than the sender or receiver without proper authorization.

Option C is incorrect. PKI (public key infrastructure) is an entire system of hardware, software, policies and procedures, and people. PKI creates, distributes, manages, stores, and revokes certificates.

Option D is incorrect. A registered authority (RA) is used to verify requests for certificates and forwards responses to the CA.

79. A. EAP-TLS uses the concepts of public key infrastructure (PKI). It eliminates the need for a shared secret between the client and the server. Digital certificates are used instead.

Options B, C, and D are incorrect. These EAP types do not use PKI.

80. B and C. Security used in SOHO environments is PSK (preshared key) authentication. WPA-Personal and WPA2-Personal use the PSK authentication method.

Options A and D are incorrect. WPA-Enterprise and WPA2-Enterprise, also known as 802.1x, use a RADIUS server for authentication purposes.

81. D. A captive portal is a web page where the user must view and agree to the terms before access to the network is granted. They are typically used by business centers, airports, hotels, and coffee shops.

Option A is incorrect. WEP (Wired Equivalent Privacy) is a security standard for 802.11b. It is designed to provide a level of security for a WLAN.

Option B is incorrect. Key stretching increases the strength of stored passwords and protects passwords from brute-force attacks and rainbow table attacks.

Option C is incorrect. MAC filtering is a technique that allows or prohibits MAC addresses to access a network. It is not a secure option since threat actors can spoof MAC addresses.

82. A and D. Elliptic curve cryptosystem (ECC) differs from other asymmetric algorithms due to its efficiency. ECC uses less processing power and works best in low power devices such as wireless devices and cellular phones. ECC generates keys faster than other asymmetric algorithms.

Option B is incorrect. ECC is not the only asymmetric algorithm that provides digital signatures, secure key distribution, and encryption.

Option C is incorrect. ECC uses less processing power than other asymmetric algorithms.

83. B. IV (initialization vector) is an arbitrary number that is used with a secret key for data encryption. IV makes it more difficult for hackers to break a cipher.

Option A is incorrect. Diffusion is a property of cryptography that makes cryptanalysis hard. A change of a single character of the input will change many characters of the output.

Option C is incorrect. A session key is a symmetric key that uses the same key for encryption and decryption.

Option D is incorrect. Hashing is a one-way encryption that transforms a string of characters into a fixed-length value or key, also known as a hash value. Hashes ensure the integrity of data or messages.

84. D. 802.1x enhances security within a WLAN by providing an authentication framework. Users are authenticated by a central authority before they are allowed within the network.

Option A is incorrect. An HIDS (host intrusion detection system) is a security management for networks and computers. It gathers information within the network or computer and identifies potential threats.

Option B is incorrect. UTM (unified threat management) is a network appliance that provides firewall, intrusion detection, anti-malware, spam, and content filtering in one integrated device.

Option C is incorrect. A VLAN allows network administrators to partition a switch within their network to provide security without having multiple switches.

85. B. The data can be decrypted with a recovery agent if the company configured one before. If there is no recovery agent, the encrypted file will be unrecoverable.

Option A is incorrect. The backup user account does not have the ability to recover the files that were encrypted by the other user.

Option C is incorrect. The encrypted file cannot be recovered by re-creating the user's account. The new user account will have a different SID even though the name is the same, and it will not be able to access the files.

Option D is incorrect. A CRL (certificate revocation list) is a list of digital certificates that have been revoked by the issuing certificate authority (CA) before their scheduled expiration date and should not be trusted.

86. B. A symmetric algorithm, also known as a secret key algorithm, uses the same key to encrypt and decrypt data.

Option A is incorrect. An asymmetric algorithm, also known as public key cryptography, uses two keys (a public and private key) to encrypt and decrypt data.

Option C is incorrect. Hashing is a one-way encryption that transforms a string of characters into a fixed-length value or key, also known as a hash value. Hashes ensure the integrity of data or messages.

Option D is incorrect. Steganography is a process of hiding data within data. This technique can be applied to images, video files, or audio files.

87. A. WPA2 CCMP replaced TKIP and is a more advanced encryption standard. CCMP provides data confidentiality and authentication.

Option B is incorrect. WEP (Wired Equivalent Privacy) is a security standard for 802.11b. It is designed to provide the least security for a WLAN.

Option C is incorrect. WPA (WiFi Protected Access) is a security standard that replaced and improved on WEP. WPA is less secure than WPA2.

Option D is incorrect. TKIP is an older encryption protocol introduced with WPA to replace the insecure WEP encryption. TKIP is considered deprecated and should not be used.

88. D. A collision occurs when a hashing algorithm creates the same hash from two different messages.

Option A is incorrect. AES (Advanced Encryption Standard) is a symmetric algorithm.

Option B is incorrect. MD5 (Message Digest 5) is a hashing algorithm.

Option C is incorrect. Hashing is a one-way encryption that transforms a string of characters into a fixed-length value or key, also known as a hash value. Hashes ensure the integrity of data or messages.

89. A. EAP-TLS is a remote access authentication protocol that supports the use of smartcards or user and computer certificates, also known as machine certificates, to authenticate wireless access clients. EAP-TLS can use tunnels for encryption by use of TLS.

Option B is incorrect. EAP-FAST is designed to increase the speed of reauthentication when a user roams from one AP to another. It authenticates the user over an encrypted TLS tunnel but uses a shared secret key.

Option C is incorrect. PEAP is an encapsulating protocol that uses a certificate on the authentication server and a certificate on the client. It supports password-based authentication but does not use TLS for encryption.

Option D is incorrect. EAP is a framework for authentication in a WLAN and point-to-point connections. EAP defines message formats and doesn't use tunnels for encryption.

90. B. A self-signed certificate will display an error in the browser stating the site is not trusted because the self-signed certificate is not from a trusted certificate authority.

Option A is incorrect. The web browser needing an update will not display an error message that the site certificate is invalid and the site is not trusted.

Option C is incorrect. A web proxy blocking the connection would not allow the site to load and display a message regarding the invalid certificate.

Option D is incorrect. If the web server was unavailable, the user would not be able to receive any information about the status of the certificate.

91. A. A CSR (certificate signing request) is a request an applicant sends to a CA for the purpose of applying for a digital identity certificate.

Option B is incorrect. Key escrow is a cryptographic key exchange process in which a key is stored by a third party. Should the original user's key be lost or compromised, the stored key can be used to decrypt encrypted material, allowing restoration of the original material to its unencrypted state.

Option C is incorrect. A CRL (certificate revocation list) is a list of digital certificates that have been revoked by the issuing certificate authority (CA) before their scheduled expiration date and should not be trusted.

Option D is incorrect. OCSP (Online Certificate Status Protocol) is a protocol that can be used to query a certificate authority about the revocation status of a given certificate. It validates certificates by returning responses such as "good," "revoked," and "unknown."

92. B. Asymmetric encryption is also known as public key cryptography and uses public and private keys to exchange a session key between two parties. It offers key management by administering the life cycle of cryptographic keys and protecting them from loss or misuse.

Option A is incorrect. Obfuscation is the action of making something difficult to read and understand.

Option C is incorrect. Symmetric encryption, also known as a secret key algorithm, uses the same key to encrypt and decrypt data.

Option D is incorrect. Hashing is a one-way encryption that transforms a string of characters into a fixed-length value or key, also known as a hash value. Hashes ensure the integrity of data or messages.

93. A. Diffie-Hellman is used to establish a shared secret between two users and is primarily used as a method of exchanging cryptography keys.

Option B is incorrect. HMAC is known as a message authentication code and is used for integrity.

Option C is incorrect. ROT13 is a substitution cipher, also known as a Caesar cipher, that replaces a letter with the 13th letter after it in the alphabet.

Option D is incorrect. RC4 is an example of a stream cipher that encrypts data one bit at a time.

94. D. RC4 is a stream cipher used for encrypting and decrypting data, but there are known weaknesses and using it is not recommended.

Option A is incorrect. MD5 is a hashing algorithm used to verify integrity.

Option B is incorrect. HMAC is known as a message authentication code and it is used for integrity.

Option C is incorrect. Kerberos is a protocol for authenticating service requests between trusted hosts across an untrusted network such as the Internet. Kerberos uses tickets to provide mutual authentication.

95. A. 3DES is a symmetric algorithm used to encrypt data by applying the DES cipher algorithm three times to the data.

Options B, C, and D are incorrect. AES, Twofish, and Blowfish do not repeat the encryption process with additional keys.

96. B. Digital signatures are created by using the user's or computer's private key that is accessible only to that user or computer. Nonrepudiation is the assurance that someone cannot deny something.

Option A is incorrect. Encryption is the process of using an algorithm to change plain text data into unreadable information to protect it from unauthorized users. The main purpose of encryption is to protect the confidentiality of digital data stored on a computer system or transmitted via a network.

Option C is incorrect. A collision occurs when a hashing algorithm creates the same hash from two different messages.

Option D is incorrect. A CA (certificate authority) is a trusted entity that issues electronic documents that verify a digital entity's identity on the Internet or computer network.

97. C. With a single number appended to the company name, the preshared key can be easily guessed. A secure preshared key is at least eight ASCII characters in length and follows the complexity rule.

Option A is incorrect. WPA (WiFi Protected Access) is a security standard that replaced and improved on WEP. Replacing WEP with WPA is not secure enough as the preshared key must follow the complexity rule and be at least eight ASCII characters in length.

Option B is incorrect. The preshared key must be at least eight ASCII characters in length and follow the complexity rule.

Option D is incorrect. WPA (WiFi Protected Access) is a security standard that replaced and improved on WEP.

98. A. A CRL (certificate revocation list) is a list of digital certificates that have been revoked by the issuing certificate authority (CA) before their scheduled expiration date and should not be trusted.

Option B is incorrect. OCSP (Online Certificate Status Protocol) is a protocol that can be used to query a certificate authority about the revocation status of a given certificate. An OCSP response contains signed assertions that a certificate is not revoked.

Option C is incorrect. Key escrow is a security measure where cryptographic keys are held in escrow by a third party and under normal circumstances, the key should not be released to someone other than the sender or receiver without proper authorization.

Option D is incorrect. A CA (certificate authority) is a trusted entity that issues electronic documents that verify a digital entity's identity on the Internet or computer network.

99. A, C, and D. The WiFi Protected Setup protocols define the following devices in a network. A registrar is the device with the authority to issue or revoke access to the network. The enrollee is a client device that is seeking to join the wireless network. The AP (access point) functions as a proxy between the registrar and the enrollee.

Option B is incorrect. A supplicant is the client that authenticates against the RADIUS server using an EAP method configured on the RADIUS server.

100. D. WPA2-Enterprise will implement AES and require an authentication infrastructure with an authentication server (RADIUS) and an authenticator. WPA2-Enterprise provides better protection of critically important information with BYOD (Bring Your Own Device).

Option A is incorrect. WEP is the weakest security protocol. WEP does not support AES or RADIUS.

Option B is incorrect. WPA does not support AES or RADIUS.

Option C is incorrect. WPA2-Personal supports AES but requires a preshared key passphrase to be entered on each device connecting to the network. This leads to shared passwords and doesn't control which device connects.

101. D. Data-at-rest is all data that is inactive and physically stored in a physical digital form such as nonvolatile memory.

Option A is incorrect. Data-in-transit is data that flows over the public or private network.

Option B is incorrect. Data-over-the-network is not defined as the three states of digital data.

Option C is incorrect. Data-in-use is all data that is active and stored in volatile memory such as RAM, CPU caches, or CPU registers.

102. B. RADIUS is a client-server protocol that enables remote access servers to communicate with a central server to authenticate users. RADIUS uses symmetric encryption for security, and messages are sent as UDP.

Option A is incorrect. TACACS+ is a Cisco proprietary authentication protocol and is used to securely access Cisco devices. TACACS+ uses TCP to send messages.

Option C is incorrect. LDAP (Lightweight Directory Access Protocol) is a software protocol to help locate individuals and other resources within a network.

Option D is incorrect. Kerberos is a protocol for authenticating service requests between trusted hosts across an untrusted network such as the Internet. Kerberos uses tickets to provide mutual authentication.

103. C. Should a hard drive be stolen, the data will not be able to be read as the data is scrambled, or encrypted, and can be read only by the corresponding key.

Option A and D are incorrect Encrypting data-at-rest will not help a user decrypt their data should they lose their password.

Option B is incorrect. Encrypting data-at-rest will not help verify the integrity of the data. Hashing is designed to verify the integrity of data.

104. C. Using AES with CCMP incorporates two cryptographic techniques that provide a more secure protocol between a mobile client and the access point.

Option A is incorrect. RC4 is an example of a stream cipher that encrypts data one bit at a time and is not used along with CCMP.

Option B is incorrect. DES is a symmetric encryption that supports a key size of 56 bits and is not used along with CCMP.

Option D is incorrect. 3DES is a symmetric algorithm that is used to encrypt data by applying the DES cipher algorithm three times to the data and is not used along with CCMP.

105. A. MD5 produces a 128-bit message digest regardless of the length of the input text.

Option B is incorrect. RIPEMD produces a 128-, 160-, 256-, and 320-bit message digest. RIPEMD was not often seen in practical implementations.

Option C is incorrect. SHA-1 produces a 160-bit message digest regardless of the length of the input text.

Option D is incorrect. AES (Advanced Encryption Standard) is a symmetric algorithm used for encryption and not considered a hashing algorithm.

106. D. A birthday attack can be used to find hash collisions. It's based off the birthday paradox stating there is a 50 percent chance of someone sharing your birthday with at least 23 people in the room.

Option A is incorrect. A Xmas attack is a specifically crafted TCP packet that turns on flags to scan the system and determine what operating system it's using.

Option B is incorrect. A denial of service (DoS) is a an attack that prevents legitimate users from accessing services or resources within a network.

Option C is incorrect. A logic bomb is a piece of code intentionally inserted into a software system that will set off a malicious function when specified conditions are met.

107. D. PKCS #12 is a file that contains both the private key and the X.509 certificate and can be installed by the user on servers or workstations. X.509 certificates can be a wildcard certificate for multiple entities under a single fully qualified domain name.

Option A is incorrect. PKCS #1 defines the mathematical properties and format of RSA public and private keys.

Option B is incorrect. PKCS #3 is a cryptographic protocol that allows two parties to jointly establish a shared key over an insecure network such as the Internet.

Option C is incorrect. PKCS #7 is used to sign and/or encrypt messages within a PKI (public key infrastructure).

108. B and D. Stream ciphers is a low latency operation that encrypt data one bit at a time, and block ciphers encrypt data one block, or fixed block, at a time.

Option A is incorrect. Stream ciphers do not encrypt data one block at a time.

Option C is incorrect. Block ciphers do not encrypt data one bit at a time.

109. A, B, and D. 3DES is a symmetric key block cipher that applies the DES cipher algorithm three times to each data block. 3DES has three keying options. First, all three keys are independent, so 3 × 56 = 168-bit key length. Second, key 1 and key 2 are independent and the third key is the same as the first key, so 2 × 56 = 112-bit key length. Third, all three keys are identical, so 1 × 56 = 56-bit key length.

Option C is incorrect. With three keying options, 3DES has effective key sizes of 56, 128, and 168 bits.

110. C. A symmetric algorithm, also known as a secret key algorithm, uses the same key to encrypt and decrypt data.

Option A is incorrect. Steganography is the process of hiding data within data. This technique can be applied to images, video files, or audio files.

Option B is incorrect. An asymmetric algorithm, also known as public key cryptography, uses public and private keys to encrypt and decrypt data.

Option D is incorrect. Hashing is a one-way encryption that transforms a string of characters into a fixed-length value or key, also known as a hash value, by using a mathematical function, not a key. Hashes ensure the integrity of data or messages.

111. D. Revoked certificates are stored on a CRL (certificate revocation list). The CA continuously pushes out CRL values to clients to ensure they have the updated CRL. OCSP (Online Certificate Status Protocol) performs this work automatically in the background and returns a response such as "good," "revoked," and "unknown." OCSP uses a process called stapling to reduce communication from the user to the CA to check the validity of a certificate.

Option A is incorrect. OCSP does not submit revoked certificates to the CRL. The CA is responsible for creating, distributing, and maintaining certificates and revoking the certificates when necessary as part of this process.

Option B is incorrect. OCSP is a more streamlined approach as it works in the background and checks a central CRL to see if a certificate has been revoked.

Option C is incorrect. OCSP, not the CRL, performs real-time validation of a certificate.

112. D. A one-time pad is a stream cipher that encrypts the plain text with a secret random key that is the same length as the plain text. The encryption algorithm is the XOR operation.

Option A is incorrect. ECDHE (Elliptic Curve Diffie-Hellman Ephemeral) is commonly used with TLS to provide perfect forward secrecy.

Option B is incorrect. PBKDF2 is a key stretching algorithm. Key stretching makes a possibly weak key, typically a password or passphrase, more secure against a brute-force attack by increasing the time it takes to test each possible key.

Option C is incorrect. Obfuscation is the action of making something difficult to read and understand.

113. A. A stream cipher encrypts one plain text digit at a time with the corresponding digit of the keystream. Stream ciphers provide the same type of protection as one-time pads do.

Option B is incorrect. RSA is an asymmetric algorithm and uses a different type of mathematics to encrypt the data.

Option C is incorrect. AES is a symmetric block cipher, and the message is divided into blocks of bits and then encrypted one block at a time.

Option D is incorrect. DES is a symmetric block cipher, and the message is divided into blocks of bits and then encrypted one block at a time.

114. C. Whole-disk encryption, such as BitLocker on a Windows OS, will protect the contents of a laptop if it is lost or stolen. If the thief were to take the hard drive out of the laptop and try reading the content, they would be unsuccessful.

Option A is incorrect. WPS (WiFi Protected Setup) is a network security standard that allows home users to easily add new devices to an existing wireless network without entering long passphrases.

Option B is incorrect. A BIOS password would prevent an unauthorized user from booting to the OS and possibly reading the data content. A BIOS password does not protect the data should the hard drive be removed and accessed.

Option D is incorrect. A cable lock is a security device designed to deter theft of a laptop. A cable lock does not protect the data from being accessed.

115. D. Steganography is a process of hiding data within data. This technique can be applied to images, video files, or audio files.

Option A is incorrect. AES (Advanced Encryption Standard) is a symmetric algorithm used to encrypt data. The question stated that you didn't have a way of encrypting the message.

Option B is incorrect. A collision occurs when a hashing algorithm creates the same hash from two different messages.

Option C is incorrect. RSA is an asymmetric algorithm used to encrypt data. The question stated that you didn't have a way of encrypting the message.

116. B. CBC (Cipher Block Chaining) mode uses feedback information to ensure the current block ciphertext differs from other blocks even if the same data is being encrypted.

Option A is incorrect. ECB (Electronic Code Book) encrypts each data block individually. Repetitive data can result in the same ciphertext.

Option C is incorrect. GCM (Galois/Counter Mode) encrypts data and checks integrity.

Option D is incorrect. CTM (counter mode), also abbreviated as CTR, is similar to CBC except it does not use a random number and does not chain the blocks.

117. B. Secure ciphers can be reverse engineered, but hashes cannot be reversed when reverse engineered attempting to re-create a data file. Hashing is a one-way encryption that is used for integrity purposes.

Options A, C, and D are incorrect. These statements are incorrect about the difference between a secure cipher and a secure hash. A secure hash creates the same size for any input size.

118. D. PFX (personal information exchange) files are typically used with Windows OSs that include digital certificates and are used for authentication processes involved in determining if a user or device can access certain files.

Option A is incorrect. DER (distinguished encoding rules) is a binary form of PEM certificate and is typically used in Java platform.

Option B is incorrect. AES is an asymmetric encryption algorithm.

Option C is incorrect. PEM (privacy-enhanced electronic mail) is a certificate format used for securing email using public key cryptography. PEM became an IETF proposed standard; it was never widely developed or used.

119. D. A session key is another name for an ephemeral key. An ephemeral key includes a private and public key, and systems use this key pair for a single session and then discard it.

Option A is incorrect. A PKI private key is held by the owner of the key pair to decrypt data or to create a digital signature.

Option B is incorrect. MD5 is a hashing algorithm that transforms a string of characters into a fixed-length value or key, also known as a hash value. Hashes ensure the integrity of data or messages.

Option C is incorrect. A PKI public key is held by the certificate authority and is available for anyone to use to encrypt data or verify a user's digital signature.

120. B. Steganography is a process of hiding data within data. This technique can be applied to images, video files, or audio files.

Option A is incorrect. Hashing is used to test integrity.

Option C is incorrect. Encryption is the process of using an algorithm to change plain text data into unreadable information to protect it from unauthorized users.

Option D is incorrect. Hashing is a one-way encryption that transforms a string of characters into a fixed-length value or key, also known as a hash value. Hashes ensure the integrity of data or messages.

121. A. AES (Advanced Encryption Standard) is a symmetric algorithm used to encrypt data that uses the least amount of CPU usage.

Option B is incorrect. SHA-1 is a hashing algorithm that transforms a string of characters into a fixed-length value or key, also known as a hash value. Hashes ensure the integrity of data or messages.

Option C is incorrect. MD5 is a hashing algorithm that transforms a string of characters into a fixed-length value or key, also known as a hash value. Hashes ensure the integrity of data or messages.

Option D is incorrect. 3DES is a symmetric algorithm used to encrypt data by applying the DES cipher algorithm three times to the data, and it uses a lot of CPU resources.

122. B. RADIUS is a client-server protocol that enables remote access servers to communicate with a central server to authenticate users. RADIUS uses symmetric encryption for security.

Option A is incorrect. RADIUS does not use asymmetric encryption. Asymmetric encryption uses a key pair, and RADIUS uses the same key to encrypt and decrypt information.

Option C is incorrect. Elliptic curve cryptography is a public key encryption based on the elliptic curve equation rather than large prime numbers.

Option D is incorrect. RSA is a public key encryption and includes hardware and software tokens.

123. A. WPA (WiFi Protected Access) is a security standard that replaced and improved on WEP. WPA is less secure than WPA2.

Option B is incorrect. WPA2 provides message authenticity and integrity verification by the use of the AES algorithm and is stronger and more reliable than WPA.

Option C is incorrect. EAP-TLS is a remote access authentication protocol that supports the use of smartcards. EAP-TLS is more secure than WPA.

Option D is incorrect. PEAP is an encapsulating protocol that uses a certificate on the authentication server and a certificate on the client. It supports password-based authentication.

124. D. RADIUS is a networking protocol that provides centralized AAA for users connecting and using a network service. EAP-TLS offers a good deal of security with the use of TLS and uses PKI to secure communication to the RADIUS authentication server.

Option A is incorrect. Kerberos is a protocol for authenticating service requests between trusted hosts across an untrusted network such as the Internet. Kerberos uses tickets to provide mutual authentication.

Option B is incorrect. LDAP (Lightweight Directory Access Protocol) is a software protocol to help locate individuals and other resources within a network.

Option C is incorrect. SAML (Security Assertion Markup Language) is an open-standard data format centered on XML. It supports the exchange of authentication and authorization details between systems, services, and devices. It does not authenticate and log connections from wireless users.

125. D. 802.1x enhances security within a WLAN by providing an authentication framework. Users are authenticated by a central authority before they are allowed within the network.

Option A is incorrect. WPA (WiFi Protected Access) is a security standard that replaced and improved on WEP and is designed to work with older wireless clients, but it does not transverse traffic from a wireless network to an internal network.

Option B is incorrect. WEP (Wired Equivalent Privacy) is a security standard for 802.11b but does not transverse traffic from a wireless network to an internal network.

Option C is incorrect. A load-balancer improves the workload by distributing traffic across multiple computer resources such as servers.

126. D. SHA-1 is a hashing algorithm that creates message digests and is used for integrity.

Options A, B, and C are incorrect. They are symmetric algorithms used for encryption.

127. C. Block ciphers encrypt data one block, or fixed block, at a time.

Option A is incorrect. Stream ciphers encrypt data one bit at a time.

Option B is incorrect. Hashing is a one-way encryption that transforms a string of characters into a fixed-length value or key, also known as a hash value. Hashes ensure the integrity of data or messages.

Option D is incorrect. Obfuscation is the action of making something difficult to read and understand.

128. B and D. MD5 and SHA are considered cryptography hashing functions that transform a string of characters into a fixed-length value.

Options A and C are incorrect. They are symmetric encryption algorithms.

129. B. Data-at-rest is all data that is inactive and physically stored in a physical digital form such as nonvolatile memory. If the device the data is stored on is stolen, the unauthorized person will not be able to read the data due to the encryption.

Option A is incorrect. SSL is designed to protect data in transit.

Option C is incorrect. Hashing is a one-way encryption that transforms a string of characters into a fixed-length value or key, also known as a hash value. Hashes ensure the integrity of data or messages.

Option D is incorrect. TLS is the successor to SSL and is designed to protect data in transit.

130. A and B. USB flash drives and smartcards can carry a token and store keys for authentication to systems. They are often used in a multifactor authentication situation.

Option C is incorrect. A PCI expansion card is internal to a PC and normally doesn't store keys for authentication purposes.

Option D is incorrect. A cipher lock is a programmable lock used for controlling access to a secure area.

131. B. AES (Advanced Encryption Standard) is a symmetric algorithm used to encrypt data that is fast and secure.

Option A is incorrect. SHA-256 is a hashing algorithm not used to encrypt data but rather to verify the integrity of the data.

Option C is incorrect. RSA is an asymmetric algorithm that is considered slow when encrypting data.

Option D is incorrect. MD5 is a hashing algorithm not used to encrypt data but rather to verify the integrity of the data.

132. C. OCSP (Online Certificate Status Protocol) is a protocol that can be used to query a certificate authority about the revocation status of a given certificate. OCSP can prepackage a list of revoked certificates and distribute them through browser updates and can be checked if there is an Internet outage.

Option A is incorrect. Key escrow is a security measure in which cryptographic keys are held in escrow by a third party, and under normal circumstances, the key should not be released to someone other than the sender or receiver without proper authorization.

Option B is incorrect. A recovery agent is a user who is permitted to decrypt another user's data in case of emergency or in special situations.

Option D is incorrect. A CSR (certificate signing request) is a request an applicant sends to a CA for the purpose of applying for a digital identity certificate. A CSR can be generated for code signing purposes.

133. D. PKI (public key infrastructure) is an entire system of hardware, software, policies and procedures, and people. PKI creates, distributes, manages, stores, and revokes certificates. A trust model is used to set up trust between CAs. A certificate has a subject alternative name (SAN) for machines (fully qualified domain names) or users (user principal name).

Option A is incorrect. ROT13 is a substitution cipher, also known as a Caesar cipher, and it replaces a letter with the 13th letter after it in the alphabet.

Option B is incorrect. PGP (Pretty Good Privacy) is a method used for encrypting and decrypting digital files and communications over the Internet. It also provides data and file integrity services by digitally signing messages.

Option C is incorrect. WPA2 is a security standard that secures computers connected to a WiFi network.

134. A and B. A threat actor can create an eavesdropping and a man-in-the-middle attack. Eavesdropping with a private key can allow the threat actor to see data in clear text. A man-in-the-middle attack can allow the threat actor to modify the data transmitting to the server, such as adding malware to the data.

Option C is incorrect. Social engineering is exploiting a person's trust to give up confidential information.

Option D is incorrect. A brute-force attack is used to obtain information such as a user password or personal identification number (PIN) by use of a trial-and-error method.

135. B. Hashing is a one-way encryption that transforms a string of characters into a fixed-length value or key, also known as a hash value. Hashes ensure the integrity of data or messages.

Option A is incorrect. A symmetric algorithm, also known as a secret key algorithm, uses the same key to encrypt and decrypt data.

Option C is incorrect. Asymmetric encryption is also known as public key cryptography, and it uses public and private keys to exchange a session key between two parties.

Option D is incorrect. PKI (public key infrastructure) is an entire system of hardware, software, policies and procedures, and people. PKI creates, distributes, manages, stores, and revokes certificates.

136. A. A CA (certificate authority) is a trusted entity that creates and digitally signs certificates so the receiver can verify the certificate came from that specific CA.

Option B is incorrect. The RA (registered authority) does not digitally sign the certificate; the CA (certificate authority) performs this action.

Option C is incorrect. The RA (registered authority) performs the certification registration duties. The RA identifies the individual requesting a certificate and initiates the certification process with the CA on behalf of the individuals. The CA creates and signs the certificate.

Option D is incorrect. The CA (certificate authority) creates and digitally signs the certificate. The RA (registered authority) performs the certification registration duties.

137. C. A digital signature is a hash value (message digest) that is encrypted with the sender's private key. The receiver performs a hashing function on the message and decrypts the sent hash value with the sender's public key and compares the two hash values. If the hash values are the same, the message actually came from the sender. This is performed by DSA (digital signature algorithm) and allows traceability to the person signing the message through the use of their private key.

Option A is incorrect. The sender will encrypt a hash value (message digest) with its own private key, not the receiver's public key. The receiver's public key is not part of the process.

Option B is incorrect. The sender encrypts the hash value (message digest) with its own private key, not the receiver's private key. The receiver's private key is always kept private by the owner.

Option D is incorrect. The receiver uses the sender's public key to decrypt the hash value (message digest) and compares the hash value produced by the receiver to verify that the message came from the sender.

138. A. AES (Advanced Encryption Standard) is a symmetric algorithm used to encrypt large amounts of data (bulk).

Option B is incorrect. Asymmetric algorithms are used to encrypt a small amount of data.

Option C is incorrect. A key escrow is a database of stored keys that can be recovered should the original user's key be lost or compromised.

Option D is incorrect. A CRL (certificate revocation list) is a list of digital certificates that have been revoked by the issuing certificate authority (CA) before their scheduled expiration date and should not be trusted.

139. A. PEAP is a protocol that encapsulates the EAP within a TLS tunnel.

Option B is incorrect. SSL was superseded by TLS and is considered not as secure as TLS.

Option C is incorrect. AES (Advanced Encryption Standard) is a symmetric algorithm used to encrypt data.

Option D is incorrect. SHA is a hashing algorithm and is used for integrity. SHA is used with SSL, and HMAC is used with TLS.

140. C. The AES-CCMP encryption algorithm used in the 802.11i security protocol uses the AES block cipher and limits the key length to 128 bits. AES-CCMP makes it difficult for an eavesdropper to spot patterns.

Options A, B, and D are incorrect. AES-CCMP is restricted to a key length of 128 bits.

141. C and D. Message Integrity Code (MIC) is a security improvement for WEP encryption within wireless networks. TKIP and CCMP use MIC, which provides an integrity check on the data packet.

Options A and B are incorrect. They are encryption algorithms and are not concerned with message integrity.

142. A and C. Preshared passphrases can be obtained from a threat actor by the use of social engineering skills and connect to the AP. WPA-Personal uses TKIP encryption, which is considered a weak option.

Option B is incorrect. WPA-Personal uses a preshared passphrase that is entered in the AP and each device that wants to connect to the network.

Option D is incorrect. WPA-Enterprise uses a RADIUS server, not WPA-Personal.

143. B. A root certificate is a public key certificate that identifies the root CA (certificate authority). Digital certificates are verified using a chain of trust (certificate chaining) and the trust anchor for the certificate is the root certificate authority (CA).

Option A is incorrect. A root certificate has an expiration date, also known as the validity period.

Option C is incorrect. A root certificate contains information about the CA (certificate authority), not the user.

Option D is incorrect. A root certificate is able to authorize subordinate CAs to issue certificates on its behalf.

144. B and C. Public and private keys work with each other to encrypt and decrypt data. If the data is encrypted with the receiver's public key, the receiver decrypts the data with their private key.

Option A is incorrect. Public and private keys are not isolated from each other. If you encrypt data with one key, the other key is used to decrypt the data.

Option D is incorrect. Data that is encrypted with the private key will be decrypted with the corresponding public key. The private key is designed to be held privately by the owner and not shared.

145. A and C. `.p12` and `.pfx` are filename extensions for PKCS #12 files.

Option B is incorrect. KEY is used for both private and public PKCS #8 keys.

Option D is incorrect. p7b is a filename extension for PKCS #7 and is used to sign and/or encrypt messages under a PKI. It also provides a syntax for disseminating certificates.

146. C and D. PGP and GPG use a web of trust to establish the authenticity of the binding between a public key and its owner.

Option A is incorrect. RC4 is a symmetric algorithm and does not use the web of trust concept.

Option B is incorrect. AES is a symmetric algorithm and does not use the web of trust concept.

147. A. A symmetric algorithm, sometimes called a secret key algorithm, uses the same key to encrypt and decrypt data and is typically used to encrypt data-at-rest.

Option B is incorrect. An asymmetric algorithm, also known as public key cryptography, uses public and private keys to encrypt and decrypt data and is typically not used to encrypt data-at-rest.

Option C is incorrect. Stream ciphers encrypt data one bit at a time.

Option D is incorrect. Hashing is a one-way encryption that transforms a string of characters into a fixed-length value or key, also known as a hash value. Hashes ensure the integrity of data or messages.

148. C. A registered authority (RA) is used to verify requests for certificates and forwards responses to the CA.

Option A is incorrect. A root CA is the top of the hierarchy and certifies intermediate CAs to issue certificates to users, computers, or services.

Option B is incorrect. An intermediate CA is certified by the root CA and can issue certificates to users, computers, or services.

Option D is incorrect. OCSP (Online Certificate Status Protocol) is a protocol that can be used to query a certificate authority about the revocation status of a given certificate. It validates certificates by returning responses such as "good," "revoked," and "unknown."

149. C. WPA2 is a security standard that secures computers connected to the 802.11n WiFi network. It provides the strongest available encryption for wireless networks.

Option A is incorrect. WEP (Wired Equivalent Privacy) is a security standard for 802.11b. It is designed to provide a level of security for a WLAN.

Option B is incorrect. WPA (WiFi Protected Access) is a security standard that replaced and improved on WEP. WPA is not as secure as WPA2.

Option D is incorrect. WPS (WiFi Protected Setup) is a network security standard that allows home users to easily add new devices to an existing wireless network without entering long passphrases. WPS is known to have vulnerabilities and is not recommended.

150. C. AES-256 can encrypt data quickly and securely with a USB flash drive.

Option A is incorrect. 3DES is an encryption algorithm but is not effective for sending information in a highly secure manner and quickly to a USB flash drive.

Options B and D are incorrect. They are examples of hash algorithms used to verify the integrity of the data.

Chapter 7: Practice Test

1. C. A virtual LAN (VLAN) is designed to allow network administrators to segment networks within a LAN. Each network will not be able to see traffic assigned to other systems within other VLANs within the same LAN.

Option A is incorrect. Media access control (MAC) is a unique identification number on a network device. This is also known as a physical address.

Option B is incorrect. Network Address Translation (NAT) is a function in a router that translates the private IP address to the public IP address and vice versa. A NAT will hide the private IP address from the Internet world and is also a solution for the limited IPv4 addresses available.

Option D is incorrect. A demilitarized zone (DMZ) is designed to protect the internal network but allow access to resources from the Internet. This provides an additional layer of protection to the LAN.

2. C. Passive reconnaissance is an attempt to obtain information about a computer system and networks without actively engaging with the system.

Option A is incorrect. Escalation of privilege attack allows an attacker to gain elevated access to the network due to programming errors or design flaws.

Option B is incorrect. Active reconnaissance is a type of network attack where the attacker engages with the targeted system. The attacker can use a port scanner to gather information about any vulnerable ports.

Option D is incorrect. Black-box testing can simulate a realistic scenario as the tester examines the functionality of a network without peering into the internal workings. Since the network administrator is an employee, he or she will have information about the internal structures of the network.

3. C. A personal identity verification (PIV) card contains the necessary data for the cardholder to be allowed to enter federal facilities.

Option A is incorrect. A proximity card is a contactless smartcard that is held near an electronic reader to grant access to a particular area.

Option B is incorrect. Time-Based One-Time Password (TOTP) is a temporary passcode that is generated for the use of authenticating to a computer system, and the passcode is valid for only a certain amount of time—for example, 30 seconds.

Option D is incorrect. HMAC-Based One-Time Password (HOTP) is a temporary passcode that is generated for the use of authenticating to a computer system; the passcode is valid until it is used by the user.

4. D. A Network Access Control (NAC) enforces security policies and manages access to a network. It enables compliant, authenticated, and trusted devices to enter the network and access resources. If the device isn't compliant, it will either be denied access or have limited access until the device becomes compliant.

Option A is incorrect. Network Address Translation (NAT) is a function in a router that translates the private IP address to the public IP address and vice versa. A NAT will hide the private IP address from the Internet world and is also a solution for the limited IPv4 addresses available.

Option B is incorrect. A host intrusion prevention system (HIPS) is used to monitor a client computer for malicious activity and performs an action based on an implemented rule.

Option C is incorrect. A demilitarized zone (DMZ) is designed to protect the internal network but allow access to resources from the Internet. This provides an additional layer of protection to the LAN.

5. A. A mantrap is a physical security access control that contains two sets of doors. When the first set of doors is closed, the second set opens. This access control prevents unauthorized access to a secure area.

Option B is incorrect. A Faraday cage is a metallic enclosure that prevents an electromagnetic field from escaping from a device such as a smartphone. The emitting of electromagnetic fields can allow an attacker to capture sensitive data.

Option C is incorrect. An airgap is the practice of isolating a computer or network to prevent it from connecting to external connections.

Option D is incorrect. Cable locks are used to prevent theft of computer equipment at the office or on the go.

6. B. A dematerialized zone (DMZ) separates the local area network (LAN) from untrusted networks such as the Internet. Resources that are placed in the DMZ are accessible from the Internet and protect resources located in the LAN.

Option A is incorrect. A honeynet is a collection of honeypots. A honeypot is a system that is set up with vulnerabilities to entice an attacker so as to view their activity and methods for research purposes.

Option C is incorrect. A proxy server sends requests on behalf of the client. Proxy servers mask the client's public IP address and can cache frequently requested websites to reduce bandwidth and improve the client's response times.

Option D is incorrect. An intranet is a private network found within a company accessed from within the LAN.

7. D. A load-balancer will distribute and manage network traffic across several servers to increase performance.

Option A is incorrect. A VPN concentrator is a router device that manages a large amount of VPN tunnels.

Option B is incorrect. A network intrusion prevention system (NIPS) is used to monitor a network for malicious activity and performs an action based on an implemented rule.

Option C is incorrect. Security incident and event management (SIEM) identifies, monitors, records, and analyzes any security event or incident in real time.

8. A. A security guard is a major role in all layers of security. A guard can execute many functions such as patrolling checkpoints, overseeing electronic access control, replying to alarms, and examining video surveillance.

Options B, C, and D are incorrect. Implementing these technologies is not as useful as employing a security guard.

9. A. A zero-day attack takes advantage of a security vulnerability on the same day the vulnerability becomes known. Attackers may find vulnerabilities before the company discovers it.

Option B is incorrect. Cross-site scripting enables attackers to insert client-side script into a webpage that other users can view.

Option C is incorrect. Address Resolution Protocol (ARP) poisoning occurs when an attacker changes the MAC address on the target's ARP cache to steal sensitive data and cause a denial of service.

Option D is incorrect. Domain hijacking occurs when an attacker uses a domain for their own purpose. Attackers can collect data about visitors.

10. B. Electromagnetic interference (EMI) will disrupt the operation of an electronic device when it is in the area of an electromagnetic field.

Option A is incorrect. A demilitarized zone (DMZ) is designed to protect the internal network but allow access to resources from the Internet. This provides an additional layer of protection to the LAN.

Option C is incorrect. A Basic Input/Output System (BIOS) manages the data between the computer's OS and the attached devices and peripherals such as the video display adapter, network interface card, wireless keyboard, and mouse.

Option D is incorrect. A Trusted Platform Module (TPM) is a specialized chip that stores RSA encryption keys that is specific to the operating system for hardware authentication.

11. C. A VPN concentrator is a device that creates a remote access or site-to-site VPN connection. A VPN concentrator is used when a company has a large number of VPN tunnels.

Option A is incorrect. A router determines the best route to pass a packet to its destination.

Option B is incorrect. A proxy server sends requests on behalf of the client. Proxy servers mask the client's public IP address and can cache frequently requested websites to reduce bandwidth and improve clients' response times.

Option D is incorrect. A firewall uses rules to control incoming and outgoing traffic in a network. Firewalls can be either hardware or software.

12. B. A key escrow is a location in where keys can be gained by authorized users to decrypt encrypted data.

Option A is incorrect. A certificate revocation list (CRL) is a list of certificates that were revoked by a CA before their expiration date. The certificates listed in the CRL should not be considered trusted.

Option C is incorrect. A trust model allows the encryption keys to be trusted; the names associated with the keys are the names associated with the person or entity.

Option D is incorrect. An intermediate certificate authority (CA) issues certificates to verify a digital device within a network or on the Internet.

13. B. Availability would be the biggest concern because the computers would not operate properly if the HVAC system does not work properly. Should the HVAC system not cool the server room adequately, the computers would not operate and become unavailable to their users.

Option A is incorrect. Confidentiality allows authorized users to gain access to sensitive and protected data.

Option C is incorrect. Integrity ensures that the data hasn't been altered and is protected from unauthorized modification.

Option D is incorrect. An airgap is the practice of isolating a computer or network to prevent it from connecting to external connections.

14. B. The correct answer is that the SSID broadcast is disabled. Disabling the SSID, the user must enter the SSID to attempt to connect the wireless access point.

Option A is incorrect. MAC filtering is the act of defining a list of devices that are permitted or prohibited on your WiFi network.

Option C is incorrect. The antenna type and placement will not prevent users from viewing the wireless SSID. The antenna type determines if the signal transmits in a 360-degree direction (omnidirectional) or in a direction between 80 and 120 degrees (directional).

Option D is incorrect. The band selection will not prevent users from viewing the wireless SSID. The band selection references the channel the wireless access point uses. In a 2.4 GHz spectrum, using channels near each other will stop the data from being received or sent.

15. B. Time-of-day restrictions are a form of logical access control where specific applications or systems are restricted access outside of specific hours.

Option A is incorrect. Job rotation is the practice of rotating employees who are assigned jobs within their employment to promote flexibility and keep employees interested in their jobs.

Option C is incorrect. Least privilege gives users the lowest level of rights so they can do their job to limit the potential chance of security breach.

Option D is incorrect. A location-based policy uses a device's location data to control features such as disabling a smartphone's camera in a sensitive area.

16. A, D, F. 3DES, RC4, and Twofish are known as symmetric algorithms. They use the same key to encrypt and decrypt data.

Options B and C are incorrect. ECDHE and RSA are known as asymmetric algorithms. They use private and public keys to encrypt and decrypt data.

Option E is incorrect. SHA is known as a hashing algorithm. Hashing transforms a string of characters into a key that represents the original string. This is also known as a one-way encryption because the hash cannot be decrypted to reveal the original string.

17. D. The correct answer is looking for weak passwords. A password-cracking tool can potentially discover users who are currently using weak passwords.

Options A, B, and C are incorrect. A password cracking program will not discover any strong passwords. It will not inform you if users are following the password complexity policy and minimum password length policy.

18. A. White-box testing refers to the process of testing a network with all information known about the network or layout.

Option B is incorrect. Black-box testing refers to the process of testing a network without any information known about the network or layout.

Option C is incorrect. Gray-box testing refers to the process of testing a network with some information known about the network or layout.

Option D is incorrect. Purple box is not a term referred to in a penetration test.

19. A. Remote Authentication Dial-In User Service (RADIUS) enables remote access servers to communicate with a central server. This central server is used to authenticate and authorize users to access network services and resources.

Option B is incorrect. TACACS+ is a protocol developed by Cisco and uses TCP for authentication, authorization, and accounting services.

Option C is incorrect. Kerberos is an authentication protocol that uses tickets to allow access to resources within the network.

Option D is incorrect. OAUTH is an authorization protocol that allows a third-party application to obtain users' data without sharing login credentials.

20. B, D. The correct answers are mitigating buffer overflow attacks and cross-site scripts (XSS) vulnerabilities. A buffer overflow attack occurs when a program attempts to place more data in a buffer (memory) than it can hold. This action can corrupt data, crash the program, or execute malicious code. XSS vulnerabilities are found in web applications and are executed by injecting malicious code to gather users' information.

Option B is incorrect. Shoulder surfing is a social engineering attack in which the attacker gathers personal information through direct observation such as looking over a person's shoulder.

Option D is incorrect. Address Resolution Protocol (ARP) poisoning is caused by an attacker sending spoofed ARP messages onto a local network. This allows the attacker to monitor data passing through the network.

21. A. The correct answer is something you do. This is an example of picture password. A user selects a photo of their choice and record gestures over it. Each gesture can be a line, a circle, or a dot, executed in an exact order. The user will repeat the gestures to log into their Windows account.

Option B is incorrect. Something you know is a knowledge factor such as a user knowing their username and password.

Option C is incorrect. Something you have is a possession factor such as a user possessing a smartcard or a security token.

Option D is incorrect. Something you are is an inherence biometric factor such as a user's fingerprint.

22. D. Account lockout prevents the hacker from accessing the user's account by guessing a username and password. It also locks the account for a determined amount of time or until an administrator has unlocked the account.

Option A is incorrect. Password complexity enforces the rule of inclusion of three of the four following character sets: lowercase letters, uppercase letters, numerals, and special characters. Password complexity will not lock out a hacker from potentially guessing a username and password.

Option B is incorrect. Account disablement is implemented when an employee has left a company, whether temporarily or permanently. Account disablement makes a user account no longer usable. This action is performed by an administrator within the company.

Option C is incorrect. Password length determines the minimum amount of alphanumeric characters a password must have. This will not lock out a hacker from potentially guessing a username and password.

23. C. DNS Security Extensions (DNSSEC) protect against attackers hijacking the DNS process and taking control of the session. DNSSEC digitally signs data so that the user can be assured the data is valid.

Option A is incorrect. Secure Socket Layer (SSL) is a protocol that secures connections between network clients and servers over an insecure network.

Option B is incorrect. Secure Shell (SSH) is a protocol that provides an administrator with a secure connection to a remote computer.

Option D is incorrect. Transport Layer Security (TLS) is a protocol that provides data integrity between two applications communicating. TLS is a successor to SSL and is more secure.

24. B. Dumpster diving is an attack performed by searching through trash for sensitive information that could be used to perform an attack on a company's network.

Option A is incorrect. Tailgating, often referred to as piggybacking, is a physical security violation where an unauthorized person follows an authorized person (an employee) into a secure area.

Option C is incorrect. Shoulder surfing is the ability to obtain information by looking over a person's shoulder. Information that can be obtained includes personal identification numbers, usernames, passwords, and other confidential information.

Option D is incorrect. A nan-in-the-middle attack is where an attacker captures and replays network data between two parties without their knowledge.

25. D. Advanced Encryption Standard (AES) uses key sizes that are 128, 192, and 256 bits.

Option A is incorrect. Data Encryption Standard (DES) uses a key size of 64 bits.

Option B is incorrect. Hash-Based Message Authentication Code (HMAC) uses a cryptographic key for messages authentication in conjunction with a hash function.

Option C is incorrect. MD5 is a 128-bit hashing algorithm.

26. C. The correct answer is penetration testing authorization. This authorization's goal is to protect the security auditor performing the work against likely attacks.

Option A is incorrect. Vulnerability testing authorization protects the security auditor from identifying and quantifying security vulnerabilities in a company's network. The question stated a simulated attack and this is referred to as penetration testing.

Option B is incorrect. Transferring risk to a third party allows the third party to manage specific types of risk, thus reducing the company's cost.

Option D is incorrect. Change management is the process of managing configuration changes made to a network.

27. C. Cloud computing is based on the concept of a hosted service provided over the Internet. Companies can have access to power processing and power storage rather than burdening the cost of creating and hosting their own system.

Option A is incorrect. Sandboxing is the concept of isolating a computing environment, such as a software developer testing new programming code.

Option B is incorrect. A demilitarized zone (DMZ) is designed to protect the internal network but allow access to resources from the Internet. This provides an additional layer of protection to the LAN.

Option D is incorrect. Data loss prevention (DLP) prevents sensitive data from leaving a company's network through scanning.

28. C. A zero-day attack takes advantage of a security vulnerability on the same day the vulnerability becomes known. Attackers may find vulnerabilities before the company discovers it.

Option A is incorrect. A buffer overflow attack occurs when a program attempts to place more data in a buffer (memory) than it can hold. This action can corrupt data, crash the program, or execute malicious code.

Option B is incorrect. Session hijacking is a method in which an attacker takes over a web user's session by capturing the session ID and impersonating the authorized user. This allows the attacker to do whatever the authorized user can do on the network

Option D is incorrect. A distributed denial of service (DDoS) occurs when an attacker uses a large number of hosts to flood a server with packets, causing the server to crash and become unavailable.

29. C, D. Wired Equivalent Privacy (WEP) and WiFi Protected Access (WPA) are security protocols for WLANs. They are known to have vulnerabilities and are prone to attacks.

Options A and B are incorrect. WPA2 Personal and WPA2 Enterprise are considered stronger choices when encrypting data between the device and the wireless access point (WAP). WPA2 Enterprise uses IEEE 802.1x authentication, and WPA2 Personal uses pre-shared keys (PSK) and is designed for home use.

30. D. Patch management consists of collecting, testing, and installing patches to a computer within a local network.

Option A is incorrect. Sandboxing is the concept of isolating a computing environment, such as a software developer testing new programming code.

Option B is incorrect. In an ad hoc network, devices are connected and communicating with each other directly.

Option C is incorrect. Virtualization allows the creation of virtual resources such as a server operating system. Multiple operating systems can run on one machine by sharing resources such as RAM, hard drives, and CPU.

31. A. FTPS (File Transfer Protocol Secure) is an extension to FTP (File Transfer Protocol) with added support for Transport Layer Security (TLS) and Secure Socket Layer (SSL) security technology.

Option B is incorrect. Secure File Transfer Protocol (SFTP) uses SSH to transfer files to remote systems and requires the client to authenticate to the remote server.

Option C is incorrect. Secure Shell is a protocol that provides an administrator with a secure connection to a remote computer.

Option D is incorrect. Lightweight Directory Access Protocol Secure (LDAPS) uses SSL (Secure Socket Layer) to securely access and maintain directory information over an IP network.

32. B. PIA (privacy impact assessment) is a tool used to collect personally identifiable information (PII). It states what is collected and how the information will be maintained and how it will be protected.

Option A is incorrect. BIA (business impact analysis) is used to evaluate the possible effect a business can suffer should an interruption to critical system operations occur. This interruption could be as a result of an accident, emergency, or disaster.

Option C is incorrect. RTO (recovery time objective) is the amount of time it takes to resume normal business operations after an event.

Option D is incorrect. MTBF (mean time between failures) is the rating on a device or component that predicts the expected time between failures.

33. D. The correct answer is quantitative. Specific dollar values are used to prioritize risk. This is why ALE (annual loss expectancy) is classified as quantitative risk analysis.

Option A is incorrect. Qualitative risk analysis involves a ranking scale to rate risk rather than specific figures.

Option B is incorrect. ROI (return on investment) cannot be calculated before a risk analysis is completed.

Option C is incorrect. SLE (single loss expectancy) is related to risk management and risk assessment and is the expected monetary loss for each risk that occurs.

34. D. Companies will use mandatory vacations policy to detect fraud by having a second person who is familiar with the duties help discover any illicit activities.

Option A is incorrect. Companies usually don't want many of their employees out at the same time. This will cause a shortage in a particular area and could compromise the security posture of the company.

Option B is incorrect. Companies have a policy of "use or lose" vacation time if not taken by the end of the calendar year. Mandatory vacations policy isn't the tool used to ensure employees are taking the correct amount of days off. This is usually maintained by the HR department.

Option C is incorrect. Companies do want their employees to be recharged to properly conduct their duties, but from a security standpoint, this isn't the best answer.

35. D. Typosquatting is used by attackers by redirecting web traffic to another website the attacker maintains. The attacker achieves this by purchasing a misspelled URL and creating a website similar to the original. The attacker can then try to sell products or install malware on a user's computer.

Option A is incorrect. Session hijacking is a method by which an attacker takes over a web user's session by capturing the session ID and impersonating the authorized user. This allows the attacker to do whatever the authorized user can do on the network.

Option B is incorrect. Cross-site scripting enables attackers to insert client-side script into a webpage that other users can view.

Option C is incorrect. Replay attack occurs when legitimate network transmission is captured by an attacker and then is maliciously retransmitted to trick the receiver into unauthorized operations.

36. D. A Trusted Platform Module (TPM) should be enabled because it is a specialized chip, also known as a hardware root of trust, that stores RSA encryption keys that are specific to the operating system for hardware authentication.

Option A is incorrect. Redundant Array of Independent Disks (RAID) provides redundancy by storing the same data in different places on multiple hard disks. If a hard drive fails, this would help protect the loss of data.

Option B is incorrect. Universal Serial Bus (USB) is an interface that allows an add-on device to connect to a computer.

Option C is incorrect. Hardware Security Module (HSM) is a physical device that manages digital keys for authentication, encryption, and decryption.

37. C. Black-box testing refers to the process of testing a network without any information known about the network or layout.

Option A is incorrect. White-box testing refers to the process of testing a network with all information known about the network or layout.

Option B is incorrect. Red box is not a term referred to as a penetration test.

Option D is incorrect. Gray-box testing refers to the process of testing a network with some information known about the network or layout.

38. B. Tailgating, often referred to as piggybacking, is a physical security violation where an unauthorized person follows an authorized person (an employee) into a secure area.

Option A is incorrect. Shoulder surfing is the ability to obtain information by looking over a person's shoulder. Information that can be obtained is personal identification numbers, usernames, passwords, and other confidential information.

Option C is incorrect. Vishing is a type of social engineering attack that tries to trick a person into disclosing secure information over the phone or a Voice over IP (VoIP) call.

Option D is incorrect. Dumpster diving is performed by searching through trash for sensitive information that could be used to perform an attack on a company's network.

39. A. Implicit deny is placed at the bottom of the list. If traffic goes through the ACL list of rules and isn't explicitly denied or allowed, implicit deny will deny the traffic as it is the last rule. In other words, if traffic is not explicitly allowed within an access list, then by default it is denied.

Option B is incorrect. Port security allows an administrator to prohibit or permit devices based on their MAC address by configuring individual physical switch ports.

Option C is incorrect. A flood guard helps prevent denial-of-service (DoS) attacks by stopping a large amount of traffic on a network in an attempt to stop a service of a device.

Option D is incorrect. Signal strength is the power of electric field transmitted by an antenna. The lower the strength, the shorter the distance devices can connect to a wireless access point.

40. D. ARP poisoning is an attack created by an attacker by sending spoofed Address Resolution Protocol (ARP) messages onto a local network. This allows the attacker to monitor data passing through the network.

Option A is incorrect. DNS poisoning is an attack where the attacker modifies the DNS server records to redirect a user to another website that can contain different types of malware.

Option B is incorrect. Injection is a computer attack where the attacker enters malicious code in an application and the malicious code is passed to the backend database.

Option C is incorrect. Impersonation is a form of social engineering where an attack impersonates another person, such as a repair technician, to access a secured area.

41. D. A Trojan is malware that is disguised as a legitimate program and can allow hackers to gain access to a user's system.

Option A is incorrect. A keylogger is a program that records every keystroke from the user and sends them to the hacker.

Option B is incorrect. A worm is a self-replicating malware that spreads to other computers in the network. It is designed to consume network bandwidth.

Option C is incorrect. Ransomware is malware that prevents and limits users from accessing their computer. This is achieved by locking the system's screen or encrypting the user's files unless a ransom is paid.

42. B. MTTR (mean time to repair) is the average time it takes for a failed device or component to be repaired or replaced.

Option A is incorrect. RTO (recovery time objective) is the amount of time it takes to resume normal business operations after an event.

Option C is incorrect. MTBF (mean time between failures) is the rating on a device or component that predicts the expected time between failures.

Option D is incorrect. RPO (recovery point objective) is the period of time a company can tolerate lost data being unrecoverable between backups.

43. B. The correct answer is life. Natural disasters and intentional man-made attacks can jeopardize the lives of employees. These attacks could include severe weather events, arson and other fires, and terrorist attacks.

Option A is incorrect. This type of impact could jeopardize the personal safety of employees and customers.

Option C is incorrect. This type of impact could cause monetary damages to a company, not jeopardize the life of employees and customers.

Option D is incorrect. This type of impact could negatively impact the image the company has in its community.

44. B. A script kiddie is an immature hacker with little knowledge about exploits. The typical script kiddie will use existing and well-known techniques and scripts to search for and exploit weaknesses in a computer system.

Answer A is incorrect. Man-in-the-middle is an attack option; an attacker captures and replays network data between two parties without their knowledge.

Option C is incorrect. White-hat hackers attempt to break into a protected network. The skills are used to improve security of a network by revealing vulnerabilities and mitigating them before malicious attackers discover them.

Option D is incorrect. A hacktivist performs hacktivism. This is the act of hacking into a computer system for a politically or socially motivated purpose.

45. B. The correct answer is users. The company's standard employees are their first line of defense. Users receive general cybersecurity awareness training.

Option A is incorrect. Based on the user's job role in the organization, different titles will receive different types of training. Data owners usually receive training on how to manage sensitive information.

Option C is incorrect. System administrators usually receive training on how to configure and maintain certain systems.

Option D is incorrect. System owners usually receive training on how to manage certain systems.

46. B. Full-disk encryption will protect the data that is not currently being accessed should the hard drive be compromised. Full-disk encryption will prevent an unauthorized individual from reading the data on the hard drive.

Option A is incorrect. Biometrics will not protect data stored on a storage device not in use, as an attacker can steal the storage device and retrieve the clear text data without the need of biometric authentication.

Option C is incorrect. A host intrusion prevention system (HIPS) is used to monitor a client computer for malicious activity and performs an action based on an implemented rule. This will not protect data stored on a storage device should it be stolen.

Option D is incorrect. A host intrusion detection system (HIDS) is used to monitor a client computer for malicious activity. An HIDS would not protect the data if the storage device is stolen.

47. B. Qualitative risk analysis uses descriptions and words to measure the amount of impact of risk. A weakness of qualitative risk analysis involves sometimes subjective and untestable methodology.

Options A, C, and D are incorrect. These statements describe quantitative risk analysis.

48. A. A stateful firewall distinguishes valid packets for different types of connections. Packets that match a known active connection will be allowed to pass through the firewall.

Option B is incorrect. A stateless firewall evaluates current packets and does not keep track of the state of network connections.

Option C is incorrect. An application firewall scans, monitors, and controls network access and operations to and by an application or service. It makes it possible to control and manage the processes of an application or service from an external network to an internal network.

Option D is incorrect. A packet filter firewall controls access to a network by watching outgoing and incoming packets. Based on the source and destination IP addresses, protocols, and ports, the firewall will allow or deny access to desired network.

49. A, C. The correct answers are fingerprint and home address. This data is often used to distinguish an individual identity as per the personally identifiable information definition used by NIST.

Option B is incorrect. The MAC address is used to identify a device that connects to a network. Anyone can use a particular device without being personally identified.

Option D is incorrect. Gender alone is less often used to characterize an individual's identity. When combined with a standalone PII element, gender can be used to identify an individual.

50. B. The correct answer is to remotely wipe the mobile device. This action will prevent sensitive data from being accessed by an unauthorized person.

Option A is incorrect. Push notification is a message that pops up on a mobile device. It can provide convenience and value to app users. Users can receive important information ranging from sports scores, new updates, flight status, to weather reports.

Option C is incorrect. Screen lock requires the user to perform a specific action and will not be able to lock the screen if they don't have possession of the mobile device.

Option D is incorrect. Geofencing defines a virtual boundary in a geographical area and can generate alerts based on defined coordinates of the geographical area.

51. B. The correct answer is full and differential. Full backup is considered the most basic type as it copies all of the files. Differential backup copies all the files that have changed since the last full backup.

Option A is incorrect. Full backup is considered the most basic type because it copies all of the files. Incremental backup copies only the files that have changed since the last full or incremental backup.

Option C is incorrect. Snapshots copy the entire architectural instance of a system. This process is also referred to as image backup.

Option D is incorrect. Full backup is considered the most basic type because it copies all of the files.

52. A. An IPv6 address is a 128-bit address that uses hexadecimal values (0–9 and A–F).

Option B is incorrect. IPv4 is a 32-bit address that uses decimal values between 0 and 255.

Option C is incorrect. A MAC address is a physical address of a device that connects to a network. It is made up of six pairs of hexadecimal values.

Option D is incorrect. Automatic Private IP Addressing is a self-assigning address when no DHCP server is available or any other automatic method for assigning IP addresses.

53. D. Bluejacking is the act of sending unsolicited messages from one Bluetooth device to another Bluetooth device such as smartphones, tablets, and laptop computers.

Option A is incorrect. Jamming can compromise a wireless network denying service to authorized users by overwhelming frequencies of illegitimate traffic.

Option B is incorrect. Bluesnarfing is the theft of information from a Bluetooth enabled device through a Bluetooth connection.

Option C is incorrect. Brute force is a trial and error method that involves guessing all possible passwords and passphrases until the correct one is discovered.

54. A. RSA is an asymmetric algorithm that uses private and public keys to encrypt and decrypt data.

Option B is incorrect. Data Encryption Standard (DES) is a symmetric key algorithm that uses the same key to encrypt and decrypt data.

Option C is incorrect. MD5 is a 128-bit hashing algorithm.

Option D is incorrect. SHA is known as a hashing algorithm. Hashing transforms a string of characters into a key that represents the original string. This is also known as a one-way encryption because the hash cannot be decrypted to reveal the original string.

55. A. Automatically encrypting outgoing emails will protect the company's sensitive email that may contain personally identifiable information. Should the email be intercepted, the attacker wouldn't be able to read the information contained in the email.

Options B and D are incorrect. Monitoring all outgoing and incoming emails will not protect the company's sensitive information. When the administrator receives a notice the email was compromised, it's too late.

Option C is incorrect. Automatically encrypting incoming emails doesn't help secure the company's sensitive information since this information is leaving the network, not entering the network.

56. B. Clean desk policy ensures that all sensitive/confidential documents are removed from an end-user workstation and locked up when the documents are not in use.

Option A is incorrect. Separation of duties is a concept of having more than one person required to complete a task.

Option C is incorrect. A job rotation policy is the practice of moving employees between different tasks to promote experience and variety.

Option D is incorrect. A privacy policy is a policy that describes the ways a party gathers, uses, discloses, and manages a customer's or client's data.

57. A. The screen lock option can be enabled to prevent an unauthorized person from viewing the data on a device should the owner leave it unattended. This option can be configured to enable within seconds to minutes if device is unattended.

Option B is incorrect. Push notification is a message that pops up on a mobile device. It can provide convenience and value to app users. Users can receive important information ranging from sports scores, new updates, flight status, to weather reports.

Option C is incorrect. Remote wipe is an action that will prevent sensitive data from being accessed by an unauthorized person by resetting the device to its default state.

Option D is incorrect. Full device encryption encodes all of the user's data on a mobile device by using an encrypted key.

58. A. Biometrics are a person's physical characteristics, such as a fingerprint, retina, hand geometry, and voice.

Option B is incorrect. A proximity card is a contactless smartcard that is held near an electronic reader to grant access to a particular area.

Option C is incorrect. Least privilege gives users the lowest level of rights so they can do their job to limit the potential chance of security breach.

Option D is incorrect. Group Policy is used by network administrators in a Microsoft Active Directory to implement certain configurations for users and computers.

59. A. A virtual private network (VPN) creates an encrypted connection between a remote client and a private network over an insecure network such as the Internet.

Option B is incorrect. Wireless LAN (WLAN) allows a mobile user to connect to a local area network (LAN) using the 802.11 wireless standard.

Option C is incorrect. Network Address Translation (NAT) is a function in a router that translates the private IP address to the public IP address, and vice versa. A NAT will hide the private IP address from the Internet world and also is a solution for the limited IPv4 addresses available.

Option D is incorrect. Ad hoc is composed of devices connected and communicating with each other directly.

60. B. A cross-site request forgery attack occurs when an attacker tricks a user into performing unwanted actions on a website the user is currently authenticated to.

Option A is incorrect. A replay attack occurs when legitimate network transmission is captured by an attacker and then is maliciously retransmitted to trick the receiver into unauthorized operations.

Option C is incorrect. Cross-site scripting enables attackers to insert client-side script into a webpage that other users can view.

Option D is incorrect. Buffer overflow attack occurs when a program attempts to place more data in buffer (memory) than it can hold. This action can corrupt data, crash the program, or execute malicious code.

61. C. The correct answer is mandatory access control (MAC). Access is controlled by comparing security labels with security clearances such as Confidential, Secret, and Top Secret.

Option A is incorrect. Role-based access control (RBAC) controls access based on the roles the users have within the system and on rules stating the access that is allowed for the users in a given role.

Option B is incorrect. Discretionary access control (DAC) controls access based on the object's owner policy.

Option D is incorrect. Attribute-based access control (ABAC) controls access on three types of attributes: the user attributes, current environmental conditions, and accessed application or system attributes.

62. B. Virtualization allows the creation of virtual resources such as a server operating system. Multiple operating systems can run on one machine by sharing the resources such as RAM, hard drive, and CPU.

Option A is incorrect. Infrastructure as a Service (IaaS) is a cloud computing concept that provides computing resources over the Internet.

Option C is incorrect. Software as a Service (SaaS) is a concept that distributes software to customers over the Internet.

Option D is incorrect. A public cloud is a cloud computing model that provides service to the public over the Internet.

63. A, C. MD5 and SHA have known cases of collisions.

Options B, D, and E are incorrect. There are no known collisions with AES, SHA-256, and RSA.

64. C. An extranet will give customers, vendors, suppliers, and other business access to a controlled private network while preventing them from accessing the company's entire network.

Option A is incorrect. An intranet is a private network found within a company accessed from within the LAN.

Option B is incorrect. The Internet is a global network of computers and devices that can communicate with anyone or any device anywhere in the world.

Option D is incorrect. A honeynet is a collection of honeypots. A honeypot is a system that is set up with vulnerabilities to entice an attacker so as to view their activity and methods for research purposes.

65. D. A property return form properly records all equipment, keys, and badges that must be surrendered to the company when the employee leaves the company.

Option A is incorrect. Job rotation is a policy that describes the practice of moving employees between different tasks to promote experience and variety.

Option B is incorrect. An NDA (nondisclosure agreement) protects sensitive and intellectual data from getting into the wrong hands.

Option C is incorrect. Background checks is a process that is performed when a potential employee is considered for hire.

66. D. Password Authentication Protocol (PAP) is an authentication protocol that sends the username and password as plain text to the authentication server.

Option A is incorrect. TACACS+ is a protocol developed by Cisco and uses TCP for authentication, authorization, and accounting services.

Option B is incorrect. Challenge-Handshake Authentication Protocol (CHAP) validates the identity of remote clients using a three-way handshake.

Option C is incorrect. NTLM authenticates the client and server using a challenge-response process that is made up of three messages.

67. B, D. BCRYPT and PBKDF2 use key stretching to reduce brute-force attacks against vulnerabilities of encrypted keys. Both are considered password hashing functions.

Option A is incorrect. ROT13 is an encrypting method by replacing each letter of the alphabet with the corresponding letter of the second half of the alphabet. A becomes N, B becomes O, and so on.

Option C is incorrect. RIPEMD is a cryptographic hashing function based on MD4 and does not offer adequate protection.

68. C. The correct answer is to reduce the signal strength for indoor coverage only. This action will prevent potential attackers from accessing the wireless access point and possibly compromising the users currently connected. Having the signal limited inside the business will help determine who is possibly connected.

Option A is incorrect. The antenna type determines if the signal transmits in a 360-degree direction (omnidirectional) or in a direction between 80 and 120 degrees (directional).

Option B is incorrect. Disabling the SSID broadcast will prevent the users from seeing the wireless access point (WAP). The users would be required to enter the name of the WAP and this will not prevent the signal from extending into the parking lot.

Option D is incorrect. Enabling MAC filtering will not prevent the signal from extending into the parking lot. MAC filtering controls who is permitted or prohibited on the network.

69. D. Least privilege gives users the lowest level of rights so they can do their job to limit the potential chance of security breach.

Option A is incorrect. Job rotation is the practice of rotating employees who are assigned jobs within their employment to promote flexibility and keep employees interested in their jobs.

Option B is incorrect. Time-of-day restriction is a form of logical access control where specific applications or systems are restricted access outside of specific hours.

Option C is incorrect. Separation of duties is a control where error and fraud are prevented by having at least two employees responsible for separate parts of a task.

70. D. Hashing transforms a string of characters into a key that represents the original string. When the string of characters is transformed and compared to the original hash, it will identify whether the string has been modified.

Option A is incorrect. Key stretching is a technique to make a weak key stronger against brute-force attacks and increase the time the attacker must spend to guess the result.

Option B is incorrect. Steganography is the practice of hiding a message such as a file within a picture.

Option C is incorrect. Key exchange is the practice of exchanging cryptographic keys between two parties.

71. C. A certificate revocation list (CRL) is a list of certificates that were revoked by a CA before their expiration date. The certificates listed in the CRL should not be considered trusted.

Option A is incorrect. An intermediate certificate authority (CA) issues certificates to verify a digital device within a network or on the Internet.

Option B is incorrect. A certificate signing request (CSR) is an encrypted message sent to a CA and validates the information that the CA requires in order to issue certificates.

Option D is incorrect. Key escrow is a location in where keys can be gained by authorized users to decrypt encrypted data.

72. C. The user is using an intimidation tactic to get the employee to take action quickly. Sometimes intimidation tactics can be combined with other principles such as urgency.

Option A is incorrect. Scarcity is a tactic that gets people to make quick decisions without thinking through the decision. An example is when people are often encouraged to take action when they think there is a limited supply of a product.

Option B is incorrect. Consensus is a tactic to get people to like what other people like.

Option D is incorrect. Authority is a tactic to get people to comply when a person of authority says to do so. The user is not in an authoritative position. The user is calling on behalf of his manager.

73. B, C. The correct answers are full-device encryption and screen locks. Full-device encryption encodes all the user's data on a mobile device by using an encrypted key, and enabling screen lock prevents an unauthorized person from viewing the data on a device should the owner leave it unattended.

Option A is incorrect. Geofencing defines a virtual boundary in a geographical area and can generate alerts based on defined coordinates of the geographical area.

Option D is incorrect. Push notification is a message that pops up on a mobile device. It can provide convenience and value to app users. Users can receive important information ranging from sports scores, new updates, flight status, to weather reports.

74. B. The correct answer is `ifconfig`. This command is used on a Linux OS to obtain a MAC address of the computer for which the OS is installed.

Option A is incorrect. The `ipconfig` command is used on a Windows OS to obtain a MAC address of the computer for which the OS is installed.

Option C is incorrect. `tracert` is a Windows command used to trace the pathway a packet takes on an IP network from the source to the destination.

Option D is incorrect. `ping` is a command used to test the connectivity between two devices. `ping` uses an ICMP to receive an echo reply to know if the device is currently running.

75. D. Account expiration policy will prevent the contracts from attempting to access the network after they leave. The provisioning team can set a date when the contract is set to leave, and the user will not be able to have access to systems within the company's network.

Option A is incorrect. Account disablement requires an administrator to manually disable the account. Should the administrator set a policy for failed logon attempts, this would disable the account. If the contractor can sign in without failed attempts, the disablement policy will not go into effect.

Option B is incorrect. Account lockout policy is set if there are failed attempts to log into the system. If the contractor can sign in without failed attempts, the lockout policy will not go into effect.

Option C is incorrect. Enforce password history is a policy that requires users to use a certain number of unique passwords before they can reuse a password. This policy will not help prevent contractors from accessing the company's network.

76. A. Password complexity is a rule that demands inclusion of three of the four following character sets: lowercase letters, uppercase letters, numerals, and special characters.

Option B is incorrect. Password length determines the minimum amount of alphanumeric characters a password must have. This will not lock out a hacker from potentially guessing a username and password.

Option C is incorrect. Password history determines the number of new passwords a user must use before an old password can be used again.

Option D is incorrect. Group Policy is used by network administrators in a Microsoft Active Directory to implement certain configurations for users and computers.

77. D. CYOD (Choose Your Own Device) allows an employee to choose from a limited number of devices. The business can also limit the usage of the device to work activities only.

Option A is incorrect. Data loss prevention (DLP) prevents sensitive data from leaving a company's network by method of scanning.

Option B is incorrect. Company-owned, personally enabled (COPE) allows companies to provide employees with devices. The company maintains ownership of these devices, and frequently monitors and controls their activity to a larger scale. With COPE devices, employees can access social media sites, email, and personal calls.

Option C is incorrect. Bring Your Own Device (BYOD) allows an employee to use their own personal device, such as a smartphone or laptop, and connect to the company's network.

78. C. Multifactor authentication requires more than one method of authentication from independent credentials: something you know, something you have, and something you are.

Option A is incorrect. Identification is used to identify a user within the system. It allows each user to distinguish itself from other users.

Option B is incorrect. Single authentication is one method of authentication from independent credentials: something you know, something you have, and something you are.

Option D is incorrect. Transitive trust is a two-way relationship that is created between parent and child domains in a Microsoft Active Directory forest. When a child domain is created, it will share the resources with its parent domain automatically. This allows an authenticated user to access resources in both the child and parent domains.

79. B, D. The correct answers are email address and fingerprint. Personally identifiable information (PII) is any information that can be used to distinguish or trace an individual's identity.

Options A and C are incorrect. Date of birth and race cannot identify an individual on its own because those items are considered general information.

80. A. The correct answer is a false positive. When legitimate data enters a system and the host intrusion prevention system (HIPS) mistakenly marks it as malicious, it is referred to as a false positive.

Option B is incorrect. False negative is the opposite of false positive, where an HIPS allows malicious data into your network by marking it as legitimate activity.

Option C is incorrect. A credentialed vulnerability scan consists of a scanning computer with an account on the computer being scanned so that the scanner can perform a deeper check for problems not seen from the network.

Option D is incorrect. A noncredentialed vulnerability scan provides a quick view of vulnerabilities by looking at network services that are exposed by the host.

81. D. The correct answer is SNMPv3. Simple Network Management Protocol (SNMP) collects and organizes information about managed devices on an IP network. SNMPv3 is the newest version and its primary feature is enhanced security.

Option A is incorrect. Secure Shell (SSH) allows users to securely log on to a remote computer and perform the same actions as though they were at the local computer.

Option B is incorrect. SNMP is the original version and doesn't provide security.

Option C is incorrect. Simple Mail Transfer Protocol (SMTP) is the standard protocol for email communication over the Internet.

82. A. A Time-Based One-Time Password (TOTP) is a temporary passcode that is generated for the use of authenticating to a computer system and the passcode is valid for a certain amount of time—for example, 30 seconds.

Option B is incorrect. An HMAC-Based One-Time Password (HOTP) is a temporary passcode that is generated for the use of authenticating to a computer system and the passcode valid until it is used by the user.

Option C is incorrect. A smartcard is a hardware token, usually the size of a credit card, with an embedded chip that connects to a reader.

Option D is incorrect. A proximity card is a contactless smartcard that is held near an electronic reader to grant access to a particular area.

83. C. Kerberos is an authentication protocol that uses tickets to allow access to resources within the network.

Option A is incorrect. Remote Authentication Dial-In User Service (RADIUS) enables remote access servers to communicate with a central server. This central server is used to authenticate and authorize users to access network services and resources.

Option B is incorrect. TACACS+ is a protocol developed by Cisco and uses TCP for authentication, authorization, and accounting services.

Option D is incorrect. Security Assertion Markup Language (SAML) is an XML standard that allows a user to log in once to an affiliate website and that supports Single Sign-On (SSO) authentication.

84. C. The correct answer is C. This is not a vulnerability, because most systems will not automatically shut down when they have reached their end-of-life period.

Options A, B, and D are incorrect. These are a vulnerability to end-of-life systems. When a system reaches its end-of-life period, attackers can exploit it since the company will no longer support the system by, for example, sending patches to further protect it.

85. B, C. A worm self-replicates itself over the network to consume bandwidth and a virus needs to be attached to a file to be replicated over the network.

Options A and D are incorrect. A worm is a stand-alone malware that does not need to copy itself to a file. A virus requires a file to be attached and requires someone to knowingly or unknowingly spread the malware without the knowledge or permission of the user.

86. B. An evil twin is a fake access point that looks like a legitimate one. The attacker will use the same network name and transmit beacons to get a user to connect. This allows the attacker to gain personal information without the end user knowing.

Option A is incorrect. A rogue access point is a wireless access point that has been installed on a network without the user's knowledge. It receives beacons transmitted by legitimate access points within the company.

Option C is incorrect. Bluejacking is the act of sending unsolicited messages from one Bluetooth device to another Bluetooth device, such as smartphones, tablets, and laptop computers.

Option D is incorrect. Bluesnarfing is the theft of information from a Bluetooth-enabled device through a Bluetooth connection.

87. A. WPA2 with CCMP provides data confidentiality and authentication. CCMP uses a 128-bit key, which is considered secured against attacks.

Option B is incorrect. Wired Equivalent Privacy (WEP) is a security protocol for WLANs and is known to have vulnerabilities that make it prone to attacks.

Option C is incorrect. WPA with CCMP does not exist. WPA adopted protocol TKIP.

Option D is incorrect. WiFi Protected Setup (WPS) uses an 8-digit PIN and is vulnerable to a brute-force attack.

88. C. Business impact analysis (BIA) usually identifies costs linked to failures. These costs may include equipment replacement, salaries paid to employees to catch up with loss of work, and loss of profits.

Option A is incorrect. A security audit tests how effective security policies are in helping protect company's assets, such as performing security vulnerability scans.

Option B is incorrect. Asset identification identifies system assets based on known information about the asset. The policy usually describes the purpose of the asset and methods for identifying assets.

Option D is incorrect. A disaster recovery plan (DRP) is a document that describes the steps for responding to an unplanned incident. Tony's job is to determine what result would occur should the SQL server go down. A DRP is a plan when a system component actually fails.

89. A. Cloud storage offers protection from cyberattacks since the data is backed up. Should the data become corrupted, the hospital can recover the data from cloud storage.

    Option B is incorrect. Wiping is the action of making data that is stored on a mobile device inaccessible.

    Option C is incorrect. A security incident and event management (SIEM) identifies, monitors, records, and analyzes any security event or incident in real time.

    Option D is incorrect. Supervisory Control and Data Acquisition (SCADA) is used in power plants to gather and analyze data information in real time from a remote location to control the equipment.

90. A. A logic bomb is a malicious code that is inserted intentionally and designed to execute under certain circumstances. It is designed to display a false message, delete or corrupt data, or have other unwanted effects.

    Option B is incorrect. A Remote Access Trojan (RAT) is a malware program that allows administrative control over a system via a back door.

    Option C is incorrect. Spyware is installed on a computer system without the user's knowledge. This is considered tracking software, and it can collect keystrokes and use cookies to track website the user visits.

    Option D is incorrect. Ransomware is malware that prevents and limits users from accessing their computer. This is achieved by locking the system's screen or encrypting the user's files unless a ransom is paid.

91. A. A hacktivist's purpose is to perform hacktivism. This is the act of hacking into a computer system for a politically or socially motivated purpose.

    Option B is incorrect. An insider is someone who threatens a company's security from within the company.

    Option C is incorrect. A script kiddie is an immature hacker. The typical script kiddie will use existing and well-known techniques and scripts to search for and exploit weaknesses in a computer system.

    Option D is incorrect. An evil twin is a rouge wireless access point that impersonates an authentic WiFi access point. The purpose of an evil twin is to have the user connect to the rouge access point to collect their personal information without the user's knowledge.

92. C. Vishing is a type of social engineering attack that tries to trick a person into disclosing secure information over the phone or a Voice over IP (VoIP) call.

    Option A is incorrect. Whaling is a form of phishing attack designed to target the head of a company.

    Option B is incorrect. Phishing is the practice of sending emails claiming to be from a reputable company to individuals in order to persuade them to disclose their personal information by clicking a fraudulent link.

    Option D is incorrect. Spear phishing is a form of phishing attack designed to target individuals to disclose confidential information.

93. A, D, E. The correct answers are third-party app store, rooting, and sideloading. Restricting these options will increase the security of a device. Third-party app stores can carry apps that may contain malware. Companies will allow certain apps to be downloaded. Rooting is the process of gaining privileged control over a device. For a user with root access, anything is possible, such as installing new applications, uninstalling system applications, and revoking existing permissions. Sideloading is installing applications on a mobile device without using an official distributed scheme.

Option B is incorrect. Biometrics is a person's physical characteristics, such as a fingerprint, retina, hand geometry, and voice.

Option C is incorrect. Content management systems are used to create and manage digital content for enterprises and web content.

94. A, C. The correct answers are IPSec and SSL. IPSec protects IP packets that are exchanged between the remote network and an IPSec gateway, which is located on the edge of a private network. Secure Socket Layer (SSL) usually supplies a secure access to a single application.

Option B is incorrect. Data Encryption Standard (DES) is a deprecated symmetric-key data encryption method.

Option D is incorrect. Secure File Transfer Protocol (SFTP) uses SSH to transfer files to a remote systems and requires the client to authenticate to the remote server.

95. D. Public Key Infrastructure (PKI) distributes and identifies public keys to users and computers securely over a network. It also verifies the identity of the owner of the public key.

Option A is incorrect. WiFi Protected Access (WPA) is a security protocol for WLANs. They are known to have vulnerabilities and are prone to attacks.

Option B is incorrect. Object identifiers are unique numeric value to identify an object to avoid conflicts with another object when different directories are combined.

Option C is incorrect. PFX is a file extension for an encrypted security file that stores secure certificates that are used for authentication.

96. D. Transitive trust is a two-way relationship that is created between parent and child domains in a Microsoft Active Directory forest. When a child domain is created, it will share the resources with its parent domain automatically. This allows an authenticated user to access resources in both the child and parent domains.

Option A is incorrect. Multifactor authentication requires more than one method of authentication from independent credentials: something you know, something you have, and something you are.

Option B is incorrect. Federation refers to a group of network providers that agree on a standard of operation in a collective manner.

Option C is incorrect. Single sign-on (SSO) is the ability to permit a user to use one set of credentials to log in and access multiple resources.

97. C. Identification is used to identify a user within the system. It allows each user to distinguish itself from other users.

Option A is incorrect. Authorization determines the user's privilege or access level to a resource such as computer programs, files and data.

Option B is incorrect. Authentication confirms a user's identity from the credentials provided.

Option D is incorrect. Accounting is the process of tracking a user's activities within a network. These activities include services accessed, amount of data accessed or transferred, and login for authentication and authorization.

98. B. Steganography is the practice of hiding a message such as a file within a picture.

Option A is incorrect. Data sanitization is the act of permanently removing data stored on a memory device.

Option C is incorrect. Tracert is a Window's command-line utility that displays the route between your computer and the specified destination through Internet.

Option D is incorrect. Network mapping discovers and displays the physical and virtual connectivity within a network.

99. B, D. The correct answers are static ARP entries and port security. Static ARP entry is the process of assigning a MAC address to an IP address to prevent an attacker from poisoning the cache. Disabling unused physical ports will prevent an attacker from plugging in their laptop and performing an ARP poisoning.

Option A is incorrect. An antivirus is designed to prevent, detect, and remove malware infections from a user's computer.

Option C is incorrect. Patching management is the process of collecting, testing, and installing patches to computers in a local network.

100. D. Implicit deny is placed at the bottom of the list. If traffic goes through the ACL list of rules and isn't explicitly denied or allowed, implicit deny will deny the traffic as it is the last rule. In other words, if traffic is not explicitly allowed within an access list, then by default it is denied.

Option A is incorrect. USB blocking is the act of prohibiting a user from inserting a USB device and possibly transferring files from a PC or infecting a network with malware from the USB device.

Option B is incorrect. Time synchronization ensures all devices have the same time. This is important since all aspects of managing, securing, and debugging networks are determined when events happen.

Option C is incorrect. MAC filtering is the act of defining a list of devices that are permitted or prohibited on your WiFi network.

Index

Note to reader: All entries with acronyms are listed alphabetically by acronym rather than by full spelled out version.

Comprehensive Online Learning Environment

Register to gain one year of FREE access to the online interactive learning environment and test bank to help you study for your CompTIA Security+ certification exam—included with your purchase of this book!

The online test bank includes:

- **Practice Test Questions** to reinforce what you learned
- **Bonus Practice Exams** to test your knowledge of the material

Go to http://www.wiley.com/go/sybextestprep to register and gain access to this comprehensive study tool package.

Register and Access the Online Test Bank

To register your book and get access to the online test bank, follow these steps:

1. Go to bit.ly/SybexTest.
2. Select your book from the list.
3. Complete the required registration information including answering the security verification proving book ownership. You will be emailed a pin code.
4. Go to http://www.wiley.com/go/sybextestprep and find your book on that page and click the "Register or Login" link under your book.
5. If you already have an account at testbanks.wiley.com, login and then click the "Redeem Access Code" button to add your new book with the pin code you received. If you don't have an account already, create a new account and use the PIN code you received.